Utilizing Cybersecurity to Foster Business Innovation and Resiliency

Filiz Mızrak
Beykoz University, Turkey

IGI Global
Scientific Publishing
Publishing Tomorrow's Research Today

Vice President of Editorial Melissa Wagner
Director of Acquisitions Mikaela Felty
Director of Book Development Jocelynn Hessler
Production Manager Mike Brehm
Cover Design Phillip Shickler

Published in the United States of America by
IGI Global Scientific Publishing
701 East Chocolate Avenue
Hershey, PA, 17033, USA
Tel: 717-533-8845
Fax: 717-533-7115
Website: https://www.igi-global.com E-mail: cust@igi-global.com

Library of Congress Cataloging-in-Publication Data

LCCN: 2025019282 (CIP Data Pending)
ISBN13: 9798369364178
Isbn13Softcover: 9798369364185
EISBN13: 9798369364192

British Cataloguing in Publication Data
A Cataloguing in Publication record for this book is available from the British Library.

Table of Contents

Detailed Table of Contents

cybersecurity across predictive maintenance, unmanned aircraft traffic management (UTM), and smart airport systems. Technologies like AI improve threat detection, blockchain ensures data integrity, and quantum cryptography enhances communication security. The chapter also highlights the importance of organizational factors—such as leadership and cybersecurity culture—in achieving resilience. Key challenges include fragmented governance and cyber vulnerabilities in low-altitude operations. Despite these, strategic opportunities exist to integrate cybersecurity into long-term innovation plans. Overall, the chapter positions cybersecurity not just as protection, but as a driver of sustainable, secure, and forward-looking aviation management.

This chapter explores how cybersecurity is strategically integrated into digital transformation in smart enterprises. With the rise of AI, IoT, and blockchain, cybersecurity is crucial not just for risk management but also for enabling innovation and resilience. It examines evolving cyber threats and the need for proactive, tailored security strategies. Using frameworks like NIST, ISO/IEC 27005, and the FAIR Model, the chapter outlines best practices in risk management, AI-driven threat detection, and secure architecture. It highlights the role of culture, leadership, and preparedness for emerging risks like quantum threats and regulatory shifts. Ultimately, it presents cybersecurity as a cornerstone of sustainable digital transformation, offering strategic guidance for innovation, collaboration, and resilience.

With the rapid advancement of digital technologies, contemporary work models have undergone a fundamental transformation, as remote and hybrid arrangements producing complex implications for organizational structures. In this shifting landscape, human resource management (HRM) has emerged as a strategic actor in safeguarding corporate information systems. The proliferation of tools such as bring-your-own-device (BYOD) policies, cloud-based infrastructures, virtual private networks (VPN), and digital surveillance platforms has required more proactive and integrated cybersecurity strategies within HRM functions. This chapter offers a comprehensive examination of cybersecurity threats relevant to HRM in the context of remote work, emphasizing the tension between digital privacy and surveillance, the co-development of security protocols through HRM–information technology (IT) collaboration, and mechanisms to foster security-oriented employee awareness. Furthermore, the chapter offers strategies to support digital resilience and sustainability.

The shift toward remote and hybrid work has transformed the cybersecurity landscape, placing increased emphasis on the human factors that influence organizational security. This chapter explores the evolving role of Human Resources (HR) in managing cyber risks within decentralized work environments. It highlights how HR functions—including policy development, employee training, behavioral monitoring, and ethical oversight—are central to building cyber resilience. Through a multidisciplinary lens, the chapter demonstrates how collaboration between HR, IT, and governance fosters a secure and adaptive digital culture. Recommendations are provided for embedding cybersecurity into organizational values, advancing workforce training, and supporting employee well-being to create a human-centered, cyber-secure workplace.

This chapter explores the strategic convergence of cybersecurity, digital innovation, and sustainability in modern supply chains. As technologies like blockchain, artificial intelligence, and IoT redefine supply chain operations, they also introduce new vulnerabilities that demand robust cyber resilience. Drawing on real-world applications across pharmaceuticals, automotive, retail, and agrifood sectors, the chapter examines how cyber-enabled solutions enhance traceability, risk forecasting, and last-mile delivery security. It introduces the Triple Nexus framework—Smart, Secure, Sustainable—as a conceptual model for aligning technological advancement with ethical and environmental goals. Through cross-sectoral analysis and strategic recommendations, the chapter underscores cybersecurity as a foundational enabler of resilient and future-ready supply chains.

Preface

INTRODUCTION

The digital revolution has ushered in an era of extraordinary opportunities, empowering businesses to innovate at unprecedented speed and scale. Yet, this same digital transformation has brought with it a complex web of cybersecurity challenges that threaten not only organizational assets but also operational integrity, reputational trust, and long-term strategic viability. *Utilizing Cybersecurity to Foster Business Innovation and Resiliency* was conceived as a response to this dual reality—where opportunity and risk are inextricably linked, and where cybersecurity is no longer an isolated IT function but a critical enabler of competitive advantage and sustainable innovation. This book aims to advance the understanding that cybersecurity, when embedded strategically across enterprise systems and decision-making processes, can serve as a dynamic force that propels innovation, enhances agility, and builds organizational resilience in an unpredictable and volatile digital environment.

Today's cybersecurity discourse is situated within a rapidly evolving global context where digital technologies—ranging from AI and blockchain to quantum computing and digital twins—are transforming industry landscapes at an accelerated pace. Across sectors, organizations are deploying these tools to reimagine processes, redefine customer experiences, and optimize complex systems. However, these advancements come with heightened exposure to cyber threats that are becoming more frequent, sophisticated, and systemic in nature. The book is therefore timely and relevant, situated at the intersection of innovation, strategic risk management, and cross-sectoral digital transformation. In a world marked by geopolitical instability, supply chain disruptions, pandemic aftershocks, and regulatory complexity, the role of cybersecurity has expanded far beyond compliance and technical protection—it has become a foundational pillar of business continuity, stakeholder trust, and long-term value creation.

The intended audience for this book is diverse, reflecting the interdisciplinary nature of cybersecurity in today's business and academic spheres. It is designed to serve as a core resource for graduate students, scholars, and researchers in the fields of cybersecurity, innovation management, digital transformation, aviation management, and industrial engineering. Simultaneously, it addresses the needs of professionals—including Chief Information Security Officers (CISOs), innovation leaders, digital strategists, human resource managers, policy-makers, and consultants—who are tasked with integrating cybersecurity into complex operational frameworks. Whether in government, corporate, academic, or nonprofit sectors, readers will find in this volume a comprehensive and actionable perspective on how cybersecurity can serve as a catalyst rather than a constraint in achieving strategic goals.

CHAPTER OVERVIEW

Chapter 1, *Cybersecurity and Strategic Innovation in the Digital Economy*, offers a wide-angle lens into how five critical sectors—finance, healthcare, aviation, manufacturing, and education—are leveraging cybersecurity to unlock innovation. The chapter presents real-world case studies to demonstrate how embedding security from the outset enhances scalability, fosters stakeholder trust, and mitigates systemic risks. It argues that cybersecurity is not merely about defense but is a core driver of the digital economy's value creation, shaping how organizations think about innovation governance, customer engagement, and ecosystem collaboration.

Chapter 2, *A Strategic Approach to Cyberattacks and Risk Management*, dives deep into the shifting terrain of cyber threats and provides a comprehensive roadmap for organizations seeking to strengthen their risk posture. It introduces the NIST Cybersecurity Framework as a strategic tool and emphasizes the integration of cybersecurity planning into broader organizational strategies. With practical insights on identifying vulnerabilities, prioritizing responses, and aligning governance structures, the chapter offers a strategic lens on defending against and preparing for the inevitability of cyber incidents.

Chapter 3, *Cybersecurity Applications in Industry 4.0*, explores how next-generation manufacturing ecosystems are reconfiguring the nature of production, automation, and logistics through technologies like cyber-physical systems and big data. It contextualizes these advancements within the Industry 4.0 paradigm and highlights how cybersecurity becomes indispensable in safeguarding interconnected infrastructures. The chapter further introduces readers to the evolution toward Industry 5.0—where human-centricity, ethical design, and sustainability are emphasized—and illustrates how cybersecurity is a precondition for realizing this next industrial frontier.

Chapter 4, *Cybersecurity Culture and Human Factor*, shifts focus to the organizational and behavioral dynamics that underpin cyber risk. It deconstructs the myth that cybersecurity is purely technical by highlighting the central role that individual behaviors, internal communication, employee engagement, and leadership culture play in building a secure digital environment. Drawing on behavioral science and organizational psychology, the chapter provides actionable guidance for embedding cybersecurity awareness into the corporate DNA, making security a shared responsibility across all levels of the organization.

Chapter 5, *Cybersecurity as a Strategic Lever for Innovation in Smart Aviation Ecosystems*, brings the discussion to one of the most technologically advanced and risk-sensitive sectors: aviation. The chapter explores how predictive analytics, unmanned aircraft systems, and smart airport infrastructures are reshaping the aviation landscape while simultaneously creating new vulnerabilities. By examining AI-driven threat detection, blockchain applications for data integrity, and quantum encryption for secure communication, the chapter offers a blueprint for embedding cybersecurity into the innovation strategies of modern aviation management.

Chapter 6, *Securing Digital Transformation: Cyber Risk Management in Smart Enterprises*, presents a holistic framework for navigating the complex journey of digital transformation in contemporary organizations. It discusses the role of AI, IoT, and blockchain in redefining business operations and proposes a set of best practices—including NIST, ISO/IEC 27005, and the FAIR Model—for managing the associated cyber risks. The chapter also addresses the strategic foresight required to anticipate emerging threats, including those posed by quantum computing and regulatory evolution, positioning cybersecurity as a foundational element of future-ready enterprise design.

Chapter 7, *Cybersecurity in Human Resource Management in the Context of Remote Work*, investigates the emerging role of HR departments in the cybersecurity landscape. With the mass shift to remote and hybrid work models, the boundaries between professional and personal digital ecosystems have blurred. This chapter analyzes how HR policies intersect with security concerns—from bring-your-own-device practices to virtual collaboration platforms—and outlines how HR can be mobilized to co-develop, implement, and monitor cybersecurity strategies in alignment with employee rights and corporate resilience.

Chapter 8, *Secure Remote Work: HR's Role in Managing Cyber Risks in Hybrid Work Environments*, delves further into the organizational changes required to secure distributed workforces. Emphasizing collaboration between HR, IT, and legal departments, the chapter introduces a human-centered cybersecurity framework that supports both technological integrity and employee well-being. It offers strategic recommendations on training, behavioral monitoring, and policy development to help organizations build cyber-aware cultures in increasingly decentralized and dynamic work environments.

Chapter 9, *The Triple Nexus of Smart, Secure, and Sustainable Supply Chains: Strategies for Resilience in the Digital Age*, proposes a forward-looking framework for aligning cybersecurity, digital innovation, and environmental sustainability in supply chains. Through detailed case analyses across sectors like pharmaceuticals, retail, and agriculture, the chapter shows how technologies like blockchain and AI can enhance transparency, reduce fraud, and improve risk forecasting. It makes the case that cybersecurity is not just a cost center but a critical enabler of ethical and sustainable value chains in the global economy.

Chapter 10, *Cyber-Resilient Sustainable Airports: Managing Digital Risks in Green Aviation Initiatives*, builds on the aviation theme by examining how airports pursuing sustainability goals must also invest in cybersecurity to protect their digitally enabled infrastructures. The chapter discusses the convergence of environmental standards and cybersecurity frameworks, proposing strategies for secure energy systems, carbon tracking platforms, and smart building technologies. By doing so, it illustrates how cybersecurity acts as a strategic bridge between environmental performance and digital innovation in airport management.

Chapter 11, *Securing the Digital Twin: Cybersecurity Strategies for Virtual Replicas in Aviation Management*, concludes the volume with a highly focused exploration of cybersecurity in digital twin systems. As aviation organizations increasingly rely on real-time simulations for predictive maintenance and operational optimization, the risks of cyber-physical disruptions rise. This chapter offers a layered architecture for securing the digital twin lifecycle and presents a series of best practices for integrating cybersecurity with enterprise planning, AI systems, and human capital development. It positions cybersecurity not as an afterthought, but as a strategic design principle for the aviation systems of tomorrow.

CONCLUSION

In sum, *Utilizing Cybersecurity to Foster Business Innovation and Resiliency* makes a significant contribution to both scholarship and practice by reframing cybersecurity from a reactive posture to a proactive, strategic lever for value creation. The book presents a cohesive vision of cybersecurity as a core component of enterprise innovation and sustainability. Through its blend of theoretical grounding, case-based evidence, and actionable frameworks, it equips readers to rethink cybersecurity as a business-critical discipline. As digital transformation continues to reshape industries, this book stands as both a guide and a call to action—for leaders, educators, and policymakers—to embrace cybersecurity not merely as a necessity, but as a powerful instrument for innovation, resilience, and societal advancement.

Filiz Mizrak
Beykoz University, Turkey

Chapter 1
Cybersecurity and Strategic Innovation in the Digital Economy

Filiz Mızrak
https://orcid.org/0000-0002-3472-394X
Beykoz University, Turkey

ABSTRACT

Cybersecurity is increasingly recognized as a key enabler of innovation in the digital economy. This chapter examines how five sectors—finance, healthcare, aviation, manufacturing, and education—are integrating cybersecurity into strategic innovation efforts. Through case studies such as blockchain in trade finance and federated learning in healthcare AI, it shows how early security integration enhances trust, scalability, and resilience. The analysis highlights sector-specific challenges, organizational capabilities, and shared success factors, while offering strategic recommendations for aligning cybersecurity with innovation governance. The chapter concludes by positioning cybersecurity as a cornerstone of sustainable digital transformation.

1. INTRODUCTION

The modern digital economy is built upon a foundation of interconnected systems, real-time data flows, and increasingly intelligent technologies that drive efficiency, innovation, and global competitiveness. From financial services and healthcare to manufacturing and education, sectors around the world are rapidly embracing digital transformation to enhance productivity and respond to shifting market demands. Yet, as this digital infrastructure becomes more pervasive, so too

DOI: 10.4018/979-8-3693-6417-8.ch001

does its exposure to a growing array of cyber threats. Cybersecurity is no longer a back-office concern confined to IT departments—it has become a fundamental enabler of trust, resilience, and strategic agility in the digital era. The reliability, integrity, and security of digital platforms, services, and data are now central to both operational continuity and competitive differentiation.

At the heart of this transformation is the evolving relationship between cybersecurity and strategic innovation. Historically viewed as a reactive function focused on risk mitigation, cybersecurity is now increasingly integrated into the core of business strategy and innovation planning. Organizations are recognizing that innovation cannot flourish without digital trust, and that security must be embedded not only in technological infrastructures but also in organizational culture, leadership, and governance. This shift is evident in the emergence of secure-by-design frameworks, real-time threat intelligence platforms, and cross-functional innovation teams that include cybersecurity experts from the outset. As new technologies like AI, blockchain, and Internet of Things (IoT) expand the boundaries of what is possible, the role of cybersecurity in enabling safe experimentation and scalable deployment has never been more critical.

This chapter adopts a sectoral case-driven approach to explore how cybersecurity can be strategically integrated into innovation ecosystems. By comparing real-world examples from finance, healthcare, aviation, manufacturing, and education, the analysis reveals both shared challenges and sector-specific responses to cybersecurity risks in digital transformation contexts. The rationale for this comparative perspective lies in the recognition that while cybersecurity principles may be universal, their application is deeply contextual. Different sectors operate under distinct regulatory, technical, and cultural constraints that shape how security and innovation interact. Understanding these dynamics through targeted case studies provides valuable insights into best practices, common pitfalls, and emerging strategies that can inform cross-sectoral learning and policy development.

The chapter is structured as follows: Section 2 reframes cybersecurity as a driver—not a barrier—of innovation, emphasizing its role in fostering digital trust and resilience. Section 3 outlines strategic models for integrating cybersecurity into innovation governance, highlighting cross-functional alignment and risk-based decision-making. Sections 4.1 through 4.5 present sector-specific case studies, detailing how cybersecurity has been embedded into innovation practices across finance, healthcare, aviation, manufacturing, and education. Section 5 examines the organizational capabilities required to sustain secure innovation, from leadership development to talent strategies. Section 6 analyzes the key tensions and constraints organizations face, including budget limitations, legacy systems, and regulatory uncertainty. Section 7 provides strategic recommendations for aligning innovation with cybersecurity objectives, while the final section, Section 8, offers concluding reflections on future directions for secure innovation in the digital economy.

2. RETHINKING CYBERSECURITY IN THE ERA OF INNOVATION

The notion that cybersecurity is merely a defensive mechanism has rapidly become outdated. In the current digital economy, cybersecurity must be recognized not only as a protector of digital assets but also as a critical enabler and driver of innovation. According to Jones (2019), cybersecurity has evolved beyond traditional threat response paradigms and now intersects with innovation processes by shaping how emerging technologies are developed, deployed, and governed. Instead of hindering progress, modern cybersecurity strategies empower organizations to innovate safely by embedding resilience into every phase of the innovation life cycle. This shift reflects a broader movement from reactive security measures toward proactive, value-driven frameworks, where cybersecurity and innovation are aligned to mutually reinforce organizational agility and competitiveness (Alevizos, Bhakuni, & Jäschke, 2025). By integrating cybersecurity early in the design phase of digital services and products, firms can avoid costly retrofitting, ensure compliance from the outset, and foster user trust—all of which are essential for successful innovation.

This paradigm shift has been particularly visible in sectors such as finance and transportation, where digital transformation initiatives often rely on trust and operational continuity. Akintoye et al. (2022) demonstrate that in the Nigerian banking sector, the implementation of advanced cybersecurity technologies has directly influenced the pace and success of financial innovations, such as mobile banking and blockchain adoption. These findings underscore the importance of treating cybersecurity as a strategic asset, one that not only safeguards data but also strengthens business models and customer engagement. The alignment between cybersecurity strategy and innovation frameworks is now seen as a critical dimension of enterprise resilience and sustainability. In a similar vein, Saeed et al. (2023) argue that organizations that proactively incorporate cybersecurity into their digital transformation initiatives are better positioned to withstand operational shocks, navigate regulatory complexity, and maintain customer loyalty in increasingly volatile environments.

Furthermore, the cyber threat landscape itself is evolving, necessitating new forms of strategic thinking and security architecture. Möller (2023) and Grima et al. (2023) emphasize the growing necessity for context-specific, adaptive cybersecurity approaches, especially as cloud computing, artificial intelligence, and IoT systems proliferate across industries. These technologies, while transformative, significantly expand the attack surface, making traditional perimeter-based security models obsolete. Organizations are now adopting zero-trust architectures, behavior-based anomaly detection, and AI-driven security operations centers to respond not only to known threats but also to predict and preempt emerging vulnerabilities. This proactive posture enables continuous innovation without compromising system integrity. Omar (2022) further illustrates how machine learning (ML) and deep learning solutions are revolutionizing threat detection and response, allowing for dynamic, real-time protection of critical assets. These systems do more than defend—they learn, adapt, and support innovation by ensuring digital environments remain secure and responsive.

Equally significant is the social dimension of cybersecurity, which is now being reframed as an organizational and behavioral challenge. As Chaudhary (2024) notes, employee awareness and cybersecurity culture are essential for embedding security into the daily operational fabric of an organization. Technological solutions alone are insufficient; strategic innovation must also account for human-centered cybersecurity that drives behavioral change. The risk of social engineering attacks, highlighted by Dabke, Dabke, and Gadgil (2023), has catalyzed innovation in user training, psychological profiling, and adaptive access controls. This awareness has led to new strategies in cybersecurity innovation that prioritize usability and human behavior alongside technical robustness. In turn, this approach cultivates a work culture that sees cybersecurity not as a burden, but as a shared responsibility that facilitates innovation and operational freedom.

Organizational resilience is deeply intertwined with the ability to adapt cybersecurity strategies as enablers of transformation. Annarelli and Palombi (2021) present a conceptual framework that places digitalization capabilities—such as real-time analytics, cross-system integration, and digital governance—at the heart of sustainable cyber resilience. These capabilities not only enhance threat visibility and response times but also support continuous innovation in product and service delivery. The work of Nkomo and Kalisz (2023) adds that organizations with strong digital transformation frameworks, aligned with clear cybersecurity principles, are better equipped to navigate uncertainty and scale innovation securely. Their emphasis on strategic planning, stakeholder alignment, and continuous evaluationprovides a roadmap for embedding cyber resilience into broader organizational transformation. This is echoed by Hokmabadi, Rezvani, and de Matos (2024), who underscore the importance of marketing and communication capabilities in supporting digital security efforts within small and medium enterprises (SMEs) and startups, where resource limitations demand creative and adaptive cybersecurity innovations.

Ultimately, the integration of cybersecurity into innovation ecosystems reflects a broader transformation in how organizations conceptualize digital value. Cybersecurity is no longer confined to the IT department—it is a strategic imperative that informs leadership, investment decisions, and innovation governance. As Kotila et al. (2023) point out in their study on defense innovation, building a robust cybersecurity ecosystem requires interdisciplinary collaboration, policy support, and continuous investment in skills and infrastructure. Innovation and cybersecurity are not competing priorities; rather, they are co-constructive forces in the digital era. As firms reimagine their strategies to stay competitive, they must rethink cybersecurity as both a protective shield and a catalytic engine—one that enables them to take bold steps into the future while staying grounded in trust, resilience, and strategic foresight.

3. STRATEGIC INNOVATION MODELS AND CYBERSECURITY INTEGRATION

As digital transformation accelerates across industries, organizations are increasingly turning to innovation frameworks such as open innovation, agile development, and design thinking to maintain competitive advantage. However, the successful implementation of these innovation models in the digital economy hinges on the strategic integration of cybersecurity throughout the innovation life cycle. Innovation is no longer viewed solely through the lens of creativity or speed to market; rather, it is being redefined to include digital trust, risk governance, and secure scalability. Mızrak (2023) highlights that embedding cybersecurity into strategic management practices ensures that innovation initiatives do not outpace an organization's ability to protect its digital infrastructure and assets. This integration is particularly crucial in environments where the consequences of cyberattacks—such as data breaches, operational disruptions, or regulatory penalties—could reverse the gains achieved through innovation.

Modern innovation processes increasingly rely on risk-based decision-making frameworks that align cybersecurity with organizational agility and responsiveness. Olaniyi et al. (2024) propose the "CyberFusion" protocol as a strategic integration model that combines enterprise risk management, ISO 27001 standards, and mobile forensics to create an advanced security ecosystem for innovative digital services. This approach exemplifies how cyber risk must be addressed not as an afterthought, but as a foundational component of the innovation architecture. The CyberFusion model promotes the idea of "security-by-design," where potential vulnerabilities are identified and mitigated early, enabling safe experimentation and faster scaling. Similarly, Rajan et al. (2021) introduce a Modified Total Interpretive Structural Model (M-TISM) that maps out the hierarchical relationships between strategic cybersecurity components in innovation-focused organizations. Their model emphasizes that leadership commitment, continuous monitoring, and cross-functional collaboration are essential for managing complex cyber risks that emerge alongside digital innovation.

In tandem with structural integration, technological advancements such as artificial intelligence (AI) and machine learning (ML) are now being leveraged to support cybersecurity in innovation ecosystems. Roshanaei, Khan, and Sylvester (2024) argue that AI/ML models provide predictive analytics and anomaly detection capabilities that allow organizations to anticipate and neutralize cyber threats in real time. These technologies serve as force multipliers in dynamic DevOps and agile pipelines, where traditional security checkpoints might delay delivery or be bypassed entirely. Manikyala et al. (2023) discuss how embedding cybersecurity best practices directly into DevOps pipelines ensures that code changes, feature releases, and microservices deployments are evaluated for risk without sacrificing development velocity. This convergence of innovation and cybersecurity engineering reflects a broader movement toward "DevSecOps," where security becomes a shared responsibility across development, operations, and security teams. Such integrated models align with agile and continuous delivery philosophies, allowing innovation to proceed at scale without compromising digital integrity.

Moreover, governance and compliance structures are increasingly seen as strategic levers that can enhance, rather than constrain, innovation. Kumar, Bhardwaj, and Lather (2024) detail how clear legal frameworks and enforcement mechanisms surrounding cybersecurity responsibilities can provide a stable regulatory environment in which innovation can thrive. Rather than viewing compliance as a hindrance, leading organizations now integrate legal and regulatory considerations into their innovation governance strategies to ensure early alignment with privacy laws (such as GDPR or HIPAA), data residency requirements, and intellectual property protection. Coutinho et al. (2023) provide a compelling case from the healthcare sector, where integrated cybersecurity methodologies have been embedded into operational information systems. These systems are designed not only to ensure real-time patient data security but also to support the continual rollout of digital health innovations such as AI-assisted diagnostics, telemedicine, and smart wearables—all within a tightly governed compliance framework.

The use of digital twin technologies in smart manufacturing further illustrates how innovation and cybersecurity can be co-developed for mutual reinforcement. Mylrea et al. (2021) describe the BioSecure digital twin model as a convergence of manufacturing innovation and cybersecurity resilience. This system enables continuous monitoring of physical assets in real time, while simultaneously scanning for anomalies or security breaches using built-in AI analytics. The integration of such digital twins into industrial control systems exemplifies how secure innovation can improve both operational performance and threat detection. In addition, Villalón-Fonseca (2022) proposes a conceptual framework for integral-comprehensive IT security modeling, where cybersecurity is treated as an interdependent, systemic function that must evolve in parallel with any form of technological advancement.

This holistic view is crucial in digital innovation, where boundaries between data, software, and infrastructure are increasingly blurred.

Importantly, national cybersecurity strategies and educational frameworks also play a significant role in supporting the secure innovation agenda. AlDaajeh et al. (2022) emphasize that without sufficient talent pipelines and institutional knowledge in cybersecurity, even the most well-structured innovation initiatives may falter under cyber threats. They argue that a forward-thinking national strategy should promote cybersecurity literacy, invest in specialized education programs, and incentivize public-private partnerships that enable co-innovation with robust security postures. Rahardja et al. (2025) reinforce this notion in their analysis of fintech ecosystems, noting that innovation in financial services must be supported by scalable, secure data infrastructures and a regulatory environment that prioritizes both performance and protection. Their study shows that scalable innovation is only achievable when cybersecurity is treated as a critical path function—one that interacts with customer experience design, data architecture, and strategic planning.

Taken together, these perspectives underline that the integration of cybersecurity into innovation frameworks is not merely a technical challenge, but a multidimensional strategic endeavor. Organizations that succeed in this integration do not treat cybersecurity as a gatekeeper to innovation, but as a foundational pillar upon which trust, agility, and resilience are built. Whether through AI-driven security models, secure-by-design development pipelines, governance-enhanced compliance, or digital twins with embedded monitoring capabilities, the digital economy demands that cybersecurity and innovation be conceived and executed in tandem. This integrated approach is what enables organizations to innovate with confidence, adapt with agility, and scale with security in an increasingly complex and interconnected world.

4. SECTOR-SPECIFIC CASE STUDIES

The integration of cybersecurity into innovation practices varies significantly across sectors, influenced by domain-specific risks, regulatory pressures, technological maturity, and organizational priorities. To illustrate the diversity of approaches and outcomes, Table 1 provides a comparative overview of five critical sectors—finance, healthcare, aviation, manufacturing, and education—highlighting how cybersecurity has been strategically embedded into digital innovation initiatives. Each row summarizes the core innovation focus, the corresponding cybersecurity priorities, strategic actions taken, resulting outcomes, and key sources supporting the case. This comparative snapshot underscores both shared principles and sector-specific adaptations, such as the use of permissioned blockchain in financial services, federated learning in healthcare AI, or anomaly detection through digital twins in manufacturing. The common thread across these examples is the proactive application of cybersecurity to enable—not impede—digital transformation.The details of each case study will be elaborated in Sections 4.1 through 4.5, offering a deeper analysis of the technical solutions, implementation strategies, and organizational lessons that emerged from each sectoral context.

Table 1. Sectoral comparison of cybersecurity-enabled innovation

Sector	Key Innovation	Cybersecurity Focus	Strategic Actions	Outcomes	Sources
Finance and Fintech	Blockchain and Smart Contracts	Digital trust, identity management, encryption	Permissioned blockchain, open APIs, compliance integration	Faster, trusted transactions; platform scalability	Decta (2021); Sinclair (2020); Synced Review (2020)
Healthcare	Federated Learning for AI Diagnostics	Data privacy, secure collaboration, compliance	Secure-by-design AI, hospital-led FL networks, encryption-by-default	Privacy-preserving diagnostics; improved patient trust	Synced Review (2020); Healthcare IT Today (2021); Nature (2021)
Aviation and Transportation	Secure UAS Systems (BFDI-AP)	Encrypted control links, automated hardening, access control	FAA partnerships, live simulations, security requirements in procurement	Safer drone operations; public and regulatory confidence	FAA (2024); NIST (2024); New Prairie Press (2020); CISA (2021)
Manufacturing and Industry 4.0	Cybersecurity-Enhanced Digital Twins	Anomaly detection, ML-based IDS, secure integration	ML training on normal behavior, SOC integration, red-teaming	Reduced attack surface; dual-use for maintenance and security	NIST (2023); ANSI (2023)
Education and Digital Learning	Secure Remote Learning Platforms (Zoom)	End-to-end encryption, authentication, digital rights management	Platform customization, policy enforcement, cyber-hygiene education	Restored platform trust; reduced classroom disruptions	NPR (2020); Chalkbeat (2020); Abto Software (2021)

4.1 Finance and Fintech

In the rapidly evolving fintech landscape, cybersecurity has emerged not only as a protective measure but as a critical trust enabler in digital financial products. This trust is especially vital in the domain of trade finance, where traditionally paper-based processes are being digitized to enhance efficiency and reduce costs. However, digitalization introduces new vulnerabilities—data tampering, fraud, and unauthorized access—which could undermine trust in digital financial ecosystems. One of the most compelling cases illustrating the strategic integration of cybersecurity in fintech innovation is HSBC's adoption of blockchain and secure smart contracts through the Contour network. This case demonstrates how cyber-resilient infrastructure can transform inherently trust-dependent financial services.

The challenge in trade finance stems from the complexity of cross-border transactions, which often require multiple intermediaries, document exchanges, and verification steps. These procedures are slow and vulnerable to fraud or error. By transitioning to a blockchain-based system, HSBC sought to resolve these issues while ensuring robust cybersecurity. The Contour network, built on the R3 Corda blockchain platform, offers a decentralized, permissioned ledger where smart contracts automatically execute upon fulfillment of predefined conditions—such as goods shipment or delivery confirmation. This approach eliminates the need for manual document processing and establishes an immutable, shared record among all parties involved. The cryptographic principles underlying blockchain ensure data integrity and authenticity, serving as a digital trust mechanism that verifies each step of the transaction lifecycle without external validation (Decta, 2021).

From a cybersecurity perspective, HSBC adopted several strategic safeguards. First, the Contour network operates as a permissioned blockchain, meaning only vetted institutions can participate. This restricts unauthorized access and reduces the surface area for potential cyberattacks. Second, all communications and transactions are encrypted, and digital identities are verified using cryptographic keys issued to participating entities. These controls are enforced through R3 Corda's enterprise-grade architecture, which supports controlled data sharing, role-based access, and auditability. HSBC also conducted live pilot transactions—most notably, the first blockchain-based cross-border letter of credit in Bangladesh in 2020—to evaluate the platform's security, scalability, and legal compliance (Sinclair, 2020). During these trials, HSBC integrated open APIs for seamless and secure interaction between existing banking systems and the blockchain network, minimizing exposure from legacy systems while promoting interoperability (Decta, 2021).

A key component of the strategy was aligning the innovation with regulatory compliance. Cybersecurity was not viewed in isolation but embedded within a broader governance framework that included privacy laws, anti-money laundering (AML) protocols, and financial reporting standards. HSBC involved legal and compliance teams early in the design process to ensure that the platform met jurisdiction-specific requirements. Penetration tests, simulated fraud scenarios, and continuous monitoring were employed to preemptively address vulnerabilities. This comprehensive, integrated approach allowed HSBC to deploy blockchain in a manner that was not only secure but strategically aligned with trust-building and regulatory resilience.

The outcomes of this cybersecurity-driven innovation were substantial. HSBC's digitized letter-of-credit transactions were processed in less than 24 hours, compared to the traditional 5–10 days—a significant improvement in operational efficiency (Sinclair, 2020). The platform's immutable audit trail greatly reduced fraud risk and increased confidence among stakeholders, including importers, exporters, and trade regulators. According to the CEO of HSBC Bangladesh, the success of the initiative has reshaped perceptions of blockchain as a practical, secure solution in financial services, offering a balance of speed, transparency, and compliance (Sinclair, 2020). By 2021, the Contour platform had been adopted by multiple global banks, confirming its scalability and reliability as a secure fintech innovation (Decta, 2021).

In conclusion, the HSBC blockchain initiative exemplifies how cybersecurity can serve as an enabler of innovation in the fintech sector. The secure deployment of smart contracts on a permissioned blockchain network transformed trade finance into a more agile, transparent, and trustworthy process. This case affirms that embedding cybersecurity features—encryption, identity management, regulatory alignment—into the core design of digital financial products is essential for sustaining user trust and achieving widespread adoption in the digital economy.

4.2 Healthcare

The digital transformation of the healthcare sector has brought forth significant advancements in service delivery, particularly in telemedicine and AI-based diagnostics. However, these innovations have also introduced new cybersecurity challenges, particularly concerning patient data protection. Telemedicine platforms routinely handle sensitive personal health information (PHI), including electronic health records (EHRs), real-time video consultations, and biometric data. As healthcare systems globally shifted to remote care models during and after the COVID-19 pandemic, incidents of unauthorized data access, system vulnerabilities, and phishing attacks surged (Healthcare IT Today, 2021). The challenge has thus been twofold: first, to maintain compliance with regulatory frameworks like HIPAA and GDPR; second, to enable medical innovation—such as AI-driven diagnostics—without centralizing or compromising sensitive health data.

To address this, healthcare innovators turned to privacy-preserving machine learning techniques and security-by-design telehealth systems. A prominent example is the federated learning initiative launched in 2020 by NVIDIA and Mass General Brigham, which aimed to predict COVID-19 patients' oxygen needs. Traditional AI models rely on aggregating massive datasets from multiple institutions—a process that poses serious privacy risks. In contrast, federated learning (FL) enables model training across multiple hospitals while keeping patient data localized. Each institution trains the model on its own data and shares only encrypted model updates with a central server, not the raw data itself (Synced Review, 2020). This technical architecture reduces the attack surface and mitigates the risk of large-scale data breaches. In parallel, telemedicine platforms began deploying end-to-end encryption, adopting HIPAA-compliant communication tools, and enforcing user authentication protocols such as multi-factor authentication and secure session management (Healthcare IT Today, 2021).

These innovations were underpinned by strategic cybersecurity actions that prioritized resilience without stalling digital progress. The federated learning model—known as EXAM (EXtreme Accuracy Model)—involved 20 hospitals across North America, Europe, and Asia. Each hospital retained full control of its data within secure IT environments. All communications between sites were encrypted and facilitated by NVIDIA's secure orchestration server, which ensured zero exposure of personally identifiable information (PII). Moreover, strict access controls and audit logging mechanisms were implemented to ensure transparency and accountability across all training nodes (Synced Review, 2020). In telemedicine platforms, similar levels of cyber-aware design were evident. Many providers adopted secure APIs for health record access, encrypted data both in transit and at rest, and conducted external audits to validate compliance with national and international cybersecurity standards (Healthcare IT Today, 2021). These layered defense mechanisms ensured that telehealth and AI systems could operate reliably, securely, and in alignment with medical ethics and privacy norms.

The impact of these cybersecurity-integrated innovations has been transformative. The EXAM federated learning model achieved an impressive 94% area-under-curve (AUC) accuracy in predicting COVID-19 patients' oxygen requirements—within just two weeks of training (Synced Review, 2020). Crucially, this was accomplished without centralizing any patient data, validating the efficacy of privacy-preserving AI in clinical applications. The model outperformed some of its centralized counterparts, demonstrating that security constraints did not hinder performance—rather, they encouraged broader data diversity as hospitals felt more confident participating (Nature, 2021). In telemedicine, patient adoption rates increased significantly as providers improved platform security. A 2021 industry survey reported that patient confidence in telehealth solutions had grown, especially when providers advertised robust data encryption and secure patient portals (Healthcare IT Today, 2021). Simultaneously, platforms that implemented these enhanced security features experienced fewer data breaches and service disruptions, particularly compared to early 2020 when ad-hoc solutions were still being deployed.

In conclusion, the healthcare sector's shift to cyber-aware design in digital services exemplifies how cybersecurity can act as an enabler—not a barrier—to innovation. Through federated learning, AI diagnostic systems were made scalable and privacy-respecting. Through encrypted, authenticated telemedicine platforms, remote care became more secure and trusted by patients. These measures reflect a broader understanding that data protection, strategic governance, and resilient design must be embedded at every level of health innovation to ensure safe, effective, and sustainable digital care delivery.

4.3 Aviation and Transportation

As smart mobility systems evolve, the adoption of Unmanned Aircraft Systems (UAS) — commonly known as drones — has increased dramatically, enabling new capabilities in logistics, infrastructure inspection, public safety, and emergency response. However, the rapid integration of drones into national airspace introduces profound cyber-physical vulnerabilities. These aerial systems, equipped with GPS, wireless communications, and onboard processors, are effectively "flying IoT devices" and are inherently susceptible to cybersecurity threats including signal jamming, data interception, and remote hijacking. Early security assessments identified widespread risks: many commercial drones were deployed with default passwords, unencrypted control links, and insecure APIs—making them easy targets for brute force attacks or man-in-the-middle exploits (CISA, 2021; New Prairie Press, 2020). In high-stakes scenarios such as surveillance, disaster relief, or medical supply transport, any breach could endanger both public safety and critical infrastructure. The challenge, therefore, is to scale drone-based innovation while embedding secure-by-design principlesthat ensure the safety, privacy, and resilience of UAS operations.

To mitigate these risks, the industry has focused on building embedded cybersecurity capabilities directly into drone systems and their operational frameworks. One standout innovation is the Brute Force Default Identification – Automated Prevention (BFDI-AP) system, developed as part of a public-private initiative led by the U.S. Federal Aviation Administration (FAA), CNA Corporation, and RIIS LLC. This system targets a well-known vulnerability: factory-default credentials and unsecured settings. BFDI-AP functions as an automated cybersecurity hardening toolthat scans drone control systems in real time for weak default configurations (such as unchanged passwords or open ports). Upon detecting such vulnerabilities, the tool autonomously updates the drone's configuration to a more secure state (e.g., generating unique passwords and closing unused ports) and alerts the operator of the intervention (NIST, 2024). This proactive mechanism ensures drones are dynamically secured before deployment, eliminating a key attack vector before it can be exploited. Parallel innovations in UAS designs now include AES-128 encrypted command-and-control links, which prevent adversaries from eavesdropping or issuing spoofed commands. The RIIS R1 quadcopter, for example, was field-tested with encrypted telemetry channels, showcasing how embedded encryption can provide a defense-in-depth model for drone operations (NIST, 2024).

Strategically, the implementation of these solutions has relied on multi-stakeholder collaboration involving federal regulators, drone manufacturers, cybersecurity experts, and end-users. In 2024, a series of live simulation exercises were conducted at the New York UAS Test Site to validate the BFDI-AP tool in real-world scenarios. Drones were pre-configured with known security flaws to mimic common field deployments. During missions simulating public safety responses—such as medical delivery and search-and-rescue—BFDI-AP successfully identified and patched these vulnerabilities mid-flight without disrupting functionality (FAA, 2024). This "cyber autopilot" capability demonstrated the feasibility of securing drone fleets at scale and in motion. Beyond technical deployments, the FAA promoted the creation of a "Blue List"—a curated catalog of UAS products that meet stringent cybersecurity criteria. Agencies and enterprises use this list to guide procurement, ensuring only pre-vetted secure drones enter their fleets. Additionally, cybersecurity training and certification protocols have been integrated into drone pilot licensing programs, emphasizing password hygiene, encryption key management, and incident response readiness. These institutional efforts illustrate how cybersecurity is being operationalized not as a stand-alone discipline but as a strategic component of UAS governance.

The outcomes of these integrated strategies have been substantial. The BFDI-AP project provided public safety agencies with a practical, low-cost solution to enhance their drone cybersecurity posture. During test campaigns, drones equipped with BFDI-AP demonstrated resilience to simulated cyberattacks, such as unauthorized login attempts or telemetry spoofing—incidents that would otherwise have resulted in drone loss or mission failure (NIST, 2024). These successful interventions significantly reduced operational risk, enabling broader deployment of drones in critical use cases. Moreover, the FAA's post-trial report highlighted the dual impact of the initiative: it not only secured the drones but also raised awareness within the UAS community about the importance of embedded security (FAA, 2024). In the commercial sector, confidence in drone technology has grown, with businesses and logistics firms increasingly willing to invest in drone delivery platforms that demonstrate robust cybersecurity safeguards. Similarly, regulators are more amenable to integrating drones into controlled airspace under the condition that secure communication links, anti-tampering protocols, and remote identification features are in place.

In sum, the UAS cybersecurity case underscores the principle that innovation in aviation must be accompanied by systemic cyber risk management. Technologies like BFDI-AP, encrypted telemetry, and authenticated identity broadcasting represent the new baseline for secure drone ecosystems. More importantly, these solutions illustrate how a proactive, multi-layered cybersecurity approach—grounded in technical rigor, regulatory foresight, and operational best practices—can enable the safe expansion of drone applications in smart mobility systems. As the industry moves toward autonomous drone corridors and integrated traffic management systems, cybersecurity must remain at the forefront to ensure that aviation innovation unfolds securely, sustainably, and with public trust.

4.4 Manufacturing and Industry 4.0

The fourth industrial revolution—commonly referred to as Industry 4.0—has ushered in a new era of connectivity between cyber and physical systems. In modern smart factories, machines such as assembly robots, 3D printers, and industrial sensors are now networked through the Industrial Internet of Things (IIoT), enabling real-time optimization and predictive maintenance. At the core of this transformation is the digital twin: a virtual model of a physical asset that mirrors its behavior and operational status using live sensor data. While digital twins enhance productivity, efficiency, and reliability, their integration into networked environments introduces serious cyber-physical vulnerabilities. Legacy industrial control systems (ICS), once safely air-gapped, are now exposed to network-based cyber threats. Malicious actors could manipulate machine parameters—such as temperature, torque, or voltage—to cause physical damage or compromise production without leaving noticeable traces in conventional security logs (NIST, 2023). This creates an innovation bottleneck: manufacturers are eager to adopt digital twins for predictive analytics but are hesitant due to cybersecurity concerns. The key challenge lies in ensuring that digital twins do not become a new attack vector in otherwise well-defended industrial environments.

A transformative solution emerged in the form of cybersecurity-augmented digital twins, a concept developed and tested through a collaboration between the National Institute of Standards and Technology (NIST) and the University of Michigan. Their 2023 pilot project focused on a 3D printer—a relatively simple yet highly programmable industrial system. The team built a high-fidelity digital twin that received continuous data from the physical printer's embedded sensors. Simultaneously, they trained machine learning (ML) models to understand what constituted normal operational behavior, including permissible variations (e.g., temperature fluctuations when a cooling fan is activated). During simulations, the researchers introduced controlled anomalies, including cyberattacks that falsified temperature or motor speed readings. The ML algorithms within the digital twin compared expected values with real sensor outputs. When discrepancies were detected—such as an actual energy draw inconsistent with reported sensor values—the system raised alerts (ANSI, 2023). This strategy effectively transformed the digital twin into a real-time intrusion detection system (IDS) that could identify and respond to subtle, process-level cyber threats that traditional network security tools might overlook (NIST, 2023).

The strategic deployment of this solution required a multidisciplinary cybersecurity framework. Control engineers, data scientists, and cybersecurity specialists worked collaboratively to integrate the ML-based anomaly detection engine directly into the operational technology (OT) environment. Instead of retrofitting an external monitoring system, they embedded the detection logic within the twin itself, allowing for native evaluation of each operational cycle. Real-time data pipelines fed the ML engine with metrics such as extruder temperature, feed rate, and current draw. Alerts could be escalated in several ways: either triggering a human-machine interface (HMI) notification for operator review or autonomously pausing the machine when a risk threshold was exceeded (NIST, 2023). Beyond the lab, industrial organizations began to mirror these cybersecurity strategies in their own facilities. Many connected digital twins to Security Operations Centers (SOCs) and integrated industrial devices into Security Information and Event Management (SIEM) platforms. Others conducted "red team" penetration tests simulating internal compromise of industrial sensors to fine-tune their detection models. Importantly, manufacturers began implementing device onboarding protocols requiring new IIoT components to support encryption, secure boot, and role-based access control before integration with digital twin systems.

The impact of this cybersecurity-enhanced digital twin model has been substantial. During controlled tests, the framework successfully detected several types of cyber manipulation that could have otherwise led to dangerous outcomes or flawed product manufacturing. In one example, the system identified a falsified input intended to trick the 3D printer into overheating—an act that could have damaged the print head and corrupted the final product. The ML engine, referencing the digital twin's simulated temperature model, recognized that the energy consumption profile didn't match the reported sensor values and halted the operation before damage occurred (NIST, 2023). As a result, manufacturers gain dual valuefrom their investment: the same infrastructure used for predictive maintenance now doubles as a cyber defense layer. This dual-functionality improves not only production efficiency but also system resilience, dramatically reducing downtime and risk exposure. The case has inspired broader adoption across sectors ranging from automotive to chemicals, with ISO and ANSI working on new standards for digital twin security and interoperability (ANSI, 2023).

In essence, by embedding cybersecurity into the predictive analytics and operational monitoring systems of Industry 4.0, manufacturers have found a pathway to secure innovation at scale. Rather than viewing cybersecurity as a constraint on efficiency, forward-thinking firms are now treating it as a foundational capability that enables more confident experimentation, faster scaling of automation, and safer integration of AI in industrial environments. The digital thread that connects machines, data, and decision-making processes is now being secured not just at the perimeter, but from within. As industrial operations become more autonomous and data-driven, cybersecurity-enhanced digital twins are emerging as a strategic pillar of smart manufacturing—ensuring that innovation remains not only productive, but also safe and sustainable.

4.5 Education and Digital Learning

The COVID-19 pandemic triggered an unprecedented shift in global education, compelling schools and universities to migrate to online platforms virtually overnight. This rapid transformation exposed severe cybersecurity and privacy vulnerabilities, especially in the use of video conferencing applications and Learning Management Systems (LMS). Initially designed for corporate use, tools like Zoom lacked adequate protections for an educational context at scale. The most notorious issue that emerged was "Zoombombing," a phenomenon in which uninvited individuals gained access to virtual classrooms and disrupted lessons with offensive or abusive content—often due to unsecured meeting links, lack of authentication, or weak access controls (NPR, 2020). The stakes were particularly high for K–12 environments, where compliance with child privacy laws such as FERPA (Family Educational Rights and Privacy Act) and COPPA (Children's Online Privacy Protection Act) required additional safeguards. Beyond classroom disruptions, educational institutions also faced the challenge of securing digital intellectual property, such as recorded lectures, assessments, and proprietary course content, against unauthorized access and distribution. The central dilemma was how to ensure secure, private, and inclusive learning experiences for millions of students across diverse digital platforms—under enormous time pressure and resource constraints.

In response, education technology providers and policymakers swiftly deployed strategic cybersecurity enhancements to re-engineer remote learning tools for secure academic use. A notable example is the transformation of Zoom into a secure education platform, which involved implementing multiple technical upgrades. These included end-to-end encryption, ensuring that only intended users—students and educators—could access the session content, with even Zoom's own servers unable to decrypt communication (Abto Software, 2021). Zoom also introduced virtual waiting rooms, meeting passwords, and participant authentication features by default. These controls gave teachers the ability to screen participants before granting access, drastically reducing the risk of unwanted intrusion (Chalkbeat, 2020). In addition, for large public school systems like New York City, Zoom developed a custom deployment integrated with the district's identity management systems. Students and staff were required to log in using official credentials, linking the platform to existing Single Sign-On (SSO) frameworks and blocking external users from joining with generic meeting links. Simultaneously, LMS platforms like Google Classroom and Canvas incorporated digital rights management (DRM) tools to prevent unauthorized downloading or screen recording of protected materials. These enhancements collectively formed a multi-layered cybersecurity strategy that addressed access control, content protection, and user verification—enabling educators to regain trust in digital learning environments.

The cybersecurity response was not limited to technical fixes; it was a coordinated effort involving policy changes, user training, and governance structures. In April 2020, school districts in New York City, Washington D.C., and Las Vegas temporarily banned Zoom due to mounting privacy concerns, prompting the company to expedite the release of education-specific security updates (NPR, 2020). This pressure proved productive: NYC's Department of Education collaborated directly with Zoom engineers to configure a version of the platform that restricted meeting domains, disabled file sharing and screen sharing for students, and provided administrator-level oversight. According to district leadership, these enhancements were non-negotiable, as they were essential for protecting minors and maintaining instructional integrity (Chalkbeat, 2020). Concurrently, schools launched cyber-hygiene campaigns to raise awareness among teachers, students, and parents. Educators were trained to lock meetings, disable public chats, and report suspicious activity, while parents received guidelines on safely managing device settings and home Wi-Fi security. Universities, particularly those offering recorded asynchronous instruction, adopted multi-factor authentication (MFA) for LMS logins and conducted risk assessments on third-party integrations. Many institutions also established cybersecurity committees or incident response teams to oversee remote learning deployments—signaling a cultural shift where digital risk management became a core component of academic operations.

The results of these integrated measures were immediate and far-reaching. By May 2020, NYC lifted its Zoom ban, enabling more than one million students to resume remote classes using a custom-secured platform compliant with federal privacy laws (Chalkbeat, 2020). Zoombombing incidents plummeted, and user confidence in digital classrooms significantly improved. Districts that had adopted customized Zoom environments or switched to secure alternatives like Microsoft Teams reported fewer service disruptions and higher levels of student engagement. Furthermore, institutions that adopted DRM and authenticated access for digital content observed a decline in intellectual property theft—professors and schools gained confidence that their recorded lectures and assessments would not be leaked or reused without consent. The broader impact has been a lasting transformation in cybersecurity awareness within the education sector. By late 2020, most educational institutions had revised their IT budgets to prioritize cybersecurity infrastructure and training. Stakeholders now routinely evaluate privacy policies and security capabilities before adopting any new digital tool for learning. This proactive mindset is shaping a more resilient educational ecosystem, one where secure digital transformation is no longer reactive but embedded into strategic planning.

In conclusion, the cybersecurity evolution of remote education platforms—particularly through the Zoom for Education case—demonstrates how strategic, multi-level interventions can turn a crisis into an opportunity for lasting digital improvement. From technical reengineering to organizational policy reform, the education sector has set a precedent for how to manage cybersecurity in times of rapid innovation. As hybrid and digital learning continue to expand globally, these foundations will ensure that privacy, trust, and access remain central to the future of education.

5. ORGANIZATIONAL CAPABILITIES FOR SECURE INNOVATION

As organizations become increasingly dependent on digital technologies to drive innovation, their capacity to integrate cybersecurity into strategic decision-making and daily operations has emerged as a defining capability. Secure innovation is not simply a matter of deploying advanced technologies or software solutions; rather, it requires the cultivation of organizational capabilities that support resilience, foresight, and agility. At the core of these capabilities lies cyber-aware leadership, where executives are expected to understand cyber risk as a strategic imperative. Moyo (2022) emphasizes that today's leaders must be able to interpret cybersecurity intelligence, allocate appropriate resources for cyber risk management, and embed security considerations into digital transformation strategies. This demands not only technical understanding but also strategic foresight, enabling leaders to anticipate future threats, navigate regulatory complexities, and respond to dynamic risk landscapes with confidence and clarity.

A key organizational asset in this process is the culture of secure experimentation—a work environment where innovation is encouraged, but not at the expense of security. As Mor and Ashta (2018) note, organizations that foster a culture of learning and experimentation tend to be more resilient, particularly when failures are framed as opportunities for improvement rather than causes for blame. This perspective is essential in cybersecurity, where unknown threats often emerge from novel attack vectors or previously unseen vulnerabilities. Ahsan (2025) further highlights the role of leadership in cultivating this environment by promoting lifelong learning, encouraging open discussions about mistakes, and supporting ongoing training programs that embed security literacy across roles and functions. These cultural attributes build the psychological safety needed for cross-functional teams to innovate securely, challenge assumptions, and report cyber risks without fear of retribution.

Effective alignment between innovation and cybersecurity also hinges on cross-functional collaboration and communication. According to Neri and Niccolini (2025), small and medium-sized enterprises (SMEs), in particular, benefit from developing internal structures that bridge the traditional divide between IT, operations, and executive management. This alignment often takes the form of interdisciplinary innovation teams that include not only developers and business strategists but also compliance officers, risk analysts, and cybersecurity professionals. Henrichsen (2024) explores this phenomenon in the context of newsrooms, where the emergence of "security champions"—individuals embedded within editorial teams who promote security best practices—has led to improved digital safety cultures. These champions act as internal connectors, translating security requirements into language that aligns with business and creative goals. Their presence supports a decentralized but cohesive model of cybersecurity awareness that is critical in fast-moving innovation contexts.

Talent development strategies are also central to securing innovation. While much attention has been paid to technical skill gaps in cybersecurity, Adams (2024) points out that the modern cybersecurity workforce must also possess communication, collaboration, and design thinking competencies. Organizations that successfully bridge the gap between innovation and security prioritize multidisciplinary recruitment—hiring individuals who can straddle roles in IT, data science, compliance, and business development. This approach not only mitigates talent shortages but also ensures that cybersecurity is treated as a shared responsibility across departments. Furthermore, educational partnerships and pipeline programs—such as articulation agreements between community colleges and four-year institutions—can expand access to cybersecurity careers and foster a more diverse talent pool (Payne et al., 2022). Such initiatives are especially valuable for building long-term organizational resilience and embedding cybersecurity into the innovation workforce from the ground up.

Finally, organizational capability building must be supported by continuous training and systemic awareness. Vasudevan, Piazza, and Carr (2023) conducted a systematic literature review using social network analysis to understand how cybersecurity training spreads within organizations. Their findings reveal that while formal training is essential, informal peer-to-peer knowledge exchange often plays a more significant role in sustaining cybersecurity practices over time. Organizations that actively map and leverage these internal knowledge networks are better positioned to institutionalize secure behaviors and adapt them to new technological contexts. As threats evolve and digital ecosystems grow more complex, organizations that invest in leadership development, cross-functional collaboration, and continuous learning will be best equipped to innovate with confidence and security.

6. CHALLENGES AND TENSIONS

While the integration of cybersecurity into digital innovation strategies has proven essential for organizational resilience, it remains fraught with persistent challenges and tensions that complicate implementation. One of the most notable issues is the trade-off between speed of innovation and security controls. In competitive markets, organizations often prioritize rapid product deployment, iterative design, and first-mover advantage. However, this can come at the expense of thorough security vetting. Li et al. (2022) argue that while model predictive control frameworks can be used to mitigate cyber threats in real-time systems, their deployment is often hindered by the latency constraints of agile innovation cycles. This tension is further exacerbated by the growing complexity of cyber-physical systems, where delays in patching vulnerabilities may lead to system-wide risks. Organizations face a constant dilemma: delaying innovation to embed comprehensive security measures can lead to competitive disadvantage, yet accelerating innovation without adequate protections increases exposure to cyberattacks.

Another substantial barrier lies in budget constraints and prioritization dilemmas, particularly for small to medium-sized enterprises (SMEs) and public institutions. Hossain, Raza, and Rahman (2023) found that cybersecurity initiatives in smaller banks often struggle with limited resources, resulting in underfunded projects and gaps in infrastructure. These financial constraints force organizations to make difficult choices about which systems to protect, often prioritizing customer-facing technologies while internal systems remain vulnerable. Mızrak (2023) further highlights that without robust multi-criteria decision-making frameworks, cybersecurity budgeting can become reactive and fragmented rather than strategic. These dilemmas are not limited to the private sector; Masombuka, Grobler, and Duvenage (2021) emphasize that local governments face similar fiscal challenges, with cybersecurity often sidelined in favor of more visible community services. This undermines long-term digital resilience and exposes critical infrastructure to threats.

A third layer of complexity involves regulatory uncertainty, especially in the context of emerging technologies such as artificial intelligence, blockchain, and decentralized finance (DeFi). Regulatory frameworks often lag behind technological developments, leaving innovators in a gray zone with unclear compliance requirements. Taeihagh, Ramesh, and Howlett (2021) identify this as a common challenge across sectors, noting that when legal guidelines are ambiguous, organizations either adopt overly cautious approaches that stifle innovation or take excessive risks that compromise security and ethics. Uzougbo, Ikegwu, and Adewusi (2024) explore this tension in the context of DeFi, where the lack of regulatory clarity has led to both groundbreaking financial services and significant cyber breaches. Regulatory fragmentation across jurisdictions also adds to the burden, especially for multinational enterprises that must navigate conflicting data protection, privacy, and cybersecurity regulations. Ulnicane et al. (2021) propose that good governance mechanisms—including anticipatory regulation and ethical foresight—can help mitigate these tensions, but widespread implementation remains limited.

Equally problematic is the prevalence of legacy systems and digital fragmentation, which pose ongoing security and integration risks. Rosenkranz et al. (2024) argue that many organizations are trapped in the "Business-Technological Age of Legacy Systems," relying on outdated infrastructure that is difficult to patch, monitor, or integrate with modern cybersecurity tools. This fragmentation creates silos of vulnerability, as older systems lack support for encryption, multifactor authentication, or modern threat detection mechanisms. Maciel et al. (2021) note that digital legacy systems often lack documentation and architectural transparency, making risk assessment and mitigation particularly difficult. Furthermore, the coexistence of modern applications and outdated systems increases attack surfaces, complicates governance, and slows down innovation. Even when new technologies are deployed, they are frequently limited by the weakest links in existing infrastructure, creating a dependency loop that hinders progress.

These challenges underscore the importance of strategic alignment between innovation and cybersecurity governance. The most resilient organizations are those that acknowledge these tensions and manage them proactively through layered defense models, adaptive budgeting, and continuous compliance monitoring. Yet, for many, these remain aspirational goals. Odebade and Benkhelifa (2023), in their comparative analysis of national cybersecurity strategies, stress the importance of cohesive national frameworks to guide organizations, particularly in developing economies where institutional support and policy coordination may be lacking.

Addressing these tensions will require more than technical innovation—it demands policy reform, leadership engagement, and the embedding of cybersecurity into the cultural DNA of digital transformation.

7. STRATEGIC RECOMMENDATIONS

As the interplay between cybersecurity and digital innovation deepens, it is imperative for organizations to transition from reactive defense mechanisms to proactive, strategic integration of cybersecurity into every phase of innovation. Insights drawn from the preceding case studies and literature review reveal a coherent path forward for securing digital transformation while sustaining agility and growth. The following strategic recommendations are designed to help organizations operationalize cybersecurity as a central component of innovation governance.

First, cybersecurity must be embedded into innovation governance frameworks from ideation through to scaling. This calls for the adoption of a "secure-by-design" philosophy, where cyber risk is considered during the earliest stages of product and process development. As demonstrated in the Zoom for Education and UAS (Unmanned Aircraft Systems) cases, waiting until post-deployment to address vulnerabilities leaves organizations exposed to reputational, operational, and regulatory risks. Instead, cybersecurity should be viewed as an enabler of trust and scalability. Moyo (2022) emphasizes that executives must treat cybersecurity not as a compliance obligation, but as a strategic priority, integrated into board-level decisions and digital strategy execution. Organizations should involve cybersecurity specialists in innovation planning teams and ensure alignment across product design, IT security, and compliance units (Henrichsen, 2024; Ahsan, 2025).

Second, organizations should develop innovation-specific risk models and cybersecurity key performance indicators (KPIs) to monitor and manage cyber risk in evolving digital ecosystems. Mızrak (2023) illustrates the importance of multi-criteria decision-making tools such as fuzzy AHP in identifying and prioritizing cybersecurity strategies that align with organizational goals. In manufacturing and healthcare contexts, digital twins and federated learning platforms have proven effective not only in achieving technical outcomes but also in measuring cybersecurity effectiveness through performance metrics such as anomaly detection accuracy, breach response time, and system availability. Embedding these KPIs into innovation dashboards allows organizations to maintain real-time situational awareness and course-correct as new threats emerge (NIST, 2023; Synced Review, 2020).

Third, fostering cross-sectoral collaboration and knowledge-sharing is vital for staying ahead of the threat curve. As seen in the collaborative approaches used in the BFDI-AP drone project and the federated learning model in healthcare, industry partnerships enable the pooling of expertise and resources to tackle shared cybersecurity challenges. Ulnicane et al. (2021) and Taeihagh et al. (2021) stress that in the face of regulatory uncertainty, cooperative governance models can promote consistency and ethical innovation practices across sectors. Organizations should participate in cybersecurity information-sharing forums, contribute to standards development initiatives, and establish public-private partnerships to address systemic vulnerabilities collectively. This ecosystem approach is particularly important in sectors with overlapping digital infrastructures, such as finance and energy, where a cyber incident can have cascading effects.

Finally, organizations must invest in real-time threat intelligence and adaptive defense mechanisms that match the pace of innovation. AI- and ML-powered systems, such as those deployed in digital twin cybersecurity and federated learning platforms, have demonstrated the ability to detect and respond to threats in real time without compromising operational performance (Roshanaei et al., 2024; NIST, 2023). These systems should be augmented with predictive analytics, behavioral baselining, and autonomous mitigation protocols to ensure resilience in high-speed, high-complexity environments. Additionally, ongoing training and upskilling efforts, as highlighted by Vasudevan et al. (2023), are essential to ensure that security teams can interpret threat intelligence data and act on it effectively. Cyber-aware leadership, as Moyo (2022) asserts, must ensure that threat intelligence insights are integrated into innovation decision-making processes and communicated across functional boundaries.

In conclusion, the secure innovation agenda must be pursued not through isolated tools or ad hoc policies, but through strategic, system-wide frameworks that align cybersecurity with digital transformation goals. By embedding cybersecurity from ideation to deployment, quantifying cyber risk with innovation-specific KPIs, promoting cross-sector collaboration, and leveraging real-time intelligence, organizations can create a resilient foundation for future-ready, secure innovation.

8. CONCLUSION

The convergence of cybersecurity and innovation is no longer a theoretical aspiration—it is a strategic imperative in today's digital economy. This chapter has demonstrated that cybersecurity, when embedded into innovation strategies from the outset, plays a critical role not only in protecting organizational assets but also in enabling trust, accelerating adoption, and sustaining long-term value creation. Across sectors—finance, healthcare, aviation, manufacturing, and education—the integration of cybersecurity into technological advancement has revealed both challenges and opportunities. Each case study reinforces a central insight: secure innovation requires a systemic, multi-dimensional approach involving governance, technology, culture, and cross-sectoral collaboration.

In finance and fintech, blockchain and smart contracts emerged as tools not only for efficiency but also for building digital trust through cryptographic security. Healthcare innovation revealed the value of privacy-preserving technologies like federated learning and encrypted telehealth platforms that allow sensitive data to remain protected while enabling scalable AI solutions. The aviation sector highlighted the need for secure-by-design frameworks, such as automated drone hardening tools, which address vulnerabilities at the infrastructure level before deployment. In manufacturing, cybersecurity-enhanced digital twins illustrated how AI and anomaly detection can secure operational continuity and process integrity. Finally, education's rapid digital transformation during the pandemic exposed initial vulnerabilities, but also demonstrated the power of policy coordination, platform re-engineering, and user awareness to turn crisis into resilience.

Several cross-cutting success factors emerged from these sectoral lessons. First, organizations that prioritized cyber-aware leadership and strategic foresight were better positioned to align innovation with resilience. Second, embedding security early—whether in product design, AI development, or platform architecture—consistently resulted in more scalable, sustainable outcomes. Third, interdisciplinary collaboration across IT, legal, operations, and innovation functions proved crucial in translating security policies into effective practices. Finally, those who treated cybersecurity not as a siloed function but as a shared organizational responsibility were more successful in building cultures of secure experimentation and continuous improvement.

Looking ahead, the future of secure innovation will be shaped by emerging technologies such as quantum computing, decentralized finance, autonomous systems, and next-generation AI. These advancements will bring new efficiencies—but also new risks. As innovation environments grow in complexity and speed, organizations must invest in real-time threat intelligence, adaptive security architectures, and agile governance models. The secure digital economy of the future will not be built solely on stronger firewalls or better encryption—it will rest on the ability of organizations to integrate cybersecurity into the very DNA of their innovation strategies, balancing speed with safety, openness with control, and experimentation with accountability.

Ultimately, securing innovation is not just about mitigating risk—it is about enabling progress with confidence. Those who succeed will be those who treat cybersecurity not as a barrier, but as a powerful enabler of transformation in an increasingly connected, data-driven world.

REFERENCES

Abto Software. (2021). *Zoom end-to-end encryption: How it works and why it matters*. Retrieved from https://www.abtosoftware.com

Adams, E. (2024). *See Yourself in Cyber: Security Careers Beyond Hacking*. John Wiley & Sons.

Ahsan, M. J. (2025). Cultivating a culture of learning: The role of leadership in fostering lifelong development. *The Learning Organization*, *32*(2), 282–306. DOI: 10.1108/TLO-03-2024-0099

Akintoye, R., Ogunode, O., Ajayi, M., & Joshua, A. A. (2022). Cyber security and financial innovation of selected deposit money banks in Nigeria. *universal Journal of Accounting and Finance, 10*(3), 643-652.

AlDaajeh, S., Saleous, H., Alrabaee, S., Barka, E., Breitinger, F., & Choo, K. K. R. (2022). The role of national cybersecurity strategies on the improvement of cybersecurity education. *Computers & Security*, *119*, 102754. DOI: 10.1016/j.cose.2022.102754

Alevizos, L., Bhakuni, L., & Jäschke, S. (2025). A value driven framework for cybersecurity innovation in transportation and infrastructure. *International Journal of Information Technology : an Official Journal of Bharati Vidyapeeth's Institute of Computer Applications and Management*, *17*(1), 321–331. DOI: 10.1007/s41870-024-02288-w

Annarelli, A., & Palombi, G. (2021). Digitalization capabilities for sustainable cyber resilience: A conceptual framework. *Sustainability (Basel)*, *13*(23), 13065. DOI: 10.3390/su132313065

ANSI. (2023). *Digital twins and cybersecurity in Industry 4.0: Standardization trends and recommendations*. American National Standards Institute. Retrieved from https://www.ansi.org

Chalkbeat. (2020, May 6). *NYC lifts Zoom ban after security improvements*. Retrieved from https://www.chalkbeat.org/newyork/2020/05/06/nyc-lifts-zoom-ban-after-security-improvements

Chaudhary, S. (2024). Driving behaviour change with cybersecurity awareness. *Computers & Security*, *142*, 103858. DOI: 10.1016/j.cose.2024.103858

CISA. (2021). *Unmanned Aircraft Systems: Cybersecurity Risks and Mitigation Approaches*. Retrieved from https://www.cisa.gov

Coutinho, B., Ferreira, J., Yevseyeva, I., & Basto-Fernandes, V. (2023). Integrated cybersecurity methodology and supporting tools for healthcare operational information systems. *Computers & Security*, *129*, 103189. DOI: 10.1016/j.cose.2023.103189

Dabke, V., Dabke, Y., & Gadgil, G. (2023). Social engineering as a driving force for innovation in cybersecurity. *Authorea Preprints.*

Decta. (2021). *Blockchain in banking: Transforming trade finance with digital trust.* Retrieved from https://www.decta.com/blog/blockchain-in-banking/

FAA. (2024). *BFDI-AP Test Report: Enhancing Cybersecurity in Public Safety UAS Operations*. Federal Aviation Administration. Retrieved from https://www.faa.gov

Grima, S., Thalassinos, E., Cristea, M., Kadłubek, M., Maditinos, D., & Peiseniece, L. (Eds.). (2023). *Digital transformation, strategic resilience, cyber security and risk management.* Emerald Publishing Limited.

Healthcare, I. T. Today. (2021). *How cybersecurity is shaping the future of telehealth platforms.* Retrieved from https://www.healthcareittoday.com

Henrichsen, J. R. (2024). Understanding Nascent Newsroom Security and Safety Cultures: The Emergence of the "Security Champion". In *Journalism and Safety* (pp. 278-297). Routledge.

Hokmabadi, H., Rezvani, S. M., & de Matos, C. A. (2024). Business resilience for small and medium enterprises and startups by digital transformation and the role of marketing capabilities—A systematic review. *Systems*, *12*(6), 220. DOI: 10.3390/systems12060220

Hossain, M. A., Raza, M. A., & Rahman, T. Y. (2023). Resource allocation and budgetary constraints for cybersecurity projects in small to medium sized banks. *Journal of Multidisciplinary Research*, *9*(01), 135–157.

Jones, N. (2019). Innovation as a Driver of Cyber Security. *Cyber Security: Threats and Responses for Government and Business*, 157.

Kotila, B., Drezner, J. A., Bartels, E. M., Hill, D., Hodgson, Q. E., Huilgol, S. S., & Wong, J. P. (2023). *Strengthening the defense innovation ecosystem.* RAND Corporation.

Kumar, V. A., Bhardwaj, S., & Lather, M. (2024). Cybersecurity and Safeguarding Digital Assets: An Analysis of Regulatory Frameworks, Legal Liability and Enforcement Mechanisms. *Productivity*, *65*(1), 1–10. DOI: 10.32381/PROD.2024.65.01.1

Li, B., Zhou, X., Ning, Z., Guan, X., & Yiu, K. F. C. (2022). Dynamic event-triggered security control for networked control systems with cyber-attacks: A model predictive control approach. *Information Sciences*, *612*, 384–398. DOI: 10.1016/j.ins.2022.08.093

Li, X., Hu, Z., & Zhang, Q. (2021). Environmental regulation, economic policy uncertainty, and green technology innovation. *Clean Technologies and Environmental Policy*, *23*(10), 2975–2988. DOI: 10.1007/s10098-021-02219-4

Maciel, C., Mendes, F. F., Pereira, V. C., & Yamauchi, E. A. (2021, April). Defining Digital Legacy Management Systems' Requirements. In *International Conference on Enterprise Information Systems* (pp. 256-279). Cham: Springer International Publishing.

Manikyala, A., Kommineni, H. P., Allam, A. R., Nizamuddin, M., & Sridharlakshmi, N. R. B. (2023). Integrating Cybersecurity Best Practices in DevOps Pipelines for Securing Distributed Systems. *ABC Journal of Advanced Research*, *12*(1), 57–70. DOI: 10.18034/abcjar.v12i1.773

Masombuka, M., Grobler, M., & Duvenage, P. (2021, June). Cybersecurity and local government: Imperative, challenges and priorities. In *ECCWS 2021 20th European Conference on Cyber Warfare and Security* (Vol. 285). Academic Conferences Inter Ltd.

Mızrak, F. (2023). Integrating cybersecurity risk management into strategic management: A comprehensive literature review. *Research Journal of Business and Management*, *10*(3), 98–108. DOI: 10.17261/Pressacademia.2023.1807

Mızrak, F. (2023). Integration of Fuzzy AHP for Cybersecurity Strategy Development in International Organizations. *Premium e-Journal of Social Sciences (PEJOSS)*, *7*(35), 1272-1292.

Möller, D. P. (2023). Cybersecurity in digital transformation. In *Guide to cybersecurity in digital transformation: Trends, methods, technologies, applications and best practices* (pp. 1–70). Springer Nature Switzerland. DOI: 10.1007/978-3-031-26845-8_1

Mor, S., & Ashta, A. (2018). Fostering the culture of learning and experimentations: An introduction. *Culture of learning and experimentation for well-being*, 1-18.

Moyo, S. (2022). *Executive's Guide to Cyber Risk: Securing the Future Today*. John Wiley & Sons. DOI: 10.1002/9781394320578

Mylrea, M., Fracchia, C., Grimes, H., Austad, W., Shannon, G., Reid, B., & Case, N. (2021). BioSecure digital twin: manufacturing innovation and cybersecurity resilience. *Engineering Artificially Intelligent Systems: A Systems Engineering Approach to Realizing Synergistic Capabilities*, 53-72.

Nature. (2021). *How federated learning is transforming healthcare AI*. Retrieved from https://www.nature.com/articles/d41586-021-00003-w

Neri, M., & Niccolini, F. (2025). On the path to cyber organizational resilience: Shedding light on the context of SMEs. *The International Journal of Organizational Analysis*, *33*(12), 105–131. DOI: 10.1108/IJOA-06-2024-4572

New Prairie Press. (2020). *Cybersecurity threats in commercial drone usage: A review of vulnerabilities and risk controls*. Retrieved from https://newprairiepress.org

NIST. (2023). *How digital twins could protect manufacturers from cyberattacks*. National Institute of Standards and Technology. Retrieved from https://www.nist.gov/news-events/news/2023/02/how-digital-twins-could-protect-manufacturers-cyberattacks

NIST. (2024). *Securing Drone Fleets with BFDI-AP: Real-World Applications and Demonstrations*. National Institute of Standards and Technology. Retrieved from https://www.nist.gov

Nkomo, L., & Kalisz, D. (2023). Establishing organisational resilience through developing a strategic framework for digital transformation. *Digital Transformation and Society*, *2*(4), 403–426. DOI: 10.1108/DTS-11-2022-0059

NPR. (2020, April 7). *'Zoombombing' is a wake-up call: Online education faces security scrutiny*. Retrieved from https://www.npr.org/2020/04/07/zoombombing-cybersecurity-education

Odebade, A. T., & Benkhelifa, E. (2023). A comparative study of national cyber security strategies of ten nations. *arXiv preprint arXiv:2303.13938*.

Olaniyi, O. O., Omogoroye, O. O., Olaniyi, F. G., Alao, A. I., & Oladoyinbo, T. O. (2024). CyberFusion protocols: Strategic integration of enterprise risk management, ISO 27001, and mobile forensics for advanced digital security in the modern business ecosystem. *Journal of Engineering Research and Reports*, *26*(6), 31–49. DOI: 10.9734/jerr/2024/v26i61160

Omar, M. (2022). *Machine learning for cybersecurity: Innovative deep learning solutions*. Springer Nature. DOI: 10.1007/978-3-031-15893-3

Payne, B., Cigularova, D., Costanzo, J., Das, S., Mann, M., & Perez, K. (2022). Impact of articulation agreements on student transfer between higher education institutions: A case study of a cybersecurity program. *Community College Journal of Research and Practice*, *46*(8), 573–588. DOI: 10.1080/10668926.2021.1887007

Rahardja, U., Miftah, M., Rakhmansyah, M., & Zanubiya, J. (2025). Revolutionizing Financial Services with Big Data and Fintech: A Scalable Approach to Innovation. *ADI Journal on Recent Innovation*, *6*(2), 118–129. DOI: 10.34306/ajri.v6i2.1180

Rajan, R., Rana, N. P., Parameswar, N., Dhir, S., & Dwivedi, Y. K. (2021). Developing a modified total interpretive structural model (M-TISM) for organizational strategic cybersecurity management. *Technological Forecasting and Social Change*, *170*, 120872. DOI: 10.1016/j.techfore.2021.120872

Rosenkranz, S., Staegemann, D., Volk, M., & Turowski, K. (2024). Explaining the Business-Technological Age of Legacy Information Systems. *IEEE Access : Practical Innovations, Open Solutions*, *12*, 84579–84611. DOI: 10.1109/ACCESS.2024.3414377

Roshanaei, M., Khan, M. R., & Sylvester, N. N. (2024). Enhancing cybersecurity through AI and ML: Strategies, challenges, and future directions. *Journal of Information Security*, *15*(3), 320–339. DOI: 10.4236/jis.2024.153019

Saeed, S., Altamimi, S. A., Alkayyal, N. A., Alshehri, E., & Alabbad, D. A. (2023). Digital transformation and cybersecurity challenges for businesses resilience: Issues and recommendations. *Sensors (Basel)*, *23*(15), 6666. DOI: 10.3390/s23156666 PMID: 37571451

Sinclair, S. (2020, November 3). *HSBC carries out Bangladesh's first blockchain letter-of-credit transaction. CoinDesk*. Retrieved from https://www.coindesk.com/markets/2020/11/03/hsbc-carries-out-bangladeshs-first-blockchain-letter-of-credit-transaction/

Synced Review. (2020, October 7). *NVIDIA and Mass General Brigham use federated learning to predict COVID-19 patient oxygen needs*. Retrieved from https://syncedreview.com/2020/10/07/nvidia-and-mass-general-brigham-use-federated-learning-to-predict-covid-19-patient-oxygen-needs/

Taeihagh, A., Ramesh, M., & Howlett, M. (2021). Assessing the regulatory challenges of emerging disruptive technologies. *Regulation & Governance*, *15*(4), 1009–1019. DOI: 10.1111/rego.12392

Ulnicane, I., Eke, D. O., Knight, W., Ogoh, G., & Stahl, B. C. (2021). Good governance as a response to discontents? Déjà vu, or lessons for AI from other emerging technologies. *Interdisciplinary Science Reviews*, *46*(1-2), 71–93. DOI: 10.1080/03080188.2020.1840220

Uzougbo, N. S., Ikegwu, C. G., & Adewusi, A. O.Ngozi Samuel UzougboChinonso Gladys IkegwuAdefolake Olachi Adewusi. (2024). Regulatory frameworks for decentralized finance (DEFI): Challenges and opportunities. *GSC Advanced Research and Reviews*, *19*(02), 116–129. DOI: 10.30574/gscarr.2024.19.2.0170

Vasudevan, S., Piazza, A., & Carr, M. (2023, March). A decade of studies on cyber security training in organizations using social network analysis: a systematic literature review through keyword co-occurrence network. In *2023 International Conference on Business Analytics for Technology and Security (ICBATS)* (pp. 1-6). IEEE. DOI: 10.1109/ICBATS57792.2023.10111127

Villalón-Fonseca, R. (2022). The nature of security: A conceptual framework for integral-comprehensive modeling of IT security and cybersecurity. *Computers & Security*, *120*, 102805. DOI: 10.1016/j.cose.2022.102805

Chapter 2
A Strategic Approach to Cyberattacks and Risk Management

Sezin Acik Tasar
https://orcid.org/0000-0002-0406-7734
Beykoz University, Turkey

ABSTRACT

Cybersecurity has become an extremely important issue that companies need to focus on to guarantee the safety of their information systems. As the need for digitalization increases, every organization must combat the ever-evolving cyberattacks. By giving a succinct summary of the current state of cyber threats, this study seeks to explore the relationship between cybersecurity risk management and cyberattacks. The study also highlights how crucial thorough risk assessment is as a first step in determining vulnerabilities, assessing the possible consequences of attacks, and setting security action priorities. Next, the five key functions of the NIST Cybersecurity Risk Management Framework were analyzed to offer a strategic perspective on how to manage cybersecurity risk throughout a business. The study emphasizes the necessity of cybersecurity, stressing the incorporation of risk management into the broader organizational strategy to better predict and prevent cyberattacks.

1. INTRODUCTION

Today's connected digital world exposes businesses to growing cyberattacks that endanger financial resources, operational continuity, and sensitive data. Cyberattacks have become more frequent and sophisticated, with adversaries using cutting-edge strategies to take advantage of weaknesses in various industries. The

DOI: 10.4018/979-8-3693-6417-8.ch002

majority of fraudulent activities involving stolen identity information are tax filings and loan applications. An estimated 8.1 million people were victims of identity theft in the United States alone in 2010 (Kavak et al., 2021; Sheppard, 2010). By 2018, the number had increased to 14.4 million people (Kavak et al., 2021; Marchini & Pascual, 2019).

Attackers escape conventional security measures by using sophisticated strategies, including malware, social engineering, and zero-day exploits. Firms must constantly modify and improve their security measures to identify and lessen these changing dangers. Additionally, enterprises must deal with new attack vectors and complications brought about by the interconnectedness of digital systems and the quick uptake of technologies like cloud computing and the Internet of Things (IoT) (Aji et al., 2023).

Implementing safeguards to protect industrial automation systems from cyberattacks is currently Industry 4.0's main objective. This entails implementing security measures, monitoring network traffic, segmenting networks, regularly training staff members in cybersecurity, and maintaining backup plans to handle incidents promptly. Stability and security in the sector depend on effective risk management and assault prevention (Pochmara & Swietlicka, 2024).

The defense of people, communities, institutions, systems, and technology against anomalous activity is known as cybersecurity. The preservation of the confidentiality, integrity, and availability (CIA) of computer resources that belong to one organization or are linked to the network of another is known as cybersecurity (Ullah et al., 2019). According to the report of Hiscox (2024), while 94.7% of workers in low-revenue companies believed they possessed the skills necessary to meet their cybersecurity goals in 2022, this percentage dropped to 49.2% in 2024. However, in 2022, 88.3% of workers at high- and medium-revenue companies believed they possessed the necessary abilities to meet their cybersecurity goals; in 2024, that percentage rose to 82.1% (World Economic Forum, 2024).

Mitigating cyberattacks requires effective risk management. Comprehensive guidelines for information security risk management are provided by international standards, which highlight the significance of a methodical approach to risk identification, assessment, and treatment. Risk management is a key discipline for effective decision-making and internal communication of outcomes inside businesses. It proactively identifies potential technical and management issues so that the appropriate steps can be taken to reduce or eliminate their likelihood and/or effects (Georgieva et al., 2009). Cybersecurity risk management is essential for today's enterprises due to the continually evolving threat landscape and the rise of increasingly complex cyberattacks. Organizations of all sizes, particularly those connected to critical infrastructure, must understand the risks to implement suitable controls for essential service delivery and overall business continuity (Kure et al., 2022).

This study aims to investigate the relationship between cybersecurity risk management and cyberattacks by providing a concise overview of the current state of cyber threats, which include malware, phishing, social engineering, Internet of Things-based threats, advanced persistent threats, and distributed denial-of-service attacks. These threats are continuously expanding in complexity and scope. The study also emphasizes the importance of doing a complete risk assessment as a preliminary step in identifying vulnerabilities, evaluating the potential outcomes of attacks, and prioritizing security actions. The NIST Cybersecurity Risk Management Framework's five main features were then examined to provide a strategic viewpoint on how to control and reduce cybersecurity risk across an organization. The study's literature review section aggregated recent studies on different risk mitigation strategies in cybersecurity risk management across different industries. To better anticipate and prevent cyberattacks, the study highlights the importance of adopting a strategic approach to cybersecurity and the integration of risk management into the larger organizational plan.

2. UNDERSTANDING CYBERATTACKS

In the twenty-first century, cybersecurity is essential since almost every aspect of our lives depends on technology to preserve social and economic security. Cyberattacks can have disastrous consequences, including monetary loss, damage to one's reputation, and even fatalities in sectors like healthcare and energy that depend on critical infrastructure (Sharma, 2012). Cyberattacks are now one of the main risks to businesses' security and financial viability. Significant financial damages, both direct and indirect, may arise from these attacks. The immediate expenses brought on by a cyberattack are considered direct economic repercussions. These include fines, legal fees, IT system recovery costs, and restitution for impacted clients (Fotis, 2024).

White-collar crime has always been challenging to define and quantify. Legal and accounting definitions, rules, and practices have changed as a result of periodic scandals (McKesson & Robbins in 1938, IOS and Equity Funding in 1973, Enron in 2001, and the banking crisis in 2008), which have prompted debate about which business practices ought to be prohibited. These developments are linked to transformations in political discourse and societal views (Andersen et al., 2019).

Cyber threats can take many different forms and can result in business interruptions that harm a company's brand and cost money. One of the primary causes of these risks stems from the company's Internet connectivity through its servers, endpoint computers, and information systems, which facilitate data communication that supports the company's operations and allows for communication with both internal and external devices via the network. Companies are now required to update their cyber protection policies and hire cyber experts who are in charge of mitigating the cyber vulnerabilities discovered in said network and computer elements because they are exposed to cyber risks by computers and network elements that are connected to the Internet (Zwilling, 2022; Amin, 2019).

The ENISA report from the European Union Agency for Cybersecurity provides an in-depth look at each of the seven primary cybersecurity threats. These threats were identified by analyzing thousands of publicly reported cybersecurity incidents and events. Threats to availability ranked highest, followed by ransomware and threats to data. These threats are (ENISA, 2024):

- ***Malware Attacks***: Malware, often known as malicious software, is a type of malicious code that can damage and destroy digital systems, computer systems, and mobile and electronic devices. The purpose of malware is to steal important data and harm digital systems (Smmarwar et al., 2024; Kumar et al., 2022). Malicious attacks include targeted attacks such as ransomware, spyware, and command and control (Zhan et al., 2024). The goal of ransomware is to prevent the victim from accessing their files or using their machine. After obtaining the equipment or data, the crooks use blackmail to get it back. Initially, the criminals tried frightening the victim by posing as police authorities. Ransomware shows a message (ransom note) outlining the terms of the ransom (O'Kane et al., 2018). These attacks are now among the most serious risks to software programs and different systems, including PCs, laptops, smart devices running Android, and Internet of Things devices (Kumar et al., 2021). The number of malware attacks globally rose by 10% from the previous year to reach 6.06 billion in 2023. In 2018, with 10.5 billion reported malware attacks, it experienced the highest number in recent memory. Worm malware was blocked over 205 million times in 2022. Emotet, another significant virus strain at that time, primarily targeted the Asia-Pacific region. According to recent industry data, malware attacks are most often transmitted via EXE files, with websites serving as the most common vectors for these attacks. Malware primarily attacked the education sector in 2022, with an average of 2,314 attacks per week. The hospital units came in second, followed by government and military agencies. In 2022, there were more than five million malware assaults in the education industry overall (Petrosyan, 2024).
- ***Phishing and Social Engineering***: Phishing is an illegal method used to find information about the identities of consumers and the passwords of financial institutions. Social engineering strategies use counterfeit emails from legitimate businesses and organizations. The purpose of those emails is to allow people to divulge financial information, such as usernames and passwords, on fraudulent websites (Phishing is a group of cyberattacks in which the attacker

uses deceit and disguising techniques to obtain the victim's private information online (Varshney et al., 2024). A global survey of 351 practitioners and decision-makers in large organizations in Asia/Pacific, Europe, North America, and the Middle East was conducted in 2021. The survey found that organizations are facing financial losses, a decline in investor confidence, a loss of intellectual property, a loss of customer trust, a disruption in business operations due to phishing attacks, and penalties from regulators (Sarker et al., 2024; Cofense, 2022; Szathmari, 2019). The frequency and sophistication of phishing attempts are rising dramatically, and they are getting more widespread. Phishing attacks have taken many different forms recently. The attackers deploy a variety of threats and channels to trap additional victims. These channels might be VoIP or social networks, and they could contain a variety of dangers, including malware attachments, URLs hidden in emails, instant messaging, scam calls, and more. Because social engineering is their preferred weapon, criminals continue to focus on social engineering attacks rather than more complex strategies and toolkits because they are aware that these tactics are successful and lucrative. Phishing assaults have increased to previously unheard-of proportions, particularly with the rise of social media and mobile devices (Alkhalil et al., 2021; Marforio et al., 2015).

- ***IoT-Based Threats:*** One of the cutting-edge technologies utilized in smart environments is the Internet of Things (IoT). It consists of billions of interconnected smart “things” that can sense, act, and process data to produce value-added services for any application area. The idea has gained traction in a variety of application areas during the past ten years, suggesting that an increasing number of devices—from wearables and smartphones to connected cars and industrial machinery—will be connected. The massive volume of data generated by these interconnected devices necessitates communication infrastructures with particular capabilities that may meet a variety of limitations, including real-time analytics, speed, scalability, storage, and data processing. To address the heterogeneity of low-level devices (at the hardware level) and simplify and improve the ultimate end-user experience (at the application level), the appropriate architecture and set of technologies must be chosen and implemented for each application situation (Patrono et al., 2020). Growing cybersecurity concerns in the IoT space necessitate prompt attention and all-encompassing solutions. IoT devices' extreme complexity and variety generate a large attack surface that draws malevolent actors looking to take advantage of flaws for various reasons (Zhang et al., 2014). Malicious actors obtain illegal access by taking advantage of flaws in IoT systems, which could lead to misuse and unlawful data access. An advanced threat vector is the development and spread of malware and botnets based on the IoT (Amoo et al., 2024; Antonakakis et al., 2017).

- ***Advanced Persistent Threats (APTs):*** Advanced Persistent Threats (APTs) are sophisticated and enduring threats that compromise the confidentiality, availability, and integrity of organizational data and services. Consequently, they pose significant security challenges for businesses (Mat et al., 2024). Due to advanced fraud techniques, APT attacks on network systems have increased in recent years. Conventional intrusion detection systems (IDSs) struggle to identify unexpected attacks, including user-to-root (U2R) and remote-to-local (R2L) attacks. They also exhibit high false-positive rates and low detection accuracy (Mutalib et al., 2024). Efficient detection techniques guard against illegal access, alteration, and destruction of an organization's systems and data. Monitoring suspicious activity, examining logs and network traffic, and utilizing security technologies like IDSs and security information and event management (SIEM) systems are some strategies for effective detection (Buchta et al., 2024). Regardless of the target's defenses, the APT selects its target and persists until it achieves a breach. Critical infrastructures, such as electric power systems, have been primary targets of APTs. Each stage of an APT attack employs different tactics, methods, and procedures (TTPs) before proceeding to the next. How the APT executes the attack from start to finish is referred to as its "tactics." The APT's technological "strategy" to achieve its objectives encompasses the methods it employs throughout the attack. Lastly, an APT's "procedure" outlines the steps the attacker takes to achieve its aims. It is useful to consider the TTP attribute as part of a specific detection technique, as it can be used to profile an APT actor and may help predict and detect APT attacks early on (Mat et al., 2024).
- ***Distributed Denial-of-Service (DDoS) Attacks:*** One of the most common and destructive types of cyber threats is flooding Distributed Denial-of-Service (DDoS) attacks, which target various industries, from critical infrastructure to finance. These attacks cause excessive traffic to overwhelm network resources, disrupting services and having a major negative economic impact (Firmansyah and Turmudi, 2024). By overloading the system with too much traffic, DDoS attacks are intended to prevent authorized users from accessing the targeted system (Qasim and Nsaif, 2024; Yan and Yu, 2015). The internet's dependability and security, as well as the services that are linked to it, are thereby exposed. Because DDoS attacks have become more frequent and intense over time, time series analysis has become the most efficient technique for identifying these attacks. DDoS attacks were identified through the use of time series analysis, which shows patterns and trends in network traffic (Qasim and Nsaif, 2024; Lau et al., 2000). DDoS attacks can be directed at

bandwidth, traffic, or applications; each attack type has a unique goal and level of success (Qasim and Nsaif, 2024). Globally, there are expected to be over 30 billion connected IoT devices by 2025 (Ahmad et al., 2024; Vailshery, 2022). By enabling unprecedented levels of monitoring, control, optimization, and automation through technologies like wearables, smart homes, driverless cars, and sensor-enabled manufacturing, this enormous increase is propelling significant advances. This high level of connection increases security concerns by introducing vulnerabilities even as it makes data sharing and automation easier. DDoS attacks, in which a large number of hacked devices are used as weapons to overload systems or services with data, are a significant new danger that disrupts availability (Ahmad et al., 2024; Le et al., 2022). DDoS attacks have become multifaceted, with several strings to their bow, so to speak, to outsmart the conventional security measures that are still in place, as attackers have evolved more sophisticated ways of presenting themselves (Reddy, 2024).

3. RISK MANAGEMENT AND CYBERSECURITY

Unauthorized access, malware attacks, DDoS attacks, social engineering, phishing, and other security problems have increased dramatically in recent years due to growing reliance on digitalization and the IoT (Sarker et al., 2020). Cybersecurity safeguards critical infrastructures, ensures the confidentiality and integrity of sensitive data, and protects personal data in small businesses, government organizations, military units, healthcare facilities, educational institutions, energy suppliers, and transportation systems (Arabo, 2015).

Cybersecurity protects Internet-connected systems, including data, hardware, and software, against online attacks. By following this procedure, organizations and individuals are shielded against unwanted access to data centers and other computerized systems. Good protection against assaults intended to access, alter, or extort a user's or organization's systems and sensitive data can be ensured with a robust cybersecurity policy. Additionally, cybersecurity works well to stop attacks that try to stop or interfere with a system's or device's functionality (Tasar, 2023; Shea et al., 2023).

Due to the growing frequency and severity of cyber incidents, a comprehensive enterprise risk management framework must include effective and integrated cyber risk management as a key component (Kosub, 2015). Businesses have implemented risk management frameworks to recognize and control cybersecurity risks. Stages are often included in all cybersecurity risk management strategies. Although the risk assessment stage is the one that firms utilize the most and is included in all risk management models, the number and names of the phases differ depending on the model (Sanchez-Garcia et al., 2023; ISACA, 2019).

The step of the risk management process that includes analyzing risks and vulnerabilities is called risk assessment. Furthermore, the mitigations offered by planned or implemented security procedures are considered in risk assessment (Sanchez-Garcia et al., 2023; NIST, 2011). In other words, identifying assets, security threats, and vulnerabilities that challenge regulated and methodical security risk management is the function of security risk management in information systems. These resources may consist of networks, software, and hardware. Certain security standards must be met to safeguard data assets in these systems. These consist of non-repudiation, accountability, availability, confidentiality, integrity, and authenticity. To identify and reduce risks, a security risk assessment is an essential element in the risk management process (Alamri et al., 2022; Dubois et al., 2010). Risk assessment is a fundamental phase in risk management that is used to determine hazards and implement appropriate control measures. Risk assessment ensures that information systems are current, safe, and economical (Leszczyna, 2021; Qiangmin et al., 2007).

Ultimately, efficient cybersecurity is not only a technological requirement but also a strategic imperative. By detecting, assessing, and reducing threats that may threaten the accessibility, safety, and integrity of digital assets, cybersecurity plays a critical role in risk assessment. The potential impact of cyber threats increases with an organization's dependence on technology; hence, it is crucial to incorporate cybersecurity into all phases of risk management. A robust cybersecurity architecture guarantees business continuity, regulatory compliance, and the maintenance of an organization's reputation, in addition to protecting sensitive data and systems.

3.1. NIST Cybersecurity Risk Management Framework

Risk management in cybersecurity requires a systematic strategy. Organizations may efficiently identify, evaluate, respond to, and monitor cybersecurity risks by using a Cybersecurity Risk Management Framework (CRMF). To guarantee data availability, confidentiality, and integrity in databases, risk assessment methodologies and techniques come in various forms, including qualitative, quantitative, and hybrid models (Phillips et al., 2024; Henrie, 2013).

The first cybersecurity directive has been implemented by the European Union (EU). It mandates critical infrastructure organizations to routinely monitor and report on their cybersecurity efforts and is based on the US National Institute of Standards and Technology's (NIST) Cybersecurity Framework (Krumay et al., 2018). The five primary roles of the NIST Cybersecurity Framework (CSF) are Identify, Protect, Detect, Respond, and Recover. These roles serve as the foundation for a cybersecurity strategy that is risk-based. Every function offers a strategic perspective of the lifecycle of managing cybersecurity risk and constitutes a high-level cybersecurity activity (Calder, 2018).

- ***Identify:*** It entails recognizing threats, weaknesses, and their effects in addition to comprehending and ranking important assets, systems, and data. Establishing governance frameworks, guidelines, and procedures for efficient risk management is another aspect of this role (Calder, 2018). By identifying important assets and business contexts, businesses can better match cybersecurity priorities with business objectives, hence increasing the effectiveness of risk mitigation (Ahmad et al., 2021).
- ***Protect:*** By taking proactive steps and protecting against potential vulnerabilities, this function seeks to prevent or lessen the impact of cybersecurity threats. It includes creating and implementing safeguards, including vulnerability management, data encryption, access limits, and security awareness training (Calder, 2018). According to Smith and Brooks (2020), lowering human-related vulnerabilities and creating a security-aware culture require protection measures like access restriction and personnel training.
- ***Detect:*** This involves proactive detection of harmful activity or security breaches through log analysis, threat intelligence collection, and real-time monitoring. Cybersecurity resilience is improved by early cyber threat identification and response (Calder, 2018). Reducing the amount of time between compromise and reaction requires real-time detection capabilities, such as continuous monitoring systems (Conti et al., 2018). Hence, the potential harm from a breach decreases with early detection.
- ***Respond:*** In addition to restoring regular operations, this entails taking prompt action to limit and minimize harm (Chidukwani et al., 2024; Thompson, 2018). Reducing the impact of occurrences is the aim. Von Solms and Van Niekerk (2013) assert that having a clear reaction plan enhances coordination and lessens chaos during high-stress situations, thereby assisting in maintaining the organization's reputation and the trust of its customers.
- ***Recover:*** Restoring operational capabilities and services following a cybersecurity event is the main goal of the NIST CSF Recover function (Calder, 2018). It covers business continuity plans, system fixes, and data restoration (Chidukwani et al., 2024). In addition to restoring operations, recovery procedures incorporate input into plans for organizational resilience. Effective recovery planning promotes long-term sustainability and system robustness following a breach (Gritzalis et al., 2019).

An organization can approach cybersecurity risk as a component of total organizational risk clearly and consistently by incorporating the NIST CSF into its risk management plan. Additionally, the framework allows businesses of all sizes to customize cybersecurity safeguards based on their unique size, level of complexity, and risk tolerance. Both the public and private sectors make substantial use of these standards, which help companies of all sizes bolster their defenses against cyberattacks.

4. LITERATURE REVIEW ON CYBERSECURITY RISK MANAGEMENT

Since every industry faces different risks and operational constraints, applying different risk mitigation strategies in cybersecurity risk management across different industries is essential.

Padmanabhan and Zhang (2018) investigated the main cyber threats now facing the additive manufacturing (AM) sector, as well as several current mitigating techniques to shield AM operations from cyber attacks. Using case examples from the literature, a novel paradigm for identifying threats and evaluating weaknesses in the AM process was suggested. Additionally, a novel method for encrypting 3D model data using 2D pictures was proposed, which could improve cybersecurity in AM sections. In conclusion of the study, the AM industry still lacks a comprehensive solution to address all cybersecurity concerns. For a complete solution to this pressing problem, cooperation between the producer of AM machines, the developer of AM software, end users, and governmental organizations is continuously required (Padmanabhan and Zhang, 2018).

Chang et al. (2019) have researched detecting cyber threats and creating risk management strategies in the maritime sector. Because the maritime sector has been depending more and more on automated and electronic technologies, cybersecurity concerns have been growing over the past ten years. Four cyber threats have been highlighted in this study: hacktivism, phishing emails, false websites, using an old IT system, and a lack of expertise and training. Additionally, four strategies for risk control are put forth: creating a cybersecurity process, educating and training people, updating and upgrading systems, and altering the cybersecurity environment. A series of interviews will be carried out as part of the subsequent study to confirm the threats and risk-control measures that have been identified and to investigate further if any have not been found in the literature review. Another questionnaire will be sent out to gather the likelihood, consequence, and probability of each threat's failure detection based on the interview results. The significance of the threats in maritime cybersecurity is assessed using Failure Modes and Effects Analysis (FMEA) using

Fuzzy Rules Bayesian Network (FRBN) and Evidential Reasoning (ER). A risk matrix will also be created to communicate the findings to the maritime sector in an easy-to-understand manner (Chang et al., 2019).

Argaw et al. (2020) conducted a study examining cyberattacks against hospitals by presenting case studies that illustrate the nature of these attacks and the responses of healthcare organizations in the past. The necessity of addressing cybersecurity proactively and preventively throughout the product lifecycle was discussed alongside a cybersecurity strategy that prioritizes high-quality IT at its core, with a solid application base and robust IT infrastructure. It is recommended to adopt a risk-based strategy, which begins with identifying at-risk IT assets and progresses to managing trade-offs between risks, benefits, and other types of risks. Along with tactics like vulnerability and patch management, the limited and regulated giving of administrative access, and the creation of incident response and business continuity plans, the emphasis is on end-user training. It is also advised that stakeholders share information to increase resilience (Argaw et al., 2020).

A review study by Ahsan et al. (2022) examined how machine learning techniques are used to make data-driven intelligent decision-making in cybersecurity systems and services. The study was motivated by the growing significance of cybersecurity and machine learning technology. It has also been discussed how it impacts security data, both in terms of analyzing the data and learning more about security incidents. Advances in machine learning and challenges in cybersecurity were the main topics of discussion. As a result, an explanation of the security dataset and associated services has been provided. The study's contribution also examined the potential impact of machine learning techniques on cybersecurity and ongoing security issues (Ahsan et al., 2022).

Physical and virtual items equipped with sensors, software, and other technologies are connected by the Internet of Things (IoT), which uses the Internet to exchange data. IoT devices have become a target for several criminals who aim to steal confidential data and jeopardize people's privacy because of their rapid global growth. Because of its distinct features and constraints, cybersecurity concerns are specific to the Internet of Things. Therefore, it's critical to recognize these threats and come up with ways to reduce their risks. Using the three layers of IoT architecture, Altulaihan et al. (2022) categorized the most prevalent dangers in the IoT environment. The most widely used mitigation strategies and countermeasures to manage IoT threats were also covered (Altulaihan et al., 2022).

The scope of the paper by Oyewole et al. (2024) includes an extensive evaluation of recent cyberattacks, an assessment of the efficacy of current cybersecurity frameworks, and the development of strategic recommendations for strengthening cybersecurity measures. The study concludes that the banking industry needs to adopt a comprehensive and flexible approach to cybersecurity, emphasized by calculated expenditures in technology, training, and cooperation. To efficiently manage the constantly changing cyber threat landscape, recommendations support the integration of Big Data analytics, artificial intelligence, and continuous risk assessment approaches. In light of the digital transformation, a clear call to action for banking institutions is made in this study by advocating for a renewed dedication to cybersecurity resilience to protect financial assets and customer trust (Oyewole et al., 2024).

Research by Aljumaiah et al. (2025) evaluates the NIST framework's ability to handle the majority of threats to critical infrastructure and points out any significant flaws. After discussing and mapping the majority of threats reported in critical infrastructure following NIST cybersecurity functions, the study will conclude with a discussion of the results. According to the findings, which are widely evident in the reviewed sources, human vulnerabilities—of which there are twelve examples—represent one of the main risks to critical infrastructure. Successful cyberattacks are much more likely when human error, carelessness, ignorance, inadequate training, and vulnerability to social engineering are present (Aljumaiah et al., 2025).

Nambundo et al. (2025) examined 41 papers from IEEE Xplore, Web of Science, and Scopus that discussed how smart meters are an essential component of the smart grid since they allow for data collecting, energy management, and real-time control. Despite technological advancements, there is still a dearth of information about the particular cybersecurity risks that these devices face, as well as the efficacy of current mitigation techniques. The study found many serious cybersecurity threats for smart meters, such as malware introduction, denial-of-service (DoS) attacks, data manipulation, illegal access, and data breaches. The study also emphasized the weaknesses that these attacks take advantage of, including obsolete software, unrecorded communications, and weak authentication. Stronger authentication and access procedures, communication system security, frequent software upgrades, code management, anomaly detection, and access control are all suggested mitigation techniques. The results show that while there are effective tactics and approaches to lessen these online dangers, there are still many unanswered questions. These gaps include differences in machine learning techniques, design requirements, software and firmware updates, physical security, vulnerability detection using big data, and user data privacy (Nambundo et al., 2025).

An article by Ibrahim and Kashef (2025) offers a comprehensive review of cyber threats to smart grids, taking into account attack surfaces, communication network layers, and the fundamental security triad of availability, confidentiality, and integrity. With an emphasis on cutting-edge technologies like artificial intelligence and large language models (LLMs) in smart grid security, this survey also discusses new threats and covers existing protection, prevention, detection, mitigation, and recovery strategies. Several threat taxonomies, a review of the growing significance of LLMs for improving grid security, and a classification of the crucial components of smart grids that are most susceptible to attack are also carried out in this paper (Ibrahim and Kashef, 2025).

Using a range of risk mitigation techniques is crucial to cybersecurity risk management to create a robust and flexible security posture. Given the dynamic, complex, and ever-changing nature of cyber attacks, no single strategy can effectively handle all threats or weaknesses. Organizations can better safeguard their digital assets, guarantee business continuity, and uphold stakeholder trust by utilizing a combination of strategies, including risk avoidance, risk reduction, risk transfer, and risk acceptance. In addition to enhancing defense in depth, a diversified mitigation approach enables more adaptable and knowledgeable decision-making when reacting to new cyber threats. In the end, proactive and thorough cybersecurity management is built on a diversified approach to risk mitigation.

5. CONCLUSION

The demands of modern cloud computing, the mobile Internet, and other elements for varied and scalable network services are becoming too much for traditional network architectures to handle due to the growing complexity of computer networks. This results from their fixed form and close integration of data-forwarding and control operations (Su et al., 2024; Chen et al., 2015).

A dynamic and strategic approach to risk management is required due to the constantly changing landscape of cyberattacks. Businesses can enhance their cybersecurity posture and protect their digital assets by utilizing well-established frameworks, carrying out in-depth risk assessments, and implementing proactive mitigation strategies.

Maintaining the efficient operation of vital assets in any organization requires ongoing risk management. This process is essential for achieving the resilience that critical infrastructures require for effective service delivery. As new tactics and increasingly complex coordinated operations emerge, the dangerous landscape continually evolves. To effectively evaluate and control risks, risk management operations must consider the current threat context (Kure et al., 2022). In the context of cybersecurity, risk management is the process of determining, assessing, and reducing the risks connected to cyber threats and vulnerabilities. Organizations that practice effective risk management can minimize operational disruption, respond to incidents promptly, and uphold stakeholder trust. Cybersecurity risk is not just a technological problem; it is a business necessity that has connections to operational, financial, legal, and reputational aspects.

To establish a strong and adaptable security posture, cybersecurity risk management requires the application of a variety of risk mitigation strategies. Since cyberattacks are dynamic, intricate, and always evolving, no one technique can adequately address every danger or vulnerability. A combination of risk avoidance, risk reduction, risk transfer, and risk acceptance tactics can help organizations better protect their digital assets, ensure business continuity, and maintain stakeholder trust. When responding to emerging cyber threats, a diverse mitigation strategy not only improves defense in depth but also makes decision-making more flexible and informed. Ultimately, a multifaceted approach to risk reduction is the foundation of proactive and comprehensive cybersecurity management.

Due to the complexity of the cybersecurity process, cybersecurity risk management necessitates a methodical approach. Using a Cybersecurity Risk Management Framework (CRMF), organizations may effectively detect, assess, respond to, and monitor cybersecurity threats. The European Union (EU) has put the first cybersecurity directive into effect. Based on the US National Institute of Standards and Technology's (NIST) Cybersecurity Framework, critical infrastructure organizations are required to regularly evaluate and report on their cybersecurity efforts (Krumay et al., 2018). Identify, Protect, Detect, Respond, and Recover are the five main functions of the NIST Cybersecurity Framework (CSF). These positions form the cornerstone of a risk-based cybersecurity approach. Each function represents a high-level cybersecurity activity and provides a strategic view of the cybersecurity risk lifecycle (Calder, 2018). NIST is significant because it offers dependable, scientifically grounded rules and guidelines that assist businesses in efficiently managing cybersecurity threats. These standards are extensively used in the public and private sectors, assisting businesses of all sizes in strengthening their defenses against online attacks.

Consequently, a more proactive, flexible, and intelligence-driven approach will be needed for cybersecurity risk management in the future. Businesses will have to spend money on continuous risk assessment frameworks, real-time reaction capabilities, and sophisticated threat detection. To guarantee resilience against changing cyber threats, a significant focus will also be on employee training, zero-trust architectures, and cross-sector cooperation.

REFERENCES

Ahmad, A., Hadgkiss, J., & Ruighaver, A. B. (2021). Incident response teams–Challenges in supporting the organizational security function. *Computers & Security*, *92*, 101768.

Ahmad, A. N., Raffei, A. F. M., Razak, M. F. A., & Ahmad, A. (2024). Distributed denial of service attack detection in IoT networks using deep learning and feature fusion: A review. *Mesopotamian Journal of Cybersecurity*, *4*(1), 47–70.

Ahsan, M., Nygard, K. E., Gomes, R., Chowdhury, M. M., Rifat, N., & Connolly, J. F. (2022). Cybersecurity threats and their mitigation approaches using machine learning- A review. *Journal of Cybersecurity and Privacy*, *2*(3), 527–555. DOI: 10.3390/jcp2030027

Aji, G. G., Widodo, S., Aji, G. N., Aji, G. G., & Prawitasari, D. (2023). Building trust in digital age: How HRM and cybersecurity collaborate for effective stakeholder relations. *Management Analysis Journal*, *12*(2), 254–260.

Alamri, B., Crowley, K., & Richardson, I. (2022). Cybersecurity risk management framework for blockchain identity management systems in health IoT. *Sensors (Basel)*, *23*(1), 218. DOI: 10.3390/s23010218 PMID: 36616816

Aljumaiah, O., Jiang, W., Addula, S. R., & Almaiah, M. A. (2025). Analyzing cybersecurity risks and threats in IT infrastructure based on NIST framework. *Journal of Cyber Security and Risk Auditing*, *2*(2), 12–26. DOI: 10.63180/jcsra.thestap.2025.2.2

Alkhalil, Z., Hewage, C., Nawaf, L., & Khan, I. (2021). Phishing attacks: A recent comprehensive study and a new anatomy. *Frontiers of Computer Science*, *3*(6), 563060. DOI: 10.3389/fcomp.2021.563060

Almomani, A., Alauthman, M., Shatnawi, M. T., Alweshah, M., Alrosan, A., Alomoush, W., Gupta, B. B., Gupta, B. B., & Gupta, B. B. (2022). Phishing website detection with semantic features based on machine learning classifiers: A comparative study. *International Journal on Semantic Web and Information Systems*, *18*(1), 1–24. DOI: 10.4018/IJSWIS.297032

Altulaihan, E., Almaiah, M. A., & Aljughaiman, A. (2022). Cybersecurity threats, countermeasures and mitigation techniques on the IoT: Future research directions. *Electronics (Basel)*, *11*(20), 3330. DOI: 10.3390/electronics11203330

Amin, Z. (2019). A practical road map for assessing cyber risk. *Journal of Risk Research*, *22*(1), 32–43. DOI: 10.1080/13669877.2017.1351467

Amoo, O. O., Osasona, F., Atadoga, A., Ayinla, B. S., Farayola, O. A., & Abrahams, T. O. (2024). Cybersecurity threats in the age of IoT: A review of protective measures. *International Journal of Science and Research Archive, 11*(1), 1304–1310. DOI: 10.30574/ijsra.2024.11.1.0217

Andersen, R., Barton, C., Böhme, R., Clayton, R., Ganan, C., Grasso, T., Levi, M., Moore, T., & Vasek, M. (2019). *Measuring the changing cost of cybercrime*. Conference Paper, The 2019 Workshop on the Economics of Information Security, Boston.

Antonakakis, M., April, T., Bailey, M., Bernhard, M., Bursztein, E., Cochran, J., Durumeric, Z., Halderman, J. A., Invernizzi, L., Kallitsis, M., Kumar, D., Lever, C., Ma, Z., Mason, J., Menscher, D., Seaman, C., Sullivan, N., Thomas, K., & Zhou, Y. (2017). Understanding the Mirai botnet. In *Proceedings of the 26th USENIX Security Symposium* (pp. 1093-1110). (Proceedings of the 26th USENIX Security Symposium). USENIX Association.

Arabo, A. (2015). Cyber security challenges within the connected home ecosystem futures. *Procedia Computer Science, 61*, 227–232. DOI: 10.1016/j.procs.2015.09.201

Argaw, S. T., Troncoso-Pastoriza, J. R., Lacey, D., Florin, M., Calcavecchia, F., Andersen, D., Burleson, W., Vogel, J., O'Leary, C., Eshaya-Chauvin, B., & Antoine, F. (2020). Cybersecurity of hospitals: Discussing the challenges and working towards mitigating the risks. *BMC Medical Informatics and Decision Making, 20*(1), 146. DOI: 10.1186/s12911-020-01161-7 PMID: 32620167

Buchta, R., Gkoktsis, G., Heine, F., & Kleiner, C. (2024). Advanced persistent threat attack detection systems: A review of approaches, challenges, and trends. *Digital Threats : Research and Practice, 5*(4), 1–37. DOI: 10.1145/3696014

Calder, A., (2018). NIST Cybersecurity Framework: A pocket Guide. Ely, IT Governance Publishing, 5–78.

Chang, C. H., Wenming, S., Wei, Z., Changki, P., & Kontovas, C. A. (2019). Evaluating cybersecurity risks in the maritime industry: a literature review. In: Proceedings of the International Association of Maritime Universities (IAMU) Conference. (International Association of Maritime Universities (IAMU), 29 October 2019 - 01 November 2019, Tokyo).

Chen, J., Zheng, X., & Rong, C. (2015). Survey on software-defined networking. In *Proceedings of the Second International Conference on Cloud Computing and Big Data in Asia*, Huangshan, China, 17–19 June 2015; Springer: Cham, Switzerland, 115–124.

Chidukwani, A., Zander, S., & Koutsakis, P. (2024). Cybersecurity preparedness of small-to-medium businesses: A Western Australia study with broader implications. *Computers & Security*, *145*, 104026. DOI: 10.1016/j.cose.2024.104026

Cofense, (2022). Keeping up with phishing. https://get.cofense.com/CRA-Keeping - Up- With- Phishing.html

Conti, M., Dehghantanha, A., & Franke, K. (2018). Cyber threat intelligence: Challenges and opportunities. *Computer Fraud & Security*, *2018*(9), 14–17.

Dubois, E., Heymans, P., Mayer, N., & Matulevicius, R. (2010). A systematic approach to define the domain of information system security risk management. In Nurcan, S., Salinesi, C., Souveyet, C., & Ralyté, J. (Eds.), *Intentional Perspectives on Information Systems Engineering*. Springer. DOI: 10.1007/978-3-642-12544-7_16

Enisa, (2024). ENISA threat landscape 2024. European Union Agency for Cybersecurity June 2023 to June 2024 Report, https://www.enisa.europa.eu/sites/default/files/2024-11/ENISA%20Threat%20Landscape%202024_0.pdf

Firmansyah, W. D., & Turmudi, A. (2024). Comprehensive review and future directions in mitigating flooding Distributed Denial of Services (DDoS) attacks. *Novice Research Exploration*, *1*(2), 46–54.

Fotis, F. (2024). Economic impact of cyber attacks and effective cyber risk management strategies: A light literature review and case study analysis. *Procedia Computer Science*, *251*, 471–478. DOI: 10.1016/j.procs.2024.11.135

Georgieva, K., Farooq, A., & Dumke, R. R. (2009). Analysis of the risk assessment methods- A survey. In *International Workshop on Software Measurement*, Springer: Berlin, Germany. DOI: 10.1007/978-3-642-05415-0_6

Gritzalis, D., Kandias, M., Stavrou, V., & Mitrou, L. (2019). History of information: From the Stone Age to the Digital Age. *Journal of Information and Communication Technology*, *13*(2), 128–145.

Henrie, M. (2013). Cybersecurity risk management in the SCADA critical infrastructure environment. *Engineering Management Journal*, *25*(2), 38–45. DOI: 10.1080/10429247.2013.11431973

Kavak, H., Padilla, J. J., Vernon-Bido, D., Diallo, S., Gore, R., & Shetty, S. (2021). Simulation for cybersecurity: State of the art and future directions. *Journal of Cybersecurity*, *7*(1), 1–13. DOI: 10.1093/cybsec/tyab005

Kosub, T. (2015). Components and challenges of integrated cyber risk management. *Zeitschrift für die gesamte Versicherungswissenschaft,* 104, 615-634.

Krumay, B., Bernroider, E. W. N., & Walser, R. (2018). Evaluation of Cybersecurity Management Controls and Metrics of Critical Infrastructures: A Literature Review Considering the NIST Cybersecurity Framework. In Gruschka, N. (Ed.), Lecture Notes in Computer Science: Vol. 11252. *Secure IT Systems. NordSec 2018*. Springer. DOI: 10.1007/978-3-030-03638-6_23

Kumar, P., Gupta, G. P., & Tripathi, R. (2021). Toward design of an intelligent cyber attack detection system using hybrid feature reduced approach for IoT networks. *Arabian Journal for Science and Engineering*, *46*(4), 3749–3778. DOI: 10.1007/s13369-020-05181-3

Kumar, R., Kumar, P., Tripathi, R., Gupta, G. P., Garg, S., & Hassan, M. M. (2022). A distributed intrusion detection system to detect DDoS attacks in blockchain-enabled IoT network. *Journal of Parallel and Distributed Computing*, *164*, 55–68. DOI: 10.1016/j.jpdc.2022.01.030

Kure, H. I., Islam, S., & Mouratidis, H. (2022). An integrated cyber security risk management framework and risk prediction for the critical infrastructure protection. *Neural Computing & Applications*, *34*(18), 15241–15271. DOI: 10.1007/s00521-022-06959-2

Lau, F., Rubin, S. H., Smith, M. H., & Trajkovic, L. (2000). Distributed denial of service attacks. 2000 IEEE International Conference on Systems, Man, and Cybernetics -Cybernetics Evolving to Systems, Humans, Organizations, and Their Complex Interactions, 3, 2275–2280

Le, K. H., Nguyen, M. H., Tran, T. D., & Tran, N. D. (2022). IMIDS: An intelligent intrusion detection system against cyber threats in IoT. *Electronics (Basel)*, *11*(4), 524. DOI: 10.3390/electronics11040524

Leszczyna, R. (2021). Review of cybersecurity assessment methods: Applicability perspective. *Computers & Security*, *108*, 102376.

Ibrahim, N., & Kashef, R. (2025). Exploring the emerging role of large language models in smart grid cybersecurity: A survey of attacks, detection mechanisms, and mitigation strategies. *Frontiers in Energy Research*, •••, 13.

ISACA. (2019). *State of Enterprise Risk Management 2020 Enterprise Risk Research Brief*. ISACA.

Marchini, K., & Pascual, A. (2019). *2019 identity fraud study: Fraudsters seek new targets and victims bear the brunt*. Javelin, 45.

Marforio, C., Masti, R. J., Soriente, C., Kostiainen, K., & Capkun, S. (2015). Personalized security indicators to detect application phishing attacks in mobile platforms. Working paper, https://arxiv.org/abs/1502.06824

Mat, N. I. C., Jamil, N., Yusoff, Y., & Kiah, M. L. M. (2024). A systematic literature review on advanced persistent threat behaviors and its detection strategy. *Journal of Cybersecurity, 10*(1).

Mutalib, N. H. A., Sabri, A. Q. M., Wahab, A. W. A., Abdullah, E. R. M. F., & AlDahoul, N. (2024). Explainable deep learning approach for advanced persistent threats (APTs) detection in cybersecurity: A review. *Artificial Intelligence Review, 57*(11), 297. DOI: 10.1007/s10462-024-10890-4

Nambundo, J. M., Gomes, O. S. M., De Souza, A. D., & Machado, R. C. S. (2025). Cybersecurity and major cyber threats of smart meters: A systematic mapping review. *Energies, 18*(6), 1445. DOI: 10.3390/en18061445

NIST. (2011). NIST Special Publication 800-39: Managing Information Security Risk; NIST: Gaithersburg, MD, USA.

O'Kane, P., Sezer, S., & Carlin, D. (2018). Evolution of ransomware. *IET Networks, 7*(5), 1–7. DOI: 10.1049/iet-net.2017.0207

Oyewole, A. T., Okoye, C. C., Ofodile, O. C., & Ugochukwu, C. E.Adedoyin Tolulope OyewoleChinwe Chinazo OkoyeOnyeka Chrisanctus OfodileChinonye Esther Ugochukwu. (2024). Cybersecurity risks in online banking: A detailed review and preventive strategies application. *World Journal of Advanced Research and Reviews, 21*(03), 625–643. DOI: 10.30574/wjarr.2024.21.3.0707

Padmanabhan, A., & Zhang, J. (2018). Cybersecurity risks and mitigation strategies in additive manufacturing. *Progress in Additive Manufacturing, 3*(1-2), 87–93. DOI: 10.1007/s40964-017-0036-9

Patrano, L., Atzori, L., Solic, P., Mongiello, M., & Almeida, A. (2020). Challenges to be addressed to realize Internet of Things solutions for smart environments. *Future Generation Computer Systems, 111*, 873–878. DOI: 10.1016/j.future.2019.09.033

Petrosyan, A. (2024). The annual number of malware attacks worldwide from 2015 to 2023. https://www.statista.com/statistics/873097/malware-attacks-per-year-worldwide/

Phillips, S. C., Taylor, S., Boniface, M., Modafferi, S., & Surridge, M. (2024). Automated knowledge-based cybersecurity risk assessment of cyber-physical systems. *IEEE Access : Practical Innovations, Open Solutions, 12*, 82482–82505. DOI: 10.1109/ACCESS.2024.3404264

Pochmara, J., & Swietlicka, A. (2024). Cybersecurity of industrial systems- A 2023 report. *Electronics (Basel)*, *13*(7), 1191. DOI: 10.3390/electronics13071191

Qasim, S. S., & Nsaif, S. M. (2024). Advancements in time series-based detection systems for distributed denial of service (DDoS) attacks: A comprehensive review. *Babylonian Journal of Networking*, *2024*, 9–17. DOI: 10.58496/BJN/2024/002

Qiangmin, W., Mengquan, L., & Jianhua, L. (2007). Method on network information system security assessment based on rough set. In *Proceedings of the 2007 Third International IEEE Conference on Signal-Image Technologies and Internet-Based System*, Shanghai, China. DOI: 10.1109/SITIS.2007.114

Reddy, R. P. (2024). A survey of Distributed Denial Service (DDoS) attack mitigation techniques. *International Journal of Computer Trends and Technology*, *72*(12), 69–77. DOI: 10.14445/22312803/IJCTT-V72I12P108

Sanchez-Garcia, I. D., Mejia, J., & Gilabert, T. S. F. (2023). Cybersecurity risk assessment: A systematic mapping review, proposal, and validation. *Applied Sciences (Basel, Switzerland)*, *13*(1), 395. DOI: 10.3390/app13010395

Sarker, I. H., Kayes, A. S. M., Badsha, S., Alqahtani, H., Watters, P., & Ng, A. (2020). Cybersecurity data science: An overview from machine learning perspective. *Journal of Big Data*, *7*(41), 1–29. DOI: 10.1186/s40537-020-00318-5

Sarker, O., Jayatilaka, A., Haggag, S., Liu, C., & Babar, M. A. (2024). A multi-vocal literature review on challenges and critical success factors of phishing education, training, and awareness. *Journal of Systems and Software*, *208*, 111899. DOI: 10.1016/j.jss.2023.111899

Sharma, R. (2012). Study of latest emerging trends on cyber security and its challenges to society. *International Journal of Scientific and Engineering Research*, *3*(6), 1–4.

Shea, S., Gillis, A. S., & Clark, C. (2023). What is cybersecurity? https://www.techtarget.com/searchsecurity/definition/cybersecurity

Sheppard, D. (2011). *ID theft down 28 percent in U.S. in 2010: A survey*. Reuters.

Smith, R., & Brooks, D. J. (2020). *Security Science: The Theory and Practice of Security*. Butterworth-Heinemann.

Smmarwar, S., Gupta, G., & Kumar, S. (2024). Android malware detection and identification frameworks by leveraging the machine and deep learning techniques: A comprehensive review. *Telematics and Informatics Reports*, *14*, 100130. DOI: 10.1016/j.teler.2024.100130

Su, Y., Xiong, D., Qian, K., & Wang, Y. (2024). A comprehensive survey of Distributed Denial of Service detection and mitigation technologies in software-defined network. *Electronics (Basel), 13*(4), 807. DOI: 10.3390/electronics13040807

Szathmari, G. (2019). Owning your legal practice's cybersecurity. https://get.cofense.com/CRA- Keeping- Up- With- Phishing.html

Tasar, S. A. (2023). Siber Güvenlik ve İç Denetim. In *Sosyal Bilimlerde Güncel Çalışmalar 2*. İksad Publishing House.

Thompson, E. C. (2018). Cybersecurity incident response: How to contain, eradicate, and recover from incidents, 1st ed. Apress, Lisle, Illinois, USA. BookWhole.

Ullah, F., Naeem, H., Jabbar, S., Khalid, S., Latif, M. A., Al-Turjman, F., & Mostarda, L. (2024). Cyber security threats detection in Internet of Things using deep learning approach. *IEEE Access : Practical Innovations, Open Solutions*, •••, 7.

Vailshery, L. S. (2022). Internet of Things (IoT) and non-IoT active device connections worldwide from 2010 to 2025. Statista. https://www.statista.com/statistics/1101442/iot-number-of-connected-devices-worldwide/#:~:text=The total installed base of,that are expected in 2021.

Varshney, G., Kumawat, R., Varadharajan, V., Tupakula, U., & Gupta, C. (2024). Anti-phishing: A comprehensive perspective. *Expert Systems with Applications, 238*, 122199. DOI: 10.1016/j.eswa.2023.122199

Von Solms, R., & Van Niekerk, J. (2013). From information security to cyber security. *Computers & Security, 38*, 97–102. DOI: 10.1016/j.cose.2013.04.004

World Economic Forum. (2024). Global cybersecurity outlook 2024: Insight report. https://www3.weforum.org/docs/WEF_Global_Cybersecurity_Outlook_2024.pdf

Yan, Q., & Yu, F. R. (2015). Distributed denial of service attacks in software-defined networking with cloud computing. *IEEE Communications Magazine, 53*(4), 52–59. DOI: 10.1109/MCOM.2015.7081075

Zhan, Y., Ahmad, S. F., Irshad, M., Al-Razgan, M., Awwad, E. M., Ali, Y. A., & Bani Ahmad Ayassrah, A. Y. A. (2024). Investigating the role of Cybersecurity's perceived threats in the adoption of health information systems. *Heliyon, 10*(1), 1–16. DOI: 10.1016/j.heliyon.2023.e22947

Zhang, Y., Wen, Y., Guan, Y., Wu, Z., & Huang, D. (2014). Security and privacy for the Internet of Things: A survey. *IEEE Internet of Things Journal, 1*(5), 381–394.

Zwilling, M. (2022). Trends and challenges regarding cyber risk mitigation by CISOs- A systematic literature and experts' opinion review based on text analytics. *Sustainability (Basel)*, *14*(3), 1311. DOI: 10.3390/su14031311

Chapter 3
Cybersecurity Applications in Industry 4.0

Esra Nur Gökhan
https://orcid.org/0000-0001-9108-3232
Beykoz University, Turkey

Pervin Ahu Çerçi
Beykoz University, Turkey

ABSTRACT

The Industry 4.0 paradigm has marked a significant turning point through the integration of technologies such as artificial intelligence, big data analytics, and cyber-physical systems. During this era—characterized by a fundamental transformation of production and operational processes—efficiency and flexibility have increased, and decision-making processes have accelerated. However, this technological advancement has also introduced serious cybersecurity threats. This study explores the historical development and technological foundations of Industry 4.0, with a particular emphasis on the scale of cybersecurity threats and potential solution strategies. It underscores the urgent need for secure digital transformation through strategic investments in cybersecurity, particularly in light of the transition toward the more human-centered paradigm of Industry 5.0.

DOI: 10.4018/979-8-3693-6417-8.ch003

1. INTRODUCTION

The Fourth Industrial Revolution, also known as Industry 4.0, marks a significant transformation in how industries operate. Technologies such as artificial intelligence, big data, and cyber-physical systems are deeply integrated into production processes, reshaping the traditional manufacturing landscape. This shift has accelerated decision-making, increased flexibility, and enhanced overall efficiency. However, this transformation also brings new and complex cybersecurity challenges. The convergence of operational technology (OT) and information technology (IT) has broadened the attack surface, exposing critical systems to cyber threats. As smart factories adopt 5G, IoT, and edge computing, every connected device becomes a potential entry point for attackers. Additionally, legal and regulatory frameworks such as the GDPR in the EU and KVKK in Türkiye aim to safeguard personal and institutional data. Yet, varying adoption levels among small and medium-sized enterprises (SMEs), infrastructural gaps, and lack of awareness make effective cybersecurity implementation inconsistent. Therefore, education and institutional investment in cybersecurity are critical. In this digital era, cybersecurity is not only a technical necessity but also a strategic national concern. Attacks threaten sectors like healthcare, finance, and education, leading to data breaches, operational disruptions, and financial loss.

The chapter will explore the core cybersecurity challenges introduced by Industry 4.0, focusing on risks related to IoT, legacy systems, human factors, and emerging threats such as AI-driven attacks and quantum computing vulnerabilities.

2. BACKGROUND

This section will provide historical and conceptual context for Industry 4.0 by reviewing the evolution of industrial revolutions, foundational technologies, and key definitions from relevant literature. It aims to highlight the technological background and strategic goals that frame current cybersecurity challenges.

The era of Industry 1.0 began in 1769 with James Watt's invention of the steam engine, leading to the widespread adoption of machinery in production. With the rise of electricity and the introduction of assembly lines, the era of Industry 2.0 emerged, marking a period of mass production. Subsequently, the use of automation systems and computers in manufacturing defined the Industry 3.0 phase, during which industrial societies began transitioning into information societies (Yoşumaz & Özkara, 2019).

Industry 4.0, which was first introduced at Germany's Hannover Trade Fair, is also referred to as the Fourth Industrial Revolution. This concept, which integrates information technologies with the industrial sector, represents a revolution built on the principles of low cost, high speed, efficiency, and quality (Yıldız Tonga & Tonga, 2022). It is anticipated that Industry 4.0 will increase the speed of production systems by 30% and improve efficiency by 25%. Furthermore, by enhancing human–machine interaction, it is expected to attract qualified intellectual capital back to Germany in response to its aging population (Kayğın et al., 2019).

The evolution of industrial revolutions has profoundly influenced modern production and technology. The First Industrial Revolution began with mechanized production powered by water and steam, exemplified by the first mechanical loom in 1784. The Second introduced mass production using electricity and labor division, seen in assembly lines like those in Cincinnati around 1870. The Third brought automation via electronics and IT systems, marked by the 1969 invention of the first PLC. Today, the Fourth Industrial Revolution features cyber-physical systems that merge digital, physical, and biological technologies, enabling smart and adaptive manufacturing. (Öztuna, 2017).

According to Banger (2018), Industry 4.0 is a vision based on the industrialization of the internet, the digitalization of production, and the ability of companies to individually adapt to customer demands.

While some view Industry 4.0 as a revolution leading automation into digitalization, others define it as the Second Machine Age or the Second Information Revolution (Brynjolfsson & McAfee, 2014). It has also been described as "a paradigm involving a new approach to production in favor of decentralized structures and a transformation in traditional centralized control systems" (Türkiye Büyük Millet Meclisi Araştırma Hizmetleri Başkanlığı, 2021).

Wascbusch (2019) outlines the key features of Industry 4.0 as follows:

- Flexible production that allows for the manufacturing of customized products,
- Safe production capable of taking preventive measures before failures occur,
- Rapid production enabled by new innovations and evolving technologies,
- Optimized logistics that reduce operational costs,
- Resource utilization that supports the reuse of materials, and
- Effective data usage that leverages large volumes of data generated during production.

According to Eğilmez (2019), Industry 4.0 has three main objectives:

- Minimizing human labor in production, thereby eliminating production errors;

- Achieving maximum flexibility in production, allowing for the customization of products based on consumer needs;
- Accelerating the production process.

In a study conducted by a global consulting firm, the goals of Industry 4.0 were categorized into strategy, organization, and processes.

Digital transformation within the Industry 4.0 framework targets strategic, organizational, and process improvements to boost competitiveness and adaptability. Strategically, it promotes new digital business models, faster time-to-market, and flexible customer response. Organizationally, it enhances job quality through better work-life balance, automation, and human-machine interaction. Process-wise, it enables time savings, dynamic planning, and efficient production for personalized goods. Smart analytics and mobile control further support agile operations. Overall, Industry 4.0 reshapes industry across multiple domains. (Özçetin, 2024).

Industry 4.0 presents a broad range of strengths, such as improved efficiency, global competitiveness, and high-skilled job creation, while offering flexibility in production and enhanced customer satisfaction. However, its dependence on advanced technologies brings high implementation costs and vulnerability to disruptions, requiring substantial investment, skilled labor, and standardization. Opportunities include strengthening Europe's industrial leadership, accessing new markets, and addressing demographic challenges. Yet, threats like cybersecurity risks, data privacy concerns, and potential socioeconomic disruptions—especially for SMEs and labor—persist. Global adoption by non-EU actors may also weaken the EU's strategic edge. Careful management of these dynamics is essential (Ötles, 2016).

3. KEY COMPONENTS OF INDUSTRY 4.0 AND THEIR CYBERSECURITY IMPLICATIONS

3.1 Internet of Things (IoT) and Industrial IoT Risks

The Internet of Things (IoT) refers to a system in which everyday devices and systems can communicate, exchange data, and interact with one another. When connected to the internet, these devices—equipped with IoT sensors—become "smart," enabling remote control, data transmission, and command execution across various domains (Serter & Serinkan, 2020).

Though widely adopted in the 2000s, the IoT concept originated in the 1960s with the development of computer networks. In 1982, engineering students at Carnegie Mellon University created the first "smart device"—a system that remotely monitored a Coca-Cola vending machine. Kevin Ashton later coined the term "Internet of Things" at MIT in 1999 (Erbey, 2025). The integration of radio-frequency identification (RFID) technology with the internet gave rise to IoT systems. These systems offer personalized marketing strategies based on user experience, improve customer engagement through big data analysis, and help mitigate risks in areas such as information systems, logistics, healthcare, and decision-making processes (Cevher, 2023).

However, IoT technologies also bring certain risks:

- A skilled workforce capable of efficiently using IoT-based systems is required.
- Integration of this high-investment technology must be continuous, and uncertainty about which solutions to adopt can pose strategic risks.
- IoT devices are vulnerable to cyberattacks, raising concerns over data privacy and theft.
- As these technologies depend on internet connectivity, infrastructure and connection issues pose significant threats.
- Installation, maintenance, and investment costs may be high, leading to concerns over return on investment.
- The collection and sharing of data raise significant privacy and legal concerns (Chen et al., 2024).

3.2 Cyber-Physical Systems (CPS) and Potential Security Threats

Cyber-Physical Systems (CPS), known for their complex and multilayered nature, integrate computer-based control mechanisms with physical processes. These systems collect data from the physical world through sensors, analyze it, and then execute actions based on this data (Yüksel et al., 2024).

Despite their advantages, CPS also come with risks:

- Inadequate integration and data exchange between systems may lead to interoperability risks, reducing overall system efficiency.
- The inability to predict system behavior may result in unpredictability risks, leading to operational difficulties.
- Though CPS are generally resilient, they must be continuously updated to avoid reliability risks.
- CPS are also vulnerable to cybersecurity threats such as Man-in-the-Middle (MITM) attacks and Denial-of-Service (DoS) attacks (Mahnamhar, 2022).

3.3 Cloud and Edge Computing Security Vulnerabilities

Cloud computing allows data, documents, software, and all types of digital information to be stored virtually and accessed via the internet using a company's own infrastructure (Çelik, 2021).

Edge computing processes data at locations closer to the user, reducing latency and improving system performance and efficiency (Wang et al., 2023). As an optimized version of cloud computing, edge computing involves positioning services at the edge of the network, offering both time and resource savings (Tay et al., 2021).

Edge computing and cloud computing offer distinct approaches to data processing, each suited to different needs. Edge computing is ideal for small data sets and localized processing, while cloud computing excels at handling large-scale data with centralized resources. Storage capacity is limited at the edge but extensive in the cloud. Security in edge systems is more complex due to distributed networks, whereas cloud computing provides stronger centralized security. Environmentally, edge computing supports local monitoring via IoT, while cloud systems are less responsive in this regard. Ultimately, their use depends on data volume, speed, and application context (Rakhade, 2024).

3.4 Protection of Big Data and AI-Supported Industrial Decision-Making Systems

Among the most innovative technologies, Big Data refers to large datasets that require specialized processing techniques to improve decision-making processes and optimize operations. It is widely used across various sectors, including social media, education, smart city transportation, and organizational management for purposes such as statistical reporting, forecasting, and trend analysis (Badshah et al., 2024; Rahul et al., 2023).

Studies emphasize the necessity of analyzing the vast amounts of raw data generated from multiple sources, making big data technology indispensable. For example, Walmart is capable of storing 2.5 petabytes of customer data in just one hour while processing over one million customer transactions. Similarly, the U.S. Library of Congress collects approximately 235 terabytes of data annually. By the mid-2000s, the number of uploaded files on Facebook had exceeded 30 billion (Ajah, 2019).

However, managing big data involves several challenges and risks, including (Abdalla, 2022):

- Breaches and data leaks resulting from the use of big data.
- Non-compliance with data protection regulations.
- Inadequate technology infrastructure for storing and processing big data.

- “Data skew” — imbalance in data distribution affecting processing efficiency.
- Significant energy loss due to inefficient operational planning.

4. CYBERSECURITY THREATS INTRODUCED BY INDUSTRY 4.0

4.1 Attacks Targeting IoT Devices

IoT technology is increasingly being used in areas such as smart homes, smart environments, and smart healthcare (Avcı, 2022). As the interaction between big data and human life intensifies, it is estimated that the number of IoT devices will reach 70 billion by 2025 (sanal.mobi, 2019). Therefore, the security of both consumer-level IoT and Industrial IoT (IIoT) devices has become a critical concern.

Common attack types targeting these systems include:

- Buffer Overflow: Excessive data overflows memory buffers.
- Code Injection: Malicious commands are inserted to hijack systems.
- Improper Input Validation: Failures to validate user input, leading to integrity attacks.
- Denial of Service (DoS): Attacks targeting system availability.
- Confidentiality Attacks: Gaining intelligence about connected devices or network policies.
- Authentication Attacks: Stealing login credentials.
- Authorization Attacks: Gaining unauthorized access to sensitive data (Zolanvari et al., 2019).

4.2 Big Data Security and Privacy Risks

Security concerns related to big data have become increasingly significant, particularly due to insufficient security testing of new products entering the market. These issues can be categorized into four main areas:

- Infrastructure Security Risks
- Data Privacy Risks
- Data Management and Integrity Risks
- Reactive Security Risks

Privacy and security in big data environments are shaped by technical, organizational, and socio-political challenges. Data quality and operational processes, such as mining and transfer, create vulnerabilities due to heterogeneous sources and formats. Legal frameworks are essential for regulating data reuse and protecting rights. Organizational policies on governance and access control support compliance, while social pressure and cultural norms influence stricter privacy measures. Individual awareness and behavior also affect data protection. Additionally, political agendas and national security concerns drive regulatory oversight, highlighting the complex landscape of big data privacy and security (Jha, 2017).

5. CYBERSECURITY MEASURES FOR INDUSTRIAL IOT

Today, Internet of Things (IoT) technologies are rapidly being adopted in order to improve manufacturing processes on an industrial scale, increase efficiency and reduce operating costs. Industrial IoT (IIoT) systems in particular have become key in automation, energy management and control of critical infrastructures. However, this technological evolution also brings with it increasing cybersecurity risks. While the highly integrated structure of devices accelerates the flow of information, it also leads to limited security certification, incomplete security measures of hardware and software, weak encryption practices and systems that are not updated, leading to vulnerability to cyber attacks in IIoT environments (Soori, Arezoo, & Dastres, 2023).

5.1 Standards and Protocols

In IIoT security, international standards serve as a fundamental reference for ensuring that device security processes are applied consistently and systematically. Notably, the IEC 62443 and ISO/IEC 27001 standards define security requirements across a broad spectrum from device design to software updates (Cindric Jurcevic, & Hadjina, 2025).

- **IEC 62443:** This standard, which has technical features such as high security in device design, controlled access, network segmentation and encryption of data, was developed for industrial automation and control systems. It specifies in detail the security procedures for the maintenance process, operation and installation phase of the relevant system (International Electrotechnical Commission, 2013).
- **ISO/IEC 27001:** Focused on information security management systems, this standard enables organizations to protect their information assets through risk assessment. At the corporate level, it encompasses organizational policies, staff training, and continuous improvement processes to ensure information security (Joint Technical Committee ISO/IEC JTC 1, 2013).

Both standards provide essential tools for maintaining security in IIoT environments; however, achieving standardization across different manufacturers and adapting to the ever-changing cyber threat landscape can pose technical and operational challenges.

5.2 Challenges in Implementation

While securing critical infrastructures, various practical challenges may arise due to high security requirements and the complexity of the systems. Factors such as technological integration, cost considerations, and the constantly evolving threat landscape may hinder the effective implementation of these standards. However, through national and international collaborations and ongoing updates to standards, these difficulties can be overcome and the protection of critical infrastructures can be strengthened.

Industry 4.0 enables digital transformation in production and automation processes while simultaneously introducing major cybersecurity, data protection, and compliance requirements. ISO 27001 and Industrial Information Security Management Systems allow organizations to systematically manage information security, while the NIST Cybersecurity Framework emphasizes risk management and continuous improvement (Folorunso, Mohammed, Wada, & Samuel, 2024). Data protection regulations such as GDPR and KVKK are key to securing industrial data flows. In addition, global and national regulations concerning IoT and industrial applications are designed to meet the needs of diverse markets. Cybersecurity standards developed to ensure the security of critical infrastructures are of great importance as they directly affect not only technical systems but also national security and social order.

In the coming years, with the rapid development of technology and the constant change of cyber threats, it will be inevitable for existing regulations and standards to be updated and harmonized. Institutions that can keep up with this process—that is, make continuous development and personnel training a part of their systems—will achieve much more successful results in their cybersecurity strategies. In the Industry 4.0 environment, attention to compliance and regulations is not only a legal obligation but also a strategic asset for institutional trust and competitive advantage (Oláh et al., 2020).

5.3 Importance and Scope of the Standards

The cybersecurity standards developed for critical infrastructures encompass not only technical measures but also organizational structures and emergency response procedures. These standards offer a comprehensive framework for detecting, preventing, and responding swiftly to attacks. In particular, standards such as NERC CIP

(North American Electric Reliability Corporation's Critical Infrastructure Protection) are decisive for organizations operating in the energy sector (Livingston, 2022).

5.4 Security Certification

Certification is among the important processes in ensuring the security of IoT devices. It ensures that the devices produced comply with international standards and that they are under warranty throughout the usage period. Certified devices are more resilient against cyberattacks. Security certifications enhance trust between manufacturers and users and increase the market competitiveness of the devices. Standards such as IEC 62443 and ISO/IEC 27001 are widely referenced to ensure the security of IIoT devices. Integrating these standards aims to elevate the overall security level of such devices. However, differing approaches among manufacturers and the diverse hardware and software characteristics of devices may occasionally lead to practical challenges (Iturbe, Mansell, Rios, & Toledo, 2023).

Although certification processes theoretically provide a solid foundation for security, in practice, the diversity of devices, the constantly evolving nature of threats, cost and time constraints, and global alignment issues make this process quite complex. This situation highlights the need for more flexible and manufacturer-oriented certification models.

5.5 Secure Hardware and Software Usage

Security in Industrial Internet of Things (IIoT) systems cannot be based solely on certification processes; at the same time, safe design and use of hardware and software is at least as important as certification (Gebremichael et al., 2020). Secure hardware and software development is the first step in integrated security measures. In this context, secure boot mechanisms and hardware-based security modules play an important role in reducing the potential attack surface of the system.

Built-in security chips, physical protection measures and post-production verification tests play an important role in protecting IIoT devices against physical interventions. Such applications are critical to protecting the integrity of both devices and the data processed through these devices.

In the process of secure software development, applying secure coding techniques, regularly updating the software and performing dynamic tests make a significant contribution to minimizing security vulnerabilities. In addition, penetration tests and constantly conducted security audits are among the key elements that increase the durability and reliability of the software (Greco & Choo, 2023).

In the coming period, it is expected that the security of IIoT systems will be increased to higher levels with automatic update systems, artificial intelligence-supported anomaly detection solutions and further strengthening of hardware-software integration.

5.6 Issues of Weak Encryption and Identity Management

In order to ensure data security in IIoT systems, strong encryption methods and effective identity management are of great importance. However, when looking at current applications, it is seen that there are serious gaps in this area. The main reasons for these weaknesses are old algorithms that are no longer considered secure, encryption keys that are easily broken, and errors made during implementation. Worse, these vulnerabilities make it much easier for attackers to access sensitive data.

In recent years, there has been increasing interest in strong and modern encryption algorithms such as AES-256 (Gaur & Kaushik, 2021). However, many systems are still protected with weak passwords and only single-factor authentication methods, which leads to serious security vulnerabilities. One of the most effective ways to reduce these risks is to switch to multi-factor authentication, because these systems make it difficult for unauthorized people to access and provide an additional layer of security. In IIoT environments, both stronger passwords are preferred and systems are regularly updated with automatic password policies to increase encryption and identity security (Sengupta, Ruj, & Bit, 2020).

5.7 Vulnerabilities of Unpatched Systems in Industrial IoT

One of the essentials for ensuring security in IIoT systems is regular and timely software updates (Mugarza, Flores, & Montero, 2020). If ignored, these updates leave systems open to malware, which can lead to both data leaks and operational disruptions. In fact, one of the most common causes of industrial security incidents is the failure to apply security patches in time (Iturbe et al., 2023). Failing to update software and firmware in production systems creates a fertile ground for many known exploits. Therefore, automated patch management, rigorous version control, and vulnerability assessments should be integral parts of the operational procedure for IIoT systems. Neglecting timely updates transforms minor vulnerabilities into critical entry points for cyberattacks, making patch management a frontline defense mechanism.

6. REAL-WORLD APPLICATIONS OF AI-BASED AUTONOMOUS SECURITY SYSTEMS

Autonomous security systems are implemented in sectors such as finance, healthcare, and critical infrastructure. For example, an energy plant can maintain continuous protection through autonomous systems, while threat hunting tools detect intrusion attempts in the early stages. These applications demonstrate the effectiveness of AI in strengthening cybersecurity (Aydın, Barışkan, & Çetinkaya, 2021).

7. DEEPFAKE AND AI-DRIVEN CYBER THREATS

Among the reasons for the emergence of new types of cyber threats is the advancement of artificial intelligence. In particular, deepfake technologies—AI systems that manipulate visual content—pose serious risks in areas such as misinformation, identity fraud, and scams (Mustak et al., 2023). Moreover, AI-enhanced threats enable attackers to design more strategic and complex methods of attack.

7.1 The Role of Deepfake Technology in Cybersecurity

Deepfake, or deep forgery, refers to the technology that enables the generation of fake but realistic audio, video, and image content. When misused, it presents serious cybersecurity threats, especially in areas such as political manipulation, reputational damage, and fraud (Westerlund, 2019). AI-powered deepfake detection systems are being developed to identify and verify these fraudulent contents.

7.2 AI-Powered Attack Techniques

Using AI technologies, attackers can execute more advanced and targeted cyberattacks. For instance, botnets—robotic networks that generate automated attack scenarios—can evolve using machine learning algorithms to bypass defense systems (Koroniotis, Moustafa, & Sitnikova, 2019). This situation necessitates the continuous update of cybersecurity strategies and the development of innovative defense methods.

7.3 Countermeasures and Recommendations

As deepfake technologies and artificial intelligence-supported cyber threats become more complex and effective every day, the development of not only the technological infrastructure but also the legal and institutional structures is of great importance in combating these threats. Establishing reliable news and content verification systems, using threat detection tools that work with artificial intelligence, and increasing cooperation at the international level are among the basic measures that can be taken.

AI-powered security solutions provide a strong and innovative defense against today's sophisticated cyber threats. Thanks to techniques such as machine learning anomaly detection, behavioral analysis, autonomous security mechanisms, AI-powered firewalls and threat hunting, threats can be detected earlier and responded to quickly (Akhtar & Rawat, 2024). However, types of attacks that can produce misleading content, such as deepfakes, constantly require new updates and stronger strategies against these systems.

In the future, with the development of artificial intelligence technologies, more integrated, flexible and durable cybersecurity systems are expected to be implemented. In this context, it is of great importance for institutions to regularly update the technologies they use by making them compatible with international standards. Studies conducted both in the academic world and in the private sector will play a decisive role in building more secure digital environments.

8. REGULATIONS, STANDARDS, AND COMPLIANCE REQUIREMENTS IN INDUSTRY 4.0

Industry 4.0 represents the most advanced point of digital transformation in production and automation processes. While innovative technologies such as IoT, artificial intelligence, robotic systems, cloud technologies and big data analytics make production processes more efficient, they also bring with them vital issues such as data security, privacy and compliance with legislation (Mahmood et al., 2024). These developments necessitate not only technological advances but also the constant review and updating of national and international regulations and standards. In order for institutions to be successful in the digitalization process, they need to both comply with legal obligations and build their technological infrastructures in a strong and secure manner.

ISO 27001 is an internationally accepted standard for the establishment and effective operation of information security management systems (ISMS). The rapid increase in data production and sharing with Industry 4.0 has made information security a more critical issue than ever. Therefore, it is of great importance to develop robust, sustainable and comprehensive information security solutions to ensure security in digitalized production environments (Uğuz, 2018). This standard is based on some basic principles such as risk management, continuous improvement, auditing and documentation. It helps institutions develop a certain systematic and sustainable security understanding in order to better protect their information assets (Folorunso et al., 2024). In particular, assessing risks and acting according to these risks is a fundamental point for industrial information security. In this way, threats can be detected before they occur and the necessary measures to ensure security can be put into effect without delay.

In industrial environments where production facilities, control systems and IoT devices work together, information security systems established according to ISO 27001 are becoming quite important. These systems both ensure that data is not corrupted and help control things like who can access what. They also provide a certain order for tasks such as auditing. ISO 27001 is not limited to technical issues; it also contributes to employees' awareness of security, and supports the preparation of plans for what to do in the event of a threat (Kitsios et al., 2023). It also foresees that security-related processes will be improved over time. In this way, institutions can develop a more robust and permanent security understanding in the long term.

The Cybersecurity Framework, developed by the National Institute of Standards and Technology (NIST), operating in the United States, provides a comprehensive guide for organizations to manage cybersecurity risks in a more controlled and effective manner. The incredible acceleration of digitalization with Industry 4.0 in recent years has led to a significant increase in both the type and complexity of threats. This clearly shows that classical security methods are no longer sufficient and that organizations need to turn to more flexible strategies that aim to take precautions in advance (Veiga Lima & Costa, 2019). The NIST Cybersecurity Framework is built on five main functions that form the foundation of cybersecurity management: Identify, Protect, Detect, Respond, and Recover. This structure allows organizations to assess their current security posture and build a more robust and resilient cybersecurity infrastructure over time. In particular, the "Identify" phase plays a vital role in identifying potential threats and vulnerabilities through risk assessments (NIST, 2018). In the "Protect" phase, technical and administrative measures are planned, security controls to be implemented are clarified, and the security of systems is proactively ensured.

The NIST-developed Cybersecurity Framework is an extremely helpful guideline to establish a secure base for automation systems, industrial control infrastructures, and IoT devices that are often implemented in Industry 4.0 scenarios. Due to the adaptable nature of the structure of the framework, organizations that function in various industries have an easy time integrating it based on their own requirement and risk scenarios. It offers an immense advantage, particularly with regards to securing critical infrastructures and managing securely production process data flows.

As digital transformation has accelerated in recent years, data privacy and the protection of personal data have become one of the most sensitive and prioritized regulatory issues. GDPR, which is valid in the European Union, and KVKK, which is valid in Türkiye, are among the main legal frameworks that form the basis of data security policies, especially in industrial environments. GDPR requires both transparency and robust security measures regarding the processing, storage and sharing of personal data. KVKK similarly aims to protect personal data and explains in detail what data controllers should pay attention to. Both regulations closely monitor how organizations work with data, and if the rules are not followed, serious sanctions are put in place (T.C. Kişisel Verileri Koruma Kurumu, 2016).

With Industry 4.0, along with the widespread use of IoT devices and production of large amounts of data, privacy policies for protecting information have become obligatory. Companies are reviewing their processes with regard to information under GDPR and KVKK regulations so that they can comply (Evren, 2023). Encryption, access controls, periodic checks etc. are some methods that they use to ensure information security. It is not only about accomplishing their legal obligations, but about ensuring digital system security and smooth function too. On the other hand, strict application of a privacy policy is giving organizations an advantage to win customer confidence and take a step ahead in their market.

The increasing prevalence of IoT devices and their integration into industrial systems necessitates the re-examination and updating of cybersecurity regulations at both national and international levels (Chen, 2019). In the field of IoT and industrial cybersecurity, there are many standards and regulations that apply worldwide. International organizations are developing common standards to ensure that both device manufacturers and users meet certain security requirements. Such regulations not only facilitate international trade, but also contribute to the establishment of a more harmonious and effective line of defense between countries against cyber threats. Each country shapes its regulatory approaches by considering its own security needs and existing infrastructure. In Türkiye, in addition to KVKK, various sector-specific cybersecurity regulations are implemented. Local regulations are designed to work in harmony with global standards while also addressing the country's economic, technological, and social dynamics (Galandarli, 2025). This is particularly important for improving region-specific security strategies in industrial applications.

Critical infrastructures—such as those in the energy, transportation, healthcare, and finance sectors—are of vital importance for both the public and private sectors. The protection of these infrastructures is crucial for national security. For this purpose, cybersecurity standards include specially designed requirements aimed at safeguarding critical infrastructures (Alcaraz & Zeadally, 2015). Cybersecurity standards developed for critical infrastructures encompass not only technical measures but also organizational structures and emergency response procedures. These standards offer a comprehensive framework for detecting, preventing, and responding swiftly to attacks.

9. FUTURE TRENDS IN CYBERSECURITY IN INDUSTRY 4.0

Industry 4.0 is driving a major transformation in manufacturing processes through digitalization, autonomous systems, and the integration of artificial intelligence. This transformation also necessitates the emergence of new trends and technologies in the field of cybersecurity. Technologies such as 5G and quantum computing, expectations surrounding Industry 5.0, cyber resilience and defense mechanisms, and next-generation industrial security solutions are among the critical components for the digital infrastructures of the future.

5G technology is revolutionizing industrial applications by offering high speed, low latency, and broad connectivity. However, these technological advancements also introduce new challenges and risks in terms of cybersecurity (Ahmad et al., 2024). 5G networks expand the attack surface by enabling a greater number of devices to connect to each other. This necessitates the development of new security protocols to ensure network protection, safeguard data privacy, and prevent unauthorized access (T.C. Sanayi ve Teknoloji Bakanlığı, 2022). Meanwhile, quantum computing has the potential to create profound changes in data processing and encryption methods. The ability of quantum computers to break existing encryption algorithms is considered a significant risk in the field of cybersecurity (Genç, 2022). Therefore, developing and implementing quantum-safe encryption methods has become a fundamental necessity to ensure future-ready cyber protection.

As Industry 5.0 emerges with its emphasis on human-centered approaches, sustainability, and flexibility, new expectations arise in terms of cybersecurity as well (Sheikh et al., 2024). The human-centered structure of Industry 5.0 requires cybersecurity strategies to take the human factor into account, including enhancing user education and developing user-friendly security solutions (Wang et al., 2024). At the same time, sustainability in cybersecurity introduces considerations such as energy efficiency and minimizing environmental impact (Demirci, 2025). Flexible and adaptable security solutions are also crucial to enable rapid and effective responses to unexpected and evolving threats.

Cyber resilience has become a core element of future cybersecurity strategies. It refers to a system's capacity to withstand cyberattacks and recover quickly after an incident, thereby ensuring business continuity (Dupont et al., 2023). In this context, proactive defense mechanisms are essential. These strategies aim to detect and block potential threats before they can cause damage, and are increasingly supported by technologies such as artificial intelligence and machine learning. These technologies are capable of identifying abnormal behavior patterns and preventing cyberattacks at their earliest stages (Efe, 2021). Automated response systems further strengthen resilience by being activated immediately upon detection of a cyberattack, limiting the impact and minimizing potential damage (Nespoli et al., 2018).

With innovations driven by Industry 4.0 and the evolution toward Industry 5.0, next-generation industrial security solutions have been developed to address both existing and emerging threats (Verma et al., 2022). These include integrated security platforms that combine various tools into a centralized system, allowing for automated processes in threat detection, analysis, intervention, and reporting. Such platforms facilitate faster and more coordinated cybersecurity responses, leading to a more effective defense mechanism overall. In addition, specialized solutions tailored to the unique needs of IoT devices and industrial control systems are becoming increasingly important. These solutions protect data integrity and prevent information leaks by securing data communication between devices, ultimately supporting uninterrupted industrial operations and establishing a more robust cybersecurity posture (Asghar et al., 2019).

CONCLUSION AND EVALUATION

Industry 4.0 represents a paradigm shift that has led to significant transformations in work styles, production structures, and decision-making processes. This transformation, which encompasses technologies such as artificial intelligence, the Internet of Things (IoT), big data analytics, and cybersecurity systems, offers notable advantages including increased efficiency and flexibility. However, alongside these benefits, it also introduces various disadvantages and risks, particularly in the domain of cybersecurity.

Manufacturing facilities have evolved into digital network nodes that transmit real-time data, moving beyond the traditional notion of production as purely physical machinery. This integration of operational technologies (OT) with information technologies (IT) has made systems more vulnerable to cyberattacks over time.

In recent years, cyberattacks have increasingly targeted critical infrastructure components, exploiting vulnerabilities in interconnected industrial environments. Such incidents underscore the need for robust cybersecurity measures in Industry 4.0 implementations. By continuing to develop adaptive and integrated security strategies that address both current and emerging threats, organizations can harness the benefits of Industry 4.0 while safeguarding their operations and data integrity for the future.

REFERENCES

Abdalla, H. B. (2022). A brief survey on big data: Technologies, terminologies, and data-intensive applications. *Journal of Big Data*, *9*(1), 107. Advance online publication. DOI: 10.1186/s40537-022-00659-3

Agyemang, E. F. (2024). Anomaly detection using unsupervised machine learning algorithms: A simulation study.

Ahmad, I. A., Osasona, F., Dawodu, S. O., Obi, O. C., Anyanwu, A. C., & Onwusinkwue, S. (2024, January 26). Emerging 5G technology: A review of its far-reaching implications for communication. *World Journal of Advanced Research and Reviews*, *21*(01), 2474–2486. DOI: 10.30574/wjarr.2024.21.1.0346

Ahmadi, S. (2024). Ocak 2). Next Generation AI-Based Firewalls: A Comparative. International. *Journal of Computers*, •••, 245–262.

Ajah, I. A., & Nweke, H. F. (2019). Big data and business analytics: Trends, platforms, success factors, and applications. *Big Data and Cognitive Computing*, *3*(2), 32. DOI: 10.3390/bdcc3020032

Madhumita, G., Das, T., Das, S., Khatri, E., Ravisankar, P., & Hemachandu, P. (2024, April). IoT and AI for Real-Time Customer Behavior Analysis in Digital Banking. In 2024 5th International Conference on Recent Trends in Computer Science and Technology (ICRTCST) (pp. 198-203). IEEE.

Akhtar, Z. B., & Rawol, A. T. (2024, August). Enhancing Cybersecurity through Artificial Intelligence (AI)-Powered Security Mechanisms. *IT Journal Research and Development*, *9*(1), 50–67. DOI: 10.25299/itjrd.2024.16852

Alcaraz, C., & Zeadally, S. (2015). Ocak). Critical Infrastructure Protection: Requirements and Challenges for the 21st Century. *International Journal of Critical Infrastructure Protection*, *8*, 53–66. DOI: 10.1016/j.ijcip.2014.12.002

Ali, M. H., Jaber, M. M., Abd, S. K., Rehman, A., Awan, M. J., Damaševicius, R., & Bahaj, S. A. (2022). Threat Analysis and Distributed Denial of Service (DDoS) Attack Recognition in the Internet of Things (IoT). Electronics MDPI.

Alnafessah, A., & Casale, G. (2020). Artificial neural networks based techniques for anomaly detection in Apache Spark. *Cluster Computing*, *23*(2), 1345–1360. DOI: 10.1007/s10586-019-02998-y

Anand, N., Saifulla, M. A., Ponnuru, R. B., Alavalapati, G. R., Patan, R., & Gandomi, A. H. (2024). Securing Software Defined Networks: A Comprehensive Analysis of Approaches, Applications, and Future Strategies against DoS Attacks. *IEEE Access : Practical Innovations, Open Solutions.*

Asghar, M. R., Hu, Q., & Zeadally, S. (2019, December 24). Cybersecurity in industrial control systems: Issues, technologies, and challenges. *Computer Networks, 165*, 165. DOI: 10.1016/j.comnet.2019.106946

Aslay, F. (2017). Siber saldırı yöntemleri ve Türkiye'nin siber güvenlik mevcut durum analizi. *International Journal of Multidisciplinary Studies and Innovative Technologies, 1*(1), 24–28.

Avcı, İ. (2022). Akıllı Evlerde IoT Teknolojileri ve Siber Güvenlik. *Avrupa Bilim ve Teknoloji Dergisi*, (34), 226–233. DOI: 10.31590/ejosat.1080228

Aydın, H., Barışkan, M. A., & Çetinkaya, A. (2021). Mayıs). *Güvenlik Bilimleri Dergisi, 10*(1), 151–174. DOI: 10.28956/gbd.941801

Badshah, A., Daud, A., Alharbey, R., Banjar, A., Bukhari, A., & Alshemaimri, B. (2024). Big data applications: Overview, challenges and future. *Artificial Intelligence Review, 57*(11), 290. DOI: 10.1007/s10462-024-10938-5

Bala, B., & Behal, S. (2024, May). AI techniques for IoT-based DDoS attack detection: Taxonomies, comprehensive review and research challenges. *Computer Science Review, 52*, 52. DOI: 10.1016/j.cosrev.2024.100631

Banger, G. (2018). *Endüstri 4.0 ve akıllı işletme* [Industry 4.0 and the smart enterprise]. Dorlion Yayınları.

Brynjolfsson, E., & McAfee, A. (2014). *The second machine age: Work, progress, and prosperity in a time of brilliant technologies.* W.W. Norton & Co.

Çelik, K. (2021). Bulut bilişim teknolojileri [Cloud computing technologies]. *Bartın Üniversitesi İktisadi ve İdari Bilimler Fakültesi Dergisi, 12*(24), 436–450. DOI: 10.47129/bartiniibf.1019898

Cevher, M. F. (2023). Bibliometric analysis of the internet of things from a marketing perspective. *Journal of Research in Business, 8*(1), 153–170. DOI: 10.54452/jrb.1181367

Chen, Y., Wang, W., Yang, Z., Deveci, M., & Delen, D. (2024). Evaluating risk of IoT adoption in the food supply chain using an integrated interval-valued spherical fuzzy generalised TODIM method. *International Journal of Production Economics, 277*, 109386. DOI: 10.1016/j.ijpe.2024.109386

Cindric, I., Jurcevic, M., & Hadjina, T. (2025). *Mapping of Industrial IoT to IEC 62443 Standards*. MDPI. DOI: 10.3390/s25030728

Claudia Greco, G. F., & Choo, K.-K. R. (2023). AI-enabled IoT penetration testing: State-of-the-art and research challenges. *Enterprise Information Systems*, *17*(9), 1223–1247.

Dehghantanha, A., Yazdinejad, A., & Parizi, R. M. (2024). Autonomous Cybersecurity: Evolving Challenges, Emerging Opportunities, and Future Research Trajectories. CCS '24: ACM SIGSAC Conference on Computer and Communications Security. Salt Lake City, U.S.A.: ACM CCS.

Deloitte University Press. (n.d.). Industry 4.0 – Is your ERP system ready for the digital era? (p. 8). Retrieved from https://www2.deloitte.com/content/dam/Deloitte/de/Documents/technology/Deloitte _ERP_ Industrie-4-0_Whitepaper.pdf as cited in Eğilmez, M. (2018). Industry 4.0. Journal of Accounting and Financial History Research, 15, 268. https://dergipark.org.tr/tr/download/issue-full-file/37137

Demirçi, Z. Ö. (2025). Şubat). Karakuri Kaizen: Yalın Üretimde Sürekli İyileştirmenin Mekanik Uygulmaları. *Anahtar Makale*, *434*, 30–32.

Dupont, B., Shearing, C., Bernier, M., & Leukfeldt, R. (2023, June 29). The tensions of cyber-resilience: From sensemaking to practice. *Computers & Security*, *132*, 103372. DOI: 10.1016/j.cose.2023.103372

Efe, A. (2021). Yapay Zekâ Odaklı Siber Risk ve Güvenlik Yönetimi. *Uluslararası Yönetim Bilişim Sistemleri ve Bilgisayar Bilimleri Dergisi*, *5*(2), 144–165. DOI: 10.33461/uybisbbd.972206

Efe, A. (2021). Yapay zekâ ve Endüstri 4.0 ilişkisinin siber güvenlik perspektifinden analizi [Analysis of the relationship between artificial intelligence and Industry 4.0 from a cybersecurity perspective]. *Aydın Adnan Menderes Üniversitesi Sosyal Bilimler Enstitüsü Dergisi*, *8*(1), 123–143. DOI: 10.30803/adusobed.936426

Eldem, M. O. (2017). Endüstri 4.0. TMMOB EMO Ankara Şubesi Haber Bülteni, 2017(3), 10. Retrieved from https://www.emo.org.tr/ekler/09287020c96f18a_ek.pdf?dergi=1111

Erbey, A. (2024). Internet of Things (IoT). In Karaca, M. F. (Ed.), *Current Topics in Management Information Systems* (pp. 15–32). Özgür Yayınları., DOI: 10.58830/ozgur.pub498.c2090

Evren, A. G. (2023, December 25). Avrupa Birliği ve Türkiye Kişisel Verilerin Korunması Kanunlarının Karşılaştırmalı Analizi: Temel İlkeler, Yasal Dayanaklar ve İlgili Kişi Hakları. *Kişisel Verileri Koruma Dergisi*, *5*(2), 39–64.

Folorunso, A., Mohammed, V., Wada, I., & Samuel, B. (2024). Ekim 21). The impact of ISO security standards on enhancing cybersecurity posture in organizations. *World Journal of Advanced Research and Reviews, 24*(01), 2582–2595. DOI: 10.30574/wjarr.2024.24.1.3169

Galandarli, A. (2025). Mitigating AI risks: A comparative analysis of Data Protection Impact Assessments under GDPR and KVKK. *Journal of Data Protection & Privacy, 7*(3), 252–273. DOI: 10.69554/ATTT2755

Gaur, P., & Kaushik, M. A. (2021, December). AES Image Encryption (Advanced Encryption Standard). [IJRASET]. *International Journal for Research in Applied Science and Engineering Technology, 9*(12), 1357–1363. DOI: 10.22214/ijraset.2021.39542

Gebremichael, T., Ledwaba, L. P., Eldefrawy, M. H., Hancke, G. P., Pereira, N., Gidlund, M., & Akerberg, J. (2020). Ağustos 28). Security and Privacy in the Industrial Internet of Things: Current Standards and Future Challenges. *IEEE Access : Practical Innovations, Open Solutions, 8*, 152351–152366. DOI: 10.1109/ACCESS.2020.3016937

Genç, S. (2022). Aralık 19). Bilişim Teknolojilerinde Blok Zincir ve Kuantum Hesaplamanın Ortak Geleceği: Kuantum Blok Zinciri. *Veri Bilimi Dergisi, 5*(2), 53–63.

Gönen, S., Yılmaz, E. N., Şanoğlu, S., Karacayılmaz, G., & Özbirinci, Ö. (2021). Endüstri 4.0'ın gelişim sürecinde unutulan bileşen: Siber güvenlik [The forgotten component in the development process of Industry 4.0: Cybersecurity]. *Düzce Üniversitesi Bilim ve Teknoloji Dergisi, 9*(4), 1152–1171. DOI: 10.29130/dubited.905340

Hermann, M., Pentek, T., & Otto, B. (2016, January). Design principles for industrie 4.0 scenarios. In 2016 49th Hawaii international conference on system sciences (HICSS) (pp. 3928-3937). IEEE.

Hossain, N. U. I., Fazio, S. A., Lezzi, M., & Islam, M. S. (2024). A decision support model for assessing and prioritization of industry 5.0 cybersecurity challenges. *Sustainable Manufacturing and Service Economics, 100018*, 100018. Advance online publication. DOI: 10.1016/j.smse.2024.100018

International Electrotechnical Commission. (2013). IEC 62443-3-3. Şubat 9, 2025 tarihinde International Electrotechnical Commission: https://webstore.iec.ch/en/iec_catalog/product/preview/?id=L3B1Yi9wZGYvcHJldmlldy9pbmZvX2l1YzYyNDQzLTMtM3tlZDEuMH1iLnBkZg== adresinden alındı

Iturbe, E., Mansell, J., Rios, E., & Toledo, N. (2023). Information security risk assessment methodology for industrial systems supporting ISA/IEC 62443 compliance. III. International Conference on Electrical, Computer and Energy Technologies (ICECET 2023). South Africa: IEEE Xplore.

Joint Technical Committee ISO/IEC JTC 1. (2013). ISO/IEC 27001:2013(en). Şubat 9, 2025 tarihinde Online Browsing Platform (OBP): https://www.iso.org/obp/ui/#iso:std:iso-iec:27001:ed-2:v1:en adresinden alındı

Karacı, A., Akyüz, H. İ., & Bilgici, G. (2017). Üniversite öğrencilerinin siber güvenlik davranışlarının incelenmesi. *Kastamonu Eğitim Dergisi*, *25*(4), 1537–1552.

Kaygin, E., Zengin, Y., & Topçuoğlu, E. (2019). Endüstri 4.0'a akademik bakış. DergiPark. Retrieved from https://dergipark.org.tr/tr/download/article-file/840401

Kişisel Verileri Koruma Kurumu, T. C. (2016, 24 3). 6698 Sayılı Kişisel Verilerin Korunması Kanunu. Ankara, Türkiye. Mart 18, 2025 tarihinde https://www.mevzuat.gov.tr/mevzuat?MevzuatNo=6698&MevzuatTur=1&MevzuatTertip=5 adresinden alındı

Kitsios, F., Chatzidimitriou, E., & Kamariotou, M. (2023, Mart 27). The ISO/IEC 27001 Information Security Management Standard: How to Extract Value from Data in the IT Sector. *MDPI.*

Koroniotis, N., Moustafa, N., & Sitnikova, E. (2019). Mayıs 23). Forensics and Deep Learning Mechanisms for Botnets in Internet of Things: A Survey of Challenges and Solutions. *IEEE Access : Practical Innovations, Open Solutions*, *7*, 61764–61785. DOI: 10.1109/ACCESS.2019.2916717

Lezzi, M., Lazoi, M., & Corallo, A. (2018). Cybersecurity for Industry 4.0 in the current literature: A reference framework. *Computers in Industry*, *103*, 97–110. DOI: 10.1016/j.compind.2018.09.004

Livingston, J. (2022). NERC CIP Standarts: Safeguarding North America's Power Grid. Verve Industrial: https://verveindustrial.com/resources/blog/what-are-the-nerc-cip-standards-in-ics-security/ adresinden alındı

Maharjan, P. (2023). *The Role of Artificial Intelligence-Driven Big Data Analytics in Strengthening Cybersecurity Frameworks for Critical Infrastructure.* Global Research Perspectives on Cybersecurity Governance, Policy, and Management.

Mahboubi, A., Luong, K., Aboutorab, H., Bui, H. T., Jarrad, G., Bahutair, M., & Gately, H. (2024). Aralık). Evolving techniques in cyber threat hunting: A systematic review. *Journal of Network and Computer Applications*, •••, 232.

Mahmood, H. S., Abdulqader, D. M., Abdullah, R. M., Ismael, H. R., Rashid, Z. N., & Sami, T. M. (2024). Conducting In-Depth Analysis of AI, IoT, Web Technology, Cloud Computing, and Enterprise Systems Integration for Enhancing Data Security and Governance to Promote Sustainable Business Practices. [JITI]. *Journal of Information Technology and Informatics*, *3*(2), 297–332.

Mahnamfar, A., & Ünlü, N. (2022). Siber Fiziksel Sistemler ve Güvenlik Sorunları. *Savunma Bilimleri Dergisi*, *41*, 97–118. DOI: 10.17134/khosbd.1100660

Manoharan, A., & Sarker, M. (2022, December). Evolutionizing Cybersecurity: Unleashing The Power Of Artificial İntelligence And Machine Learning For Next Generation Threat Detection. *International Research Journal of Modernization in Engineering Technology and Science*, *04*(12).

Mobi, S. (2019). Siber Saldırılar Nesnelerin İnternetini (IoT) Etkiler mi? Sanal Mobi. Retrieved from https://sanal.mobi/tr/Blog/165-siber-saldirilar-nesnelerin-internetini-iot-etkiler-mi?utm_source

Moura, J., & Serrão, C. (2016). Security and Privacy Issues of Big Data. arXiv. https://arxiv.org/pdf/1601.06206

Mugarza, I., Flores, J. L., & Montero, J. L. (2020). Security Issues and Software Updates Management in the Industrial Internet of Things (IIoT) Era. Sensors MDPI.

Tay, M., & Şentürk, A. (2021). Kenar, Sis ve Bulut Bilişimin IoT Açısından İncelenmesi. *Avrupa Bilim ve Teknoloji Dergisi*, (32), 68–75.

Muneer, S., Farooq, U., Athar, A., Raza, M. A., Ghazal, T. M., & Sakib, S. (2024). A Critical Review of Artificial Intelligence Based Approaches in Intrusion Detection: A Comprehensive Analysis. Hindawi Journal of Engineering.

Mustak, M., Salminen, J., Mantymaki, M., Rahman, A., & Dwivedi, Y. K. (2023). Deepfakes: Deceptions, mitigations, and opportunities. *Journal of Business Research*, •••, 154.

Nespoli, P., Dimitrios Papamartzivanos, F. G., & Kambourakis, G. (2018). Optimal Countermeasures Selection Against Cyber Attacks: A Comprehensive Surveyon Reaction Frameworks. *IEEE Communications Surveys and Tutorials*, *20*(2), 1361–1396. DOI: 10.1109/COMST.2017.2781126

NIST. (2018). Framework for Improving Critical Infrastructure Cybersecurity (Version 1.1). ABD: National Institute of Standards and Technology.

Oláh, J., Aburumman, N., Popp, J., Khan, M. A., Haddad, H., & Kitukutha, N. (2020, June 8). Impact of Industry 4.0 on Environmental Sustainability. *MDPI, 12*(11).

Ötleş, S. (2016). *Vasfiye Hazal Özyurt, "Büyüme ve Verimlilik İçin Dijitalleşme"*. Ege Üniversitesi Gıda Mühendisliği Bölümü Dergisi.

Özçetin, N. (2024). Endüstri 4.0 ve Endüstri 5.0 perspektiflerinde muhasebe: Teorik bir inceleme [Accounting in Industry 4.0 and Industry 5.0 Perspectives: A Theoretical Review]. Yönetim Bilimleri Dergisi- Journal of Administrative Sciences, 22(Özel Sayı), 1324-1344. DOI: 10.35408/comuybd.1490646

Öztuna, B. (2017). *The Future of Working Life with Industry 4.0 (The Fourth Industrial Revolution)* (1st ed.). Gece Kitaplığı.

Rahul, K., Banyal, R. K., & Arora, N. (2023). A systematic review on big data applications and scope for industrial processing and healthcare sectors. *Journal of Big Data, 10*(1), 133. DOI: 10.1186/s40537-023-00808-2

Rajenda, S., & Kaliappan, V. K. (2022). Sensor Data Based Anomaly Detection in Autonomous Vehicles using Modified Convolutional Neural Network. *Intelligent Automation & Soft Computing, 32*(2), 859–875. DOI: 10.32604/iasc.2022.020936

Rakhade, V. M. (2024, December). Security challenges in edge computing. Paper presented at the International Journal of Futuristic Innovation in Arts, Humanities and Management (IJFIAHM), Shri Sai College of Engineering & Technology, Chandrapur, India.

Salah, K., Elbadawi, K., & Boutaba, R. (2012, March). Performance Modeling and Analysis of Network Firewalls. *IEEE Transactions on Network and Service Management, 9*(1), 12–21. DOI: 10.1109/TNSM.2011.122011.110151

Teknolojileri, B., & Kurumu, İ. (2020). Sektörel Araştırma ve Strateji Geliştirme Dairesi.

Sengupta, J., Ruj, S., & Bit, S. D. (2020). A Comprehensive Survey on Attacks, Security Issues and Blockchain Solutions for IoT and IIoT. *Journal of Network and Computer Applications, 149*, 149. DOI: 10.1016/j.jnca.2019.102481

Serter, H., & Serinkan, C. (2020). Endüstri 4.0 ve yenilik yönetimi. In M. Dalkılıç (Ed.), New Developments in Education and Social Sciences (Bölüm 34, s. 677-692). Gece Kitaplığı.

Sheikh, A. M., Islam, M. R., Habaebi, M. H., Zabidi, S. A., Najeeb, A. R. B., & Kabani, A. (2025). A survey on edge computing (EC) security challenges: Classification, threats, and mitigation strategies. Preprints, Version 1. DOI: 10.20944/preprints202502.1500.v1

Soori, M., Arezoo, B., & Dastres, R. (2023). Internet of things for smart factories in industry 4.0, a review. *Internet of Things and Cyber-Physical Systems*, *3*, 192–204. DOI: 10.1016/j.iotcps.2023.04.006

Uğuz, S. (2018). Kurumsal Bilgi Güvenliği Yönetim Sistemi Yazılımları: Örnek Bir Yazılım Geliştirilmesi. Uluslararası Yönetim Bilişim Sistemleri ve Bilgisayar Bilimleri Dergisi, 2(1).

Vaia Rousopoulou, T. V., Nizamis, A., Iakovidis, I., Samaras, L., Kirtsoglou, A., Georgiadis, K., & Tzovaras, D. (2022). Cognitive analytics platform with AI solutions for anomaly detection. *Computers in Industry*, *134*, 134. DOI: 10.1016/j.compind.2021.103555

Veiga, G. L., Lima, E. P., & Costa, S. E. (2019). Ağustos). Efficiency Frontier Identification Based on Operations Strategy- A Retrospective Analysis of Leading Authors. *Procedia Manufacturing*, *39*, 775–785. DOI: 10.1016/j.promfg.2020.01.431

Verma, A., Bhattacharya, P., Madhanı, N., Trıvedı, C., Bhushan, B., Tanwar, S., Sharma, G., Bokoro, P. N., & Sharma, A. R. (2022, July 5). Blockchain for Industry 5.0: Vision, Opportunities, Key Enablers, and Future Directions. *IEEE Access : Practical Innovations, Open Solutions*, *10*, 69160–69199. DOI: 10.1109/ACCESS.2022.3186892

Wang, T., Liang, Y., Shen, X., Zheng, X., Mahmood, A., & Sheng, Q. Z. (2023). Edge computing and sensor-cloud: Overview, solutions, and directions. ACM Computing Surveys, 55(13s). *ACM Computing Surveys*, *281*(13s), 1–37. DOI: 10.1145/3582270

Waschbusch, L., & Mundt, E. (2019, 27. Mai). Was bedeutet Industrie 4.0? Definition, Merkmale und Anwendung. Industry of Things. https://www.industry-of-things.de/was-bedeutet-industrie-40-definition-merkmale-und-anwendung-a-828236/

Westerlund, M.MikaWesterlund. (2019). Ekim). The Emergence of Deepfake Technology: A Review. *Technology Innovation Management Review*, *9*(11), 39–52. DOI: 10.22215/timreview/1282

Yıldız Tonga, M., & Tonga, M. (2022). Endüstri 4.0'a genel bir bakış: Sanayinin geleceği [Overview of Industry 4.0: The Future of the Industry]. G. Ü. İslahiye İİBF Uluslararası E-Dergi, 6(6), 40-60.

Yoşumaz, İ., & Özkara, B. (2019). Endüstri 4.0 sürecinin hazır giyim işletmeleri üzerindeki etkileri: hugo boss türkiye örneği. İşletme Araştırmaları Dergisi, 11(4), 2587-2600.

Yüksel, A., Eren, T., & Güven, E. (2024). Siber fiziksel sistemler alanında Türkiye'deki akademik eğilimler: Bir bibliyometrik analiz. *Bilgisayar Bilimleri ve Teknolojileri Dergisi*, *5*(2), 24–35. DOI: 10.54047/bibted.1530609

Zhou, Y., Cheng, G., Zhao, Y., Chen, Z., & Jiang, S. (2022, April). Toward Proactive and Efficient DDoS Mitigation in IIoT Systems: A MovingTarget Defense Approach. *IEEE Transactions on Industrial Informatics*, *18*(4), 2734–2744. DOI: 10.1109/TII.2021.3090719

Zolanvari, M., Teixeira, M. A., Gupta, L., Khan, K. M., & Jain, R. (2019). *Machine Learning Based Network Vulnerability Analysis of Industrial Internet of Things*. IEEE. DOI: 10.1109/JIOT.2019.2912022

Chapter 4
Cybersecurity Culture and Human Factor

Aslihan Bekaroğlu Özatar
https://orcid.org/0000-0002-5502-227X
Beykoz University, Turkey

Aysun Varan
https://orcid.org/0000-0001-6401-9542
Beykoz University, Turkey

ABSTRACT

In today's digital environment, the business world has to go beyond seeing cyber security as a defence tool in order to adapt to rapidly changing threats and maintain its competitive advantage. Cyber security should be considered not only as a protection mechanism but also as a fundamental component of business continuity and innovation. With the evolution of technology, the threats faced by both individuals and organisations have increased. In this chapter, while examining the role of people in cyber security culture, it aims to explain the effects of individuals' behaviours and personal characteristics in this area. A strong cyber security culture not only eliminates threats by increasing employee awareness and engagement, but also makes business processes more resilient and innovative. The study examines how security awareness can be integrated into corporate culture, how the human factor shapes cyber risks and what steps organisations should take to create a more resilient structure.

DOI: 10.4018/979-8-3693-6417-8.ch004

1. INTRODUCTION

In today's digital environment, the business world has to go beyond seeing cyber security as a defence tool in order to adapt to rapidly changing threats and maintain its competitive advantage. Cyber security should be considered not only as a protection mechanism but also as a fundamental component of business continuity and innovation. With the evolution of technology, the threats faced by both individuals and organisations have increased. Cyber attacks, data breaches and other security issues are not only related to technical solutions, but also to people's behaviour and awareness levels. While the business world has great opportunities with rapidly developing technology, it also faces increasingly complex cyber threats. Cyber security has become a critical element not only for data protection but also for business continuity, customer confidence, competitive advantage and innovation. According to IBM's 2024 Cost of Data Breach report, which interviewed more than 600 organisations worldwide, the average global cost of a data breach in 2024 reached approximately $4.88 million, while according to the 2023 Cost of Data Breach Report, the average cost of a data breach was $4.45 million, the biggest jump since the pandemic (IBM, 2024). See Figure 1.This increase shows that cyber threats are becoming more intense and preventing such incidents is becoming more complex. This shows that cyber security plays a critical role in ensuring business continuity and maintaining competitive advantage.

Figure 1. Global average total cost of a data breach

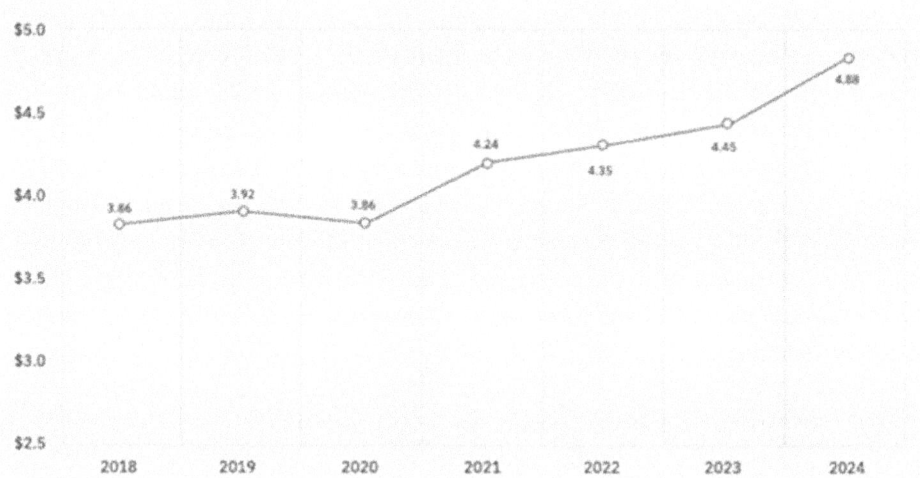

Source: Cost of a Data Breach Report 2024

Cyber attacks not only cause financial losses, but also undermine customer confidence. A study by the Ponemon Institute reveals that 65 per cent of consumers would avoid using the services of a company that suffered a data breach (Ponemon, 2022). In this context, a strong cyber security strategy should be considered not only as a defence mechanism against attacks, but also as an element that increases customer confidence and supports innovation.

In this chapter, while examining the role of people in cyber security culture, it aims to explain the effects of individuals' behaviours and personal characteristics in this area. A strong cyber security culture not only eliminates threats by increasing employee awareness and engagement, but also makes business processes more resilient and innovative. The study examines how security awareness can be integrated into corporate culture, how the human factor shapes cyber risks and what steps organisations should take to create a more resilient structure.

The chapter effectively highlights the historical background of cybersecurity issues, tracing incidents back to the late 1980s. This contextualization is crucial as it demonstrates that cybersecurity concerns are longstanding and not merely a contemporary phenomenon. The identification of vulnerabilities (human, hardware, and software) laid out by Warner (2012) sets a broad framework for understanding the complexities involved in cybersecurity today. Also this chapter synthesizes findings from various studies (e.g., Gcaza et al. 2017; Uchendu et al. 2021) that explore the interplay between cybersecurity culture and organizational behavior. This integration of existing literature helps support the assertion that a robust cyber security culture is vital for protecting information assets. By referencing a mix of academic and industry perspectives, the chapter lends credibility to its analysis of cybersecurity culture .

The emphasis on human factors aligns well with contemporary findings in the field. It reflects a shift in the literature from purely technical approaches to the importance of behavioral aspects in enhancing cybersecurity. The chapter further highlights how organizational support, leadership involvement, and awareness programs contribute to cultivating a culture of security, thereby reinforcing the significance of these human-centric elements in cybersecurity strategies

In the literature review part of the study, the conceptual models used in the field of human role in cyber security culture were explained. Additionally, "**Human Role in Cyber Security Culture**" section address the key theories contributing to the formation of cybersecurity culture, particularly how the Theory of Planned Behavior (TPB), Protection Motivation Theory (PMT), Information Security Awareness Capability Model (ISACM) have been applied in existing studies to develop effective cybersecurity strategies. The prominent models on the subject are given in the table below. See Table 1.

Table 1. Conceptual models

Conceptual Model	Main Academic	Objective
HAIS-Q	Parsons et al. (2014)	Security awareness and behaviour measurement
SCF	Roer & Petric (2017)	Structural analysis of safety culture
TPB	Ifinedo (2012)	Psychological explanation of compliance with security policies
Schein	Schlienger & Teufel (2003)	Impact of organisational values on security
ISACM	Tsohou et al. (2015)	Assessment of organisational awareness capacity

2. CONCEPTUAL FRAMEWORK

2.1. Evolution from Information Security to Cybersecurity Culture

In the last decade, the issue of security culture has featured heavily in practice and research as organisations seek to combat the increase in attacks by exploiting human factors. Various terms are used in this field such as security culture, information security culture and more recently cyber security culture. Although cyber security is often used synonymously with information security, the nature of the two terms differs (Uchendu, R.C. Nurse, Bada, & Furnell, 2021). In order to understand cyber security culture, it is necessary to first understand the formation of the field. For this reason, the emergence of cyber security culture will be explained by starting from the field of information security and information technologies. Information Security is a multidisciplinary field of study and professional activity that emerged with the aim of protecting Information Technologies from various dangers and securing these technologies. Initially, information security is defined as a more technical approach and left to those who are technically specialised in the field. However, those responsible for information security practices realised that senior management should also be involved in this process, leading to the integration of information security into organisational structures and the appointment of information security managers. Subsequently, security policies and procedures were established, which led to the need to understand the effectiveness of these policies and procedures and to evaluate their results. In particular, previously ignored elements of information security have been identified and an effort has begun to standardise, certify and assess information security and to address the human factor as an important security element (Georgiadou, Mouzakitis, Boun, & Askounis, 2022).

An organisation's greatest threat to privacy and security is often seen as its own employees, and this is often not openly acknowledged. Employee security awareness is a critical link in an organisation's security chain. Even the best-protected organisational structures are vulnerable without an effective security culture. The term ‘security culture’ has come to the fore in discussions on this topic and various definitions have been made. Most definitions state that a security culture exists when each individual in the information society, in accordance with his or her role, is aware of relevant security risks and preventive measures, takes responsibility and takes steps to improve the security of information systems and networks (Rantos, Fysarakis, & Manifavas, 2012). In this context, security culture is related to the level of awareness of employees in understanding, implementing and developing information security policies. An inadequate security culture can open the door to potential cyber threats due to employee carelessness or unconsciousness. Therefore, it is critical for the overall security status of the organisation that each individual acts in a security-conscious and responsible manner.

Security culture is developed through a long and time-consuming process in which various factors have different weights. Many factors play a role in this process, such as the structure of the organisation, employee behaviour, leadership style, communication channels and training programmes. Each factor can have a different degree of influence on how a safety culture takes shape. For example, strong leadership and a supportive work environment can increase employee engagement and responsibility for security, while inadequate training and lack of communication can negatively impact this culture.

However, while information security assessment techniques generally focus on specific and standardised methods, no similar standardisation has been achieved for the assessment of security culture. In other words, methods for measuring the effectiveness and robustness of security culture are not yet widely accepted or standardised. This makes it difficult for organisations to effectively assess and improve their safety culture. The inadequacy of security culture assessment methods may lead to ineffective practices in this area and cyber security vulnerabilities in the long term. Therefore, it is an important need to develop more holistic and systematic assessment methods for security culture.

The complexity of human nature in terms of information security has been the subject of research in different scientific disciplines. These disciplines have tried to understand how employees' emotions, beliefs, behaviours and attitudes can affect the information security of the organisation. Getting to the root of the problem can provide effective solutions and create a healthy security culture by developing applicable security policies and training programmes.

Employee compliance with information security policies has been the starting point of many studies using various theories (Theory of Planned Behaviour, Rational Choice Theory, Protection Motivation Theory, etc.). It has been observed that employees' attitudes, normative beliefs and habits have significant effects on compliance with these policies. In addition, the fact that individuals have security knowledge and skills but are unable to apply them effectively in their daily work routines has led to new research on the concept of self-efficacy. In this context, self-efficacy refers to an employee's confidence in his/her ability to comply with the organisation's safety controls (Aurigemma & Panko, 2012).

Research has shown that individuals who demonstrate high self-efficacy have greater beliefs about mobilising the motivational and cognitive resources needed to successfully implement security policies. It has also been found that individuals' habits and subjective norms directly influence their behaviour and reduce the effectiveness of **compliance** behaviours. It was concluded that security technologies should be user-oriented in order to be effective, and the effects of the individual's social and work environment on security behaviours and compliance were emphasised. In order to better understand the interactions in these areas, researchers have identified the need for a **formalised** examination **of individual and organisational security dimensions**.

2.2. Behavioral Models in Cybersecurity Context

Employee compliance with information security policies has been the starting point of many scientific researches. These studies use various theories to explain employee behaviour and compliance with information security policies. The focus of each of these theories is to understand how individuals' behaviours are shaped and to examine the factors that affect these behaviours.

1. **Theory of Planned Behaviour (TPB)**: This theory was developed by Icek Ajzen in 1985 as an extension of the Theory of Reasoned Action. This theory focuses on the analysis of factors (attitudes, normative beliefs and perceived behavioural control) that determine individuals' behavioural intentions (Ajzen, 1991).. Compliance with information security policies is directly related to the development of individuals' intentions based on these factors.
2. **Rational Choice Theory (RCT)**: Rooted in economics and philosophy, this theory was significantly developed by Gary Becker in1968 (Becker, 1968). This theory suggests that individuals' decision-making processes are associated with a rational analysis. Employees evaluate the benefits and harms of complying or not complying with information security policy; hence this theory describes how compliance with information security policies is linked to rational thinking.

3. **Protection Motivation Theory (PMT)**: First proposed by R.W. Rogers in 1975 to explain how the appeal of fear motivates individuals to adopt protective behaviours (Rogers, 1975).. This theory examines how individuals are motivated in the face of a threat (for example, situations that threaten information security) and how this motivation affects their behaviour. Employees can adapt to these policies by focusing on their fear of information security threats and the protection strategies they will develop against these threats.
4. **General Deterrence Theory (GDT)**: Rooted in classical criminology, this theory was first developed by Cesare Beccaria (1764) and later extended by Jeremy Bentham (1789). Modern empirical applications have been explored by scholars such as Gibbs (1975). This theory emphasises how penalties and sanctions influence the behaviour of individuals. Employees who are aware of the consequences of not complying with information security policies may take fewer risks to comply (Gibbs, 1975).
5. **Social Cognitive Theory (SCT)**: Developed by Albert Bandura in the 1980s as an extension of the earlier Social Learning Theory. This theory addresses how individuals' behaviour is shaped through observation, social interactions and personal experiences. Employees' behaviour in relation to information security can be shaped by their social environment and the influence of other individuals.
6. **Theory of Rationalised Action (TRA)**: This theory considers two main factors (attitudes and normative beliefs) that influence individuals' behaviour. Individuals' attitudes towards information security practices can influence their decisions to adopt or avoid policies.
7. Human Aspects of Information Security Questionnaire (HAIS-Q) designed by Parsons, K., McCormac, A., Butavicius, M., Pattinson, M., & Jerram, C. (2014) to measure the relationship between security awareness, attitude and behaviour of employees and to understand the security culture by making the human factor measurable,
8. Information Security Awareness Capability Model (ISACM) developed by Tsohou, A., Karyda, M., & Kokolakis, S. (2015) to assess the human-centred security awareness levels of organisations with a maturity model and to plan training and behavioural development stages,
9. The Security Culture Framework, designed by Roer, K., & Petric, G. (2017), to analyse the current security culture maturity of the organisation and integrate human behaviours into the corporate security framework (This model was also used in Alshaikh, M., Maynard, S. B., Ahmad, A., & Chang, S. (2015), Information security policy: A management practice perspective)

These theories provide a framework for understanding employees' tendencies to comply with information security policies and for developing strategies to encourage such compliance. By addressing the different aspects that influence employee compliance with security policy, each theory adds depth to research and, in aggregate, lays the groundwork for more effective information security strategies.

Security reports published in 2018 and 2019 show that a significant proportion of cybersecurity breaches are caused by employees not complying with **corporate information security policies** (NTT, 2023). Security researchers have consistently argued that it is necessary to create a cybersecurity culture to change attitudes, perceptions and instil good security behaviours (Da Veiga, Astakhova, Botha, & Herselman, 2020).

In general, security culture is the set of sensitivities, attitudes, behaviours and norms towards security in an organisation or society. It can cover physical security, health security and other areas. Cyber security culture is an understanding of security that focuses on the protection of information technologies and digital assets. It refers to the behaviours, attitudes and norms that enable individuals and organisations to be aware of cyber threats and to effectively combat these threats (Georgiadou, Mouzakitis, Boun, & Askounis, 2022).

Cyber security culture is a concept that covers the awareness, behaviour and attitudes of all members of an organisation regarding information security. This culture plays an important role in the adoption and implementation of cyber security policies within the organisation. Cyber security culture can be defined as a set of values, beliefs and norms that shape individuals' attitudes and reactions to cyber threats (Wamala, 2012).

When the studies in the literature are examined, it is seen that there has been a transition from security culture or information security issues to cyber security and cyber security culture building issues in recent years. Uchendu, Nurse, Bada, and Furnell (2021) analysed 58 research articles published between 2010 and 2020 to determine how cyber security culture has been defined in past academic studies, what factors are involved in building and maintaining this culture, what are the frameworks proposed to develop a security culture and what are the criteria proposed to evaluate it. As a result of the research, top management support, policies and procedures, and awareness were found to be critical in establishing a cyber security culture. The conceptual frameworks examined revealed common foundations with organisational culture, which plays an important role in building appropriate cybersecurity culture models (Uchendu, R.C. Nurse, Bada, & Furnell, 2021).

Alshaikh (2021), in his study on creating a cybersecurity culture that will influence employee behaviour, identifies and explains five key initiatives that three Australian organisations have implemented to develop their cybersecurity cultures. These initiatives, defined as identifying key cybersecurity behaviours, establishing a network of 'cybersecurity champions', developing a brand for the cybersecurity team, establishing a cybersecurity centre, and aligning security awareness activities with internal and external campaigns, have been found to help organisations move beyond minimum standard compliance to establish functional cybersecurity cultures. Security researchers have consistently argued that creating a cybersecurity culture is essential to change attitudes and perceptions and instil good security behaviours (Da Veiga & Eloff, 2010).

Cyber security culture is 'contextualised in the behaviour of people in an organisational context to protect information processed by the organisation through compliance with information security policy and an understanding of how to apply the requirements in a careful and diligent manner embedded through regular communication, awareness, education and training initiatives. This current and inclusive definition of security culture emphasises the importance of normal communication and security education, training and awareness (SETA) initiatives in building a cyber security culture (Alshaikh, 2020). In order to create a cybersecurity culture, organisations need to meet and even exceed the minimum requirements of the security awareness training approach (AlHogail, 2015).

3. CYBER SECURITY CULTURE

The International Telecommunication Union (ITU), a special agency of the United Nations (UN), which sets global telecommunication standards, regulates frequency spectrums and promotes the development of information and communication technologies (ICT), defines cyber security culture as a set of shared values, attitudes and behaviours that enable individuals, organisations and societies to act in an informed, responsible and secure manner against cyber threats. According to ITU, cyber security culture is a holistic approach to security, supported not only by technical measures, but also by user awareness, education and policy development. The basic elements are as follows:

- Awareness: Individuals' and organisations' understanding of cyber threats and adoption of security measures.
- Education: Instilling safe digital habits in employees and general users.
- Policies: Setting security standards and best practices.
- Responsibility: All stakeholders see cyber security as a priority and take proactive measures.

Cyber security culture is an issue that has come to the forefront in recent years and plays an important role in achieving the development goals of countries. In this context, ITU-D Working Groups have been established to support the Telecommunications Development Bureau information sharing and capacity building agenda. Working Group 1, appointed for the period 2010-2014, examined nine issues in the areas of enabling environment, cybersecurity, ICT applications and Internet-related issues. The report prepared by the working group on the topic 'Securing information and communications networks: best practices for the development of a cybersecurity culture' stated that building a cybersecurity culture consists of many activities, such as raising awareness and educating private citizens about online risks, educating national stakeholders about the impact of virtual activities on their organisations and the impact of their activities on cyber and information security (ITU, 2014).

Cyber security culture needs to be examined in two dimensions: cyber security culture in the public sector and cyber security culture in commercial enterprises.

Governments own and operate only a small part of the information infrastructure worldwide. However, governments have ambitious Electronic Government (eGovernment) projects. Governments also have law enforcement and counter-terrorism responsibilities. Yet the networks supporting government activities face increasing threats from hostile countries seeking confidential data, as well as from hackers and cybercriminals. Therefore, governments need strict data handling procedures to protect the integrity and confidentiality of sensitive and classified information. Governments have spent significant amounts of money to build technological defences. However, these measures are useless unless all government employees, contractors and third-party users have the right knowledge and skills to mitigate cyber threats. However, even in developed countries, cases of loss of government data show that the cyber security culture is not sufficiently developed.

The private sector owns and operates most of the critical information infrastructure. Businesses should therefore understand the risks involved, preventive measures and effective responses. While large companies have larger systems, small and medium-sized companies often lack the human and organisational capacity to address threats, so it is important to address cybersecurity risks in these companies. Governments should work with industry associations to develop and implement cybersecurity education and training programmes. It would be useful to produce cybersecurity manuals, guides, handbooks and model policies for commercial enterprises. Where possible, governments should produce company-specific security self-assessment tools. Countries may also consider using tax incentives and financial assistance to encourage the development of secure systems (Wamala, 2012). .

National governments have the ultimate responsibility for leading a systematic effort to create a culture of cybersecurity in co-operation with other relevant stakeholders. A culture of security is in line with the sixth GCA Strategic objective, which deals with capacity building mechanisms to raise awareness, transfer knowledge and enhance cybersecurity on the national policy agenda. The United Nations General Assembly (UNGA) has also encouraged the promotion, development and implementation of a strong global cybersecurity culture because trust and security in the use of ICTs are among the main pillars of the information society (UN, 2010).

There is a consensus in the literature that organisations need to develop a cyber security culture to protect their information assets. The process of building a cybersecurity culture has become an important focus in the cybersecurity literature, and early work in this area aimed to establish and understand the concept (Gcaza N., Solms, Grobler, & Vuuren, 2017).

Uchendu, Nurse, Bada, and Furnell (2021) analysed 58 research articles published between 2010 and 2020 with the PRISMA systematic literature review technique and as a result; they found that while most of the articles (42) examine information security culture, there are fewer articles (10) dealing with cyber security culture. However, it is also among the findings that the majority of the publications in the last five years have focused on cyber security (Uchendu, R.C. Nurse, Bada, & Furnell, 2021).

In their study, Karayel and Akbıyık (2023) analysed 4252 articles published between 1980 and 2021 indexed in the database of Web of Science and found that research published in the field of cyber security showed an increasing trend over the years, while publications on information security showed a decreasing trend (Karayel & Akbıyık, 2023).

In the study conducted by Sanlı et al. (2024), comparative data on 408 postgraduate theses in the archive of the National Thesis Centre of the Higher Education Institution under the keyword cyber security were analysed and as a result of the analysis in the field of 'Cyber Security', it was seen that the most theses were published in 2022 (Sanlı, Baltacı, Güven, & Eren, 2024).

3.1. Cyber Threat Trends and the Human Factor

The contemporary cyber threat landscape is marked by an increasing sophistication of attack techniques that exploit not only technical vulnerabilities but also human behaviors. Threat actors are leveraging social engineering, insider manipulation, and behavioral predictability to bypass traditional security controls. This section outlines key threat categories—ransomware, phishing, and insider threats—and discusses how each targets human vulnerabilities, thereby underlining the need for a security-aware workforce.

The cybersecurity landscape has evolved to recognize that human factors are as critical as technological defenses. Threat actors increasingly exploit psychological and behavioral vulnerabilities, making the human element a pivotal point of failure or defense in cybersecurity (Prabhu & Thompson, 2021).

Table 2. Examples of cases in latest trends and threat types.

Threat Type	Latest Trend	Human Vulnerability Exploited	Cases
Ransomware	Multi-extortion, AI-driven targeting	Clicking malicious links, poor password hygiene	MGM Resorts attack (2023)
Phishing	AI-generated messages, deepfakes, quishing	Trust in urgency/authority, unfamiliarity with new formats	Microsoft Teams phishing (2024, KnowBe4)
Insider Threats	Rise in remote/hybrid misuse, third-party access misuse	Negligence, over-permissioning, lack of training	Twitter source code leak by former contractor

Ransomware has evolved from a relatively straightforward malware threat into a multifaceted, **multi-extortion strategy**, combining data encryption, data theft, and reputational pressure (Coveware, 2024). The rise of **Ransomware-as-a-Service (RaaS)** platforms has also lowered the barrier to entry for attackers, democratizing access to advanced ransomware toolkits. Ransomware attacks have surged, often leveraging social engineering tactics to deceive users into executing malicious software. The infamous WannaCry attack exploited human error and outdated systems, highlighting the need for user awareness and timely system updates (Gregory, 2020).

Phishing and Social Engineering

Phishing has become the most frequently reported cyber threat due to its evolving complexity and human-centric design. Using **AI and deepfake technologies**, attackers can now craft hyper-personalized emails, voice messages, and even video content to mimic trusted entities (ENISA, 2024).

Variants such as **spear phishing**, **vishing** (voice phishing), **smishing** (SMS phishing), and **quishing** (QR code phishing) are increasingly used to exploit emotional and cognitive biases. Studies show that phishing attacks now account for **36% of breaches**, often leveraging authority, urgency, or fear to manipulate victims (Verizon, 2023).

Human factors contributing to success in phishing attacks include:

- Over-trust in digital communication.
- Lack of awareness of modern phishing formats.
- Inadequate organizational training and reinforcement (Vance, Siponen, & Pahnila, 2012).

Insider Threats

Insider threats—both **malicious** and **unintentional**—have risen with the growth of **remote work** and **cloud-based collaboration** tools. Accidental insiders may leak data due to **misconfigurations**, while malicious actors might exploit their access for sabotage or profit (Ponemon Institute, 2023).

- **Human Vector:** Often caused by **lack of training**, **over-permissioned access**, or **inadequate monitoring** (CERT, 2023).

4. THE ROLE OF HUMAN FACTOR IN CYBER SECURITY

The problem of cyber security is not a phenomenon that emerged in the twenty-first century. The existence of incidents related to cyber security can be traced back to the late 1980s. Even during this period a number of cybercrimes were recorded, including espionage, theft and hacking. According to Warner (2012), at that time, three categories of vulnerabilities were identified that were responsible for compromising cyber security. The categories are human vulnerabilities, hardware vulnerabilities and software vulnerabilities. In this classification, the category of human vulnerabilities includes accidental or intentional activities that users may perform that may compromise the security of systems. Hardware vulnerabilities include physical systems and, in addition, vulnerabilities arising from the software running on these systems. In order to mitigate the identified security risks, technology-centred measures are considered to offer the most important solution. Modern solutions have largely adopted this parochial view of cybersecurity: using technology-centric measures alone. However, following a legacy of failed technological endeavours, such solutions alone have proved insufficient to mitigate cyber risks. One of the reasons for these results is 'human vulnerabilities'. These vulnerabilities are nowadays referred to as the 'human factor' (Gcaza, Solms, Grobler, & Jansen van Vuuren, 2017)..

In the context of cyber security, the term 'human factor' is related to the roles that users play in the security process. Users have certain perceptions that can positively or negatively affect the security process. In a study conducted by Rughinis and Rughinis (2014) in the European Union, three types of end-users were identified that explain cybersecurity-related misbehaviours. These users are cognitively lazy users, economically rational users and social users. Lazy users typically have insufficient awareness and tend to favour comfort even if security is compromised. Economically rational users choose to offset costs and consequently show low levels of compliance with security requirements. Finally, social users are only interested in the online service they want and trust the service provider on all security issues. These users are ideal prey for social engineering scams (Rughiniş & Rughiniş, 2014).

With the rapid adoption of computer systems by society in recent years, researchers have identified new security and privacy issues arising from the interaction between users and systems. This has led to the study of human factors. In this context, most research has emerged as part of either (i) the design of secure and usable systems or (ii) empirical studies of problems related to how users interact with systems and services. The first approach is design-orientated. Data on users are collected as part of a design process or evaluation of an existing system. Consider eliciting user requirements or validating the performance of the designed system with real users. Organised around the concepts of usability and human-computer interaction, researchers have worked to create safe and usable systems. The second approach to human factors research is descriptive, i.e. it focuses on requesting empirical data about users' behaviour. Users are studied in a variety of security-related contexts to learn more about their behaviour in general, not directly linked to the design process of a particular system or service (Gcaza N., Solms, Grobler, & Vuuren, 2017).

Research on cyber security culture and the human element is complex. Studies in this field need to 'decompose' the field of cyber security culture, i.e. to break it down and define it more clearly. This is important to draw the direction of the research clearly and to prevent misunderstandings in the research community. In this context, Gcza, Solms, Grobler, and Vuuren (2017) state in their study that the cyber security culture research field is practically divided into two main perspectives: technical perspective and human-centred perspective.

1. **Technical Perspective**: This perspective focuses on technology solutions such as security systems and tools. This approach argues that secure applications can meet cyber security requirements when running on secure platforms and using secure networks.
2. **Human Centred Perspective**: This approach emphasises human factors and the impact of human behaviour on cyber security. Human-centred research suggests that technical measures are insufficient in cyber security, so it is emphasised that human behaviour should be taken into account.

As a result, both perspectives play an important role in cyber security; however, it is stated that human-centred research emphasises the importance of understanding human behaviour as well as technical solutions.

Studies focusing on the human factor in the field of cybersecurity emphasise the importance of human beings in the creation of cybersecurity culture and theories in the field of behavioural psychology are used to understand the dynamics of human behaviour in cybersecurity culture. These theories are used in studies such as the development of cyber security awareness campaigns in order to understand the attitudes and behaviours of users regarding cyber security and to influence these behaviours (Gcaza N., Solms, Grobler, & Vuuren, 2017).

When the studies in the field are examined; it is seen that human-centred research in the field of cyber security is conceptualised by using theories from psychology studies such as rational choice theory and theory of planned behaviour. **Theory of Planned Behavior** and **Theory of Reasoned Action**, which are behavioural models that are also used in the creation of the conceptual framework of cyber security culture, have been applied in many studies to explore human behaviour associated with cyber security culture.

In addition, the issue of cyber criminals, which is an element that should be considered in the creation of cyber security culture, has also been addressed in the literature. It emphasises that cybercriminals have an increased interest in human error and therefore organisations need to develop strategies to address behavioural risks. It is stated that traditional awareness campaigns are not sufficient for this purpose; instead, it is necessary to explore the applicability of behavioural sciences in this area (Steen, 2025).

In his study, Steen (2025) proposes a five-stage approach to develop a behavioural cyber security strategy. The approach supports the effective implementation of behavioural cyber security strategies to help organisations become more cyber secure. This approach is designed to enable organisations to increase their cyber security by addressing the human factor (Steen, 2025).

In their study, Karayel, Aktaş, and Akbıyık (2025) examine the cyber hygiene practices of remote workers. The research was conducted using two instruments: first, the Cyber Hygiene Inventory scale, which measures users' information and computer security behaviours; second, the Recsem Inventory, which was developed to assess the cyber security measures adopted by organisations for remote workers. The research findings show that there is a significant correlation between the security measures implemented by companies and employees' cyber hygiene practices. In addition, there are significant differences in cyber hygiene levels between public and private sector employees (Karayel, Aktaş, & Akbıyık 2025).

Human factors are generally recognised as the weakest link in cyber security systems. Research shows that individuals' non-compliance with security practices is the main cause of security breaches. There are many studies on the impact of employee behaviour on organisations' information security. For example, the IBM (2015) report reveals that more than 95 per cent of security breaches are caused by human error. It is also stated that improving employee behaviour can reduce the risk of security breaches by 45-70%. This emphasises the importance of human factors in security strategies.

Building a Security-Aware Workforce

Creating a resilient cybersecurity posture requires more than just technology; it depends on cultivating **security-aware behavior** across the organization. **Awareness training** reduces click rates on phishing emails by up to 70% (KnowBe4, 2024). **Behavioral reinforcement**, such as simulations, gamification, and feedback loops, promotes habitual secure conduct (Herath & Rao, 2009). **Security culture** fosters shared responsibility and vigilance, which is critical for sustaining long-term resilience (Schlienger & Teufel, 2003; Roer & Petric, 2017).

"Security is not just an IT issue; it's a **human and cultural** issue." Tsohou et al., 2015

5. FINDINGS

This study focuses on the effects of human factors in cyber security culture. The results of human behaviours and attitudes on cyber security are revealed through bibliometric analysis and current literature. The findings obtained are aimed at identifying various dimensions of the human factor in the field of cyber security.

First of all, it has been determined **that the human factor is** an area where creating a cyber security culture is not only possible with technical measures, but also shaped by the behaviours and attitudes of individuals. Studies show that most cyber security breaches are caused by human errors. While creating a cyber security culture, raising awareness and training of employees is of critical importance. In this context, the implementation of an effective training programme increases the awareness of users and ensures the adoption of security protocols. Another component that needs to be evaluated together with the human factor is **Awareness and Awareness Raising**. Individuals' awareness of cyber security directly affects the organisational cyber security culture. In particular, cyber security awareness training increases employee compliance with security rules and leads to behavioural changes. In the articles analysed, it is emphasised that regular seminars, workshops and providing up-to-date information are effective in raising cyber security awareness, In addition to awareness and awareness raising; **Organisational Support and Policy Formation** gain importance in terms of support by the management following the formation of cyber security culture. **Behavioural Factors** are important in terms of taking into account the behavioural aspects of individuals in the understanding of the human factor in cyber security. Studies show that social interactions and organisational identity affect individuals' compliance with cyber security protocols. In particular, social norms and group dynamics have important roles in the development of cyber security culture,

The exploration of the role of human factors in shaping a cyber security culture reveals several critical insights that underscore the importance of integrating behavioral awareness into organizational security strategies. Through extensive analysis of current literature and empirical research, the findings illuminate key dimensions of the human factor within the realm of cyber security.

Firstly, it is evident that human errors are a primary contributor to security breaches in organizations. Research indicates that a staggering 95% of all security incidents can be attributed to human mistakes, emphasizing the need for organizations to recognize their personnel as both a vulnerable point and a potential line of defense against cyber threats. This statistic highlights the critical necessity for dedicated efforts in training and awareness-raising initiatives, which can significantly reduce the likelihood of breaches stemming from human error. By implementing effective training programs tailored to employees' varying levels of understanding, organizations can enhance their workforce's capabilities in recognizing threats.

Secondly, the findings indicate that an individual's awareness and understanding of cyber security directly influence organizational cyber security culture. Enhanced awareness not only improves compliance with security measures but also fosters a proactive mindset towards identifying and mitigating potential risks. Comprehensive cyber security awareness training initiatives are shown to lead to notable behavioral changes among employees. This is particularly vital as engaged employees are more likely to report suspicious activities and follow security protocols diligently. Strategies such as regular seminars, workshops, and updated informational bulletins are recognized as effective in instilling a culture of vigilance regarding cyber threats.

Moreover, the study reveals the significance of leadership and organizational support in cultivating a robust cyber security culture. Organizations with strong leadership commitment to security practices typically showcase higher levels of employee engagement and compliance. This commitment manifests through clear communication of security policies, involvement in awareness programs, and the establishment of a supportive environment for employees to discuss their security concerns openly. The findings highlight that management's active participation in security initiatives sends a powerful message that the safeguarding of information assets is a collective responsibility.

Additionally, findings indicate that existing approaches to cyber security training often fail to address the complexities of human behavior adequately. Traditional awareness initiatives are often insufficient in effectively altering attitudes and behaviors relating to cyber security. The importance of applying behavioral science principles, such as the Theory of Planned Behavior, comes to the forefront, offering insights into by what factors drive employee behaviors in relation to security compliance. By understanding the motivations behind employees' choices, organizations can design more effective training interventions that align with these behavioral drivers.

Finally, the exploration of social dynamics reveals that social interactions and organizational identity play substantial roles in shaping compliance with cyber security protocols. The influence of group norms and dynamics—where employees feel the sway of peer behavior—underscores the necessity for fostering a security-focused community within organizations. Creating a culture where security is a shared value and collective responsibility can significantly enhance adherence to security policies and procedures.

In summary, the findings underscore the unequivocal importance of human factors in the development of a cyber security culture. As organizations navigate an increasingly complex cyber threat landscape, comprehensive efforts focused on employee awareness, behavior modification, and organizational commitment are critical for mitigating cyber risks effectively. By implementing structured training programs, engaging leadership, and fostering a supportive security culture, organizations can substantially enhance their overall resilience against cyber threats and ensure the protection of their critical information assets. This multifaceted approach not only addresses existing vulnerabilities but also empowers employees to become proactive defenders within the cyber security framework.

10. CONCLUSION

In conclusion, the pivotal role of human factors in fostering a robust cyber security culture cannot be overstated. As organizations increasingly face complex cyber threats in a rapidly evolving digital landscape, it becomes imperative for them to recognize that cyber security extends beyond technical measures. A proactive approach that emphasizes the integration of human behavior, awareness, and engagement into cyber security strategies is essential for achieving comprehensive protection against cyber threats.

The findings of this study underscore that a strong cyber security culture is built upon the collective understanding, attitudes, and behaviors of all employees within an organization. Despite the most advanced technological safeguards in place, the human element remains the most vulnerable aspect of an organization's security posture. Data shows that a significant percentage of security breaches can be traced back to employee missteps, either through ignorance or negligence. Consequently, organizations must prioritize the development of a culture that promotes security awareness and accountability among all staff members.

To effectively integrate security awareness into corporate culture, organizations should adopt a multifaceted strategy. This strategy should encompass tailored training programs aimed at enhancing employees' understanding of cyber threats, the importance of security practices, and their individual responsibilities in safeguarding sensitive information. Regular workshops and seminars can also serve to reinforce this knowledge and keep employees informed of the latest threats and best practices in cyber security. Moreover, initiatives that encourage open communication about security concerns can foster a supportive environment where employees feel empowered to report suspicious activities without fear of repercussions.

Furthermore, the role of leadership is critical in shaping a cyber security culture. Senior management should actively endorse and participate in awareness programs, demonstrating a commitment to cyber security that resonates throughout the organization. By establishing clear security policies and procedures and by communicating these effectively, leaders can set the tone for the organizational culture. The visible involvement of management in security initiatives reinforces the message that cyber security is a shared responsibility that requires everyone's participation.

Moreover, a comprehensive assessment framework should be developed to continually evaluate the effectiveness of the security culture initiatives. This framework should measure not only compliance rates but also the overall understanding and attitudes towards cyber security among employees. Utilizing surveys and feedback mechanisms can provide valuable insights into the strengths and weaknesses of the current culture, guiding organizations in making necessary adjustments to their training and awareness initiatives.

The incorporation of behavioral science theories, such as the Theory of Planned Behavior and the Theory of Reasoned Action, can provide invaluable insights into why employees may or may not comply with security policies. Understanding the cognitive processes behind decision-making can enable organizations to develop strategies that align with employees' motivations and encourage positive cyber security behaviors.

Additionally, as cyber threats evolve, organizations must remain agile in their approaches to training and engagement. The emergence of new technologies, such as artificial intelligence and machine learning, can be leveraged to create personalized and adaptive training programs that respond to the unique needs and learning speeds of individual employees. Such innovations can enhance the effectiveness of security awareness programs, making them more engaging and impactful.

Overall, developing a potent cyber security culture is an ongoing process that requires dedicated effort, continuous learning, and adaptation. By recognizing that humans are a critical component of the cyber security framework, organizations can better prepare themselves to mitigate risks and respond effectively to potential threats. Cultivating a culture where security awareness is ingrained in daily operations will not only protect organizations from financial and reputational damage but will also enhance consumer trust and loyalty. The proactive involvement of every member of the organization in building a resilient cyber security culture will ultimately be the cornerstone of creating a safer digital environment. By taking these steps, organizations can transform cyber security from a compliance necessity into a strategic asset that supports innovation and growth in the digital age.

REFERENCES

Ajzen, I. (1991). The theory of planned behavior. *Organizational Behavior and Human Decision Processes, 50*(2), 179–211. DOI: 10.1016/0749-5978(91)90020-T

AlHogail, A. (2015). *Design and validation of information security culture framework.* Computer Human Behaviour. DOI: 10.1016/j.chb.2015.03.054

Alshaikh, M. (2020, August 21). Developing cybersecurity culture to influence employee behavior: A practice perspective. *Computers & Security, 98*, 2–10. DOI: 10.1016/j.cose.2020.102003

Aurigemma, S., & Panko, R. (2012). A composite framework for behavioralcompliance with information security policies. In 45th HawaiiInternational Conference on Systems Sciences. Maui, Hawaii.

Becker, G. (1968). Crime and punishment: An economic approach. *Journal of Political Economy, 76*(2), 169–217. DOI: 10.1086/259394

Brilingaitė, A., Bukauskas, L., Domarkienė, I., Rančelis, T., Ambrozaitytė, L., Pirta, R., & Knox, B. J. (2025). Towards projection of the individualised risk assessment for the cybersecurity workforce. *Computer Standards & Interfaces, 93*, 103962.

Burns, S., & Roberts, L. (2013). Applying the theory of planned behaviour to predicting online safety behaviour. *Crime Prevention and Community Safety, 15*, 48–64.

Da Veiga, A., Astakhova, L., Botha, A., & Herselman, H. (2020, May 30). Defining organisational information security culture—Perspectives from academia and industry. *Computers & Security, 92*, 101713. DOI: 10.1016/j.cose.2020.101713

Da Veiga, A., & Eloff, J. (2010, March 1). A framework and assessment instrument for information security culture. *Computers & Security, 29*(2), 196–207. DOI: 10.1016/j.cose.2009.09.002

DBIR. (2023) Data Breach Investigations Report Public Sector Snapshot, Verizon. https://www.verizon.com/business/resources/Te46/reports/2023-dbir-public-sector -snapshot.pdf

Dudorov, D., Stupples, D., & Newby, M. (2013), "Probability analysis of cyber attack paths against business and commercial enterprise systems", *European Intelligence and Security Informatics Conference (EISIC)*, Uppsala. DOI: 10.1109/EISIC.2013.13

Gcaza, N., Solms, R., Grobler, M., & Jansen van Vuuren, J. (2017). A general morphological analysis: Delineating a cyber-security culture. *Information and Computer Security, 25*(3), 259–278. DOI: 10.1108/ICS-12-2015-0046

Gcaza, N., Solms, R., Grobler, M., & Vuuren, J. (2017). A general morphological analysis: Delineating a cyber-security culture. *Information and Computer Security, 25*(3), 259–278. DOI: 10.1108/ICS-12-2015-0046

Georgiadou, A., Mouzakitis, S., Boun, K., & Askounis, D. (2022). A Cyber-Security Culture Framework for Assessing Organization Readiness. *Journal of Computer Information Systems, 62*(3), 452–462. DOI: 10.1080/08874417.2020.1845583

Gibbs, J. P., & Poston, D. L.Jr. (1975). The Division of Labor: Conceptualization and Related Measures. *Social Forces, 53*(3), 468–476. DOI: 10.2307/2576589

Gregory, J. (2020), Wannacry: how the widespread ransomware changed cybersecurity, IBM, https://www.ibm.com/think/x-force/wannacry-worm-ransomware-changed-cybersecurity

Healey, J. (2013). *A Fierce Domain: Conflict in Cyberspace, 1986 to 2012.* Cyber Conflict Studies.

IBM. (2024). Cost of a Data Breach Report 2024. NewYork: July.

ITU. (2014). Fınal Report Itu-D Study Group 1. Geneva: International Telecommunication Union(ITU) Telecommunication Development Bureau (BDT).

Karayel, T., & Akbıyık, A. (2023, July). Siber Güvenlik Araştırmalarına Küresel Bir Bakış: Yayın Trendleri ve Araştırma Yönelimleri. Bilişim Teknolojileri Dergisi, s. 221-235.

Karayel, T., Aktaş, B., & Akbıyık, A. (2025). Human factors in remote work: Examining cyber hygiene practices. *Information and Computer Security, 33*(1), 96–116. DOI: 10.1108/ICS-11-2023-0215

NTT. (2023). Global Threat Intelligence Report. Information Asset Classification: Public NTT Security Holdings.

Parsons, K., McCormac, A., Butavicius, M., Pattinson, M., & Jerram, C. (2014, May). Determining employee awareness using the Human Aspects of Information Security Questionnaire (HAIS-Q). *Computers & Security, 42*, 165–176. DOI: 10.1016/j.cose.2013.12.003

Ponemon (2022). Cost of a Data Breach Report 2022.

Prabhu, S., & Thompson, N., A primer on insider threats in cybersecurity. (2022). Information. *Security Journal, 31*(5), 602–611.

Rantos, K., Fysarakis, K., & Manifavas, H. (2012). *How effective is your security awareness program? An evaluation methodology*. Inf Sec J Global Perspect. DOI: 10.1080/19393555.2012.747234

Rogers, R. (1975). A protection motivation theory of fear appeals and attitude change. *The Journal of Psychology*, *91*(1), 93–114. DOI: 10.1080/00223980.1975.9915803 PMID: 28136248

Rughiniş, C., & Rughiniş, R. (2014). Nothing ventured, nothing gained. Profiles of online activity cyber-crime exposure, and security measures of end-users in european union. *Computers*, •••, 111–125.

Sanlı, Y., Baltacı, F., Güven, E., & Eren, T. (2024, July). Siber Güvenlik Çalışmaları Üzerine Bibliyometrik Analiz. Bilişim Teknolojileri Dergisi, s. 223-229.

Steen, T. (2025). Developing a behavioural cybersecurity strategy: A five-step approach for organisations. *Computer Standards & Interfaces*, *92*, 1–8. DOI: 10.1016/j.csi.2024.103939

European Union Agency for Cybersecurity. Lella, I., Theocharidou, M., Magonara, E., Malatras, A., Svetozarov Naydenov, R., Ciobanu, C., & Chatzichristos, G. (2024). ENISA threat landscape 2024 : July 2023 to June 2024. https://data.europa.eu/doi/10.2824/0710888

Uchendu, B. R. C., Nurse, J., Bada, M., & Furnell, S. (2021, June 30). Developing a cyber security culture: Current practices and future needs. *Computers & Security*, *109*, 1–23. DOI: 10.1016/j.cose.2021.102387

Wamala, F. (2012). *ITU National Cybersecurity Strategy Guide*. International Communication Union.

Warner, M. (2012). Cybersecurity: A pre-history. *Intelligence and National Security*, *27*(5), 781–799. DOI: 10.1080/02684527.2012.708530

Chapter 5
Cybersecurity as a Strategic Lever for Innovation in Smart Aviation Ecosystems:
A Review of Emerging Trends

Tuncel Oz
https://orcid.org/0000-0001-6603-0841
Istanbul Ticaret University, Turkey

ABSTRACT

As aviation undergoes digital transformation, cybersecurity has become essential to innovation and operational resilience. This chapter reviews recent advancements in cybersecurity across predictive maintenance, unmanned aircraft traffic management (UTM), and smart airport systems. Technologies like AI improve threat detection, blockchain ensures data integrity, and quantum cryptography enhances communication security. The chapter also highlights the importance of organizational factors—such as leadership and cybersecurity culture—in achieving resilience. Key challenges include fragmented governance and cyber vulnerabilities in low-altitude operations. Despite these, strategic opportunities exist to integrate cybersecurity into long-term innovation plans. Overall, the chapter positions cybersecurity not just as protection, but as a driver of sustainable, secure, and forward-looking aviation management.

DOI: 10.4018/979-8-3693-6417-8.ch005

1. INTRODUCTION

The aviation industry has undergone a transformative evolution in recent decades, shifting from analog, compartmentalized systems toward highly digitized, interconnected, and intelligent operational ecosystems. This transformation, often captured under the umbrella term *smart aviation ecosystems*, encompasses a wide range of technological advancements—from automated air traffic control and biometric boarding to predictive aircraft maintenance, drone traffic integration, and real-time passenger service personalization. These developments are underpinned by the increasing adoption of AI, IoT, blockchain, and data-driven platforms that span across airports, aircraft systems, maintenance hubs, and passenger interfaces. As smart environments continue to redefine the operational fabric of aviation, they also bring with them a growing dependence on digital infrastructure, creating both opportunities and vulnerabilities that are unprecedented in scale and complexity.

This increasing reliance on digital systems has brought cybersecurity to the forefront as a foundational concern for aviation stakeholders. The shift to digital airspaces, e-enabled aircraft, and interconnected maintenance ecosystems has significantly expanded the attack surface, making aviation systems more attractive to cybercriminals, state-sponsored actors, and insider threats. As emphasized by Ukwandu et al. (2022), the aviation sector faces a dual challenge: while striving to integrate emerging technologies to enhance efficiency and competitiveness, it must simultaneously manage escalating cybersecurity risks that can impact flight safety, data integrity, and operational continuity. Moreover, the highly regulated and safety-critical nature of aviation means that any cybersecurity lapse can have far-reaching implications, not just financially or operationally, but also in terms of public trust and international cooperation. Garcia et al. (2021) and Dave et al. (2022) have shown that vulnerabilities in aircraft communication systems, navigation protocols, and surveillance networks can disrupt critical systems, calling for a new generation of cybersecurity tools that are proactive, intelligent, and adaptive to dynamic threat environments.

However, this chapter argues that cybersecurity should not be viewed solely as a protective mechanism or compliance requirement. Rather, it must be understood as a strategic enabler that supports innovation, fosters business resilience, and facilitates the secure evolution of the aviation sector. The literature increasingly supports this perspective, emphasizing the potential of cybersecurity to act as a catalyst for digital transformation when it is integrated early and strategically into system design, organizational planning, and innovation frameworks (Mızrak, 2023a; Pigola & da Costa, 2025). For example, AI-powered threat detection not only enhances safety but also enables data-informed decisions that drive operational innovation. Similarly, blockchain technologies can provide immutable and verifiable maintenance records, streamlining compliance and facilitating predictive logistics across global aviation supply chains (Bakyt et al., 2025; Kabashkin & Perekrestov, 2024).

The purpose of this chapter, therefore, is to explore the intersection of cybersecurity, innovation, and strategic resilience within the context of smart aviation ecosystems. Drawing upon a comprehensive review of current literature, the chapter investigates how cybersecurity is evolving beyond its traditional role and is increasingly integrated into aviation's strategic decision-making processes. The analysis will highlight how emerging technologies such as AI, blockchain, and quantum cryptography are reshaping aviation cybersecurity capabilities while also identifying organizational, cultural, and regulatory challenges that must be addressed to fully leverage cybersecurity as a driver of innovation. Ultimately, this chapter positions cybersecurity not as a constraint but as a critical enabler of the aviation industry's digital future—supporting smart, sustainable, and secure growth across all layers of the ecosystem.

2. THEORETICAL AND CONCEPTUAL BACKGROUND

The aviation industry is undergoing a profound transformation driven by digitalization, automation, and interconnected technologies, forming what is now referred to as smart aviation ecosystems. These ecosystems integrate digital infrastructure across airports, aircraft, and air traffic management systems to enhance operational efficiency, safety, and customer experience. However, this transformation has significantly increased the industry's exposure to cybersecurity risks, making cybersecurity not only a technical necessity but a strategic lever for innovation and business resiliency. Within this context, cybersecurity is no longer confined to IT departments or regulatory compliance frameworks; it is increasingly positioned as a cross-cutting enabler that empowers innovation while safeguarding digital assets and operational continuity. The conceptual evolution of cybersecurity in aviation is therefore deeply intertwined with the sector's innovation agenda, where interconnected platforms—such as biometric passenger processing, AI-assisted predictive maintenance, and real-time air traffic management—require not only speed and agility but also robust and adaptive security frameworks.

Smart aviation ecosystems are defined by the seamless integration of digital technologies that interconnect airport operations (e.g., smart check-ins, automated baggage systems), aircraft systems (e.g., avionics, fly-by-wire control, and inflight connectivity), and communication, navigation, and surveillance (CNS) infrastructure. As noted by Kagalwalla and Churi (2019), while these technologies promise improved efficiency, safety, and customer satisfaction, they also create new entry points for cyber threats. Their study emphasizes that the increased surface area of attack in smart aviation settings—especially through IoT systems and satellite communication links—renders traditional security models ineffective. The transition from isolated systems to connected infrastructures necessitates a more integrated cybersecurity approach that anticipates sophisticated threat actors targeting aviation's mission-critical systems. These include real-time disruptions to cockpit communications, data manipulation in navigation systems, and unauthorized access to passenger data in smart terminal environments.

Central to understanding aviation cybersecurity is the application of the core security principles—confidentiality, integrity, availability (CIA)—as well as resilience, which is gaining recognition as an equally critical dimension. Elmarady and Rahouma (2021) argue that civil aviation's cybersecurity frameworks must evolve beyond static risk models and adopt dynamic assessment methods that reflect real-time system dependencies, cyber-physical interactions, and emerging threat landscapes. Their work on aviation cybersecurity risk assessment frameworks underlines the need to develop models that address the cascading impacts of cyber incidents across multiple nodes in the aviation ecosystem, from aircraft onboard systems to interconnected ground operations. In line with this, they advocate for the integration of resilience indicators—such as recovery speed, adaptability, and learning capacity—into security models, thereby positioning cybersecurity as a proactive and innovation-supportive function rather than merely a reactive control mechanism.

In a complementary analysis, Ukwandu et al. (2022) provide a comprehensive review of current and future cybersecurity challenges in aviation, framing the issue within the broader digital transformation of the industry. They highlight that aviation faces a dual challenge: modernizing its systems to accommodate emerging technologies while simultaneously addressing vulnerabilities introduced by legacy systems. The study identifies key threat vectors including data breaches, denial-of-service (DoS) attacks, insider threats, and supply chain vulnerabilities, which are compounded by the slow pace of cybersecurity standardization across international jurisdictions. More importantly, the authors emphasize that the integration of cybersecurity in aviation should not be viewed solely through the lens of threat prevention, but as a foundation for building stakeholder trust, enabling digital innovations such as AI-driven operations, and supporting resilient business models. Their insights reinforce the strategic dimension of cybersecurity, particularly in high-reliability environments where safety and continuity are non-negotiable.

The strategic importance of artificial intelligence (AI) and machine learning (ML) in aviation cybersecurity is thoroughly explored by Garcia, Babiceanu, and Seker (2021), who outline how these technologies are being deployed for advanced threat detection, anomaly recognition, and intelligent system management. AI and ML applications offer aviation operators the ability to analyze vast amounts of data in real time—ranging from sensor data on aircraft performance to behavioral patterns of airport network users—to detect abnormal activity indicative of potential cyber intrusions. These technologies not only enhance security but also serve as enablers of innovation, facilitating more efficient maintenance cycles, intelligent passenger flow control, and responsive air traffic systems. The authors also highlight that these AI-based systems require equally robust security frameworks to protect their data pipelines and algorithms from manipulation, further reinforcing the interdependence between cybersecurity and technological innovation in aviation.

This interdependence is acutely evident in the protection of communication, navigation, and surveillance (CNS)systems, which form the backbone of modern aviation safety. Dave et al. (2022) provide a focused review of the cybersecurity challenges facing CNS systems, identifying attack techniques such as GPS spoofing, signal jamming, and man-in-the-middle attacks that can compromise flight integrity and endanger both crew and passengers. Their findings reveal a pressing need for encryption protocols, intrusion detection systems, and multilayered verification mechanisms tailored specifically to the aviation context. The study also underscores the strategic role of cybersecurity in enabling next-generation CNS capabilities—such as satellite-based navigation and integrated airspace management—by ensuring the reliability, confidentiality, and integrity of transmitted data across diverse and often transnational systems.

A broader perspective on aviation safety and cybersecurity is provided by Stastny and Stoica (2022), who argue that cybersecurity is intrinsically linked to the core safety mission of the aviation industry. Their review presents cybersecurity not only as a protective layer but as a critical component of aviation safety systems that are increasingly reliant on digital technologies. They discuss the emerging need for safety certification processes that incorporate cybersecurity assessments, particularly for aircraft with digital flight controls, automated systems, and remote access capabilities. This position aligns closely with the argument that cybersecurity is essential to aviation's operational resilience, enabling organizations to maintain safety standards even in the face of ongoing or attempted cyber disruptions.

Further insights into systemic challenges and gaps are offered by Shah, Jhanjhi, and Brohi (2024), who examine the civil aviation sector's struggle to institutionalize comprehensive cybersecurity practices. Their chapter in Cybersecurity in the Transportation *Industry* identifies persistent issues such as fragmented regulatory oversight, insufficient cyber awareness among operational staff, and inconsistent adoption of international standards. The authors argue for a unified and forward-looking governance model that recognizes cybersecurity as a strategic resource that must be woven into the DNA of innovation and change management processes in aviation. This includes aligning cybersecurity with business continuity planning, digital transformation agendas, and the development of cyber-resilient infrastructure.

An equally important dimension in positioning cybersecurity as a strategic enabler lies in the human factor. As Sabillon and Bermejo Higuera (2023) emphasize, human behavior remains both a point of vulnerability and a potential asset in aviation cybersecurity. Their study highlights the critical importance of cybersecurity awareness training in enabling early threat detection and fostering a proactive security culture. They argue that even the most advanced technical solutions can be undermined by untrained personnel, poor cyber hygiene, and inadequate organizational commitment to cybersecurity knowledge development. Training initiatives, they suggest, must be continuous, role-specific, and embedded within broader innovation strategies to ensure that cybersecurity becomes an enabler rather than a bottleneck in the smart aviation transformation journey.

This perspective is echoed in Mizrak and Akkartal (2024), who develop a fuzzy multi-criteria framework to prioritize cybersecurity initiatives in aviation based on their systemic impact. Using a DEMATEL-QSFS methodology, they demonstrate how aviation organizations can identify which cybersecurity measures most significantly affect innovation potential, system stability, and operational efficiency. Their study reveals that cybersecurity initiatives focused on system integration, AI algorithm protection, and data governance rank highest in strategic importance—thereby validating the proposition that cybersecurity is a driver of business value and innovation. In a related study, Mızrak (2024) further expands this discussion by emphasizing the role of human resources management in aligning AI deployment with cybersecurity objectives in aviation. Her findings suggest that strategic workforce planning, cross-functional collaboration, and cybersecurity leadership development are essential to creating adaptive and innovation-oriented cybersecurity cultures. These human-centric approaches, when paired with technological investments, position cybersecurity not only as a protective measure but as a catalyst for transformation.

Taken together, these studies provide a multi-dimensional theoretical and conceptual foundation for understanding cybersecurity in smart aviation ecosystems. They converge on a critical insight: cybersecurity, when strategically integrated into aviation management, does more than defend against threats—it unlocks new capabilities, accelerates innovation, and reinforces organizational resilience. As aviation continues to digitalize, cybersecurity must be embedded across governance, operations, and human capital strategies to support the sector's evolving role in global mobility and economic development.

3. LITERATURE REVIEW: CYBERSECURITY-DRIVEN INNOVATIONS IN AVIATION

The aviation industry is entering a new era shaped by cyber-physical convergence, where cybersecurity plays a central role not only in protecting infrastructure but also in enabling innovations across smart airports, digital aircraft systems, unmanned traffic management, and personalized passenger experiences. As aviation ecosystems evolve into highly interconnected, data-intensive environments, cybersecurity becomes a fundamental enabler of operational innovation and strategic value creation. The transformation of traditional infrastructure into smart and sustainable systems has accelerated the integration of Internet of Things (IoT), artificial intelligence (AI), machine learning (ML), and data analytics. These technologies introduce vast new opportunities for automation, predictive management, and personalization but simultaneously expose aviation organizations to unprecedented cybersecurity threats. A growing body of literature underscores how cybersecurity-driven innovations are reshaping aviation business models and service paradigms.

Recent contributions highlight that smart airport ecosystems are undergoing rapid digitalization through biometric identity systems, automated baggage handling, connected ground vehicles, and cloud-based terminal operations. Chang et al. (2024) provide a compelling case in their study on Taoyuan Smart Aviation City, showing how digital services and IoT infrastructure have enhanced efficiency and sustainability but also raised significant cybersecurity concerns related to data governance and operational integrity. Similarly, Demir and Paksoy (2025) propose a conceptual framework for smart and sustainable operations that depends heavily on secure data exchange and robust system interoperability, positioning cybersecurity as essential for sustaining innovation. Kabashkin (2024) extends this discussion to communication networks by arguing that the deployment of next-generation 6G technology in aviation maintenance requires secure data routing and encryption protocols to prevent data breaches during inter-system coordination. These innovations in airport and ground operations are supported by a robust cybersecurity infrastructure that enables scalability, system trust, and continuous operational improvement. As Fiorentino et al. (2020) illustrate in their study of an air navigation service provider, the successful implementation of smart technologies for sustainable business models hinges on transparent and secure data management, where cybersecurity is integrated into organizational strategy and not treated as a reactive technical layer.

The transformation of digital aircraft systems through AI-powered predictive maintenance, digital twins, and e-enabled aircraft functionalities has revolutionized maintenance efficiency and safety assurance. Kabashkin and Perekrestov (2024) explore this transition from aircraft health monitoring to intelligent health management systems, emphasizing the synergy of IoT and AI in proactively identifying maintenance needs before system failures occur. However, such systems depend critically on the integrity and authenticity of data flows between sensors, aircraft systems, and maintenance platforms, making them prime targets for cyber intrusion. Giacotto et al. (2021) similarly emphasize the necessity for "Ecosystem 4.0" models to support "Maintenance 4.0," highlighting that aviation assembly lines require encrypted and authenticated data transmission to maintain reliability and quality standards. The incorporation of machine learning models into operational frameworks is further supported by Garcia et al. (2021), who review AI and ML approaches for aviation cybersecurity, pointing out that these technologies are not only used for enhancing operational efficiency but also for real-time threat detection and vulnerability management. Merlo (2024) extends this by demonstrating how predictive maintenance models, driven by AI, depend on cybersecurity protocols to ensure that their underlying algorithms are not manipulated or corrupted by malicious actors. Ukwandu et al. (2022) reinforce this view by identifying cybersecurity as a primary challenge facing digital aircraft systems, particularly with respect to safeguarding avionics, in-flight communications, and onboard data processing units from both internal and external threats.

One of the most dynamically evolving domains in aviation is air traffic management (ATM) and unmanned aircraft system traffic management (UTM), where cybersecurity vulnerabilities pose risks to national security, airspace safety, and the scalability of autonomous systems. Scott and Andritsos (2023) propose a strategic framework for a smart and sustainable drone ecosystem in Europe, underlining that cybersecurity is foundational for operational trust, especially in densely trafficked urban environments where drones operate alongside traditional aircraft. Sampigethaya et al. (2018)laid the groundwork for this understanding by identifying cybersecurity risks in UTM architectures, such as unauthorized control commands and location spoofing, which can result in systemic disruptions. More recently, Hamissi and Dhraief (2023) provided a comprehensive survey of UTM systems, noting that while automation and AI offer improved efficiency, they must be tightly integrated with real-time security monitoring systems to ensure safety. Aposporis (2024)adds that global and regional frameworks for UAS integration remain fragmented, and a lack of cybersecurity standardization can hinder effective coordination and real-time decision-making across jurisdictions. As operational altitude decreases and the number of autonomous aerial vehicles increases, Xie, Gardi, and Sabatini (2022) stress that cybersecurity must address the unique characteristics of low-altitude operations, where traditional radar and CNS protections are insufficient. Their analysis of cybersecurity trends in low-altitude air traffic management identifies the need for adaptive encryption, secure communication protocols, and AI-based intrusion detection to prevent exploitation of these emerging platforms.

The passenger experience, long viewed through the lens of service quality, is now undergoing a transformation driven by personalization, real-time services, and digital engagement. However, this innovation frontier depends heavily on responsible data collection and cybersecurity-enabled data governance. Vredenborg et al. (2025) offer a systematic review of personalization in public transport systems, proposing a framework where cybersecurity and privacy-by-design principles are central to passenger trust. In the aviation context, Mwesiumo et al. (2023) investigate how passengers' willingness to share personal data for digital services at airports is contingent on their perceived benefits and assurance that their data will be protected. Their findings suggest that innovation in customer experience cannot proceed without strong cybersecurity frameworks that enhance user confidence. Masseno and Santos (2019) provide a legal perspective on the profiling of tourists in smart tourism destinations, arguing that excessive data collection without adequate data protection measures can lead to reputational and regulatory risks. Pina et al. (2023) further this narrative by showing how sustainable and personalized travel behaviors must be balanced against data privacy obligations to ensure ethical digital engagement. From a governance standpoint, Yallop et al. (2023) argue that data ethics and cybersecurity policies are no longer optional in the era of the "digital traveler," where biometric boarding, personalized recommendations, and loyalty program integration have become standard expectations.

To provide a structured overview of the existing body of knowledge on cybersecurity-driven innovations in aviation, Table 1 summarizes 20 key studies selected from recent academic and industry literature. These studies span various domains within the aviation ecosystem, including smart airport infrastructure, digital aircraft systems, unmanned aircraft traffic management, and data-driven passenger services. Each entry outlines the authors, publication year, methodology employed, and the primary findings related to cybersecurity implications and strategic innovations.

Table 1. Literature review summary table

Author(s)	Year	Methodology	Key Findings
Scott & Andritsos	2023	Policy review	Cybersecurity is vital for sustainable drone strategies in Europe.
Kabashkin	2024	Conceptual modeling	6G tech enables unified aviation maintenance with secure data flow.
Demir & Paksoy	2025	Conceptual framework	Smart operations require integrated cybersecurity frameworks.
Kabashkin & Perekrestov	2024	Technical analysis	IoT and AI synergy enhances predictive maintenance but demands security.

continued on following page

Table 1. Continued

Author(s)	Year	Methodology	Key Findings
Giacotto et al.	2021	Case study	Maintenance 4.0 needs robust cybersecurity for industrial automation.
Pereira et al.	2022	Longitudinal review	Technological trajectories create value but expose cyber risks.
Fiorentino et al.	2020	Case-based analysis	Smart tech supports sustainability when paired with cybersecurity.
Carayannis et al.	2022	Theoretical framework	Techno-centric innovation must be aligned with cyber ethics.
Jiang et al.	2023	Technology review	ML and XR applications in aviation raise new security concerns.
Chang et al.	2024	Empirical case study	Smart city aviation models must address data and system security.
Garcia et al.	2021	Literature review	AI can detect threats but needs secure integration with systems.
Ukwandu et al.	2022	Scoping review	Cybersecurity challenges stem from tech adoption and legacy systems.
Merlo	2024	Theoretical analysis	AI-driven predictive maintenance must ensure data integrity.
Sampigethaya et al.	2018	System architecture analysis	UTM systems vulnerable to spoofing and signal hijacking.
Hamissi & Dhraief	2023	Systematic review	UTM adoption needs standardized cybersecurity protocols.
Aposporis	2024	Comparative review	Integration frameworks must close regulatory cyber gaps.
Xie et al.	2022	Trend analysis	Low-altitude traffic management faces rising cyber threats.
Vredenborg et al.	2025	Systematic review	Personalization systems need secure data practices.
Mwesiumo et al.	2023	Quantitative survey	Willingness to share data depends on perceived cybersecurity.
Masseno & Santos	2019	Legal review	Tourist profiling raises concerns about data misuse and breaches.

4. EMERGING TRENDS, CHALLENGES, AND STRATEGIC OPPORTUNITIES

The rapid evolution of smart aviation ecosystems has prompted the emergence of transformative technologies such as artificial intelligence (AI), blockchain, and quantum cryptography as foundational tools in the next generation of aviation cybersecurity frameworks. These technologies not only offer powerful mechanisms for detecting and mitigating cyber threats but also reshape how cybersecurity is conceptualized in relation to business innovation and resilience. The integration of AI-driven anomaly detection systems into aviation cybersecurity has become increasingly critical, particularly in complex, data-rich environments where traditional rule-based approaches struggle to detect novel attack patterns. As explored by Bakyt et al. (2025), aerospace systems—particularly those leveraging low Earth orbit (LEO) satellite communication—are now experimenting with hybrid cybersecurity frameworks that integrate quantum key distribution, blockchain-based integrity verification, and AI-enabled real-time threat monitoring. Their framework suggests that the convergence of these technologies can create an adaptive, distributed, and resilient cybersecurity architecture, particularly useful in aviation's high-availability and real-time operational contexts. Supporting this, Denis et al. (2025) provide an in-depth survey on the synergy between AI and blockchain for cybersecurity in smart cities, many principles of which are transferable to aviation. They demonstrate that blockchain can offer immutability and traceability for aviation data flows—especially relevant in distributed maintenance logs, flight data records, and autonomous drone operations—while AI strengthens the system's proactive threat detection capacity.

The move toward quantum resilience in aviation cybersecurity is also gaining traction, with quantum-safe encryption models and post-quantum cryptographic standards becoming necessary to prepare aviation networks for the disruptive capabilities of quantum computing. This is particularly critical given aviation's reliance on secure communication in CNS systems and satellite-dependent navigation, where cryptographic disruption could cause catastrophic failures. While this area is still emerging, Garcia et al. (2021) and Xie et al. (2022) already point toward the necessity of future-proofing aviation infrastructure by integrating flexible and scalable encryption standards. The literature clearly signals that aviation cybersecurity is no longer just a technical subdomain but is becoming a platform for strategic innovation—facilitating secure digital transformation and laying the groundwork for resilient smart aviation systems that can withstand not only current threats but also future unknowns.

However, the promise of these technologies cannot be fully realized without addressing the human and organizational dimensions of cybersecurity, which remain among the most persistent and complex challenges facing the aviation industry. Several studies, including AlDaajeh and Alrabaee (2024) and Sallos et al. (2019), emphasize that technical tools alone are insufficient in achieving robust cyber resilience if they are not matched with a security-oriented organizational culture and leadership commitment. Strategic cybersecurity requires not just operational execution but alignment with organizational knowledge flows, managerial awareness, and cross-departmental collaboration. Sallos et al. (2019) frame this issue within the "knowledge-problem" perspective, suggesting that many cybersecurity failures stem from gaps in shared understanding and institutionalized learning mechanisms rather than purely technological shortcomings. Similarly, Al-ma'aitah (2022) presents evidence from the public sector in Jordan, revealing that the effectiveness of cybersecurity programs significantly depends on managerial buy-in, employee engagement, and national strategic alignment.

From a strategic management perspective, Mızrak (2023a) outlines how cybersecurity risk management must be systematically integrated into strategic planning, particularly for organizations operating in dynamic and high-risk industries such as aviation. Her comprehensive literature review suggests that cybersecurity is often siloed within technical units, detached from innovation planning, investment prioritization, and performance management—an oversight that leaves firms vulnerable to both internal and external threats. In a related study, Mızrak (2023b) uses Fuzzy AHP to model how cybersecurity strategy can be hierarchically structured to align with an organization's innovation capacity and strategic vision. These insights are echoed by Pigola and da Costa (2025), who empirically validate a dynamic capabilities framework for enhancing cybersecurity intelligence. Their findings demonstrate that organizations with strong absorptive, adaptive, and transformative capacities are more likely to translate cyber insights into strategic action, thereby fostering innovation rather than inhibiting it.

The importance of cybersecurity education and workforce development is another vital theme, particularly as aviation systems become more reliant on autonomous and AI-based technologies. AlDaajeh et al. (2022) examine how national cybersecurity strategies influence educational priorities and institutional readiness, concluding that policy-level alignment is essential for developing the cyber competencies needed in high-tech industries like aviation. This points to a broader shift: cyber innovation must be accompanied by organizational learning and workforce reskilling. Innovation strategies that embed cybersecurity into their structure—not only technically but also behaviorally—are far more likely to succeed in developing resilient digital ecosystems.

Despite the promising developments and evolving awareness around cybersecurity's strategic role, the aviation sector continues to grapple with several persistent challenges, the most notable of which are fragmented governance structures and the continually evolving threat landscape. As highlighted by Ukwandu et al. (2022), the lack of unified international standards and regulatory enforcement mechanisms in aviation cybersecurity creates significant vulnerabilities, especially given the cross-border nature of air transport. Many nations and agencies operate in silos, with incompatible systems and varying definitions of cyber incidents and response protocols, which hampers collective action and real-time information sharing. This fragmentation is particularly problematic when confronting novel threats such as AI-generated deepfakes, synthetic identities used for unauthorized access, or coordinated drone swarms capable of disrupting flight operations. Shah, Jhanjhi, and Brohi (2024) further emphasize that current cybersecurity frameworks are often reactive and compliance-focused, failing to account for the speed, scale, and sophistication of emerging attacks. These gaps not only limit innovation but also erode public trust and delay the safe adoption of new technologies.

Yet, within these challenges lie significant strategic opportunities. As demonstrated across multiple studies—including those by Demir and Paksoy (2025), Fiorentino et al. (2020), and Carayannis et al. (2022)—cybersecurity can be positioned as a catalyst for innovation rather than a barrier. The integration of cybersecurity into strategic planning and innovation roadmaps allows aviation organizations to move beyond a defensive posture toward a proactive and adaptive model. This includes embedding cybersecurity considerations into early-stage technology development, procurement policies, AI governance, and customer experience design. For instance, the strategic use of AI and blockchain not only enhances operational resilience but also opens new pathways for secure innovation in air traffic automation, predictive maintenance, and hyper-personalized passenger services. Carayannis et al. (2022) conceptualize this as part of a broader techno-centric and human-centric innovation system, where knowledge flows across institutional boundaries to co-create smart, sustainable, and inclusive solutions. Applied to aviation, this view encourages the development of cybersecurity strategies that are not only risk-informed but also value-oriented—supporting business growth, stakeholder trust, and societal safety.

In sum, the intersection of emerging technologies, strategic management practices, and cybersecurity imperatives presents a rich and complex terrain for innovation in the aviation sector. The literature reviewed clearly underscores that while the aviation industry faces serious cybersecurity threats and governance challenges, it is also uniquely positioned to lead in the development of integrated, intelligent, and resilient systems. Realizing this potential depends on a strategic shift—one that recognizes cybersecurity not as a constraint, but as a foundational element of the digital aviation ecosystem and a key enabler of competitive advantage and long-term sustainability.

5. CONCLUSION AND FUTURE RESEARCH DIRECTIONS

The comprehensive review presented in this chapter demonstrates that cybersecurity is no longer a peripheral or reactive function within aviation management but has become a central strategic pillar supporting innovation, operational continuity, and long-term organizational resilience. Across various domains—smart airports, digital aircraft systems, unmanned traffic management, and passenger data services—cybersecurity plays a foundational role in enabling the deployment, scalability, and trustworthiness of emerging technologies. Literature from multiple perspectives consistently reveals that as aviation ecosystems grow more intelligent and interconnected, they also become increasingly vulnerable to cyber threats that evolve in both scope and sophistication. Studies by Garcia et al. (2021), Ukwandu et al. (2022), and Bakyt et al. (2025) collectively underscore that cybersecurity must be reframed from a defensive necessity into a proactive enabler of business value and digital transformation.

One of the most significant findings emerging from the literature is the synergistic potential of integrating advanced technologies—such as artificial intelligence, blockchain, and quantum cryptography—into aviation cybersecurity frameworks. AI-driven anomaly detection can dramatically reduce response times and false positives in threat detection, while blockchain ensures data immutability and traceability across aircraft maintenance, baggage handling, and crew identity systems. These technological advances, when coupled with robust governance and ethical implementation strategies, offer aviation stakeholders a means to not only protect assets but also unlock new models of innovation and service delivery. Furthermore, quantum resilience, though still an emerging field, is poised to revolutionize encryption standards in communication, navigation, and surveillance (CNS) systems, particularly in satellite-dependent aviation contexts where information integrity is mission-critical.

The role of human factors and organizational culture also emerged as a critical theme throughout the chapter. Despite the promise of technical innovation, studies by Sallos et al. (2019), AlDaajeh and Alrabaee (2024), and Mızrak (2023a) consistently point to the fact that cybersecurity success hinges on how well it is embedded into organizational structures, leadership mindsets, and employee behavior. Aviation organizations that cultivate a culture of cybersecurity awareness—through training, cross-functional collaboration, and clear communication—are better positioned to adapt to changing threat landscapes and integrate secure innovation. Managerial capacity to interpret and act on cybersecurity intelligence, particularly in fast-changing operational environments such as airports or air traffic control centers, will increasingly define organizational resilience and competitiveness in the aviation sector.

From a strategic and managerial standpoint, aviation stakeholders must rethink how cybersecurity is positioned within their enterprise architecture. Rather than treating cybersecurity as a cost center or a compliance obligation, it should be integrated into core strategic planning, digital transformation roadmaps, and innovation processes. For example, smart airport development projects should include cybersecurity assessments at every stage—from vendor selection to infrastructure design and passenger-facing services. Similarly, aircraft manufacturers and MRO (Maintenance, Repair, and Overhaul) providers should align cybersecurity protocols with predictive maintenance systems, digital twins, and AI-driven diagnostics.

This integration will not only reduce vulnerabilities but also improve operational efficiencies and regulatory compliance, while enhancing customer trust and brand reputation.

Policy makers and regulatory bodies also have an instrumental role in shaping an international aviation cybersecurity framework that supports innovation without compromising safety. As emphasized by Shah, Jhanjhi, and Brohi (2024) and Aposporis (2024), fragmented governance and the absence of globally standardized cybersecurity protocols are major obstacles to secure aviation operations. ICAO, EASA, IATA, and other regional authorities must work collaboratively to harmonize threat classification systems, incident response procedures, and cyber maturity benchmarks. These frameworks should be scalable and adaptable to various organizational sizes and technological maturity levels, from global airlines to regional airports. Moreover, incentives should be provided to invest in cybersecurity innovation—such as R&D grants, public-private partnerships, and workforce development programs targeting cybersecurity skills in aviation.

Future research should delve deeper into sector-specific cybersecurity challenges and how emerging technologies can be tailored to address them. For instance, while AI and blockchain have demonstrated broad applicability, their integration into specific aviation subsystems—such as cargo logistics, biometric access control, and drone airspace management—requires focused studies that assess real-world constraints, interoperability challenges, and ethical risks. Longitudinal studies tracking cybersecurity performance metrics across digitally transformed aviation organizations could also offer critical insights into best practices and ROI (Return on Investment). Moreover, qualitative research involving aviation professionals—pilots, cybersecurity officers, ground staff, and IT architects—would enrich our understanding of the socio-technical dynamics shaping cybersecurity adoption in aviation.

Another promising direction for future research lies in the development of composite cybersecurity resilience indices for aviation organizations. These indices could integrate technical, organizational, and strategic dimensions and offer benchmarking tools for self-assessment and regulatory audits. Furthermore, as aviation embraces Industry 5.0 and the rise of human-machine collaboration, research should explore how cybersecurity can support not just automation, but human-centric innovation—ensuring that digital transformation enhances not only efficiency and safety, but also trust, well-being, and inclusivity. The incorporation of cybersecurity into Environmental, Social, and Governance (ESG) metrics may also emerge as a valuable framework for aligning aviation sustainability goals with digital ethics and risk governance.

In conclusion, the convergence of cybersecurity and innovation in the aviation sector represents both a profound challenge and a powerful opportunity. As this chapter has shown, cybersecurity can and should be strategically leveraged to enable smart, secure, and sustainable growth in aviation. By adopting a proactive, integrated approach that combines technological innovation with organizational readiness and policy support, aviation stakeholders can move beyond reactive security postures toward building future-ready ecosystems. These ecosystems, grounded in resilience, transparency, and ethical digital governance, will form the bedrock of aviation's continued evolution in the face of both digital transformation and global uncertainty.

REFERENCES

Al-ma'aitah, M. A. (2022). Investigating the drivers of cybersecurity enhancement in public organizations: The case of Jordan. *The Electronic Journal on Information Systems in Developing Countries*, *88*(5), e12223. DOI: 10.1002/isd2.12223

AlDaajeh, S., & Alrabaee, S. (2024). Strategic cybersecurity. *Computers & Security*, *141*, 103845. DOI: 10.1016/j.cose.2024.103845

AlDaajeh, S., Saleous, H., Alrabaee, S., Barka, E., Breitinger, F., & Choo, K. K. R. (2022). The role of national cybersecurity strategies on the improvement of cybersecurity education. *Computers & Security*, *119*, 102754. DOI: 10.1016/j.cose.2022.102754

Aposporis, P. (2024). A review of global and regional frameworks for the integration of an unmanned aircraft system in air traffic management. *Transportation Research Interdisciplinary Perspectives*, *24*, 101064. DOI: 10.1016/j.trip.2024.101064

Bakyt, M., La Spada, L., Zeeshan, N., Moldamurat, K., Atanov, S., Konyrkhanova, A., & Tilenbayev, A. (2025). Advanced Cybersecurity Framework for LEO Aerospace: Integrating Quantum Cryptography, Artificial Intelligence Anomaly Detection, and Blockchain Technology. [JRC]. *Journal of Robotics and Control*, *6*(2), 695–714.

Carayannis, E. G., Dezi, L., Gregori, G., & Calo, E. (2022). Smart environments and techno-centric and human-centric innovations for Industry and Society 5.0: A quintuple helix innovation system view towards smart, sustainable, and inclusive solutions. *Journal of the Knowledge Economy*, *13*(2), 926–955. DOI: 10.1007/s13132-021-00763-4

Chang, K. Y., Chen, C. D., & Ku, E. C. (2024). Enhancing smart tourism and smart city development: Evidence from Taoyuan smart aviation city in Taiwan. *International Journal ofTourism Cities*, *10*(1), 146–165. DOI: 10.1108/IJTC-05-2023-0088

Dave, G., Choudhary, G., Sihag, V., You, I., & Choo, K. K. R. (2022). Cyber security challenges in aviation communication, navigation, and surveillance. *Computers & Security*, *112*, 102516. DOI: 10.1016/j.cose.2021.102516

Demir, S., & Paksoy, T. (2025). A Conceptual Framework for Smart and Sustainable Operations in the Aviation Industry. In *Smart and Sustainable Operations Management in the Aviation Industry* (pp. 1–14). CRC Press.

Denis, A., Thomas, A., Robert, W., Samuel, A., Kabiito, S. P., Morish, Z., Sallam, M., Ali, G., & Mijwil, M. M. (2025). A Survey on Artificial Intelligence and Blockchain Applications in Cybersecurity for Smart Cities. *SHIFRA, 2025*, 1–45. DOI: 10.70470/SHIFRA/2025/001

Elmarady, A. A., & Rahouma, K. (2021). Studying cybersecurity in civil aviation, including developing and applying aviation cybersecurity risk assessment. *IEEE Access : Practical Innovations, Open Solutions, 9*, 143997–144016. DOI: 10.1109/ACCESS.2021.3121230

Fiorentino, R., Grimaldi, F., Lamboglia, R., & Merendino, A. (2020). How smart technologies can support sustainable business models: Insights from an air navigation service provider. *Management Decision, 58*(8), 1715–1736. DOI: 10.1108/MD-09-2019-1327

Garcia, A. B., Babiceanu, R. F., & Seker, R. (2021, April). Artificial intelligence and machine learning approaches for aviation cybersecurity: An overview. In *2021 integrated communications navigation and surveillance conference (ICNS)*(pp. 1-8). IEEE.

Giacotto, A., Costa Marques, H., Pereira Barreto, E. A., & Martinetti, A. (2021). The need for ecosystem 4.0 to support maintenance 4.0: An aviation assembly line case. *Applied Sciences (Basel, Switzerland), 11*(8), 3333. DOI: 10.3390/app11083333

Hamissi, A., & Dhraief, A. (2023). A survey on the unmanned aircraft system traffic management. *ACM Computing Surveys, 56*(3), 1–37. DOI: 10.1145/3617992

Jiang, Y., Tran, T. H., & Williams, L. (2023). Machine learning and mixed reality for smart aviation: Applications and challenges. *Journal of Air Transport Management, 111*, 102437. DOI: 10.1016/j.jairtraman.2023.102437

Kabashkin, I. (2024). Unified Aviation Maintenance Ecosystem on the Basis of 6G Technology. *Electronics (Basel), 13*(19), 3824. DOI: 10.3390/electronics13193824

Kabashkin, I., & Perekrestov, V. (2024). Ecosystem of aviation maintenance: Transition from aircraft health monitoring to health management based on IoT and AI synergy. *Applied Sciences (Basel, Switzerland), 14*(11), 4394. DOI: 10.3390/app14114394

Kagalwalla, N., & Churi, P. P. (2019, September). Cybersecurity in aviation: An intrinsic review. In *2019 5th international conference on computing, communication, control and automation (ICCUBEA)* (pp. 1-6). IEEE.

Masseno, M. D., & Santos, C. (2019). Personalization and profiling of tourists in smart tourism destinations–a data protection perspective. *Revista Argumentum-Argumentum Journal of Law*, *20*(3), 1–215.

Merlo, T. R. (2024). Emerging role of artificial intelligence (AI) in aviation: using predictive maintenance for operational efficiency. In *Harnessing Digital Innovation for Air Transportation* (pp. 25–41). IGI Global. DOI: 10.4018/979-8-3693-0732-8.ch002

Mızrak, F. (2023a). Integrating cybersecurity risk management into strategic management: A comprehensive literature review. *Research Journal of Business and Management*, *10*(3), 98–108. DOI: 10.17261/Pressacademia.2023.1807

Mızrak, F. (2023b). Integration of Fuzzy AHP for Cybersecurity Strategy Development in International Organizations. *Premium e-Journal of Social Sciences (PEJOSS)*, *7*(35), 1272-1292.

Mızrak, F. (2024). Integrating AI with aviation cybersecurity: The strategic role of human resources. *Business & Management Studies: An International Journal*, *12*(3), 610–628. DOI: 10.15295/bmij.v12i3.2396

Mizrak, F., & Akkartal, G. R. (2024). Prioritizing cybersecurity initiatives in aviation: A dematel-QSFS methodology. *Heliyon*, *10*(16), e35487. DOI: 10.1016/j.heliyon.2024.e35487 PMID: 39687858

Mwesiumo, D., Halpern, N., Bråthen, S., Budd, T., & Suau-Sanchez, P. (2023). Perceived benefits as a driver and necessary condition for the willingness of air passengers to provide personal data for non-mandatory digital services at airports. *Transportation Research Part A, Policy and Practice*, *171*, 103659. DOI: 10.1016/j.tra.2023.103659

Pereira, B. A., Lohmann, G., & Houghton, L. (2022). Technology trajectory in aviation: Innovations leading to value creation (2000–2019). *International Journal of Innovation Studies*, *6*(3), 128–141. DOI: 10.1016/j.ijis.2022.05.001

Pigola, A., & da Costa, P. R. (2025). Cybersecurity management: An empirical analysis of dynamic capabilities framework for enhancing cybersecurity intelligence. *Information and Computer Security*. Advance online publication. DOI: 10.1108/ICS-08-2024-0185

Pina, N., Brito, C., Vitorino, R., & Cunha, I. (2023). Promoting sustainable and personalised travel behaviours while preserving data privacy. *Transportation Research Procedia*, *72*, 2768–2775. DOI: 10.1016/j.trpro.2023.11.819

Sabillon, R., & Bermejo Higuera, J. R. (2023, July). The importance of cybersecurity awareness training in the aviation industry for early detection of Cyberthreats and vulnerabilities. In *International Conference on Human-Computer Interaction* (pp. 461-479). Cham: Springer Nature Switzerland. DOI: 10.1007/978-3-031-48057-7_29

Sallos, M. P., Garcia-Perez, A., Bedford, D., & Orlando, B. (2019). Strategy and organisational cybersecurity: A knowledge-problem perspective. *Journal of Intellectual Capital*, *20*(4), 581–597. DOI: 10.1108/JIC-03-2019-0041

Sampigethaya, K., Kopardekar, P., & Davis, J. (2018, April). Cyber security of unmanned aircraft system traffic management (UTM). In *2018 Integrated Communications, Navigation, Surveillance Conference (ICNS)* (pp. 1C1-1). IEEE.

Scott, B. I., & Andritsos, K. I. (2023). A drone strategy 2.0 for a smart and sustainable unmanned aircraft eco-system in Europe. *Air and Space Law*, *48*(3). Advance online publication. DOI: 10.54648/AILA2023041

Shah, I. A., Jhanjhi, N. Z., & Brohi, S. (2024). Cybersecurity issues and challenges in civil aviation security. *Cybersecurity in the Transportation Industry*, 1-23.

Stastny, P., & Stoica, A. M. (2022, February). Protecting aviation safety against cybersecurity threats. [). IOP Publishing.]. *IOP Conference Series. Materials Science and Engineering*, *1226*(1), 012025. DOI: 10.1088/1757-899X/1226/1/012025

Ukwandu, E., Ben-Farah, M. A., Hindy, H., Bures, M., Atkinson, R., Tachtatzis, C., Andonovic, I., & Bellekens, X. (2022). Cyber-security challenges in aviation industry: A review of current and future trends. *Information (Basel)*, *13*(3), 146. DOI: 10.3390/info13030146

Vredenborg, M., van Kasteren, A., & Masthoff, J. (2025). Personalization in Public Transport Passenger Information Systems: A Systematic Review and Framework. *ACM Computing Surveys*, *57*(9), 1–38. DOI: 10.1145/3721478

Xie, Y., Gardi, A., & Sabatini, R. (2022, September). Cybersecurity trends in low-altitude air traffic management. In *2022 IEEE/AIAA 41st Digital Avionics Systems Conference (DASC)* (pp. 1-9). IEEE. DOI: 10.1109/DASC55683.2022.9925840

Yallop, A. C., Gică, O. A., Moisescu, O. I., Coro , M. M., & Séraphin, H. (2023). The digital traveller: Implications for data ethics and data governance in tourism and hospitality. *Journal of Consumer Marketing*, *40*(2), 155–170. DOI: 10.1108/JCM-12-2020-4278

Chapter 6
Securing Digital Transformation:
Cyber Risk Management in Smart Enterprises

Turhan Karakaya
https://orcid.org/0000-0003-0818-8522
Dogus University, Turkey

ABSTRACT

This chapter explores how cybersecurity is strategically integrated into digital transformation in smart enterprises. With the rise of AI, IoT, and blockchain, cybersecurity is crucial not just for risk management but also for enabling innovation and resilience. It examines evolving cyber threats and the need for proactive, tailored security strategies. Using frameworks like NIST, ISO/IEC 27005, and the FAIR Model, the chapter outlines best practices in risk management, AI-driven threat detection, and secure architecture. It highlights the role of culture, leadership, and preparedness for emerging risks like quantum threats and regulatory shifts. Ultimately, it presents cybersecurity as a cornerstone of sustainable digital transformation, offering strategic guidance for innovation, collaboration, and resilience.

1. INTRODUCTION

Digital transformation (DT) in smart enterprises represents a comprehensive shift in how organizations leverage technology to optimize processes, create value, and enhance stakeholder engagement. Far beyond the digitization of analog processes, DT encompasses the integration of artificial intelligence (AI), Internet of Things (IoT), blockchain, edge computing, and advanced analytics into the core functions

DOI: 10.4018/979-8-3693-6417-8.ch006

of businesses. These transformations reshape organizational culture, supply chains, human resource systems, and customer interfaces. According to Annarelli and Palombi (2021), digitalization capabilities are key enablers of sustainable cyber resilience, creating new opportunities for innovation and efficiency. However, the very technologies that drive these changes also generate new vulnerabilities. As enterprises adopt increasingly intelligent and interconnected systems, the attack surface broadens dramatically, introducing strategic cyber risks that demand holistic and proactive management approaches. Mızrak (2023a) emphasizes that integrating cybersecurity risk management into broader strategic management processes is essential to sustain the transformative momentum without compromising digital integrity or stakeholder trust.

The convergence of innovation and cyber risk has become one of the defining features of the digital economy. Technologies such as AI, while central to predictive decision-making and automation, are susceptible to adversarial attacks, data poisoning, and bias, which can distort outputs and damage reputation (Camacho, 2024; Ferrara, 2023). Similarly, IoT systems introduce significant risk through device vulnerabilities, inadequate encryption, and interoperability gaps (Waheed et al., 2020; Hafeez et al., 2018). As Mızrak and Akkartal (2024) point out in their aviation-sector-specific study, these risks are particularly critical in high-reliability domains where cyber breaches may not only result in data loss but also disrupt operational safety and continuity. The incorporation of blockchain technology, while providing decentralization and transparency, adds complexity around smart contract integrity and identity authentication (Tu et al., 2019). As Mızrak (2024b) notes in the context of AI-integrated aviation cybersecurity, human resource functions must also evolve to support secure innovation, indicating that cybersecurity is no longer confined to IT departments—it is a cross-cutting organizational priority. Thus, the intersection of digital transformation and cyber risk presents both opportunity and challenge, requiring enterprises to manage innovation and vulnerability as interdependent variables.

In this evolving digital landscape, cybersecurity can no longer be perceived as a reactive control mechanism or regulatory checkbox. It must instead be embedded as a strategic foundation in all digital initiatives. Mızrak (2023b) underscores this shift by proposing a Fuzzy AHP-based framework for cybersecurity strategy development in international organizations, highlighting the importance of dynamic, data-driven prioritization aligned with institutional goals. Similarly, Safitra et al. (2023) propose that cybersecurity frameworks must be anticipatory and integrative, supporting enterprise innovation rather than constraining it. When cybersecurity is incorporated from the design phase of digital transformation projects—whether it involves AI deployment, IoT integration, or enterprise architecture redesign—it enhances organizational agility, stakeholder confidence, and long-term competitiveness (Kosutic & Pigni, 2022). Moreover, Mızrak (2024a) emphasizes that integrating human resource management (HRM) into cybersecurity frameworks strengthens internal risk mitigation and reinforces an organization's capacity to adapt to complex digital environments. This integration is particularly critical given emerging challenges such as cybersecurity fatigue and employee mental health risks, which further underscore the socio-technical dimensions of secure digital transformation (Mizrak et al., 2025).

This chapter aims to provide a comprehensive analysis of how cybersecurity frameworks, tools, and cultural practices are strategically integrated into the digital transformation efforts of smart enterprises. It begins by examining the evolving cyber risk landscape driven by AI, IoT, and blockchain technologies, highlighting their vulnerabilities and associated threat vectors. The next section explores how cybersecurity principles are embedded into digital technologies through technical safeguards and governance mechanisms. This is followed by an overview of cyber risk management frameworks—such as the NIST Cybersecurity Framework, ISO/IEC 27005, and the FAIR model—along with advanced threat detection tools powered by AI. The chapter then discusses the broader organizational transformation enabled by cybersecurity integration, including leadership roles, cultural adaptation, and cross-sector resilience ecosystems. By structuring the discussion around these interlinked dimensions, the chapter demonstrates how cybersecurity can serve not only as a defense mechanism but also as a strategic enabler for sustainable, innovative, and resilient digital enterprises.

2. THE EVOLVING CYBER RISK LANDSCAPE

The evolving cyber risk landscape in smart enterprises has grown increasingly complex, driven by the rapid integration of emerging technologies such as artificial intelligence (AI), the Internet of Things (IoT), and blockchain systems. As businesses become more connected and data-driven, the avenues for exploitation by malicious actors have multiplied. AI, while widely adopted for its predictive and automation capabilities, also introduces new vulnerabilities. According to Camacho (2024), the misuse of AI can enable the development of more sophisticated phishing techniques, deepfake-driven identity fraud, and evasion-aware malware, which collectively escalate the threat landscape. Zaman et al. (2021) echo these concerns, identifying adversarial AI attacks as a critical security concern in smart systems. These attacks, where malicious inputs are designed to deceive AI models, pose a significant risk to smart enterprise applications that rely on real-time analytics and machine learning models.

IoT networks, which form the backbone of many smart enterprises, are particularly vulnerable due to their distributed nature and limited built-in security capabilities. Humayun et al. (2024) underscore that with billions of IoT devices globally, many lack the computational power for robust encryption, making them easy targets for intrusion, botnet enlistment, and data exfiltration. Waheed et al. (2020) and Attkan and Ranga (2022) further highlight that the deployment of machine learning and blockchain can mitigate these threats through decentralized authentication and anomaly detection systems. Nonetheless, the effective implementation of such defenses remains a challenge due to heterogeneity in devices, software interoperability issues, and varying compliance levels. Meanwhile, Singh et al. (2021) emphasize the rising number of blockchain-specific attacks, such as 51% attacks and smart contract vulnerabilities, which compromise the integrity of distributed systems and complicate risk management strategies in enterprise environments.

Smart enterprise environments are also incorporating complex cyber-physical systems such as autonomous vehicles, which demand advanced cybersecurity protocols. Bendiab et al. (2023) discuss how AI and blockchain technologies are increasingly leveraged to secure vehicular networks, route data integrity, and prevent unauthorized control. However, these same systems are targets for coordinated cyber-attacks due to their interconnected control systems. Malik, Malik, and Naim (2024) note that although AI, ML, and blockchain open up opportunities for autonomous cybersecurity response mechanisms, they simultaneously introduce new attack surfaces, such as data poisoning and model inversion, which traditional defenses are not yet equipped to handle. Consequently, as the functionality and autonomy of systems increase, so too does the scale and impact of potential breaches.

The cost and complexity associated with cyber risks in digital enterprises have surged in recent years. Dreyer et al. (2018) estimated that the global annual cost of cybercrime could reach trillions of dollars, factoring in direct financial losses, reputational damage, and business disruption. Orlando (2021) introduced the concept of Cyber Value at Risk (CyVaR) to provide a quantifiable financial impact metric, highlighting how organizations can estimate the potential economic losses associated with specific cyber incidents. Kavallieratos et al. (2021) add that cyber risk in complex systems can propagate through interconnected components, exacerbating the damage and necessitating multi-layered defense mechanisms. In such settings, choosing the right mix of cybersecurity controls becomes not only a technical decision but also a strategic one, involving risk appetite, resource availability, and long-term resilience planning.

In addition to technical and financial concerns, legal and regulatory frameworks significantly shape how organizations address cybersecurity risks. Elendu et al. (2024) highlight that in sectors such as healthcare, the legal liability for data breaches extends beyond financial penalties to include professional sanctions and reputational harm. Thummala and Bindewari (2024) argue that compliance-based cybersecurity models—such as those aligned with the NIST Cybersecurity Framework or ISO/IEC 27001—offer structured approaches for identifying, assessing, and mitigating risks. Yet, they also caution that compliance alone does not equate to security; proactive monitoring and incident response remain essential. Kumar, Bhardwaj, and Lather (2024) further emphasize the increasing complexity of regulatory obligations across jurisdictions, noting that multinational corporations must navigate overlapping laws related to digital asset protection, data localization, and cross-border data flows. Allahrakha (2023) draws attention to the ethical dilemmas faced in balancing cybersecurity with user privacy, warning that overly aggressive surveillance measures can undermine civil liberties and public trust, especially when enterprises operate in data-rich environments such as e-commerce or smart cities.

Together, these studies illustrate the multifaceted nature of cyber risk in the digital age, where technological advancement brings both opportunity and exposure. Organizations must rethink their cybersecurity postures not just as a matter of defense, but as an enabler of innovation and trust in increasingly interconnected and intelligent enterprise ecosystems.

3. INTEGRATING CYBERSECURITY INTO DIGITAL TECHNOLOGIES

Integrating cybersecurity into artificial intelligence (AI) applications has become an essential task for smart enterprises aiming to maintain both ethical responsibility and system resilience. As AI systems increasingly drive decisions across sectors—from finance to healthcare—their vulnerability to bias, data poisoning, and adversarial attacks poses serious challenges. Muvva (2021) presents a structured framework for bias mitigation and privacy preservation in large-scale data pipelines, underlining that both input data and model training processes must be audited to ensure ethical AI deployment. Schwartz et al. (2022) further emphasize the necessity for standardized methods to identify, measure, and manage algorithmic bias, proposing guidelines for transparency and stakeholder accountability. Ferrara (2023) categorizes bias into data-driven, societal, and algorithmic types, stressing that unchecked biases can propagate systemic inequalities and undermine trust in digital systems. Real-world instances reinforce these concerns: Facebook's internal "Red Team" initiative, as reported by Wired (Heaven, 2021), systematically probes

AI models for vulnerabilities including bias and malicious manipulation, highlighting how tech firms are operationalizing AI security through offensive testing. As smart enterprises scale their AI usage, embedding cybersecurity features—like secure model training, adversarial robustness, and explainability—into every stage of the AI lifecycle is imperative for ethical innovation.

The Internet of Things (IoT), with its proliferation of interconnected sensors and smart devices, introduces a vast and often undersecured digital surface area. These devices are frequently limited in processing power and memory, which constrains the implementation of conventional cybersecurity protocols. Hafeez et al. (2018) demonstrate the efficacy of real-time IoT activity detection using edge network monitoring, which enables early identification of malicious or anomalous behavior. Edge security is especially critical, as processing data closer to the source reduces latency but increases exposure to physical and remote attacks. Li et al. (2020) highlight authentication and encryption techniques that protect edge devices, including trusted execution environments and key exchange protocols. Furthermore, Shahidinejad et al. (2021) propose "Light-edge," a lightweight and scalable authentication framework suitable for edge-cloud ecosystems. Commercial implementations of these principles are seen in Microsoft's Azure IoT Hub, which integrates secure device provisioning, authentication, and real-time telemetry analysis for enterprise-grade IoT security (Microsoft, 2024). These approaches illustrate that cybersecurity in IoT must be not only robust but also scalable and adaptive, accounting for device heterogeneity and resource constraints.

Blockchain technology, while often heralded for its inherent security features, also demands careful cybersecurity integration—particularly in areas like smart contract integrity, key management, and decentralized identity. Tu et al. (2019) propose a decentralized identity authentication and key management model aimed at reducing single points of failure in traditional systems. Similarly, Dua et al. (2020) introduce "Trustful," a decentralized public key infrastructure (PKI) that enhances identity verification through blockchain-based consensus. As noted by Agarkar et al. (2024), secure identity management systems must address access control, data privacy, and revocation mechanisms, especially in public blockchain networks. A high-profile example of blockchain's real-world application is China's "RealDID" initiative, which leverages decentralized identifiers (DIDs) to establish national digital identities while protecting user privacy via encrypted credentials and blockchain registries (Wikipedia, 2024). These examples highlight how blockchain's decentralization benefits can be maximized only when accompanied by well-designed cybersecurity protocols addressing both cryptographic and operational risks.

Cybersecurity cannot be a stand-alone function but must be woven into the broader enterprise architecture and operational workflows. Kelley and Moyle (2023) advocate for "cybersecurity-by-design" principles that align technical safeguards with business objectives, urging cybersecurity professionals to collaborate with enterprise architects, DevOps teams, and compliance officers. This integration facilitates proactive risk identification, threat modeling, and security automation within digital transformation projects. A compelling case is presented by Sophos, a cybersecurity firm that implemented a comprehensive enterprise architecture framework using the Avolution ABACUS platform to align business processes with threat intelligence and resilience metrics (Avolution, 2024). This alignment enabled Sophos to standardize response protocols, prioritize digital assets, and support secure innovation across its global operations. Embedding cybersecurity into workflows—from procurement to product development—not only reduces vulnerability but also builds a security culture that adapts alongside technological evolution. In increasingly smart enterprises, such integration is not optional but foundational.

4. FRAMEWORKS AND TOOLS FOR CYBER RISK MANAGEMENT

Effectively managing cyber risk in smart enterprises requires the adoption of comprehensive frameworks that integrate both preventive and responsive security strategies. Cybersecurity-by-design is a foundational principle that encourages organizations to embed security into all stages of system development and organizational architecture rather than treating it as an afterthought. As Lee (2021) outlines, incorporating security as an integral component of business and IT operations allows for more cost-effective mitigation of threats, ensuring investment decisions around cybersecurity are both strategic and impactful. Similarly, Alamri, Crowley, and Richardson (2022) present a risk management framework specifically tailored to blockchain-based identity systems in health IoT, demonstrating how a security-first approach is critical in highly sensitive data environments. Blin et al. (2022) also highlight the application of cybersecurity frameworks in securing national land transaction systems, reinforcing that such models must be adapted to sector-specific data integrity requirements and governance practices. These studies underscore the importance of contextualizing frameworks to sectoral, technical, and geographic needs while preserving a core philosophy of proactive security engineering.

Several standardized models have emerged as cornerstones of cybersecurity risk management. The NIST Cybersecurity Framework (CSF) and ISO/IEC 27005 are among the most widely adopted international standards, guiding organizations through the processes of identifying, protecting, detecting, responding to, and recovering from cyber threats. The FAIR (Factor Analysis of Information Risk) model, meanwhile, provides a quantifiable approach to cyber risk, helping organizations translate technical risk into financial terms. Echeverría et al. (2021) introduce a hardening-based IoT cybersecurity model that aligns well with these frameworks by recommending layered security techniques to prevent unauthorized access. In parallel, Brezavšček and Baggia (2025) conducted a comprehensive literature review showing an increasing trend toward cybersecurity maturity assessments, emphasizing the need for organizations to evolve from mere compliance toward continuous security optimization. In the domain of conceptual modeling, Martins et al. (2022) propose a framework for ontology-based characterization of cybersecurity processes, which helps harmonize technical definitions and processes across complex IT environments. These structured approaches enable enterprises to not only comply with regulatory expectations but also to benchmark and improve their cyber risk posture over time. To support the strategic selection of a suitable framework, Table 1 compares three widely recognized cyber risk models—NIST CSF, ISO/IEC 27005, and the FAIR Model—highlighting their scope, methodology, and strengths across different enterprise needs.

Table 1. Comparison of key cyber risk management frameworks

Framework	Focus Area	Main Components	Strengths	Typical Use Cases
NIST CSF	Risk-based cybersecurity posture	Identify, Protect, Detect, Respond, Recover	Widely adopted; flexible and scalable; sector-neutral	Critical infrastructure, enterprise IT, digital strategy
ISO/IEC 27005	Information security risk management	Risk identification, analysis, evaluation, treatment, communication, monitoring	Internationally standardized; strong regulatory alignment	Compliance audits, risk governance, structured enterprise risk
FAIR Model	Financial quantification of cyber risk	Loss Event Frequency, Probable Loss Magnitude, Risk Scenarios	Converts cyber risk into monetary terms; supports decision-making	Budgeting, cyber insurance valuation, board-level reporting

Adapted and synthesized from:Lee (2021); Echeverría et al. (2021); Brezavšček & Baggia (2025); Martins et al. (2022); National Institute of Standards and Technology (NIST, 2018); International Organization for Standardization (ISO/IEC 27005:2018); The Open Group (2019).

Advances in artificial intelligence and machine learning have also revolutionized the landscape of threat intelligence and detection. AI-enabled security operations centers (SOCs) can now process vast streams of data in real time, identifying patterns indicative of emerging threats far faster than traditional methods. Kavitha and Thejas (2024) explore how AI models are increasingly leveraged for anomaly detection, predictive threat assessment, and automated incident response, dramatically improving security responsiveness. Paracha et al. (2024) present a conceptual overview of AI's role in network threat detection, highlighting that deep learning algorithms can detect advanced persistent threats (APTs), zero-day exploits, and insider threats through behavioral modeling and unsupervised learning. This automated intelligence not only shortens the time-to-response for cyber incidents but also alleviates the pressure on human analysts in monitoring complex environments. Enterprises such as IBM have incorporated AI-powered threat detection into their QRadar suite, enabling contextual and automated threat prioritization—a critical capability in today's high-volume cyber threat landscape.

Measuring cyber readiness and digital resilience has become a strategic imperative for organizations navigating digital transformation. Bahyan, Ajmal, and Saber (2024) provide empirical evidence from the energy sector showing that human capital and innovation readiness are pivotal enablers of organizational cyber resilience. Zighan (2024) outlines a transition framework that helps businesses move from traditional continuity planning toward digital resilience, incorporating adaptability, learning agility, and integrated IT-risk alignment. Similarly, Annarelli and Palombi (2021) propose a framework for sustainable cyber resilience that focuses on digitalization capabilities, advocating for synergy between technological assets and organizational processes. This resonates with the findings of Kumar et al. (2024), who model digital resilience enablers for small and medium enterprises, identifying knowledge management, dynamic resource allocation, and risk communication as critical components. Together, these studies reflect a shift in focus—from managing isolated risks to building holistic resilience capacities that support long-term business continuity, innovation, and trust in digital systems.

Overall, the integration of well-established risk management frameworks, advanced AI tools, and resilience measurement models equips organizations to navigate the increasingly complex cybersecurity landscape. Whether through formalized standards like NIST and FAIR or AI-driven SOCs, the key lies in combining strategic foresight, operational discipline, and adaptive innovation to transform cybersecurity into a driver of sustainable digital growth.

5. STRATEGIC IMPACTS AND ORGANIZATIONAL TRANSFORMATION

In today's increasingly digitized economy, robust cybersecurity strategies have evolved from being merely a defensive mechanism into a catalyst for strategic innovation and competitive differentiation. Kosutic and Pigni (2022) argue that organizations that proactively invest in cybersecurity not only reduce exposure to digital threats but also unlock new opportunities for innovation, particularly through secure digital infrastructure that builds stakeholder trust. This proactive investment perspective aligns cybersecurity with long-term value creation rather than short-term cost containment. Safitra, Lubis, and Fakhrurroja (2023) further reinforce this by proposing a forward-looking cybersecurity framework that anticipates the evolution of cyber threats and treats cybersecurity as a platform for resilience-led innovation. From a sustainability perspective, Annarelli and Palombi (2021) emphasize that cybersecurity capabilities are tightly linked to an enterprise's broader digitalization and innovation agenda, helping organizations maintain operational continuity while experimenting with emerging technologies. When cyber strategies are robust, agile, and integrated across organizational functions, they enhance digital confidence—enabling faster time-to-market, seamless collaboration, and scalable business models that would otherwise be constrained by risk concerns.

Organizational culture and leadership are key drivers in successfully embedding cybersecurity into enterprise transformation. A cybersecurity-focused culture does not emerge solely from technical controls but is cultivated through values, leadership behavior, and strategic alignment. Willie (2023) stresses the significance of building a "security-first" culture that permeates all levels of the organization, noting that employees' routine behaviors often dictate the effectiveness of even the most sophisticated technical safeguards. Fisher, Porod, and Peterson (2021) provide empirical evidence that motivational techniques—such as rewards, continuous training, and shared accountability—can significantly increase employees' adherence to cybersecurity protocols. Moreover, Al-Somali et al. (2024) show that in small and medium-sized enterprises (SMEs), organizational culture not only moderates the impact of cybersecurity initiatives on business performance but also enhances resilience by embedding cyber awareness into strategic decision-making. Möller (2023) adds a macro view, suggesting that leadership in the digital age must combine technical literacy with transformation leadership competencies, enabling CISOs and executives to jointly champion cybersecurity as a strategic pillar of organizational growth. Without such cultural and leadership alignment, even well-funded cybersecurity initiatives risk fragmentation, inefficiency, or poor adoption across enterprise units.

Preparing for the future of cybersecurity demands anticipatory governance and technological foresight, especially as organizations face quantum-enabled threats, regulatory volatility, and increasingly hybrid digital infrastructures. Khan et al. (2024) explore the importance of post-quantum cryptography in securing next-generation technologies, such as unmanned aerial vehicles (UAVs), which are susceptible to decryption by quantum algorithms. These threats are no longer theoretical; their potential impact on encrypted financial transactions, identity systems, and defense infrastructure is substantial. Elmisery et al. (2025) raise alarms over the dual challenge posed by AI-generated attacks and quantum computing in the financial sector, underscoring the need for adaptable cybersecurity architectures. As organizations migrate to cloud-native environments, edge networks, and 5G systems, traditional security frameworks must evolve toward flexible, modular, and interoperable models that accommodate rapid technological shifts. Regulatory developments—ranging from GDPR to sector-specific mandates such as the EU's NIS2 directive—further necessitate agile compliance mechanisms embedded within cybersecurity strategy. Thus, future-proofing is not simply a technical adjustment; it is a strategic orientation toward resilience, adaptability, and ethical stewardship in the digital economy.

The increasingly interconnected nature of digital ecosystems makes cross-sector collaboration a critical dimension of cybersecurity transformation. Organizations no longer operate in isolated silos but within complex, interdependent networks that include suppliers, infrastructure providers, regulators, and customers. Dentoni, Pinkse, and Lubberink (2021) argue that sustainable business models must be embedded within socio-ecological resilience frameworks, which often require cross-sector partnerships to address systemic risks like cybersecurity. Oukes et al. (2024) extend this perspective by exploring resilience strategies in developing countries, showing how collaborations between public and private actors help overcome institutional voids and resource asymmetries in managing digital risk. Sonesson, Johansson, and Cedergren (2021) emphasize the role of governance mechanisms in coordinating interdependencies across critical infrastructure sectors, identifying shared risk assessment tools and interoperable cybersecurity standards as essential to cross-sector resilience. In practical terms, examples like the Global Forum on Cyber Expertise (GFCE) and cross-industry working groups within the financial services and energy sectors illustrate how shared intelligence, capacity building, and coordinated incident response enhance the collective cyber posture. Building resilience ecosystems through such collaborative mechanisms amplifies the reach and effectiveness of individual organizations' cybersecurity efforts and creates a broader, more adaptive shield against evolving threats.

6. REAL-WORLD CASE APPLICATIONS IN SECURE DIGITAL TRANSFORMATION

Real-world implementations of secure digital transformation demonstrate how strategic cybersecurity integration enables organizations to innovate confidently while safeguarding critical systems and data. These cases span multiple sectors—healthcare, manufacturing, government, finance, and logistics—each highlighting distinct technological approaches and cybersecurity strategies that align with sector-specific demands.

In the healthcare industry, ensuring patient data security while enabling interoperable digital services has become a priority. A recent development in this space is an Ethereum-based electronic health record (EHR) management system that empowers patients with secure, decentralized control over their medical data.

The system utilizes Role-Based Access Control, digital signatures, and modular smart contracts to overcome traditional data privacy and interoperability challenges, allowing healthcare institutions to adhere to both cybersecurity and regulatory requirements simultaneously (Ali et al., 2024). This approach not only enhances patient trust and data accuracy but also introduces scalable, tamper-resistant structures into healthcare infrastructure—representing a blueprint for secure digital innovation in health systems globally.

In manufacturing, digital transformation is largely driven by the adoption of AI and IoT technologies. Samsung SDS has deployed a smart factory platform, Nexplant, which integrates AI-driven analytics and real-time monitoring of factory environments using sensor data. This system not only improves productivity and operational agility but also embeds cybersecurity directly into the production lifecycle by detecting anomalies, managing vulnerabilities, and ensuring secure device communication (Samsung SDS, 2024). The strategic combination of AI and IoT within the cybersecurity architecture exemplifies how manufacturing enterprises can transform traditional operations into secure, intelligent production ecosystems.

Government-led digital transformation efforts have also prioritized cybersecurity, particularly in public education systems. The Hawai'i State Department of Education (HIDOE), for example, has launched a robust initiative to modernize its IT infrastructure while embedding security frameworks to protect student and administrative data. By implementing comprehensive cybersecurity policies and deploying secure cloud-based learning systems, HIDOE improved its digital resilience and ensured compliance with national privacy laws. This transformation was bolstered by continuous training programs for staff and leadership, illustrating how cybersecurity awareness can be institutionalized at the organizational level (Medina & Dela Cruz, 2023).

The financial services sector, heavily dependent on data confidentiality and customer trust, has aggressively adopted AI and cybersecurity tools to manage cyber risks in digital operations. A large Indian financial institution successfully deployed AI-enabled threat detection and identity governance systems to secure its privileged access management structure and internal networks. The deployment allowed the firm to monitor access behavior, apply real-time policy enforcement, and respond swiftly to potential insider threats, thereby protecting sensitive data while improving regulatory compliance and operational continuity (Inspira Enterprise, 2024). This case illustrates how financial institutions are leveraging AI not just for fraud detection but as a core component of proactive cybersecurity architecture.

In the logistics sector, blockchain technology has been used to secure international trade operations. Samsung SDS, in collaboration with ABN AMRO and the Port of Rotterdam, developed the DELIVER platform—a blockchain-based logistics system aimed at securing documentation processes, preventing double payments, and ensuring traceability across global supply chains. By digitizing bill-of-lading transactions and implementing smart contracts, the system enhances supply chain transparency while ensuring data integrity and reducing fraud (Samsung SDS, 2024). Such applications demonstrate how logistics providers can simultaneously innovate and mitigate operational risk by leveraging decentralized technologies.

These case studies underscore the multifaceted nature of secure digital transformation. They collectively show that cybersecurity, when treated as a strategic function, enables rather than hinders innovation. Across diverse industries, organizations that embed cybersecurity into their digital infrastructure, governance practices, and cultural frameworks not only reduce their exposure to cyber threats but also build trust, achieve compliance, and accelerate value creation.

7. CONCLUSION

This chapter has underscored a fundamental shift in how cybersecurity must be perceived and implemented in the age of digital transformation. Rather than serving as a mere protective layer or regulatory obligation, cybersecurity today is a strategic enabler—integral to fostering innovation, sustaining operational continuity, and ensuring competitive advantage. As smart enterprises increasingly depend on interconnected digital infrastructures powered by artificial intelligence, blockchain, IoT, and cloud systems, the attack surface expands, making cybersecurity a critical factor in enterprise viability and resilience.

A key insight derived from this exploration is that cybersecurity must be embedded at every level of digital transformation—technological, organizational, procedural, and cultural. The evidence presented in studies by Camacho (2024), Mızrak and Akkartal (2024), and Annarelli and Palombi (2021) points to the fact that smart technologies, while empowering, carry inherent risks that cannot be managed retroactively. For instance, AI systems are vulnerable to adversarial manipulation, IoT devices suffer from limited encryption capacity, and blockchain smart contracts can be exploited through coding vulnerabilities. Therefore, organizations must adopt a "cybersecurity-by-design" approach, where risk mitigation strategies are integrated into the earliest stages of digital system development and enterprise architecture planning.

Moreover, this chapter has demonstrated that effective cybersecurity strategies do not hinder innovation—they accelerate it. As highlighted by Kosutic and Pigni (2022), enterprises that treat cybersecurity as a strategic investment rather than a compliance necessity are better positioned to unlock new digital capabilities. These organizations create trust with customers, partners, and regulators, enabling them to scale faster, enter new markets, and experiment more freely with emerging technologies. To achieve this, enterprises must align cybersecurity initiatives with innovation goals—such as launching new digital platforms, automating workflows, or leveraging AI for customer insights—ensuring that each innovation pathway is secure and resilient from inception.

Organizational culture and leadership also emerged as decisive enablers of cybersecurity transformation. Technical controls alone are insufficient without a culture of shared responsibility and informed vigilance. As emphasized by Willie (2023) and Mızrak (2024a), cultivating a "security-first" culture requires leadership at all levels to model cyber-aware behavior, reinforce secure practices through training, and integrate cybersecurity expectations into employee performance systems. Fisher, Porod, and Peterson (2021) found that when employees are incentivized and educated about cyber risks—rather than merely warned or policed—they are more likely to adhere to protocols and report anomalies early. Thus, developing a security-focused culture must be a deliberate initiative, supported by continuous training, cross-functional governance, and transparent communication around risk and accountability.

Future-readiness is another dominant theme, particularly in light of rapid technological and regulatory evolution. The anticipated rise of quantum computing, for instance, will render many current encryption methods obsolete. Studies by Khan et al. (2024) and Elmisery et al. (2025) caution that organizations failing to prepare for post-quantum cryptography could face major breaches in sectors ranging from aviation to financial services. At the same time, global regulations—such as GDPR, NIS2, and sector-specific cybersecurity acts—are becoming more stringent and fragmented. Enterprises must therefore adopt flexible, modular cybersecurity architectures that allow for rapid compliance updates, secure integration of third-party services, and hybrid deployment across cloud-edge infrastructures. This level of agility requires ongoing investment in AI-powered security tools, predictive analytics, and adaptive response mechanisms.

Additionally, the chapter highlighted the importance of cross-sector collaboration and ecosystem-level resilience. In an era where critical infrastructures are interdependent, no organization can afford to manage cyber risk in isolation. Collaborations with regulatory bodies, suppliers, competitors, and research institutions enhance shared threat intelligence, establish common standards, and support coordinated responses to large-scale threats. Studies by Dentoni et al. (2021) and Sonesson et al. (2021) illustrate that multi-stakeholder partnerships—particularly in sectors like transportation, energy, and healthcare—are essential to maintaining resilience across interconnected systems. Enterprises should actively participate in national and international cybersecurity alliances and adopt interoperable standards that facilitate rapid information exchange and joint crisis response.

In conclusion, cybersecurity is no longer a technical add-on or a compliance checkbox—it is the foundation of digital trust, innovation, and resilience in modern enterprises. To harness the full potential of digital transformation, organizations must:

- Integrate cybersecurity into strategic planning and innovation design, not just system implementation.
- Develop dynamic risk governance models that are adaptable to new technologies, threat vectors, and compliance regimes.
- Invest in AI-driven, behavior-based threat detection systems to improve response times and reduce human workload in security operations centers.
- Establish a security-conscious workforce through targeted education, performance incentives, and psychological well-being support to combat cybersecurity fatigue.
- Anticipate future challenges by preparing for quantum-era encryption threats and continuously assessing cyber readiness.
- Embed cybersecurity into cross-sector partnerships and critical infrastructure networks to build a shared resilience framework.

Ultimately, the ability to thrive in an era of pervasive digital innovation will not belong to those who innovate fastest, but to those who innovate securely, strategically, and sustainably. Cybersecurity is the backbone of that future.

REFERENCES

Agarkar, A. A., Karyakarte, M., Chavhan, G., Patil, M., Talware, R., & Kulkarni, L. (2024). Blockchain aware decentralized identity management and access control system. *Measurement. Sensors*, *31*, 101032. DOI: 10.1016/j.measen.2024.101032

Al-Somali, S. A., Saqr, R. R., Asiri, A. M., & Al-Somali, N. A. (2024). Organizational cybersecurity systems and sustainable business performance of small and medium enterprises (SMEs) in Saudi Arabia: The mediating and moderating role of cybersecurity resilience and organizational culture. *Sustainability (Basel)*, *16*(5), 1880. DOI: 10.3390/su16051880

Alamri, B., Crowley, K., & Richardson, I. (2022). Cybersecurity risk management framework for blockchain identity management systems in health IoT. *Sensors (Basel)*, *23*(1), 218. DOI: 10.3390/s23010218 PMID: 36616816

Ali, H. A., Abid, A., Ammar, M., Qamar, A., Khalid, R., & Shahid, A. R. (2024). Ethereum based electronic health record management system for secure and controlled access. *arXiv preprint arXiv:2412.02851*. Retrieved from https://arxiv.org/abs/2412.02851

Allahrakha, N. (2023). Balancing cyber-security and privacy: Legal and ethical considerations in the digital age. *Legal Issues in the digital. The Age (Melbourne, Vic.)*, (2), 78–121.

Annarelli, A., & Palombi, G. (2021). Digitalization capabilities for sustainable cyber resilience: A conceptual framework. *Sustainability (Basel)*, *13*(23), 13065. DOI: 10.3390/su132313065

Attkan, A., & Ranga, V. (2022). Cyber-physical security for IoT networks: A comprehensive review on traditional, blockchain and artificial intelligence based key-security. *Complex & Intelligent Systems*, *8*(4), 3559–3591. DOI: 10.1007/s40747-022-00667-z

Avolution. (2024). *Case Study: Sophos and Cybersecurity Architecture*. Retrieved from https://www.avolutionsoftware.com/our-resources/sophos/

Bahyan, H., Ajmal, M. M., & Saber, H. (2024). Going resilient with digital transformation, human capabilities and innovation readiness: Empirical evidence from the energy sector. *Benchmarking*. Advance online publication. DOI: 10.1108/BIJ-10-2023-0699

Bendiab, G., Hameurlaine, A., Germanos, G., Kolokotronis, N., & Shiaeles, S. (2023). Autonomous vehicles security: Challenges and solutions using blockchain and artificial intelligence. *IEEE Transactions on Intelligent Transportation Systems, 24*(4), 3614–3637. DOI: 10.1109/TITS.2023.3236274

Blin, P. F., Aditya, T., Claramunt, C., Kermarrec, Y., & Santosa, P. B. (2022). Cybersecurity Risk-Management to Maintain Integrity Land Data Transactions: Application to Indonesian and French Land Administration Systems. *The International Archives of the Photogrammetry, Remote Sensing and Spatial Information Sciences, 48*, 29–31. DOI: 10.5194/isprs-archives-XLVIII-4-W3-2022-29-2022

Brezavšček, A., & Baggia, A. (2025). Recent Trends in Information and Cyber Security Maturity Assessment: A Systematic Literature Review. *Systems, 13*(1), 52. DOI: 10.3390/systems13010052

Camacho, N. G. (2024). The role of AI in cybersecurity: Addressing threats in the digital age. *Journal of Artificial Intelligence General science (JAIGS) ISSN: 3006-4023, 3*(1), 143-154.

Dentoni, D., Pinkse, J., & Lubberink, R. (2021). Linking sustainable business models to socio-ecological resilience through cross-sector partnerships: A complex adaptive systems view. *Business & Society, 60*(5), 1216–1252. DOI: 10.1177/0007650320935015

Dreyer, P., Jones, T., Klima, K., Oberholtzer, J., Strong, A., Welburn, J. W., & Winkelman, Z. (2018). Estimating the global cost of cyber risk. [*-WFHF, Rand Corporation.*]. *Research Reports (Montgomery)*, ●●●, RR-2299.

Dua, A., Barpanda, S. S., Kumar, N., & Tanwar, S. (2020, December). Trustful: A decentralized public key infrastructure and identity management system. In *2020 IEEE Globecom Workshops (GC Wkshps* (pp. 1-6). IEEE. DOI: 10.1109/GCWkshps50303.2020.9367444

Echeverría, A., Cevallos, C., Ortiz-Garces, I., & Andrade, R. O. (2021). Cybersecurity model based on hardening for secure internet of things implementation. *Applied Sciences (Basel, Switzerland), 11*(7), 3260. DOI: 10.3390/app11073260

Elendu, C., Omeludike, E. K., Oloyede, P. O., Obidigbo, B. T., & Omeludike, J. C. (2024). Legal implications for clinicians in cybersecurity incidents. *Revista de Medicina (São Paulo), 103*(39), e39887. PMID: 39331908

Elmisery, A. M., Sertovic, M., Zayin, A., & Watson, P. (2025). Cyber Threats in Financial Transactions—Addressing the Dual Challenge of AI and Quantum Computing. *arXiv preprint arXiv:2503.15678.*

Ferrara, E. (2023). Fairness and bias in artificial intelligence: A brief survey of sources, impacts, and mitigation strategies. *Sci*, *6*(1), 3. DOI: 10.3390/sci6010003

Fisher, R., Porod, C., & Peterson, S. (2021). Motivating employees and organizations to adopt a cybersecurity-focused culture. *Journal of Organizational Psychology*, *21*(1), 114–131.

Hafeez, I., Ding, A. Y., Antikainen, M., & Tarkoma, S. (2018, August). Real-time IoT device activity detection in edge networks. In *International Conference on Network and System Security* (pp. 221-236). Cham: Springer International Publishing. DOI: 10.1007/978-3-030-02744-5_17

Heaven, W. D. (2021, June 24). Facebook's "Red Team" is hunting for bias in its AI. *WIRED*. Retrieved from https://www.wired.com/story/facebooks-red-team-hacks-ai-programs/

Humayun, M., Tariq, N., Alfayad, M., Zakwan, M., Alwakid, G., & Assiri, M. (2024). Securing the Internet of Things in artificial intelligence era: A comprehensive survey. *IEEE Access : Practical Innovations, Open Solutions*, *12*, 25469–25490. DOI: 10.1109/ACCESS.2024.3365634

Inspira Enterprise. (2024). *Banking and financial case study: Next-gen network access control and identity governance*. Retrieved from https://inspiraenterprise.com/case-studies/

International Organization for Standardization. (2018). *ISO/IEC 27005:2018 Information technology—Security techniques—Information security risk management*. ISO.

Kavallieratos, G., Spathoulas, G., & Katsikas, S. (2021). Cyber risk propagation and optimal selection of cybersecurity controls for complex cyberphysical systems. *Sensors (Basel)*, *21*(5), 1691. DOI: 10.3390/s21051691 PMID: 33804503

Kavitha, D., & Thejas, S. (2024). Ai enabled threat detection: Leveraging artificial intelligence for advanced security and cyber threat mitigation. *IEEE Access : Practical Innovations, Open Solutions*.

Kelley, D., & Moyle, E. (2023). *Practical Cybersecurity Architecture: A guide to creating and implementing robust designs for cybersecurity architects*. Packt Publishing Ltd.

Khan, M. A., Javaid, S., Mohsan, S. A. H., Tanveer, M., & Ullah, I. (2024). Future-proofing security for UAVs with post-quantum cryptography: A review. *IEEE Open Journal of the Communications Society*, *5*, 6849–6871. DOI: 10.1109/OJCOMS.2024.3486649

Kosutic, D., & Pigni, F. (2022). Cybersecurity: Investing for competitive outcomes. *The Journal of Business Strategy*, *43*(1), 28–36. DOI: 10.1108/JBS-06-2020-0116

Kumar, V., Sindhwani, R., Behl, A., Kaur, A., & Pereira, V. (2024). Modelling and analysing the enablers of digital resilience for small and medium enterprises. *Journal of Enterprise Information Management*, *37*(5), 1677–1708. DOI: 10.1108/JEIM-01-2023-0002

Kumar, V. A., Bhardwaj, S., & Lather, M. (2024). Cybersecurity and Safeguarding Digital Assets: An Analysis of Regulatory Frameworks, Legal Liability and Enforcement Mechanisms. *Productivity*, *65*(1), 1–10. DOI: 10.32381/PROD.2024.65.01.1

Lee, I. (2021). Cybersecurity: Risk management framework and investment cost analysis. *Business Horizons*, *64*(5), 659–671. DOI: 10.1016/j.bushor.2021.02.022

Li, X., Chen, T., Cheng, Q., Ma, S., & Ma, J. (2020). Smart applications in edge computing: Overview on authentication and data security. *IEEE Internet of Things Journal*, *8*(6), 4063–4080. DOI: 10.1109/JIOT.2020.3019297

Malik, S., Malik, P. K., & Naim, A. (2024). Opportunities and challenges in new generation cyber security applications using artificial intelligence, machine learning and block chain. *Next-generation cybersecurity: AI, ML, and Blockchain*, 23-37.

Martins, B. F., Serrano Gil, L. J., Reyes Román, J. F., Panach, J. I., Pastor, O., Hadad, M., & Rochwerger, B. (2022). A framework for conceptual characterization of ontologies and its application in the cybersecurity domain. *Software & Systems Modeling*, *21*(4), 1437–1464. DOI: 10.1007/s10270-022-01013-0

Medina, C., & Dela Cruz, R. (2023). Hawai'i state department of education: Strategic transformation of secure education infrastructure. In *Proceedings of the 2023 International Conference on Digital Learning Ecosystems.*

Microsoft. (2024). *Azure IoT Hub*. Retrieved from https://azure.microsoft.com/en-us/products/iot-hub/

Mızrak, F. (2023a). Integrating cybersecurity risk management into strategic management: A comprehensive literature review. *Research Journal of Business and Management*, *10*(3), 98–108. DOI: 10.17261/Pressacademia.2023.1807

Mızrak, F. (2023b). Integration of Fuzzy AHP for Cybersecurity Strategy Development in International Organizations. Premium e-Journal of Social Sciences (PEJOSS), 7(35), 1272-1292.

Mızrak, F. (2024a). Enhancing Cybersecurity risk management through conceptual analysis of Hrm integration. *Yönetim Bilimleri Dergisi*, *22*(51), 96–118. DOI: 10.35408/comuybd.1342408

Mızrak, F. (2024b). Integrating AI with aviation cybersecurity: The strategic role of human resources. *Business & Management Studies: An International Journal*, *12*(3), 610–628. DOI: 10.15295/bmij.v12i3.2396

Mizrak, F., & Akkartal, G. R. (2024). Prioritizing cybersecurity initiatives in aviation: A dematel-QSFS methodology. *Heliyon*, *10*(16), e35487. DOI: 10.1016/j.heliyon.2024.e35487 PMID: 39687858

Mizrak, F., Demirel, H. G., Yaşar, O., & Karakaya, T. (2025). Digital detox: Exploring the impact of cybersecurity fatigue on employee productivity and mental health. *Discover Mental Health*, *5*(1), 1–21. DOI: 10.1007/s44192-025-00149-x PMID: 39998759

Möller, D. P. (2023). Cybersecurity in digital transformation. In *Guide to cybersecurity in digital transformation: Trends, methods, technologies, applications and best practices* (pp. 1–70). Springer Nature Switzerland.

Muvva, S. (2021). Ethical AI and Responsible Data Engineering: A Framework for Bias Mitigation and Privacy Preservation in Large-Scale Data Pipelines. *International Journal of Scientific Research in Engineering and Management*, *5*(09).

National Institute of Standards and Technology. (2018). *Framework for Improving Critical Infrastructure Cybersecurity*(Version 1.1). NIST. DOI: 10.6028/NIST.CSWP.04162018

Orlando, A. (2021). Cyber risk quantification: Investigating the role of cyber value at risk. *Risks*, *9*(10), 184. DOI: 10.3390/risks9100184

Oukes, T., Beninger, S., Derks, M., & Nijhof, A. (2024). Navigating disturbances in developing countries: Resilience strategies for cross-sector partnerships. *Business Strategy & Development*, *7*(4), e70020. DOI: 10.1002/bsd2.70020

Paracha, M. A., Jamil, S. U., Shahzad, K., Khan, M. A., & Rasheed, A. (2024). Leveraging ai for network threat detection—A conceptual overview. *Electronics (Basel)*, *13*(23), 4611. DOI: 10.3390/electronics13234611

Safitra, M. F., Lubis, M., & Fakhrurroja, H. (2023). Counterattacking cyber threats: A framework for the future of cybersecurity. *Sustainability (Basel)*, *15*(18), 13369. DOI: 10.3390/su151813369

Samsung, S. D. S. (2024). *Smart manufacturing and blockchain-powered logistics solutions*. Retrieved from https://en.wikipedia.org/wiki/Samsung_SDS

Schwartz, R., Schwartz, R., Vassilev, A., Greene, K., Perine, L., Burt, A., & Hall, P. (2022). *Towards a standard for identifying and managing bias in artificial intelligence* (Vol. 3, p. 00). Gaithersburg, MD: US Department of Commerce, National Institute of Standards and Technology.

Shahidinejad, A., Ghobaei-Arani, M., Souri, A., Shojafar, M., & Kumari, S. (2021). Light-edge: A lightweight authentication protocol for IoT devices in an edge-cloud environment. *IEEE Consumer Electronics Magazine*, *11*(2), 57–63. DOI: 10.1109/MCE.2021.3053543

Singh, S., Hosen, A. S., & Yoon, B. (2021). Blockchain security attacks, challenges, and solutions for the future distributed iot network. *IEEE Access : Practical Innovations, Open Solutions*, *9*, 13938–13959. DOI: 10.1109/ACCESS.2021.3051602

Sonesson, T. R., Johansson, J., & Cedergren, A. (2021). Governance and interdependencies of critical infrastructures: Exploring mechanisms for cross-sector resilience. *Safety Science*, *142*, 105383. DOI: 10.1016/j.ssci.2021.105383

The Open Group. (2019). *FAIR Factor Analysis of Information Risk*. https://www.opengroup.org/fair

Thummala, V. R., & Bindewari, S. (2024). Optimizing Cybersecurity Practices through Compliance and Risk Assessment. *International Journal of Research Radicals in Multidisciplinary Fields, ISSN*, 910-930.

Tu, Y., Gan, J., Hu, Y., Jin, R., Yang, Z., & Liu, M. (2019, November). Decentralized identity authentication and key management scheme. In *2019 IEEE 3rd Conference on Energy Internet and Energy System Integration (EI2)* (pp. 2697-2702). IEEE. DOI: 10.1109/EI247390.2019.9062013

Waheed, N., He, X., Ikram, M., Usman, M., Hashmi, S. S., & Usman, M. (2020). Security and privacy in IoT using machine learning and blockchain: Threats and countermeasures. [csur]. *ACM Computing Surveys*, *53*(6), 1–37. DOI: 10.1145/3417987

Wikipedia. (2024). *China RealDID*. Retrieved from https://en.wikipedia.org/wiki/China_RealDID

Willie, M. M. (2023). The role of organizational culture in cybersecurity: Building a security-first culture. *Journal of Research. Innovation and Technologies*, *2*(2 (4)), 179–198.

Zaman, S., Alhazmi, K., Aseeri, M. A., Ahmed, M. R., Khan, R. T., Kaiser, M. S., & Mahmud, M. (2021). Security threats and artificial intelligence based countermeasures for internet of things networks: A comprehensive survey. *IEEE Access : Practical Innovations, Open Solutions*, *9*, 94668–94690. DOI: 10.1109/ACCESS.2021.3089681

Zighan, S. (2024, February). Navigating the cyber landscape: A framework for transitioning from business continuity to digital resilience. In *2024 2nd International Conference on Cyber Resilience (ICCR)* (pp. 01-06). IEEE. DOI: 10.1109/ICCR61006.2024.10532999

Chapter 7
Cybersecurity in Human Resource Management in the Context of Remote Work:
Policy, Practice, and Risk Management

Ümit Deniz İlhan
https://orcid.org/0000-0003-3565-0938
Beykoz University, Turkey

ABSTRACT

With the rapid advancement of digital technologies, contemporary work models have undergone a fundamental transformation, as remote and hybrid arrangements producing complex implications for organizational structures. In this shifting landscape, human resource management (HRM) has emerged as a strategic actor in safeguarding corporate information systems. The proliferation of tools such as bring-your-own-device (BYOD) policies, cloud-based infrastructures, virtual private networks (VPN), and digital surveillance platforms has required more pro-active and integrated cybersecurity strategies within HRM functions. This chapter offers a comprehensive examination of cybersecurity threats relevant to HRM in the context of remote work, emphasizing the tension between digital privacy and surveillance, the co-development of security protocols through HRM–information technology (IT) collaboration, and mechanisms to foster security-oriented employee awareness. Furthermore, the chapter offers strategies to support digital resilience and sustainability.

DOI: 10.4018/979-8-3693-6417-8.ch007

INTRODUCTION

The accelerated integration of digital technologies into organizational processes has fundamentally transformed structural dynamics, leading to the emergence of new strategic responsibilities—most notably within the domain of human resource management (HRM). The transition from conventional office-based settings to remote and hybrid work models has necessitated comprehensive adjustments not only in operational workflows but also in corporate approaches to information security (Waizenegger et al., 2020). In this evolving context, core security concerns—such as employee data protection, access governance, system integrity, and digital privacy—have increasingly shifted beyond the remit of information technology (IT) departments and become integral to the strategic functions of HRM departments (Brougham & Haar, 2018; Colbert et al., 2016).

The widespread use of personal devices in remote work settings (BYOD), alongside cloud-based applications, virtual private networks (VPN), and digital communication platforms, has significantly accelerated corporate data flows. However, these technological developments have concurrently exacerbated cybersecurity vulnerabilities, including increased exposure to cyberattacks, data breaches, and unauthorized access (Ferdousi, 2022). Within this shifting digital infrastructure, HRM departments are no longer confined to administrative functions related to data management; instead, they are progressively repositioned as critical stakeholders in the protection and governance of organizational data. The binding force of data protection frameworks—such as the General Data Protection Regulation (GDPR) and Turkey's Personal Data Protection Law (KVKK)—at both national and supranational levels has further intensified the strategic imperative for HRM. This includes the institutionalization of authority audits, access governance mechanisms, ethical surveillance protocols, and comprehensive digital privacy policies (Evren, 2023; Kaya, 2023).

However, the increasing prevalence of practices such as digital employee surveillance, algorithmic performance evaluation, and real-time monitoring of online activities has elevated ethical concerns to a level of strategic significance—coexisting and often in tension with institutional goals related to security and operational efficiency. Chief among these concerns is the right to privacy, which frequently intersects—if not collides—with organizational surveillance frameworks designed to safeguard digital assets and ensure compliance. This tension obliges HRM to develop policy architectures that do not merely conform to legal standards but are also grounded in ethical reasoning and sensitive to power asymmetries within the employment relationship (Ball, 2014). Within this evolving paradigm, the pursuit of a sustainable and ethically defensible balance between data governance and employee autonomy is increasingly conceptualized as a core dimension of corporate security culture, with long-term implications for institutional trust, legitimacy, and employee engagement (Ajunwa, 2023; Möhlmann & Zalmanson, 2017).

This chapter explores the evolving role of HRM within organizational cybersecurity policies under the conditions of remote and hybrid work, adopting a multidimensional analytical lens. It offers a theoretically informed and empirically grounded examination of critical domains including BYOD policies, access management protocols, employee monitoring systems, HRM–IT interdepartmental coordination, and the cultivation of security awareness across organizational levels. By integrating these components, the chapter seeks to articulate the strategic imperatives of HRM in shaping cyber-resilient infrastructures and advancing institutional capacity for sustainable digital work environments. In doing so, it contributes to an emerging body of research that positions HRM not only as an administrative facilitator but as a key actor in organizational digital governance and risk management frameworks.

1. REMOTE WORK AND CYBERSECURITY THREATS

1.1. BYOD Policies and Personal Device Usage

With remote work becoming a permanent work model, many organizations have implemented bring your own device (BYOD) policies that allow employees to use their personal devices within corporate systems. While these practices provide employees with flexibility and mobility, they also create new risk areas in terms of data security, access control, and system integrity for corporate information systems (Stallings & Brown, 2018). The implementation of BYOD policies may lead to various security vulnerabilities; particularly, threats such as data leakage, malware, and unauthorized access come to the forefront (see Table 1) (Tipton & Krause, 2022). The security risks increase when personal devices are connected to corporate networks, especially due to factors such as the use of unauthorized software, outdated security updates, and non-standard access protocols (Panko, 2020).

Table 1. Common security threats encountered in BYOD practices and their causes

Types of Threat	Cause
Data Leakage	Inadequate encryption or insecure storage of corporate data on personal devices.
Malware	Absence of up-to-date antivirus software and security patches on personal devices.
Unauthorized Access	Lack of centralized authorization systems or use of weak passwords on BYOD devices.

continued on following page

Table 1. Continued

Types of Threat	Cause
Phishing	Devices being compromised due to users clicking on fraudulent emails or links.
Hardware Insecurity	Use of unregistered personal devices that do not comply with corporate security standards.

Source: Synthesized from Panko, 2020; Stallings & Brown, 2018; Tipton & Krause, 2022

On devices not provided by the organization and managed directly by users, it is frequently observed that software updates are neglected, antivirus protection is insufficient, and data encryption is lacking (Zetter, 2015). These conditions increase the risk of malware infiltrating systems, facilitate the execution of ransomware attacks, and make data breaches more likely. Furthermore, the use of the same device for both personal and professional purposes complicates the technical separation between work and private life, thereby making data classification and control processes more complex (Furnell & Clarke, 2012).

BYOD practices are not solely shaped by technical infrastructure; they also represent a multilayered structure influenced by organizational governance, interdepartmental coordination, and employee behavior. In the evaluation of such practices, hardware-based precautions must be considered alongside policy design, user guidance, and process-based control mechanisms (Downer & Bhattacharya, 2022). The literature emphasizes that BYOD policies should not be handled solely by information technology departments; rather, they must be addressed through an integrated approach involving HRM, legal departments, and broader governance structures (Doargajudhur & Dell, 2018).

The roles assumed by HRM and IT departments in these systems are decisive for the transparency of data flow within the organization, the functioning of authorization processes, and the standardization of user-level practices (Lam et al, 2024). In this context, the way BYOD policies are implemented and communicated directly affects employees' perceptions of corporate security norms, their level of organizational commitment, and their individual usage behaviors (Alkhazi et al., 2022).

1.2. VPN, Cloud-Based Systems, and Access Protocols

With the widespread adoption of remote work, organizations have begun integrating various technological solutions into their business processes to ensure secure employee access to corporate systems. Among these, one of the most commonly used technologies is the virtual private network (VPN) (Mandadi et al., 2024). VPN infrastructures allow employees to securely access corporate resources regardless of their physical location. However, the growing use of VPNs has also introduced new security challenges, such as increased data traffic, a higher number of connection points, and an expanded surface vulnerable to cyberattacks (Thabit et al., 2021).

Cloud-based systems used in conjunction with VPNs have emerged as platforms that facilitate remote access, enable location-independent data retrieval, and support multi-user infrastructures. Among the primary tools utilized by HRM departments during the digital transformation process are cloud-based solutions such as online recruitment systems, performance management dashboards, and digital payroll platforms (Marin et al., 2022). However, the operation of these platforms through third-party service providers extends data security concerns beyond internal measures, necessitating a broader security perspective that also accounts for supply chain risks (Destriani et al., 2024).

Access control models that define which users can access what resources, when, and to what extent are foundational to risk mitigation policies in corporate data security. Among the most widely used approaches are Role-Based Access Control (RBAC), Task-Based Access Control (TBAC), the Least Privilege Principle (LPP), and Multi-Factor Authentication (MFA) (see Table 1). Access protocols, which determine the scope, depth, and duration of users' access to digital systems, play a critical role in the context of remote work. Approaches such as RBAC, the LPP, and MFA are considered vital in preventing unauthorized access and preserving data integrity (Aluvalu & Muddana, 2015). Structuring access protocols in a manner that is responsive to user behavior ensures that systems are accessible not only to authenticated individuals but also specifically to those with role-based authorization. In this regard, access policies must align not only with technical architecture but also with the organization's internal workflow processes (Sha et al., 2020).

Table 2. Definitions, advantages, and limitations of access control models

Model	Definition	Advantages
Role-Based Access Control (RBAC)	Users are granted access permissions based on predefined roles.	Easy to manage; access is granted according to user roles.
Task-Based Access Control (TBAC)	Users are granted access based on the tasks they perform.	Provides controlled task-specific access; dynamic in structure.
Least Privilege Principle (LPP)	Users are granted only the minimum access required to perform their tasks.	Reduces privilege misuse and data leakage.
Multi-Factor Authentication (MFA)	The authentication process is strengthened by using multiple verification factors.	Offers strong protection against identity fraud.

Source: Synthesized from Aluvalu & Muddana, 2015; Sha et al., 2020

In parallel, the literature frequently emphasizes that integration between different systems can create security vulnerabilities (Zissis & Lekkas, 2012). Especially during transitions between cloud systems and in-house data centers, discrepancies in encryption levels, inconsistencies in authentication methods, or the lack of centralized log management are regarded as factors that can compromise the overall security of the system (Dawood et al., 2023).

1.3. Data Security in Hybrid Network Structures

With the widespread adoption of hybrid work models at the organizational level, hybrid network structures—enabling access from both office environments and external networks within the same organization—have come to the forefront. Although such network environments increase flexibility and support business continuity, they present a more complex threat profile compared to traditional centralized network architectures in terms of data security (Kitsiou et al., 2025). In particular, data traffic flowing through multiple access points, device types, and connection protocols necessitates the comprehensive reconfiguration of institutional control mechanisms in a multilayered manner (Zhao & Song, 2022).

Among the main elements that pose security threats in hybrid network environments are the sharing of data over the same network by both corporate and personal devices, simultaneous access from different physical locations, and the combined use of wired and wireless connection types (Badawy et al., 2024). These factors highlight the insufficiency of traditional network security policies; consequently, necessitating an integrated evaluation of technical solutions such as network segmentation, traffic encryption, endpoint protection, and anomaly detection (Lekkala & Gurijala, 2024)

Network segmentation is considered an effective method for limiting the lateral spread of security threats by ensuring isolation between systems. Different segmentation strategies vary both technically and administratively depending on the organizational structure (see Table 3). Another important element in the context of network security is the principle of end-to-end transparency and traceability. Since connections in hybrid systems are not established from a fixed center but from various access points, centrally tracking user identities and access levels, and maintaining comprehensive log records, stand out as fundamental security practices (Ko et al., 2011). Furthermore, when individuals operate across multiple systems and platforms simultaneously—connecting to various cloud services or Software-as-a-Service (SaaS) solutions—it creates an environment in which vulnerabilities may stem not only from within the organization but also from the service providers themselves (Abdulsalam & Hedabou, 2022).

Table 3. Network segmentation strategies and implementation examples

Strategy	Definition	Implementation Example
Physical Segmentation	Separation of the network using physically distinct hardware infrastructures (e.g., separate switches, routers).	Locating financial and human resources systems on separate physical servers.
Logical (VLAN) Segmentation	Creation of logically isolated traffic zones using VLANs.	Assigning accounting and marketing departments to different VLAN IDs.
Application-Based Segmentation	Running specific applications in isolated network zones, separate from other systems.	Restricting CRM application access to a specific IP range only.
Role-Based User Segmentation	Restricting network access based on the user's role within the organization.	IT personnel have full access to all systems, while other employees access only certain services.

Source: Synthesized from Kitsiou et al., 2025; Ko et al., 2011

The literature also emphasizes that internal segmentation within hybrid network architectures directly affects the overall level of security. Specifically, the placement of critical systems within isolated network zones, task-based segregation of access permissions, and the configuration of data traffic in a traceable manner are cited as key factors in limiting the spread of attacks (Sha et al., 2020). In this regard, hybrid network environments are considered structures that require not only technological but also managerial and behavioral dimensions of a multidimensional organizational security approach (Aboobaker & Shanujas, 2025).

2. EMPLOYEE MONITORING SYSTEMS AND THE PRIVACY BALANCE

2.1. Digital Surveillance Applications

As remote and hybrid work arrangements have become firmly embedded in organizational practice, the monitoring of employee activities beyond traditional office settings has emerged as a strategic priority—driven by both operational oversight and cybersecurity imperatives (Ball, 2022). In this context, digital surveillance applications have been developed to record employees' online presence, software and system usage durations, data access behaviors, and overall activity levels through dedicated systems (Andrejevic, 2025). These technologies are used not only for workflow monitoring but also for security-oriented purposes such as detecting unauthorized access, monitoring data leaks, and identifying abnormal activity patterns at an early stage (Ajunwa, 2023).

Digital surveillance systems encompass a wide range of technological solutions. For example, tools such as screen capture software, keyboard and mouse activity trackers, browser history logs, behavior modeling based on application usage frequency, and monitoring of microphone and camera activity enable surveillance at varying levels (Ozobu et al., 2025; Tomlinson & Schnackenberg, 2022). Additionally, they directly and indirectly construct a digitized profile of employee activities, allowing employers to systematically analyze indicators such as productivity, task duration, and workload (Olsen, 2019).

Although such applications offer institutional benefits on a technical level, the HRM literature increasingly examines the psychological and experiential effects of digital surveillance on individual employees (Andrejevic, 2025). It has been noted that constant monitoring creates a "visibility pressure" on employees, which may lead to behavioral distortions that focus not on performance but on appearing visible (West & Bowman, 2016). Moreover, feeling continuously monitored has been found to negatively affect employees' sense of autonomy, trust, and perception of privacy (Ajunwa, 2023; Bennett & Raab, 2020).

The scope and intensity of digital surveillance technologies vary depending on industry, organizational size, and cultural norms (Graham & Wood, 2017). Surveillance systems are more extensively implemented in sectors that require high levels of oversight, such as finance, customer service, and data security; in contrast, these systems tend to be applied more sparingly in creative or knowledge-based work environments (Westerlund et al., 2021). Nevertheless, it is emphasized that digital surveillance is not solely a technical matter but also a subject of normative regulation, being restricted through data protection laws, employee contracts, and internal organizational policies (Bennett & Raab, 2020; Ball, 2022).

2.2. Data-Driven Performance Monitoring

In remote and digital work environments, performance metrics are increasingly being structured based on digital data rather than physical observation to evaluate employee productivity (Majam & Jarbandhan, 2022). Accordingly, performance monitoring systems have been developed to generate data based on measurable indicators such as employee login and logout times, document production, email response times, software usage rates, and project-based completion speed (Ball, 2010). The analysis of such data enables the quantification of employee activity, serving as a decision-support tool for managers, while also being used to assess the alignment between corporate objectives and individual outcomes (Andrejevic, 2025).

Among the most commonly used tools in data-driven performance monitoring are task management systems (e.g., Trello, Asana), time-tracking applications (e.g., RescueTime), and surveillance software that offers screen recording or application analytics (e.g., Hubstaff, ActivTrak, Teramind). Through these tools, detailed datasets can be generated at the level of individual employees—such as how long they use specific platforms, when particular files are produced, and the temporal distribution of these interactions (Ozobu et al., 2025). When these structures are supported by algorithms, predictive modeling of employee behavior can also be carried out (Kitsiou et al., 2025).

Although the use of digital performance data offers advantages in providing objectivity and measurability in organizational decision-making processes, it may also result in various negative psychological and behavioral consequences for employees. The literature notes that when employees are aware they are being constantly measured, they may engage in strategic manipulation of their work processes—for instance, interacting with software unnecessarily to appear productive (Hanandeh, 2025). Moreover, it is stated that performance systems based on numerical data may not always accurately reflect the quality of individual contributions, particularly in roles requiring creativity, cognitive effort, or collaborative output (Stankeviciute, 2024).

Algorithmic decision-making processes also play a determining role in the functioning of data-driven evaluation systems. Examples such as automatically classifying employees with performance metrics below certain threshold values as low performers, or labeling them as "unproductive" by the system, have sparked discussions around principles such as transparency, accountability, and ethical responsibility in employment relationships (Binns et al., 2018). Furthermore, questions regarding the criteria on which such systems collect data, which behaviors are considered indicators of productivity, and how this data is interpreted are viewed as issues that human resource management must address at both technical and normative levels (Ball, 2022).

2.3. Employee Privacy, Ethical Boundaries, and Legal Framework

The widespread use of digital surveillance technologies has necessitated a renewed discussion on the boundaries between employee privacy and institutional security policies. Particularly in remote and hybrid work environments, surveillance practices conducted outside the physical office directly interact with employees' perception of private space (Ball, 2010; Ajunwa, 2023). Such an interaction raises multidimensional questions such as what constitutes the scope of the workplace, which types of data may be monitored by the organization, and for what purposes this data may be used (Bennett & Raab, 2020). The literature emphasizes the importance of defining these boundaries in a way that does not violate the balance between organizational authority and individual rights (Andrejevic, 2025).

One of the central areas of debate regarding employee privacy revolves around the concepts of consent and informed authorization. The monitoring of employees who are unaware of the presence of surveillance systems or who do not know what types of data are being collected poses significant ethical concerns (Ball, 2022). Furthermore, even when employees have formally given consent to such systems, questions arise about whether this consent is truly based on free will (Jeske & Santuzzi, 2015). Particularly within the hierarchical structure of the employer–employee relationship, the validity of the concept of "consent" remains a continuous point of debate (Gao et al., 2024).

In defining ethical boundaries, not only individual and organizational values but also sectoral norms and cultural context play a decisive role. Privacy, in particular, is recognized as a sociotechnical concept—referring not only to the right to protect one's physical or digital presence but also to the societal agreements that shape how this presence may be accessed or interfered with (Andrew & Baker, 2021; Wang et al., 2023). Therefore, for surveillance systems to be ethically legitimate, compliance with legal regulations alone is not sufficient; they must also align with the principles of transparency, necessity, proportionality, and auditability (Jeske & Santuzzi, 2015; Ozobu et al., 2025).

From a legal standpoint, digital surveillance practices are directly linked to data protection legislation in many countries. Regulations such as the European Union's General Data Protection Regulation (GDPR), Turkey's Law on the Protection of Personal Data (KVKK), and the California Consumer Privacy Act (CCPA) in the United States are grounded in fundamental principles including explicit consent, data minimization, purpose limitation, and the right to erasure (Bennett & Raab, 2020; Wright & Kreissl, 2014). These legal frameworks place human resources departments within an integrated domain of operational, legal, and ethical responsibility (Andrejevic, 2025).

3. HRM-IT COLLABORATION AND POLICY DEVELOPMENT

3.1. The Role of HRM in Institutional Cybersecurity Protocols

While cybersecurity is typically considered an activity focused on protecting technical infrastructure, it is increasingly evaluated as a multilayered process that is directly related to corporate governance, employee behavior, and organizational culture. In this context, HRM departments assume roles that are not technical but strategic in ensuring cybersecurity within increasingly digitalized work environments (Jeske & Santuzzi, 2015; Sha et al., 2020). Especially in remote work models, how employees access systems, interact with digital platforms, and engage with data directly intersects with HRM processes. This intersection positions HRM as a natural stakeholder in cybersecurity governance (Ajunwa, 2023).

The role of HRM departments in institutional cybersecurity protocols is generally addressed under three main areas: policy development, behavioral compliance monitoring, and internal organizational integration. Within the scope of policy development, HR contributes to the preparation of documents that define employees' responsibilities regarding data usage—such as confidentiality agreements, system access guidelines, remote work protocols, and digital device usage policies (Bennett & Raab, 2020). These documents serve as essential tools for both legal compliance and the construction of a security culture. HRM's influence on these documents is critical for aligning internal communication with the language of security and for fostering shared security norms among employees (Liorens, 2023)

On the other hand, the collaboration between HRM and IT departments extends beyond document production to operational domains such as monitoring employee behavior, auditing systemic compliance, and overseeing assignments in high-risk positions (Nica et al., 2024). Especially in detecting potential data leaks, unauthorized access attempts, or possible security violations at an early stage, the involvement of HR professionals—who understand the organizational context—is just as important as technical tools. Therefore, HRM not only defines security policies but also assumes the role of ensuring their alignment across the organization and acts as a bridge between employees and technical systems (Manoharan, 2024; Ozobu et al., 2025).

3.2. Proactive Risk Management: Access, Permission, and Authorization Control

In sustaining corporate cybersecurity, a proactive risk management approach is based on anticipating potential threats before they occur and taking preventive action (Sha et al., 2020). This approach is manifested particularly through practices such as regulating how employees access systems, limiting their interactions with data, and aligning authorization levels with job descriptions (Calvard & Jeske, 2018). In remote and hybrid work environments, the diversification of access points, the use of multiple devices connecting to the same systems, and the physical detachment of users from the organizational setting have made these types of risks more apparent (Kitsiou et al., 2025).

Access management systems constitute the institutional infrastructure that determines which user can access which data, when, and under what conditions. Among the most commonly used models in these systems are role-based access control (RBAC), task-based access control (TBAC), and the principle of least privilege (Muppalaneni et al., 2025). In the RBAC model, employees are assigned to specific roles and granted access only to resources related to those roles; in contrast, the least privilege principle ensures that users are granted access only to the systems necessary for them to perform their tasks. The implementation of such structures significantly reduces the risk of data breaches and misuse, especially in large-scale organizations (Hajnić & Boshkoska, 2022).

Moreover, in the functioning of authorization control processes, HRM stands out as a department that contributes substantially to the technical dimension of the system. Job descriptions defined at the time of recruitment are considered fundamental data for determining the boundaries of access permissions; when there is a change in role or position, the automatic updating of authorization levels is considered critical for the effectiveness of the system (Ozobu et al., 2025). The literature indicates that the digitization of workflow diagrams produced by HRM departments in coordination with IT departments ensures coherence in access management and reduces the need for manual intervention (Sha et al., 2020).

Additionally, the use of audit trails, the logging of access behaviors, and the analytical monitoring of abnormal access patterns are complementary practices that support risk management in authorization control systems. These monitoring mechanisms are emphasized as being functional not only in terms of security but also for institutional accountability and regulatory compliance (Bennett & Raab, 2020). In particular, under data protection regimes such as the GDPR and KVKK, the regular maintenance of access logs and the ability to trace activities retrospectively have become explicit legal requirements (Andrejevic, 2025; Ko et al., 2011).

3.3. HRM–IT Integration: Sustainable Security Approaches

The sustainable implementation of cybersecurity within organizational structures depends not only on the strengthening of technical systems but also on the holistic configuration of organizational processes and collaboration among institutional actors. In this regard, establishing structural integration between HRM and IT departments enhances the applicability of security policies and facilitates a more manageable relationship between employee behavior and system security (Mızrak, 2024). The literature views HRM–IT integration as critical not only at the level of information sharing but also in terms of joint decision-making mechanisms, coordinated protocol development, and the continuity of organizational security awareness (Makedon et al., 2019).

One of the most important conditions for institutionalizing this type of integration is embedding data-driven security practices into HRM processes. For example, digital commitments during the recruitment phase, data security modules used in training, and compliance indicators embedded in performance evaluation systems enable the procedural framework of HRM to be directly aligned with the security practices of IT (Badawy et al., 2024; Sha et al., 2020). These structures contribute to embedding both operational workflows and the organization's holistic risk perception at the employee level (Kioskli et al., 2025).

The integration process often faces challenges due to differences in language, priorities, and performance metrics between HRM and IT departments. While IT departments generally operate with technical priorities related to system security, HRM departments tend to focus on more normative areas such as employee satisfaction, compliance, and workplace ethics (Roul et al., 2024). This divergence can lead to resistance from employees toward security practices or hinder their internalization. For this reason, the literature emphasizes that integration processes should be evaluated not only in structural terms but also under the theme of cultural alignment (Bennett & Raab, 2020).

From the perspective of a sustainable security approach, HRM–IT collaboration is defined not merely as a reactive response during crises but as a continuous, preventive, and improvement-oriented structure (Roul et al., 2024). Regularly updated protocols, jointly conducted risk analyses, and organization-wide security training programs are mechanisms that institutionalize this collaboration at the level of practical implementation (Ko et al., 2011).

4. EDUCATION, AWARENESS, AND BUILDING A SECURITY CULTURE

4.1. Employee Training and Awareness Programs

The effectiveness of corporate cybersecurity systems depends not only on the quality of technical infrastructure but also on the knowledge, awareness, and behavioral competence of the employees who use these systems (Hu et al., 2022). Especially in remote and hybrid work environments, where individuals interact with systems independently of centralized supervision, the internalization of secure behaviors has become increasingly critical (Sha et al., 2020). In this context, cybersecurity training and awareness programs for employees are regarded as strategic priority initiatives that fall under the shared responsibility of HRM and IT departments (Andrejevic, 2025; Badawy et al., 2024).

It is important that training programs go beyond technical instruction to develop decision-making skills, risk perception, and personal accountability. The literature highlights that case-based content, in particular, enhances employees' capacity to recognize suspicious situations and respond promptly (Ozobu et al., 2025). The use of pedagogically supportive methods such as gamification, simulation, and interactive modules is cited among the factors that increase learning retention Hu et al., 2022).

On the other hand, the effectiveness of training increases when programs are designed not in a generalized manner, but rather based on specific tasks and tailored to risk profiles. For example, it is noted that specialized content for IT personnel should differ in structure from modules provided to general office staff (Hwang et al., 2021). Such differentiation ensures that employees not only gain relevant knowledge but also understand how to behave in accordance with the nature of their roles (Jeske & Santuzzi, 2015).

The sustainability of organizational awareness initiatives is also a critical concern. Limiting training to the onboarding process reduces its long-term impact; therefore, annual refresher sessions, microlearning content, and updates based on internal audit feedback are recommended (Bennett & Raab, 2020). Furthermore, training should be approached not as a calendar-based obligation, but as a continuous process aimed at behavioral transformation (Ko et al., 2011).

In this regard, the success of training programs is closely tied not only to the quality of the content but also to how they are perceived within the organization. Programs that are visibly supported by top management and modeled by supervisors tend to have a more lasting impact on employees (Ajunwa, 2023). When HRM departments position such programs not merely as procedural requirements but as strategic components of shaping a security culture, their institutional impact is significantly enhanced (Jeske & Santuzzi, 2015).

4.2. Organizational Resilience Against Social Engineering

Social engineering refers to types of attacks that target not the technological systems themselves, but rather the vulnerabilities of individuals who use these systems (Hadnagy, 2018). These attacks are commonly carried out through methods such as phishing emails, fake call centers, impersonated technical support scenarios, or physical intrusion attempts, often bypassing technical safeguards to exploit human behavior (Siddiqi et al., 2022). Due to factors such as the absence of an embedded security culture within the organization, weak password policies, insufficient skepticism, and a lack of questioning reflexes, the success rate of such attacks can be quite high (Andrejevic, 2025).

Organizational resilience against social engineering depends not only on individual awareness but also on designing institutional structures in accordance with behavioral security principles. In this context, employees are expected to question data requests even when they appear ordinary, develop reflexes against non-standard communication channels, and recognize unusual behavioral patterns (Agozie et al., 2022). The literature emphasizes that organization-specific attack scenarios, interactive case-based training, and simulation techniques strengthen employees' defensive reflexes and reduce response times in the face of such threats (Jeske & Santuzzi, 2015; Ozobu et al., 2025).

In addition to individual training, restructuring organizational procedures is also essential for enhancing resilience against social engineering threats. For instance, standardizing multi-factor authentication in identity verification processes, linking even internal requests to defined protocols, and managing data access through permission-based systems are structural measures that effectively limit social engineering risks (Sha et al., 2020). Moreover, recognizing these threats not only within IT departments but also within HRM, and incorporating them into policy documents, helps expand the perspective on this issue beyond purely technical boundaries (Saeed et al., 2023).

5. DISCUSSION AND CONCLUSION

This chapter has examined the evolving role of human resource management (HRM) within the context of cybersecurity in increasingly digital work environments from a multidimensional perspective. In particular, the widespread adoption of remote and hybrid work models has made it necessary to rethink not only technical security measures but also human-centered security policies. Security vulnerabilities arising from BYOD policies, cloud systems, VPN access, and hybrid network structures have emerged as areas that require the active involvement of not only IT departments but also HRM departments at the institutional level. As seen in the example of BYOD, coordination between HRM and IT departments in areas ranging from device management to access control is considered a critical factor in ensuring data security (see Table 1).

Employees' interactions with digital systems and their access to multi-source network infrastructures from outside the organization necessitate a dynamic and risk-oriented approach to access management. In this context, access protocol models such as RBAC, TBAC, Least Privilege, and MFA have been comparatively evaluated, with each model's strengths and limitations analyzed at both technical and managerial levels (see Table 2). The functionality of these models depends not only on the security level of the system in which they are implemented but also on how well they are aligned with job definitions, task-based authorizations, and principles of organizational transparency. Similarly, system-level structuring strategies such as network segmentation are also categorized as tools that reinforce the technical architecture of cybersecurity (see Table 3).

Accordingly, it has been observed that cybersecurity policies extend beyond system access and are integrated with mechanisms that monitor employee behavior and measure performance through digital data. While digital surveillance applications and data-driven performance tracking systems offer operational benefits for organizations, they are also deeply intertwined with human factors such as privacy, ethical boundaries, and employee psychology. The various applications of surveillance technologies present a risk of these systems being perceived not as security tools but as instruments of behavioral control—thus increasing HRM's responsibility to guide security policies in a more inclusive, transparent, and balanced manner.

The sustainability of all these processes depends largely on positioning the collaboration between HRM and IT departments within a strategic governance model. This collaboration must encompass not only the coordination of technical processes but also the alignment of organizational behaviors with security principles. Embedding security policies into the organizational culture—beyond the operational level—requires HRM departments to act as strategic agents in building institutional resilience. Approaching training policies from a lifecycle perspective, strengthening organizational resilience against social engineering threats, and supporting ethical compliance through communication-centered approaches are among the key priorities that must be addressed within HRM's strategic management function.

In conclusion, the relationship established between HRM and cybersecurity strategies in the context of remote work presents a multilayered security approach aimed at reducing organizational vulnerabilities. This approach concerns both the management of individual risks and the structuring of the institution's overall risk perception. Addressing corporate security culture through a strategic management lens necessitates that data protection policies go beyond technical regulations to include behavioral and managerial dimensions. Placing HRM at the center of this structure makes it possible to design security processes that are human-centered, sustainable, and integrated into institutional governance. In this framework, HRM becomes a core management function within contemporary organizations that recognize cybersecurity not merely as a technical issue, but as a strategic approach.

REFERENCES

Abdulsalam, Y. S., & Hedabou, M. (2022). Security and privacy in cloud computing: Technical review. *Future Internet, 14*(1), 11. DOI: 10.3390/fi14010011

Aboobaker, N., & Shanujas, V. (2025). Towards a sustainable workplace: Investigating workplace cyberbullying and its relationship with employee wellbeing and intention to stay in remote and hybrid work settings. *International Journal of Productivity and Performance Management, 74*(2), 453–470. DOI: 10.1108/IJPPM-12-2023-0662

Agozie, D. Q., Edu, A. S., & Nat, M. (2022). Toward building organizational resilience to social engineering among higher educational institution professionals. In *Delivering distinctive value in emerging economies* (pp. 347–367). Productivity Press. DOI: 10.4324/9781003152217-29

Ajunwa, I. (2023). *The quantified worker*. Cambridge University Press. DOI: 10.1017/9781316888681

Alkhazi, B., Alshaikh, M., Alkhezi, S., & Labbaci, H. (2022). Assessment of the impact of information security awareness training methods on knowledge, attitude, and behavior. *IEEE Access: Practical Innovations, Open Solutions, 10*, 132132–132143. DOI: 10.1109/ACCESS.2022.3230286

Aluvalu, R., & Muddana, L. (2015). A survey on access control models in cloud computing. In S. Satapathy, A. Govardhan, K. Raju, & J. Mandal (Eds.), Emerging ICT for bridging the future – Proceedings of the 49th Annual Convention of the Computer Society of India (CSI) Volume 1 (Vol. 337, pp. 611–619). Springer. DOI: 10.1007/978-3-319-13728-5_73

Andrejevic, M. (2025). Labor and surveillance: The productivity of being watched. In *The handbook of digital labor* (pp. 119–131). Cambridge University Press. DOI: 10.1002/9781119981831.ch7

Andrew, J., & Baker, M. (2021). The general data protection regulation in the age of surveillance capitalism. *Journal of Business Ethics, 168*(3), 565–578. DOI: 10.1007/s10551-019-04239-z

Badawy, M., Sherief, N. H., & Abdel-Hamid, A. A. (2024). Legacy ICS cybersecurity assessment using hybrid threat modeling—An oil and gas sector case study. *Applied Sciences (Basel, Switzerland), 14*(18), 8398. DOI: 10.3390/app14188398

Ball, K. (2010). Workplace surveillance: An overview. *Labor History, 51*(1), 87–106. DOI: 10.1080/00236561003654776

Ball, K. (2014). Electronic surveillance at work: An ethical analysis. *Public Administration Review, 74*(3), 348–359.

Ball, K. (2022). Surveillance in the workplace: Past, present, and future. *Surveillance & Society, 20*(4), 455–461. DOI: 10.24908/ss.v20i4.15805

Bennett, C. J., & Raab, C. D. (2020). *The governance of privacy: Policy instruments in global perspective* (3rd ed.). MIT Press.

Bernstein, E., Shore, J., & Lazer, D. (2022). How intermittent breaks improve productivity. *Harvard Business Review, 100*(1), 94–101.

Binns, R., Veale, M., Van Kleek, M., & Shadbolt, N. (2018). "It's reducing a human being to a percentage": Perceptions of justice in algorithmic decisions. In Proceedings of the 2018 CHI Conference on Human Factors in Computing Systems (pp. 1–14). ACM. DOI: 10.1145/3173574.3173951

Brougham, D., & Haar, J. (2018). Smart technology, artificial intelligence, robotics, and algorithms (STARA): Employees' perceptions of future workplaces. *Journal of Management & Organization, 24*(2), 239–257. DOI: 10.1017/jmo.2016.55

Calvard, T. S., & Jeske, D. (2018). Developing human resource data risk management in the age of big data. *International Journal of Information Management, 43*, 159–164. DOI: 10.1016/j.ijinfomgt.2018.07.011

Colbert, A., Yee, N., & George, G. (2016). The digital workforce and the workplace of the future. *Academy of Management Journal, 59*(3), 731–739. DOI: 10.5465/amj.2016.4003

Dawood, M., Tu, S., Xiao, C., Alasmary, H., Waqas, M., & Rehman, S. U. (2023). Cyberattacks and security of cloud computing: A complete guideline. *Symmetry, 15*(11), 1981. DOI: 10.3390/sym15111981

Destriani, R., Adhitama, R. Y., Sensuse, D. I., Hidayat, D. S., & Purwaningsih, E. H. (2024). Challenges and technology trends in implementing a human resource management system: A systematic literature review. *Journal of Information Systems Engineering and Business Intelligence, 10*(3), 355–367. DOI: 10.20473/jisebi.10.3.355-367

Doargajudhur, M. S., & Dell, P. (2018). The effect of bring your own device (BYOD) adoption on work performance and motivation. *Journal of Computer Information Systems, 60*(6), 518–529. DOI: 10.1080/08874417.2018.1543001

Downer, K., & Bhattacharya, M. (2022). BYOD security: A study of human dimensions. *Informatics (MDPI), 9*(1), 16. DOI: 10.3390/informatics9010016

Evren, A. G. (2023). Comparative analysis of the European Union and Turkish personal data protection laws: Basic principles, legal grounds, and rights of data subjects. *Kişisel Verileri Koruma Dergisi*, *5*(2), 39–64.

Ferdousi, B. J. (2022). Cyber security risks of bring your own device (BYOD) practice in workplace and strategies to address the risks. *International Journal of Science Academic Research*, *3*(10), 4554–4558.

Furnell, S., & Clarke, N. (2012). Power to the people? The evolving recognition of human aspects of security. *Computers & Security*, *31*(8), 983–988. DOI: 10.1016/j.cose.2012.08.004

Gao, S., Jia, Y., Liu, B., & Mu, W. (2024). Algorithmic monitoring increases unethical behavior in gig workers: The mediating role of moral disengagement. *Information Technology & People*. Advance online publication. DOI: 10.1108/ITP-07-2023-0693

Graham, S., & Wood, D. (2017). Digitizing surveillance: Categorization, space, inequality. In *Surveillance, crime and social control* (pp. 537–558). Routledge. DOI: 10.4324/9781315242002-25

Hadnagy, C. (2018). *Social engineering: The science of human hacking* (2nd ed.). Wiley. DOI: 10.1002/9781119433729

Hajnić, M., & Boshkoska, B. M. (2022). Integration of the decision support system with the human resources management and identity and access management systems in an enterprise. In *Rational decisions in organisations* (pp. 203–222). Auerbach Publications. DOI: 10.1201/9781003030966-15

Hanandeh, R., Alkhazali, Z., Alhyasat, K. M., Mistarihi, A. M., & Kilani, Q. A. (2025). The impact of data-driven decision-making, real-time analytics, and ethical data practices on HR performance and employee satisfaction

Hu, S., Hsu, C., & Zhou, Z. (2022). Security education, training, and awareness programs: Literature review. *Journal of Computer Information Systems*, *62*(4), 752–764. DOI: 10.1080/08874417.2021.1913671

Hwang, I., Wakefield, R., Kim, S., & Kim, T. (2021). Security awareness: The first step in information security compliance behavior. *Journal of Computer Information Systems*, *61*(4), 345–356. DOI: 10.1080/08874417.2019.1650676

Jeske, D., & Santuzzi, A. M. (2015). Monitoring what and how: Psychological implications of electronic performance monitoring. *New Technology, Work and Employment*, *30*(1), 62–78. DOI: 10.1111/ntwe.12039

Kaya, M. (2023). ISO 27001, KVKK, and GDPR: A comparison of information security standards and regulations. *Journal of Emerging Technologies*, *5*(1), 15–30.

Kioskli, K., Seralidou, E., & Polemi, N. (2025). A practical human-centric risk management (HRM) methodology. *Electronics (Basel)*, *14*(3), 486. DOI: 10.3390/electronics14030486

Kitsiou, A., Pantelelis, M., Mazarakis, P.-A., Mavroeidi, A.-G., Simou, S., Tzortzaki, E., Stavridis, S., Koutzamanis, G., & Kalloniatis, C. (2025). Self-adaptive privacy in cloud computing environments: Developing an integrated framework and a beta tool for social media platforms. *Electronics (Basel)*, *14*(7), 1412. DOI: 10.3390/electronics14071412

Ko, R. K. L., Lee, B. S., & Pearson, S. (2011). Towards achieving accountability, auditability and trust in cloud computing. In Hemanth, D. J., Guru, D. S., & Mohapatra, D. P. (Eds.), *Advances in computing and communications* (Vol. 193, pp. 432–444). Springer., DOI: 10.1007/978-3-642-22726-4_45

Lam, H., Beckman, T., Harcourt, M., & Shanmugam, S. (2024). Bring your own device (BYOD): Organizational control and justice perspectives. *Employee Responsibilities and Rights Journal*, •••, 1–19. DOI: 10.1007/s10672-024-09498-1

Lekkala, S., & Gurijala, P. (2024). *Security and privacy for modern networks: Strategies and insights for safeguarding digital infrastructures*. Springer., DOI: 10.1007/979-8-8688-0823-4

Llorens, J. J. (2023). The role of human resource management in cybersecurity. In *Public personnel management* (pp. 175–184). Routledge. DOI: 10.4324/9781003403401-13

Majam, T., & Jarbandhan, D. B. (2022). Data-driven human resource management in the Fourth Industrial Revolution (4IR). *Africa's Public Service Delivery and Performance Review*, *10*(1), 588. DOI: 10.4102/apsdpr.v10i1.588

Makedon, V., Hetman, O., Yemchuk, L., Paranytsia, N., & Petrovska, S. (2019). Human resource management for secure and sustainable development. *Journal of Security & Sustainability Issues*, *8*(3), 345–354. DOI: 10.9770/jssi.2019.8.3(5)

Mandadi, S., Gochhayat, S. P., Torremocha, V., & Kethar, J. (2024). Cybersecurity risks in remote work and learning environments and methods of combating them. *Journal of Student Research*, *13*(2). Advance online publication. DOI: 10.47611/jsrhs.v13i2.6808

Manoharan, P. (2024). A review on cybersecurity in HR systems: Protecting employee data in the age of AI. *Regul. GDPR*, *4*, 605–612. DOI: 10.48175/IJARSCT-18492

Maqueira Marín, J. M., Oliveira-Dias, D. D., Jafari Navimipour, N., Gardas, B., & Unal, M. (2022). Cloud computing and human resource management: Systematic literature review and future research agenda. *Kybernetes*, *51*(6), 2172–2191. DOI: 10.1108/K-05-2021-0420

Mızrak, F. (2024). Enhancing cybersecurity risk management through conceptual analysis of HRM integration. *Yönetim Bilimleri Dergisi*, *22*(51), 96–118. DOI: 10.35408/comuybd.1342408

Möhlmann, M., & Zalmanson, L. (2017). Hands on the wheel: Navigating algorithmic management and Uber drivers' autonomy. *Journal of Business Ethics*, *152*(1), 1–16. DOI: 10.1007/s10551-019-04204-w

Muppalaneni, R., Inaganti, A. C., Ravichandran, N., & Nersu, S. R. K. (2025). AI-powered role-based access control (RBAC): Automating policy enforcement in enterprise environments. *Journal of Advanced Computing Systems*, *5*(2), 1–12.

Nica, E., Burcea, . G., & Sabie, O. M. (2024). The critical role of human resources in mitigating and managing cybersecurity risks in modern organizations: A strategic approach. *Psychosociological Issues in Human Resource Management*, *12*(2).

Olsen, M. (2019). Using data analytics in the management of employees: Digital means of tracking, monitoring, and surveilling worker activities. *Psychosociological Issues in Human Resource Management*, *7*(2), 43–48. DOI: 10.22381/PIHRM7220197

Ozobu, C. O., Adikwu, F. E., Cynthia, O. O., Onyeke, F. O., & Nwulu, E. O. (2025). Developing an AI-powered occupational health surveillance system for real-time detection and management of workplace health hazards. *World Journal of Innovation and Modern Technology*, *9*(1), 156–185.

Panko, R. R. (2020). *Corporate computer and network security*. Pearson Education.

Roul, J., Mohapatra, L. M., Pradhan, A. K., & Kamesh, A. V. S. (2024). Analysing the role of modern information technologies in HRM: Management perspective and future agenda. *Kybernetes*. Advance online publication. DOI: 10.1108/K-11-2023-2512

Saeed, S., Suayyid, S. A., Al-Ghamdi, M. S., Al-Muhaisen, H., & Almuhaideb, A. M. (2023). A systematic literature review on cyber threat intelligence for organizational cybersecurity resilience. *Sensors (Basel)*, *23*(16), 7273. DOI: 10.3390/s23167273 PMID: 37631808

Sha, K., Yang, T. A., Wei, W., & Davari, S. (2020). A survey of edge computing-based designs for IoT security. *Digital Communications and Networks*, *6*(2), 195–202. DOI: 10.1016/j.dcan.2019.08.006

Siddiqi, M. A., Pak, W., & Siddiqi, M. A. (2022). A study on the psychology of social engineering-based cyberattacks and existing countermeasures. *Applied Sciences (Basel, Switzerland), 12*(12), 6042. DOI: 10.3390/app12126042

Stallings, W., & Brown, L. (2018). *Computer security: Principles and practice* (4th ed.). Pearson Education.

Stankevičiūtė, Ž. (2024). Data-driven decision making: Application of people analytics in human resource management. In *Digital transformation: Technology, tools, and studies* (pp. 239–262). Springer Nature Switzerland. DOI: 10.1007/978-3-031-55952-5_12

Thabit, F., Alhomdy, S. A.-H., Alahdal, A., & Jagtap, S. B. (2020). Exploration of security challenges in cloud computing: Issues, threats, and attacks with their alleviating techniques. *Journal of Information and Computational Science, 12*(10). https://ssrn.com/abstract=3749271

Tipton, H. F., & Krause, M. (Eds.). (2022). *Information security management handbook* (6th ed.). Auerbach Publications.

Tomlinson, E. C., & Schnackenberg, A. (2022). The effects of transparency perceptions on trustworthiness perceptions and trust. *Journal of Trust Research, 12*(1), 1–23. DOI: 10.1080/21515581.2022.2060245

Waizenegger, L., McKenna, B., Cai, W., & Bendz, T. (2020). An affordance perspective of team collaboration and enforced working from home during COVID-19. *European Journal of Information Systems, 29*(4), 429–442. DOI: 10.1080/0960085X.2020.1800417

Wang, H., Ding, H., & Kong, X. (2023). Understanding technostress and employee well-being in digital work: The roles of work exhaustion and workplace knowledge diversity. *International Journal of Manpower, 44*(2), 334–353. DOI: 10.1108/IJM-08-2021-0480

West, J. P., & Bowman, J. S. (2016). Electronic surveillance at work: An ethical analysis. *Administration & Society, 48*(5), 628–651. DOI: 10.1177/0095399714556502

Westerlund, M., Isabelle, D. A., & Leminen, S. (2021). The acceptance of digital surveillance in an age of big data. *Technology Innovation Management Review, 11*(3), 32–44. DOI: 10.22215/timreview/1427

Wright, D., & Kreissl, R. (Eds.). (2014). *Surveillance in Europe*. Routledge. DOI: 10.4324/9781315851365

Zetter, K. (2015). *Countdown to zero day: Stuxnet and the launch of the world's first digital weapon*. Crown.

Zhao, G., Song, J., & Li, X. (2020). Network security model based on active defense and passive defense hybrid strategy. *Journal of Intelligent & Fuzzy Systems*, *39*(6), 8897–8905. DOI: 10.3233/JIFS-189287

Zissis, D., & Lekkas, D. (2012). Addressing cloud computing security issues. *Future Generation Computer Systems*, *28*(3), 583–592. DOI: 10.1016/j.future.2010.12.006

Chapter 8
Secure Remote Work: HR's Role in Managing Cyber Risks in Hybrid Work Environments

Kagan Cenk Mizrak
https://orcid.org/0000-0002-3472-394X
Nisantasi University, Turkey

ABSTRACT

The shift toward remote and hybrid work has transformed the cybersecurity landscape, placing increased emphasis on the human factors that influence organizational security. This chapter explores the evolving role of Human Resources (HR) in managing cyber risks within decentralized work environments. It highlights how HR functions—including policy development, employee training, behavioral monitoring, and ethical oversight—are central to building cyber resilience. Through a multidisciplinary lens, the chapter demonstrates how collaboration between HR, IT, and governance fosters a secure and adaptive digital culture. Recommendations are provided for embedding cybersecurity into organizational values, advancing workforce training, and supporting employee well-being to create a human-centered, cyber-secure workplace.

1. INTRODUCTION

The COVID-19 pandemic precipitated one of the most rapid and widespread transformations in the global workplace, ushering in a new era of remote and hybrid work models. What began as a reactive shift to maintain continuity during a public health crisis has now evolved into a long-term strategic realignment of how organizations operate. In this new paradigm, employees frequently access sensitive company resources from home networks, personal devices, and third-party cloud

DOI: 10.4018/979-8-3693-6417-8.ch008

services—systems that are often outside the traditional perimeter of corporate security infrastructure. This decentralization of the workplace has expanded the attack surface exponentially, exposing organizations to new and more complex cyber threats. The digital workplace—defined by distributed teams, virtual collaboration, and mobile access—demands a reimagining of cybersecurity strategy, with a specific focus on human behavior, cross-functional coordination, and the integration of non-technical roles into the defense architecture.

The hybrid work model has introduced unique vulnerabilities that challenge conventional security frameworks. In the past, cybersecurity defenses relied heavily on perimeter-based controls—firewalls, in-house monitoring, and tightly managed enterprise systems. In contrast, the modern workforce operates across geographies and devices, often relying on unsecured Wi-Fi connections, unmonitored cloud services, and a mix of personal and corporate hardware. This fluid environment enables agility and innovation but also creates gaps in oversight, weakens access control, and introduces greater variability in user behavior. As Aslan et al. (2023) noted in their comprehensive review, threats like phishing, credential stuffing, and ransomware have surged in remote contexts, where users are more isolated, fatigued, and susceptible to deceptive tactics. Moreover, shadow IT—where employees adopt unauthorized tools to improve productivity—has emerged as a persistent issue in remote work scenarios, often bypassing established protocols and introducing unmanaged entry points into the system (Flores et al., 2023; Nwankpa & Datta, 2023).

In light of these changes, cybersecurity can no longer be viewed solely as a technical or IT-centric function. It must become a shared organizational responsibility that spans departments, roles, and hierarchies. The traditional notion that cybersecurity lies within the exclusive domain of IT departments is not only outdated but also dangerous. As Mizrak and Akkartal (2024) emphasize in their aviation-focused study, risk prioritization and cybersecurity investment must be rooted in a multi-stakeholder framework, incorporating both strategic and operational considerations. This same logic applies across sectors and work models: HR leaders, line managers, and executive boards must collaborate with IT experts to shape holistic cybersecurity strategies that balance technological safeguards with behavioral controls and organizational culture. In particular, Human Resources has emerged as a critical actor in managing the "human factor" of cybersecurity—overseeing employee training, establishing ethical guidelines, tracking behavioral compliance, and mitigating the psychological risks (such as burnout or fatigue) that contribute to cyber-risky behavior (Fisher et al., 2021; Mizrak et al., 2025).

Moreover, HR is uniquely positioned to design and enforce remote work policies that are not only operationally efficient but also security-conscious. Through targeted interventions—such as onboarding protocols, cyber hygiene training, behavioral monitoring systems, and performance-linked accountability—HR can reinforce security as a core organizational value. It is also tasked with protecting employee privacy and autonomy in environments increasingly shaped by surveillance technologies and AI-driven monitoring tools. As cybersecurity threats become more adaptive and AI-enabled, ethical governance and employee trust will become key battlegrounds. In this context, HR must serve as both a strategic partner in risk mitigation and an ethical steward of organizational resilience (Dhirani et al., 2023; Kaushik et al., 2024).

The purpose of this chapter is to explore how cybersecurity practices and organizational resilience are shaped by the interplay between HR strategy, IT infrastructure, and governance. The chapter begins by examining the specific risks introduced by remote and hybrid work models and the evolving human factor in cybersecurity. It then analyzes how HR departments can design strategic interventions—from policy development to mental health support—to cultivate a culture of cyber awareness and secure behavior. Next, the discussion shifts to how HR and IT departments can co-lead cybersecurity implementation and how technologies such as AI and analytics can support both protection and prevention. Finally, the chapter highlights ethical and governance challenges, emphasizing the need for transparent, values-driven cybersecurity frameworks in the modern workplace.

By bridging behavioral, technical, and ethical dimensions, this chapter aims to demonstrate that cybersecurity is not just about protecting systems—it's about protecting people and enabling innovation in a secure and resilient manner.

2. UNDERSTANDING REMOTE WORK RISKS: THE HUMAN FACTOR IN CYBERSECURITY

The accelerated adoption of remote and hybrid work environments has profoundly altered the cybersecurity landscape, introducing a complex array of human-centered vulnerabilities. In decentralized settings, employees routinely access corporate systems through home networks and personal devices, often bypassing traditional security perimeters. This shift has dramatically expanded the attack surface for malicious actors, creating multiple entry points vulnerable to exploitation. Remote workers, in particular, may use insecure Wi-Fi networks, rely on weak or reused passwords, or install unauthorized applications—commonly known as shadow IT—to compensate for a lack of IT-supported tools. These practices make it easier for attackers to infiltrate organizational systems using tactics such as credential stuffing, malware deployment, or ransomware injections. Compounding these issues is the fact that many home devices do not have updated security patches or enterprise-grade antivirus software, rendering them soft targets for cyber threats. The increased dependency on cloud services and digital collaboration tools further complicates the risk matrix, especially when users lack adequate training on secure usage practices. These risks are particularly prevalent in hybrid work settings where security controls are inconsistent across locations and devices (Aslan et al., 2023; Brilingaitė et al., 2020).

What makes these risks even more concerning is the dual role employees play in cybersecurity ecosystems. On one hand, they represent a critical layer of defense against threats, capable of identifying suspicious activity and preventing breaches through vigilant behavior. On the other hand, they also constitute the most unpredictable variable in the cybersecurity equation—prone to human error, carelessness, or lack of awareness. This paradox is especially prominent in organizations that view cybersecurity primarily as a technical issue, often delegating responsibility solely to IT departments. In reality, effective cybersecurity in hybrid environments depends on cultivating a workforce that is both technically aware and behaviorally aligned with organizational policies. When employees are not properly trained or do not understand the rationale behind security protocols, they are more likely to engage in risky digital behaviors, such as clicking on phishing links or disabling security settings for convenience. Cultural and psychological elements also matter; when cybersecurity is framed as a compliance burden rather than a shared value, employees become disengaged and resistant to best practices. Building a security-aware culture that empowers employees to act as responsible cyber stewards is therefore a crucial strategy in mitigating risk across hybrid environments (Fisher et al., 2021; Victor-Mgbachi, 2024).

The psychological pressures of remote work environments further exacerbate cybersecurity vulnerabilities. In hybrid setups, the boundaries between personal and professional life are blurred, often resulting in extended screen time, irregular work hours, and constant digital engagement. Over time, this leads to digital fatigue—a state of cognitive exhaustion stemming from information overload and prolonged exposure to digital interfaces. Employees experiencing digital fatigue are more prone to overlook suspicious cues, misjudge the authenticity of emails, or bypass security steps to save time. This behavior increases susceptibility to phishing, social engineering, and other targeted attacks that exploit cognitive shortcuts. Additionally, employees suffering from burnout may disengage from organizational policies, ignore routine system updates, or fall behind on mandatory cybersecurity training. A recent study on cybersecurity fatigue found that chronic digital exhaustion not only compromises security performance but also has measurable impacts on mental health and overall productivity. These conditions are further intensified when employees feel they are under constant surveillance or lack sufficient support from leadership, leading to decreased morale and increased error rates. Traits such as impulsivity, low self-control, and high levels of stress have also been empirically linked to unsafe online behaviors, reinforcing the need for HR-driven interventions that address the psychological dimensions of cybersecurity (Mizrak et al., 2025; Raywood-Burke et al., 2021; Gan et al., 2024).

Numerous real-world data breach incidents illustrate the direct consequences of human error in hybrid work environments. During the COVID-19 pandemic and beyond, several high-profile breaches were traced not to sophisticated hacking tools, but to simple mistakes—employees sharing passwords via unsecured channels, clicking on malicious links, or failing to update software on personal devices used for work. In one case, a healthcare provider suffered a significant breach due to an employee accessing sensitive electronic health records through a personal tablet on a public Wi-Fi connection. Investigations later revealed that the employee had never received formal training on remote access protocols. Another case involved a large financial services firm where a staff member unknowingly downloaded ransomware after clicking on a fake meeting invitation. Such examples highlight how insufficient training, poor communication, and lack of oversight in remote setups contribute directly to security failures. Furthermore, organizations often underestimate their legal liability in such cases, assuming that remote workers bear individual responsibility for their devices. However, courts increasingly recognize that employers must provide the necessary tools, education, and policies to mitigate risk, regardless of work location. These case studies demonstrate that in the age of hybrid work, the human element is not just a variable—it is a central pillar of cybersecurity strategy (Golubock, 2024; Ozer et al., 2024; Yeo & Banfield, 2022; Kari & Steinert, 2021).

Collectively, the evidence points to the urgent need for integrated, human-centered cybersecurity strategies tailored to the realities of remote and hybrid work. Technical controls alone are insufficient if the human component is neglected. HR departments must therefore collaborate with IT, compliance, and legal teams to develop training programs, behavioral monitoring tools, and well-being initiatives that empower employees to act securely and sustainably. Cybersecurity must become a shared organizational value embedded in everyday behavior, not just a checklist to satisfy compliance standards. Recognizing and addressing the psychological, behavioral, and legal dimensions of remote work risks is a prerequisite for building truly resilient and innovative digital organizations.

3. STRATEGIC HR INTERVENTIONS FOR CYBER-RESILIENT WORKFORCES

The development of strategic HR interventions has become indispensable in ensuring organizational cyber resilience, particularly as hybrid and remote work become standard practice. Effective cybersecurity can no longer rely solely on technological safeguards—it must also be embedded in human-centered policies and practices that actively shape employee behavior and organizational culture. HR professionals play a key role in aligning cybersecurity goals with strategic human resource management, integrating resilience-focused practices into workforce development, training, and governance. Cybersecurity risk is increasingly viewed through the lens of organizational adaptability and long-term sustainability, requiring HR functions to adopt proactive measures in promoting awareness, behavior change, and supportive digital environments. This integration of cybersecurity with HRM practices offers a holistic pathway to strengthening enterprise-wide resilience in the face of growing cyber threats (Alhidaifi et al., 2024; Mızrak, 2023; Mızrak, 2024).

One of the most critical responsibilities of HR in cyber-resilient organizations is the design and enforcement of remote work policies that incorporate robust security measures. Policies must go beyond general IT guidelines and include clear expectations about acceptable device use, password protocols, secure data sharing practices, and reporting procedures for suspicious activity. These guidelines should also be tailored to reflect the specific risks posed by remote environments, such as shared networks, device access by family members, or data exposure in public spaces. Research shows that comprehensive cybersecurity policies significantly reduce risky behavior among remote workers, especially when they are supported by ongoing communication and accountability mechanisms. Moreover, the inclusion of behavioral norms and values in remote work policy documents reinforces a security-oriented culture across all departments. Importantly, effective policy implementation requires more than documentation—it demands clear dissemination, accessible language, and the empowerment of team leaders to champion compliance across distributed teams (Nwankpa & Datta, 2023; Georgiadou et al., 2022; Hijji & Alam, 2022; Flores et al., 2023).

HR departments must also lead efforts in awareness training, secure onboarding and offboarding processes, and behavioral monitoring—components that form the foundation of a resilient workforce. Onboarding should include mandatory cybersecurity orientation sessions, teaching new hires how to recognize phishing attempts, use virtual private networks (VPNs), manage digital credentials, and safely handle sensitive company data. Offboarding, conversely, must include steps to immediately revoke access rights, disable user accounts, and secure intellectual property—especially in cases of remote or contract-based employees. Continuous training, delivered in engaging and interactive formats, helps reinforce secure behavior over time. Behavioral monitoring tools, when ethically applied, can support early detection of suspicious activities such as login anomalies or unauthorized file transfers. These tools must be carefully integrated to protect both organizational assets and employee privacy, reinforcing the notion that cyber monitoring is not about surveillance but about shared risk management. A security-first mindset can only be cultivated when employees understand the logic behind monitoring and see it as a means of protecting both personal and organizational integrity (Flores et al., 2023; Mihailović et al., 2021)

To ensure cybersecurity remains an integral part of the organizational fabric, HR leaders should consider embedding cyber hygiene practices into performance appraisal systems, feedback cycles, and routine compliance evaluations. When employees are evaluated not just on productivity, but also on secure behavior, policy adherence, and participation in security training, the message becomes clear: cybersecurity is a shared responsibility and a performance metric. This alignment reinforces organizational accountability and normalizes digital diligence as part of everyday work culture. Such integration also allows HR departments to identify training gaps, reward proactive cyber behavior, and tailor interventions to individual and departmental risk profiles. Additionally, tracking cyber engagement through HR analytics enables organizations to forecast risk exposure, assess workforce readiness, and fine-tune training programs for higher impact (Trim & Lee, 2021; Vagal & Dillon, 2021).

However, building cyber resilience through HR cannot rely solely on surveillance or metrics; it must also prioritize employee trust, autonomy, and well-being. Excessive monitoring can erode morale, especially in environments where employees feel they are being scrutinized rather than supported. Transparent communication, opt-in digital health tools, and employee participation in the design of cyber initiatives help maintain trust while still achieving oversight goals. HR must walk a fine line between protecting the organization and respecting the privacy and autonomy of its workforce. This balance is particularly important when dealing with issues like digital fatigue, burnout, and stress—conditions that directly affect employees' ability to adhere to security practices. Cyber-risky behavior often stems not from negligence but from cognitive overload, emotional exhaustion, or lack of recovery time. HR-led initiatives that promote psychological safety, encourage digital detox periods, and offer counseling or mental health support contribute not only to workforce resilience but also to stronger cybersecurity outcomes (Dangheralou & Jahankhani, 2022; Mızrak et al., 2025).

In sum, the strategic integration of cybersecurity into HR policies, training, performance systems, and well-being initiatives constitutes a critical pillar of organizational resilience. HR departments must move beyond traditional boundaries and actively engage in cyber governance, policy co-creation, and behavior modeling. This human-centric approach ensures that employees are not only informed and equipped but also motivated and supported to act as the first line of defense in increasingly complex digital ecosystems.

4. COLLABORATION AND TECHNOLOGY: BRIDGING HR, IT, AND GOVERNANCE

The need for integrated collaboration between Human Resources (HR), Information Technology (IT), and organizational governance has grown significantly in the context of hybrid work, where cybersecurity vulnerabilities arise not just from technical gaps, but from behavioral inconsistencies and policy misalignments. HR and IT must act as co-leaders in the development of cyber-resilient strategies that reflect both technological requirements and human behavior dynamics. Eltayeb (2024) emphasizes that anticipating cyber threats using Cyber Threat Intelligence (CTI) is more effective when organizational units share information and take joint ownership of risk mitigation. This interdepartmental synergy ensures that cybersecurity is not treated as a siloed technical matter, but as an enterprise-wide issue requiring both infrastructural solutions and people-focused interventions. Ranganathan et al. (2024) further stress that future cybersecurity readiness depends on bridging disciplines—including behavioral science and HRM—to prepare workforces that are technically capable and culturally resilient.

A major area where this collaboration becomes operational is the implementation of secure technology stacks for distributed workforces. Tools such as multi-factor authentication (MFA), virtual private networks (VPNs), endpoint protection software, and centralized mobile device management (MDM) systems must be universally adopted across employee platforms. However, technological implementation alone is not enough—HR must ensure that employees are properly trained in using these tools and understand their importance. Stefanidou et al. (2024) note that cloud-driven network security infrastructure is only as effective as its users' ability to engage with it securely, highlighting the importance of usability and training alongside deployment. When HR collaborates with IT to co-create onboarding procedures and digital literacy sessions that embed these tools into daily workflows, organizations experience a higher rate of secure behavior adherence and fewer user-driven breaches.

Beyond tool deployment, HR analytics can be leveraged to detect early warning signs of insider threats and behavioral non-compliance, helping to identify trends before they escalate into security incidents. Ranganathan et al. (2024) demonstrate that by integrating cybersecurity metrics into HR dashboards—such as phishing test results, frequency of password resets, or training completion—organizations can perform predictive risk modeling and customize employee training needs accordingly. This data-driven approach supports proactive intervention strategies and contributes to building a more adaptive cyber-resilient workforce. Furthermore, HR data can complement IT access logs and authentication histories to provide a fuller picture of risky behavior patterns, making cross-functional collaboration not only strategic but also operationally actionable.

However, this data-driven security environment introduces ethical concerns related to employee monitoring, data privacy, and autonomy. The line between justified cybersecurity measures and invasive surveillance is increasingly difficult to draw, especially in remote settings where employees often use personal devices or share spaces with others. Dhirani et al. (2023) provide a comprehensive review of ethical dilemmas in emerging technologies, identifying employee trust erosion as a significant consequence of poorly communicated or overly intrusive monitoring practices. Similarly, Tronnier et al. (2022) argue that digital service chains pose a complex ethical challenge in cybersecurity, where privacy risks often emerge from interconnected third-party systems and unregulated data flows. HR must therefore play a critical governance role in designing transparent monitoring frameworks, ensuring that employees are informed about what data is being collected, why it's being collected, and how it will be used. This ethical stewardship not only upholds organizational integrity but also preserves the psychological contract between employer and employee.

The integration of artificial intelligence (AI) in cybersecurity systems adds another layer of ethical and operational complexity. AI-powered security tools—such as anomaly detection engines, behavior-based access controls, and AI-driven incident response systems—offer immense potential for identifying and responding to threats in real time. However, as Kaushik et al. (2024) point out, these tools can introduce risks of algorithmic bias, lack of transparency, and automation-induced unfairness, especially when used for workforce monitoring or access decisions. Alawida et al. (2023) caution that while tools like ChatGPT and large language models can support cybersecurity tasks, they also pose concerns regarding misuse, misinformation, and unintended privacy violations if not properly governed. Yu and Carroll (2022) further argue that AI applications in national security contexts—such as cybersecurity threat prevention—must include ethical safeguards, especially when used to monitor citizens or employees. This reinforces the necessity of HR involvement in evaluating and implementing AI tools within the workplace, ensuring that these technologies align with organizational values, employee rights, and legal frameworks.

To ensure effective cybersecurity governance in hybrid work environments, organizations must move beyond siloed departmental strategies and embrace integrated, cross-functional collaboration. Figure 1 illustrates the triangular relationship between Human Resources (HR), Information Technology (IT), and Governance as a foundational model for enabling a collaborative cybersecurity strategy. Each unit plays a distinct yet interdependent role—HR oversees ethical workforce engagement and behavior monitoring, IT manages the technological infrastructure and threat detection systems, while Governance ensures compliance, policy alignment, and ethical oversight. At the center of this framework lies the collaborative strategy that unites these domains, promoting shared ownership of risk, data-driven decision-making, and ethically grounded cybersecurity innovation.

Figure 1. Triangular collaboration model: HR, IT & governance in cybersecurity.

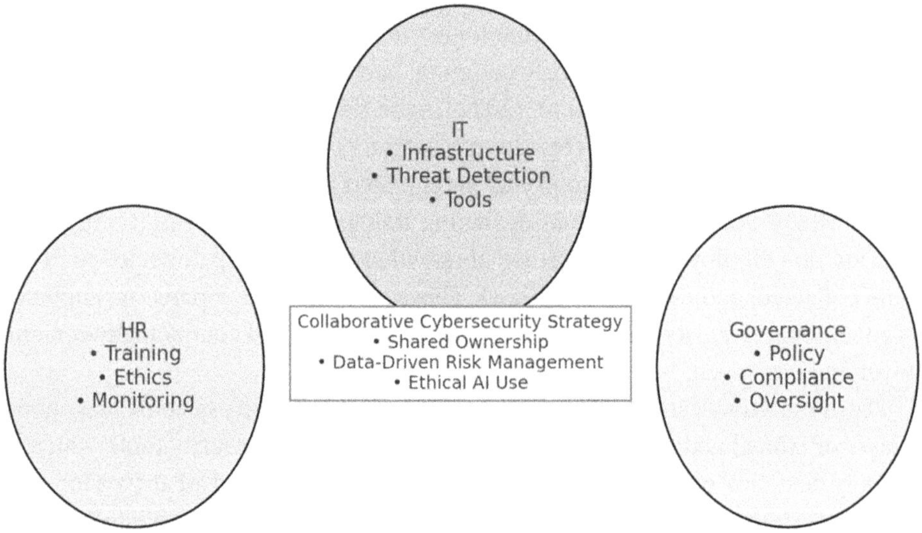

In conclusion, cybersecurity success in the hybrid era depends on a triangular alliance between HR, IT, and governance. When HR understands the tools, IT understands the people, and governance ensures ethical oversight, cybersecurity strategies become holistic, defensible, and future-ready. Cross-departmental collaboration transforms cybersecurity from a reactive function into a proactive, values-driven element of organizational design—protecting not only digital infrastructure but also employee trust and workplace culture.

5. DESIGNING INCLUSIVE CYBERSECURITY POLICIES FOR DIVERSE WORKFORCES

As organizations adopt remote and hybrid work models, the effectiveness of cybersecurity strategies increasingly depends on their inclusivity and accessibility. Cyber threats do not discriminate, but the ability of employees to recognize, respond to, or report those threats often varies based on age, gender, cognitive diversity, cultural background, and digital literacy. A one-size-fits-all approach to cybersecurity training and policy development can unintentionally exclude or underserve segments of the workforce, thereby undermining the overall resilience of the organization. Inclusive cybersecurity policy design is not just a matter of equity—it is a practical necessity for operational security.

Digital literacy is a foundational factor that influences how employees engage with cybersecurity practices. Older employees, or those with limited exposure to digital environments, may find cybersecurity protocols intimidating or confusing. In contrast, younger, digitally native workers may overlook protocols out of overconfidence or habitual multitasking. Georgiadou et al. (2022) emphasize that the shift to remote work revealed significant discrepancies in cybersecurity culture based on demographic variables, with generational gaps contributing to varied perceptions of risk and responsibility. Training programs must therefore be adaptable in format, content, and delivery. While digital simulations and gamified phishing tests may work well for some employees, others may benefit more from live instruction, assistive learning tools, or scenario-based walkthroughs tailored to their experience level.

Neurodiverse employees may process information differently or have specific learning needs that are often overlooked in traditional training environments. Flores et al. (2023) stress the importance of considering cognitive variability in the design of cybersecurity awareness programs, especially in remote work settings where asynchronous learning and self-paced modules are the norm. Adaptive training tools that allow for repetition, visual cues, audio instructions, and simplified language are essential in ensuring comprehension across neurodiverse populations. Accessibility standards should also be incorporated into all cybersecurity communication—ranging from font readability to video captioning and screen reader compatibility—to ensure equitable access for employees with visual, auditory, or learning impairments.

Gender and cultural factors also play a role in cybersecurity engagement. Studies suggest that women in male-dominated technical environments may be less likely to ask questions during training or report suspicious activities due to concerns about credibility or confidence (Abrahams et al., 2024). Moreover, cultural attitudes toward authority and technology can affect how employees interact with security protocols. Organizations operating across borders must therefore localize cybersecurity policies and training content to reflect regional norms and language preferences. Dangheralou and Jahankhani (2022) point out that misalignment between global security protocols and local user behavior often leads to policy non-compliance, especially in multicultural workforces.

Inclusive policy development must also address varying levels of trust and psychological safety within teams. Surveillance-heavy approaches—such as aggressive monitoring software or frequent password resets—can have disparate effects depending on an employee's personal background or sense of agency. Mizrak et al. (2025) highlight that cybersecurity fatigue disproportionately affects employees who feel over-managed or under-informed, leading to disengagement and increased vulnerability. To prevent this, organizations should solicit feedback from diverse employee groups when designing policies, ensuring that those policies are not only effective but also perceived as fair and respectful.

Inclusion must be embedded not only in training materials but also in how policies are communicated, enforced, and evaluated. HR departments should collaborate with diversity and inclusion teams to audit cybersecurity policies through an equity lens and revise them accordingly. Evaluating the outcomes of cybersecurity interventions should also consider whether improvements in awareness and compliance are distributed evenly across demographic groups. If certain populations continue to underperform or disengage, it may indicate that the policy, rather than the individual, needs to adapt.

Ultimately, cybersecurity culture can only be resilient if it is inclusive. By designing policies and training frameworks that account for the full range of employee needs, organizations enhance both their security posture and their commitment to equitable digital transformation.

6. FUTURE OUTLOOK: HR'S EXPANDING ROLE IN CYBER-RESILIENCE STRATEGY

As organizations continue to embrace digital transformation, the future of cybersecurity will be shaped by emerging technologies such as artificial intelligence (AI), blockchain, and quantum computing. These technologies hold great promise for enhancing operational efficiency and threat mitigation but also introduce unprecedented complexity and ethical challenges. In this rapidly evolving landscape, the role of Human Resources will extend far beyond compliance and training. HR will become a central stakeholder in designing, governing, and sustaining human-centered cybersecurity strategies that are aligned with organizational values, regulatory frameworks, and the evolving digital threat environment.

One of the most transformative developments in cybersecurity is the use of predictive analytics to identify and mitigate insider threats. Advanced algorithms can analyze vast streams of employee behavior data—such as login times, document access patterns, email usage, and response latency—to detect anomalies that may signal malicious intent or high-risk activity. While traditionally this domain belonged to IT and security operations, HR is uniquely positioned to contextualize these patterns through employee history, performance records, and engagement levels. When integrated responsibly, predictive analytics can serve as an early warning system that enables intervention before a security breach occurs. For instance, a disengaged employee with declining performance and unusual data activity may trigger an HR-led support or counseling process, addressing the root cause of risk rather than resorting immediately to punitive measures. This collaboration between HR and IT in behavioral analytics not only strengthens organizational resilience but also enables a more proactive and humane approach to insider risk management (Ranganathan et al., 2024; Mizrak, 2024).

In parallel, AI-driven cybersecurity solutions are becoming increasingly prevalent, automating threat detection, response workflows, and even compliance reporting. However, the use of AI in workplace surveillance and decision-making brings significant ethical implications—many of which fall squarely within HR's domain. AI systems used to evaluate employee behavior, detect anomalies, or assign risk scores can reinforce biases if not properly governed. Kaushik et al. (2024) caution that ethical considerations such as transparency, accountability, and fairness must be central to the deployment of AI in cybersecurity. HR professionals will therefore play a vital role in establishing ethical AI governance frameworks, ensuring that AI tools respect employee rights, are aligned with labor laws, and support inclusive and fair workplace practices. HR's involvement in algorithmic auditing, impact assessments, and employee communication strategies will be essential in building trust in AI-enhanced security systems.

Blockchain technology also presents opportunities for secure identity management, audit trails, and decentralized access control—especially valuable in hybrid and multi-cloud work environments. While blockchain adoption is still in its early stages in workforce management, its potential to create tamper-proof digital records of credentialing, device access, and policy adherence will likely expand. HR departments may soon be responsible for maintaining blockchain-based employee credential systems that integrate with cybersecurity protocols, enabling real-time verification of user authenticity and secure role-based access to systems and data.

Looking even further ahead, quantum computing—with its ability to break traditional encryption algorithms—will redefine the cybersecurity landscape. While quantum threats are not yet mainstream, preparing the workforce to understand and adapt to post-quantum cryptography will be a future concern for HR-led training initiatives. As Stefanidou et al. (2024) suggest, cloud-driven cybersecurity will increasingly depend on adaptable, scalable, and intelligent infrastructures—making employee adaptability and literacy a strategic priority. HR will be tasked with identifying and closing knowledge gaps through agile learning ecosystems, ensuring that employees are not only compliant but continuously prepared for evolving technological paradigms.

Ultimately, the future will demand a paradigm shift in HR's identity—from administrative support to strategic co-leadership in cybersecurity governance. HR will sit at the intersection of people, technology, and ethics—responsible not just for developing a security-aware culture but for influencing the design and governance of the systems that shape employee behavior. This includes participating in executive cybersecurity committees, leading human-factor risk assessments, and managing crisis response protocols in collaboration with IT and legal teams.

As the digital frontier expands, resilient organizations will be those that empower their HR leaders to drive human-centered cybersecurity innovation, ensuring that technology enhances security without compromising dignity, inclusion, or trust. In this future, the question is no longer whether HR should be involved in cybersecurity, but how well it can lead.

7. CONCLUSION

As organizations continue to adapt to the demands of hybrid and remote work, the importance of integrating cybersecurity into the very fabric of human resource management has become unmistakably clear. This chapter has demonstrated that cybersecurity is no longer the sole domain of IT departments—it is a shared strategic responsibility that hinges on the collaboration between HR, IT, and governance structures. In hybrid work environments, where physical boundaries are blurred and digital behaviors become central to daily operations, HR functions are uniquely positioned to shape the human aspects of cybersecurity. From policy design and awareness training to mental health support and ethical oversight, HR plays a pivotal role in building a cyber-resilient workforce.

Human Resources is not only responsible for disseminating knowledge and ensuring compliance, but also for fostering a culture where security is normalized, understood, and valued by employees at all levels. Through secure onboarding and offboarding procedures, HR can close critical access gaps that often serve as entry points for malicious activity. By embedding cybersecurity into performance appraisals and compliance routines, HR can incentivize good practices and create accountability. Moreover, by addressing the psychological dimensions of digital fatigue and stress—factors shown to correlate with increased cyber-risky behavior—HR can help reduce vulnerability at its source. The effectiveness of these initiatives is amplified when HR collaborates closely with IT to deploy secure infrastructure and analytics systems, and when governance bodies provide ethical frameworks to protect employee trust and privacy.

To advance this integration, HR leaders and executives should consider the following key recommendations:

- Embed cybersecurity into company culture by treating it not as a compliance requirement but as a collective organizational value. This involves leadership modeling secure behavior, weaving cybersecurity themes into internal communications, and recognizing employees who contribute to organizational security through responsible digital conduct.

- Create engaging, ongoing learning programs that go beyond static training modules. Cybersecurity education should be interactive, scenario-based, and tailored to different roles and risk levels. Gamified phishing simulations, refresher workshops, and just-in-time learning are all examples of how learning can be continuous and adaptive.
- Collaborate across departments for integrated security, ensuring that HR, IT, and compliance teams regularly share insights, co-develop policies, and align their goals. As seen throughout this chapter, the most effective cybersecurity strategies emerge when technological tools, behavioral science, and ethical governance are interconnected.

In closing, resilience in the digital age is not merely about having strong firewalls or advanced threat detection systems—it is about cultivating empowered, informed, and secure people. Employees are the first and last line of defense in any cybersecurity framework, particularly in remote work contexts where autonomy is high and supervision is limited. When HR functions as a proactive architect of human-centered cybersecurity, organizations are not only better protected from breaches—they are also positioned to thrive with confidence and integrity in an increasingly volatile digital landscape.

REFERENCES

Abrahams, T. O., Farayola, O. A., Kaggwa, S., Uwaoma, P. U., Hassan, A. O., & Dawodu, S. O. (2024). Cybersecurity awareness and education programs: A review of employee engagement and accountability. *Computer Science & IT Research Journal*, *5*(1), 100–119. DOI: 10.51594/csitrj.v5i1.708

Alawida, M., Mejri, S., Mehmood, A., Chikhaoui, B., & Isaac Abiodun, O. (2023). A comprehensive study of ChatGPT: Advancements, limitations, and ethical considerations in natural language processing and cybersecurity. *Information (Basel)*, *14*(8), 462. DOI: 10.3390/info14080462

Alhidaifi, S. M., Asghar, M. R., & Ansari, I. S. (2024). A survey on cyber resilience: Key strategies, research challenges, and future directions. *ACM Computing Surveys*, *56*(8), 1–48. DOI: 10.1145/3649218

Aslan, Ö., Aktuğ, S. S., Ozkan-Okay, M., Yilmaz, A. A., & Akin, E. (2023). A comprehensive review of cyber security vulnerabilities, threats, attacks, and solutions. *Electronics (Basel)*, *12*(6), 1333. DOI: 10.3390/electronics12061333

Brilingaitė, A., Bukauskas, L., & Juozapavičius, A. (2020). A framework for competence development and assessment in hybrid cybersecurity exercises. *Computers & Security*, *88*, 101607. DOI: 10.1016/j.cose.2019.101607

Dangheralou, A., & Jahankhani, H. (2022). The Impact of GDPR Regulations on Cyber Security Effectiveness Whilst Working Remotely. In *Artificial Intelligence in Cyber Security: Impact and Implications: Security Challenges, Technical and Ethical Issues, Forensic Investigative Challenges* (pp. 253–279). Springer International Publishing.

Dhirani, L. L., Mukhtiar, N., Chowdhry, B. S., & Newe, T. (2023). Ethical dilemmas and privacy issues in emerging technologies: A review. *Sensors (Basel)*, *23*(3), 1151. DOI: 10.3390/s23031151 PMID: 36772190

Eltayeb, O. (2024). Cyber Defense Using Cyber Threat Intelligence to Anticipate and Avoid Future Cyber Attacks. *Journal of Ecohumanism*, *3*(4), 2435–2455. DOI: 10.62754/joe.v3i4.3766

Fisher, R., Porod, C., & Peterson, S. (2021). Motivating employees and organizations to adopt a cybersecurity-focused culture. *Journal of Organizational Psychology*, *21*(1), 114–131.

Flores, C., Gonzalez, J., Kajtazi, M., Bugeja, J., & Vogel, B. (2023). Human Factors for Cybersecurity Awareness in a Remote Work Environment. In *9th International Conference on Information Systems Security and Privacy (ICISSP 2023)*, Lisbon, Portugal, 22–24 February 2023 (Vol. 1, pp. 608-616). SciTePress. DOI: 10.5220/0011746000003405

Gan, C. L., Lee, Y. Y., & Liew, T. W. (2024). Fishing for phishy messages: Predicting phishing susceptibility through the lens of cyber-routine activities theory and heuristic-systematic model. *Humanities & Social Sciences Communications*, *11*(1), 1–17. DOI: 10.1057/s41599-024-04083-1

Georgiadou, A., Mouzakitis, S., & Askounis, D. (2022). Working from home during COVID-19 crisis: A cyber security culture assessment survey. *Security Journal*, *35*(2), 486–505. DOI: 10.1057/s41284-021-00286-2

Golubock, D. G. (2024). Remote Workers, Ever-Present Risk: Employer Liability for Data Breaches in the Era of Hybrid Workplaces. *Case W. Res. JL Tech. & Internet*, *15*, 305.

Hijji, M., & Alam, G. (2022). Cybersecurity awareness and training (CAT) framework for remote working employees. *Sensors (Basel)*, *22*(22), 8663. DOI: 10.3390/s22228663 PMID: 36433259

Kari, R., & Steinert, M. (2021). Human factor issues in remote ship operations: Lesson learned by studying different domains. *Journal of Marine Science and Engineering*, *9*(4), 385. DOI: 10.3390/jmse9040385

Kaushik, K., Khan, A., Kumari, A., Sharma, I., & Dubey, R. (2024). Ethical considerations in AI-based cybersecurity. In *Next-generation cybersecurity: AI, ML, and Blockchain* (pp. 437–470). Springer Nature Singapore. DOI: 10.1007/978-981-97-1249-6_19

Mihailović, A., Cerović Smolović, J., Radević, I., Rašović, N., & Martinović, N. (2021). COVID-19 and beyond: Employee perceptions of the efficiency of teleworking and its cybersecurity implications. *Sustainability (Basel)*, *13*(12), 6750. DOI: 10.3390/su13126750

Mızrak, F. (2023). Integrating cybersecurity risk management into strategic management: A comprehensive literature review. *Research Journal of Business and Management*, *10*(3), 98–108. DOI: 10.17261/Pressacademia.2023.1807

Mızrak, F. (2024). Enhancing Cybersecurity risk management through conceptual analysis of Hrm integration. *Yönetim Bilimleri Dergisi*, *22*(51), 96–118. DOI: 10.35408/comuybd.1342408

Mizrak, F., & Akkartal, G. R. (2024). Prioritizing cybersecurity initiatives in aviation: A dematel-QSFS methodology. *Heliyon*, *10*(16), e35487. DOI: 10.1016/j.heliyon.2024.e35487 PMID: 39687858

Mizrak, F., Demirel, H. G., Yaşar, O., & Karakaya, T. (2025). Digital detox: Exploring the impact of cybersecurity fatigue on employee productivity and mental health. *Discover Mental Health*, *5*(1), 1–21. DOI: 10.1007/s44192-025-00149-x PMID: 39998759

Nwankpa, J. K., & Datta, P. M. (2023). Remote vigilance: The roles of cyber awareness and cybersecurity policies among remote workers. *Computers & Security*, *130*, 103266. DOI: 10.1016/j.cose.2023.103266

Ozer, M., Kose, Y., Bastug, M., Kucukkaya, G., & Varlioglu, E. R. (2024). The Shifting Landscape of Cybersecurity: The Impact of Remote Work and COVID-19 on Data Breach Trends. *arXiv preprint arXiv:2402.06650.*

Ranganathan, P., Jangula, J., Kose, U., Goveas, N., & Balaji, S. R. A. (2024). Designing Effective Cybersecurity Curriculum: Bridging Disciplines for Next Generation Workforce.

Raywood-Burke, G., Bishop, L. M., Asquith, P. M., & Morgan, P. L. (2021, July). Human individual difference predictors in cyber-security: exploring an alternative scale method and data resolution to modelling cyber secure behavior. In *International Conference on Human-Computer Interaction* (pp. 226-240). Cham: Springer International Publishing. DOI: 10.1007/978-3-030-77392-2_15

Stefanidou, M., Maraslidis, G. S., Antoniadis, I., & Fragulis, G. F. (2024, October). Cloud-driven network security: A survey of methods, challenges, and innovations. In *AIP Conference Proceedings* (Vol. 3220, No. 1). AIP Publishing. DOI: 10.1063/5.0234978

Trim, P. R., & Lee, Y. I. (2021). The global cyber security model: Counteracting cyber attacks through a resilient partnership arrangement. *Big Data and Cognitive Computing*, *5*(3), 32. DOI: 10.3390/bdcc5030032

Tronnier, F., Pape, S., Löbner, S., & Rannenberg, K. (2022). A discussion on ethical cybersecurity issues in digital service chains. In *Cybersecurity of digital service chains: challenges, methodologies, and tools* (pp. 222–256). Springer International Publishing. DOI: 10.1007/978-3-031-04036-8_10

Vagal, V., & Dillon, R. (2021). Reducing cyber risk in remote working. In *Digital Transformation in a Post-Covid World* (pp. 155–170). CRC Press. DOI: 10.1201/9781003148715-8

Victor-Mgbachi, T. O. Y. I. N. (2024). Navigating cybersecurity beyond compliance: Understanding your threat landscape and vulnerabilities. *Iconic Research and Engineering Journals*, •••, 7.

Yeo, L. H., & Banfield, J. (2022). Human factors in electronic health records cybersecurity breach: An exploratory analysis. *Perspectives in Health Information Management*, *19*(Spring), 1i. PMID: 35692854

Yu, S., & Carroll, F. (2022). Implications of AI in national security: understanding the security issues and ethical challenges. In *Artificial intelligence in cyber security: Impact and implications: Security challenges, technical and ethical issues, forensic investigative challenges* (pp. 157–175). Springer International Publishing.

Chapter 9
The Triple Nexus of Smart, Secure, and Sustainable Supply Chains:
Strategies for Resilience in the Digital Age

Filiz Mızrak
https://orcid.org/0000-0002-3472-394X
Beykoz University, Turkey

ABSTRACT

This chapter explores the strategic convergence of cybersecurity, digital innovation, and sustainability in modern supply chains. As technologies like blockchain, artificial intelligence, and IoT redefine supply chain operations, they also introduce new vulnerabilities that demand robust cyber resilience. Drawing on real-world applications across pharmaceuticals, automotive, retail, and agrifood sectors, the chapter examines how cyber-enabled solutions enhance traceability, risk forecasting, and last-mile delivery security. It introduces the Triple Nexus framework—Smart, Secure, Sustainable—as a conceptual model for aligning technological advancement with ethical and environmental goals. Through cross-sectoral analysis and strategic recommendations, the chapter underscores cybersecurity as a foundational enabler of resilient and future-ready supply chains.

DOI: 10.4018/979-8-3693-6417-8.ch009

1. INTRODUCTION

The global supply chain landscape is undergoing an unprecedented digital transformation, driven by advances in Industry 4.0 technologies such as artificial intelligence (AI), the Internet of Things (IoT), blockchain, cloud computing, and advanced analytics. These technologies are enabling supply chains to evolve from linear, siloed models into real-time, interconnected ecosystems that offer enhanced agility, transparency, and predictive capability. From automated inventory systems and smart logistics platforms to end-to-end traceability and autonomous last-mile delivery, the digitization of supply chains is redefining operational paradigms across sectors such as pharmaceuticals, automotive, retail, and agrifood. This transformation, however, brings with it new vulnerabilities. As supply chains become more digitally integrated and dependent on data flows, they also become more exposed to cyber threats. Malicious actors increasingly target critical supply chain nodes—from third-party software systems to IoT-enabled infrastructure—exploiting security gaps to launch ransomware attacks, exfiltrate sensitive data, and disrupt operations on a global scale.

In this context, cybersecurity is no longer a standalone technical function but a strategic imperative that must be embedded across the innovation and sustainability agendas of modern supply chains. The intersection of cybersecurity, digital innovation, and sustainability represents a critical frontier for research and practice. Secure data systems underpin accurate environmental, social, and governance (ESG) reporting, blockchain-based traceability enables ethical sourcing and regulatory compliance, and AI-driven risk forecasting supports proactive disruption management while safeguarding data integrity. These interdependencies call for a holistic perspective that aligns technological advancement with cyber resilience and sustainability goals. Yet, many organizations still treat these domains in isolation, underestimating how cybersecurity directly supports supply chain transparency, trust, and long-term viability. Therefore, addressing the convergence of these elements is not only timely but essential for designing robust, responsible, and future-ready supply chains.

This chapter addresses three core research questions: (1) How are cyber-enabled technologies being adopted across key supply chain sectors to enhance transparency, resilience, and sustainability? (2) What are the real-world challenges and benefits associated with integrating cybersecurity into digital supply chain strategies? (3) What strategic frameworks and governance models can organizations use to align cybersecurity with innovation and sustainability in supply chain operations? To answer these questions, the chapter draws on recent case studies, industry initiatives, and academic literature, providing a cross-sectoral analysis of how cybersecurity is operationalized in digital supply chains. The chapter offers both a conceptual model—the Triple Nexus of Smart, Secure, and Sustainable Supply Chains—and a practical roadmap for cyber-sustainability integration.

The structure of the chapter is as follows: Section 2 traces the evolution of modern supply chains, highlighting the shift from linear to dynamic ecosystems and the rise of Industry 4.0 technologies. Section 3 introduces the Triple Nexus framework, conceptualizing the convergence of smartness, security, and sustainability. Section 4 explores cybersecurity as a strategic enabler of supply chain innovation, drawing on cross-sector insights. Section 5 presents real-world applications across four industries—pharmaceuticals, automotive, retail, and agrifood—demonstrating how cyber-enabled technologies are transforming operations. Section 6 analyzes governance, regulatory, and ethical challenges, while Section 7 discusses the strategic trade-offs and barriers organizations face in implementation. Section 8 offers strategic recommendations and an integration roadmap. Finally, Section 9 concludes with key insights and directions for future research and practice. Together, these sections aim to advance both the theoretical understanding and practical implementation of secure, sustainable digital supply chains.

2. THE EVOLUTION OF MODERN SUPPLY CHAINS

The structure and behavior of global supply chains have undergone a profound transformation over the past two decades. Traditional supply chains were predominantly linear and functionally siloed, where goods and information flowed in a unidirectional manner—from raw material suppliers to manufacturers, distributors, retailers, and ultimately, consumers. These models operated with a clear division of responsibilities and limited transparency among nodes, leading to inefficiencies in responsiveness and coordination. However, the pressures of globalization, rising consumer expectations, and the volatility of global markets have driven the shift toward dynamic, interconnected, and ecosystem-based supply chains (Nikookar, Stevenson, & Varsei, 2024). In this contemporary model, actors across the supply chain—suppliers, logistics providers, manufacturers, and retailers—collaborate in real time, supported by integrated digital infrastructures and mutual visibility. Ivanov and Dolgui (2022) emphasize that supply chains are no longer discrete pipelines but rather resilient ecosystems, characterized by their capacity to absorb shocks and dynamically reconfigure in the face of disruption. The COVID-19 pandemic, geopolitical tensions, and environmental crises have further underscored the limitations of linear systems, catalyzing investments in interoperable and decentralized structures that can anticipate, respond to, and recover from disturbances efficiently.

Central to this evolution is the incorporation of Industry 4.0 technologies such as the Internet of Things (IoT), artificial intelligence (AI), blockchain, digital twins, and advanced robotics. These technologies are not merely add-ons but serve as strategic enablers of supply chain agility, transparency, and sustainability (Al-Okaily, Younis, & Al-Okaily, 2024). IoT sensors allow for the real-time monitoring of goods, equipment, and environmental conditions, thereby enabling predictive maintenance and reducing delays caused by unforeseen breakdowns. AI and machine learning algorithms, as discussed by Jampani et al. (2023), optimize demand forecasting, inventory management, and routing by processing vast volumes of structured and unstructured data, leading to enhanced efficiency and responsiveness. Blockchain technologies, on the other hand, play a critical role in ensuring data transparency, traceability, and trust across multiple stakeholders (Hellani et al., 2021; Khan et al., 2022). The integration of blockchain has proven especially effective in industries with high regulatory and ethical requirements, such as pharmaceuticals and food, where authenticity and origin tracking are vital. Furthermore, the advent of digital twins—virtual replicas of physical systems—enables organizations to simulate supply chain operations, test contingency plans, and make informed strategic decisions before real-world implementation (Pan et al., 2021). Together, these technologies shift supply chains from being reactive systems to becoming proactive, intelligent networks capable of continuous adaptation and optimization.

Another defining feature of modern supply chains is the convergence of cyber-physical systems (CPS), which represent the fusion of digital computation, networking, and physical processes. Cyber-physical integration empowers supply chains to operate autonomously and self-organize in response to real-time stimuli, significantly enhancing both operational efficiency and resilience. This convergence is especially visible in the Physical Internet (PI) paradigm, which Pan et al. (2021) identify as a transformative approach toward logistics and transportation interoperability. CPS facilitate the synchronization of data, resources, and physical flow by interlinking smart warehouses, connected vehicles, and autonomous distribution centers into a cohesive system. These infrastructures operate in harmony through shared data protocols and secure digital platforms, often reinforced by blockchain's decentralized verification mechanisms (Rejeb et al., 2021). As digital twins and AI further evolve, the CPS paradigm will enable predictive scenario planning, wherein disruptions (e.g., supplier failure or geopolitical risks) are preemptively mitigated through automated rerouting and resource reallocation. According to Abaku, Edunjobi, and Odimarha (2024), such CPS-enabled frameworks allow for resilient and responsive decision-making with minimal human intervention—an imperative in high-velocity global markets.

The integration of sustainability and ethics into supply chain operations has become another hallmark of the modern era. Increasingly, organizations are expected not only to deliver goods efficiently but also to do so in ways that align with environmental and social governance (ESG) principles. Esan, Ajayi, and Olawale (2024) argue that contemporary supply chains must internalize ethical sourcing, carbon footprint reduction, and social compliance as core components of strategy, not merely public relations concerns. Digital technologies support this goal by offering real-time environmental data and traceability, enabling organizations to document sustainable practices and meet regulatory obligations. In parallel, supply chain actors are now developing antifragile capabilities—those that allow systems to grow stronger from volatility and uncertainty rather than merely surviving them (Nikookar et al., 2024). These capabilities, often grounded in digital infrastructure and data-sharing agreements, ensure that supply chains do not return to the old norm post-disruption but instead evolve with enhanced adaptive potential.

In sum, the evolution of supply chains from linear models to cyber-physical ecosystems reflects a strategic transformation shaped by technology, sustainability, and resilience imperatives. As highlighted by Mızrak (2024) and Akkartal & Mızrak (2024), these modern systems require cross-functional collaboration, digital fluency, and governance structures that embrace continuous innovation. Supply chain leaders must be prepared to operate within a digitally dynamic, ethically aware, and cyber-secure ecosystem, where data becomes the key currency of trust, agility, and strategic decision-making. The old paradigms of static production planning and siloed logistics are being replaced by real-time visibility, predictive analytics, and adaptive digital twins—building a foundation for supply chains that are not only smarter and faster, but also more sustainable, transparent, and future-ready.

3. CONCEPTUAL FRAMEWORK: THE TRIPLE NEXUS

The transformation of supply chains through digitalization is no longer a linear or siloed evolution but a multidimensional convergence of intelligence, integrity, and impact. To conceptualize this, we propose the Triple Nexus Framework, which positions smartness, security, and sustainability as interdependent pillars of modern supply chain excellence. Rather than pursuing these dimensions independently, organizations must integrate them into cohesive strategies that align operational innovation with ethical, resilient, and environmentally responsible practices. This section defines each pillar in detail, demonstrating how their integration supports the development of digitally empowered, cyber-resilient, and environmentally sound supply chain ecosystems.

3.1 Smart: Automation, Predictive Analytics, and AI-Based Logistics

The "smart" dimension of the framework refers to the strategic integration of digital technologies that enhance supply chain visibility, efficiency, and adaptability. Smartness is primarily operationalized through automation, predictive analytics, artificial intelligence (AI), and real-time decision systems. These tools enable supply chains to operate as intelligent, adaptive systems that can respond dynamically to internal inefficiencies and external disruptions. As described by Jampani et al. (2023), AI-driven logistics optimization facilitates real-time inventory control, route planning, and demand forecasting, thereby reducing waste and increasing service reliability. Edge-cloud computing architectures further support this smart infrastructure by distributing processing power closer to physical assets, which is essential for high-speed responsiveness in sectors such as automotive and perishable logistics (Yang et al., 2022; Wu et al., 2020).

Moreover, the use of digital twins—virtual replicas of supply chain entities—enables organizations to simulate operations, assess risks, and test scenarios before physical execution (Ivanov & Dolgui, 2022). These systems are increasingly being used to perform predictive risk assessments in global sourcing, allowing companies to anticipate disruptions before they impact operations (e.g., VW Mexico's AI-based risk matrix discussed in Section 5). Thus, smartness not only delivers operational agility but also builds the cognitive capacity for proactive and data-driven supply chain decision-making, reducing reliance on manual interventions and static forecasting models.

3.2 Secure: Data Protection, Threat Detection, and Blockchain Traceability

The second pillar of the framework, security, ensures the integrity, confidentiality, and availability of data across increasingly complex and digitized supply chain networks. As digital transformation expands the attack surface, cybersecurity has emerged as a foundational enabler of innovation, not a constraint. Hammi, Zeadally, and Nebhen (2023) emphasize that the most critical threats to digital supply chains include data breaches, ransomware, supply chain impersonation, and vulnerabilities in third-party systems. These threats necessitate a multilayered defense strategy encompassing threat detection, secure-by-design architecture, identity management, and continuous risk monitoring.

Key to this pillar is the adoption of blockchain technologies for secure, immutable traceability. In sectors such as pharmaceuticals and agrifood, blockchain supports provenance verification and cold-chain monitoring, providing shared access to tamper-proof records that enhance regulatory compliance and stakeholder trust (Khan et al., 2022; Hellani et al., 2021). Meanwhile, the implementation of Zero Trust Architecture (ZTA) reinforces identity and access controls by continuously validating users and devices, thereby eliminating blind spots in security coverage (Patel & Chaudhary, 2024; Rivera et al., 2024). ZTA, when paired with multi-factor authentication and behavior analytics, establishes a trustworthy digital environment that protects the real-time flows of data underpinning smart supply chains. Overall, the secure dimension ensures that innovation is grounded in reliability and trust, empowering organizations to deploy technologies with confidence in their cyber-resilience.

3.3 Sustainable: Low-Carbon Logistics, Waste Minimization, and Ethical Sourcing

The sustainable dimension of the Triple Nexus reflects a long-term commitment to reducing environmental impact, ensuring ethical practices, and aligning supply chains with global sustainability standards. As outlined by Esan, Ajayi, and Olawale (2024), sustainable supply chains internalize carbon footprint reduction, resource efficiency, circular logistics, and social responsibility as strategic priorities rather than compliance burdens. In this context, smart technologies play a critical role by enabling precise measurement of emissions, fuel consumption, and waste levels, while AI-based analytics improve load consolidation and inventory optimization to prevent overproduction and reduce excess capacity (Singh, 2023; Khoa, 2024).

Blockchain-enabled traceability platforms further advance sustainability by verifying ethical sourcing and environmental performance of suppliers, creating end-to-end transparency that facilitates ESG reporting and regulatory compliance (Rejeb et al., 2021). Secure IoT systems, such as encrypted ambient sensors used in cold-chain logistics (e.g., Wiliot's IoT tags), enable real-time monitoring of temperature-sensitive goods, preventing spoilage and minimizing food waste (Yang et al., 2022). Moreover, sustainable logistics must be ethically governed—Hao and Demir (2024) propose that AI models used in supply chain planning should incorporate environmental and social governance (ESG) triggers, ensuring that decision-making algorithms do not prioritize efficiency at the expense of equity or ecological responsibility. As climate resilience and social equity rise on corporate agendas, sustainability becomes not only a reputational asset but a structural requirement for long-term supply chain viability.

3.4 Integrating the Triple Nexus

The convergence of these three pillars—smartness, security, and sustainability—forms the basis for the Smart-Secure-Sustainable Supply Chain Model (Figure 1). This model illustrates that these dimensions are not mutually exclusive but mutually reinforcing. Smart technologies require robust security to function reliably; sustainability efforts demand data transparency and traceability supported by both smart infrastructure and secure systems; and security measures must account for ethical and environmental impacts to remain socially acceptable. For instance, the integration of AI-based risk forecasting (smart) with blockchain-based provenance systems (secure) and ESG-aligned logistics planning (sustainable) enables a supply chain that is not only efficient but resilient, ethical, and future-proof.

Organizations that strategically operate at the intersection of this nexus are better positioned to withstand disruptions, comply with evolving regulations, and meet the demands of digitally conscious consumers and regulators. As demonstrated across the real-world cases and sectoral applications discussed in this study, embedding the Triple Nexus as a design principle fosters supply chains that are simultaneously agile, trusted, and responsible—meeting the challenges of Industry 4.0 with integrity and foresight.

Figure 1. Smart-secure-sustainable supply chain model

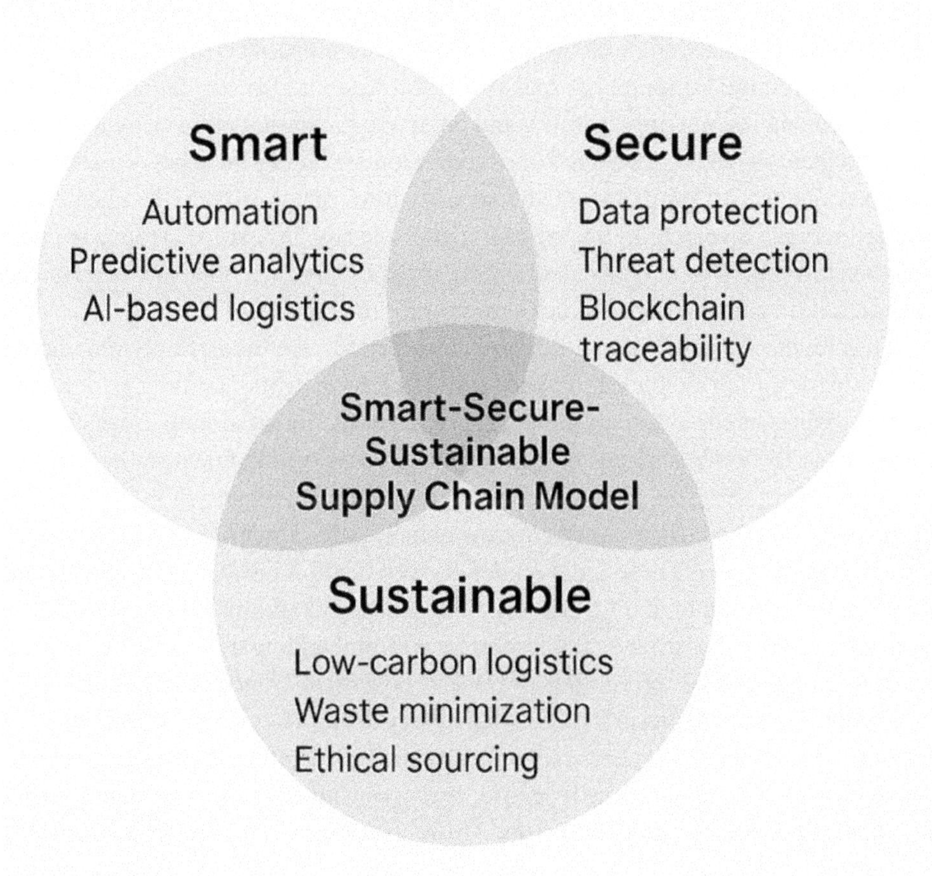

4. CYBERSECURITY AS A STRATEGIC ENABLER IN SUPPLY CHAIN INNOVATION

The digital transformation of supply chains has undeniably enhanced operational agility, visibility, and responsiveness. However, this transformation has also exposed organizations to a rapidly evolving threat landscape. As digital ecosystems become increasingly interconnected, cyber threats in supply chains have grown in both frequency and sophistication, often targeting third-party vendors, interconnected platforms, and critical infrastructure. Hammi, Zeadally, and Nebhen (2023) argue that cyberattacks in digital supply chains are no longer isolated incidents but are part of complex, multi-stage campaigns exploiting weak links across global networks.

These include ransomware attacks on logistics systems, phishing schemes aimed at procurement personnel, and advanced persistent threats targeting IoT endpoints and cloud storage. Pandey et al. (2020) highlight that in globalized supply chains, risk is not only inherited through internal vulnerabilities but also accumulated through interdependencies, making visibility and proactive threat modeling critical. Recent cyber incidents—such as the SolarWinds and Colonial Pipeline breaches—underscore the consequences of insufficient cybersecurity governance, especially when external partners are involved. In this context, cybersecurity has evolved from a support function to a strategic enabler and differentiator in supply chain innovation, ensuring that digital transformation does not compromise resilience.

To mitigate these escalating threats, organizations are increasingly embracing secure-by-design principles and cyber-resilience frameworks tailored to complex supply chain structures. Secure-by-design refers to the integration of cybersecurity measures at the earliest stages of system and process development, rather than as an afterthought. Boyson, Corsi, and Paraskevas (2022) emphasize that designing systems with embedded security controls enhances the integrity and longevity of digital supply chains. These include identity verification mechanisms, end-to-end encryption, immutable audit trails via blockchain, and automated incident detection. Cha (2022) also stresses the importance of embedding cybersecurity culture across the organization, promoting awareness, governance, and accountability from boardrooms to operational units. Complementary to this, Gaudenzi and Baldi (2024) introduce the concept of cyber resilience as a strategic posture that extends beyond prevention to include real-time response, recovery, and adaptive learning. As digital supply chains face compound risks—from geopolitical disruptions to zero-day vulnerabilities—this resilience becomes foundational. Sadeghi, Azadegan, and Ojha (2023) provide empirical evidence that firms with high absorptive capacity and operational visibility—facilitated by digital twins, AI, and blockchain—are more capable of absorbing cyber shocks and emerging stronger post-disruption.

Cybersecurity implementation strategies in the supply chain have also evolved from rigid controls to adaptive and intelligence-driven architectures, particularly in the logistics sector. Odimarha, Ayodeji, and Abaku (2024) identify best practices among shipping and logistics firms, such as risk-based authentication, segmentation of critical systems, and penetration testing across transport nodes. Sindiramutty et al. (2024) further highlight how global logistics firms like Maersk and FedEx have shifted toward real-time monitoring platforms that integrate predictive analytics, cyber incident forensics, and supplier risk assessments. These firms not only protect internal IT infrastructure but also assess the cyber maturity of their third-party partners. Aarland (2025) proposes a Digital Supply Chain Management Framework (DSCMF) that places cybersecurity at the center of procurement, inventory, and logistics decision-making. This approach emphasizes interoperability between systems, secure contract negotiations through smart contracts, and traceability using distributed ledger technology. The strategic emphasis on cyber resilience is not simply a matter of compliance but a means to ensure continuity, safeguard reputational capital, and sustain innovation even during systemic disruptions.

A central technological pillar in securing modern supply chains is the Zero Trust Architecture (ZTA), which operates on the premise of "never trust, always verify." In contrast to perimeter-based security models, ZTA continuously authenticates all entities—users, devices, and applications—regardless of their location. Patel and Chaudhary (2024) provide a comprehensive overview of how zero trust disrupts traditional access control by enforcing micro-segmentation, strict identity management, and adaptive authentication policies. Rivera, Muhammad, and Song (2024) explore the use of blockchain-integrated multi-factor authentication (MFA) systems to enhance digital identity assurance within ZTA, particularly for remote procurement and logistics staff. This decentralized approach improves resistance to credential theft and insider threats. Onwuegbuzie and Alabi (2025) emphasize the growing efficiency of authorization mechanisms under zero trust, particularly when combined with behavior analytics and AI-based anomaly detection. The integration of ZTA into logistics platforms ensures that unauthorized data access, lateral movement of threats, and supply chain impersonation attacks are minimized. Azad et al. (2024) extend this discourse by examining zero trust in the Internet of Things (IoT) context, arguing that ZTA provides a scalable and secure model for the heterogeneous devices that now populate supply chain environments—from warehouse sensors to delivery drones. These strategies not only mitigate threats but also instill digital trust across supply chain networks, facilitating seamless and secure innovation.

Equally transformative is the adoption of secure edge-cloud computing infrastructures, which enable real-time processing, scalability, and localized control over supply chain operations. As Industry 4.0 demands faster and smarter decision-making, organizations are migrating from centralized architectures to distributed edge-cloud models that reduce latency, support autonomous operations, and enhance data sovereignty. Wu, Dai, and Wang (2020) present a compelling framework for the convergence of blockchain and edge computing in industrial IoT (IIoT), asserting that the decentralized ledger system ensures integrity while edge nodes provide agility and speed. Yang et al. (2022) illustrate a practical application in the form of a blockchain-enabled quality management platform for perishable logistics, integrating edge-cloud infrastructure to track, validate, and respond to deviations in environmental conditions. This is especially critical for time- and temperature-sensitive products like pharmaceuticals and fresh food. Okwuibe et al. (2021) demonstrate how Software-Defined Networking (SDN) and edge orchestration enhance the resource allocation and reliability of industrial IoT deployments, allowing for dynamic reconfiguration during supply chain disruptions. Similarly, Guo et al. (2019) apply deep reinforcement learning (DRL) to optimize service function chaining across cloud-edge nodes, ensuring secure and efficient resource utilization. These solutions collectively create a resilient and decentralized digital infrastructure for supply chains, ensuring that cybersecurity is not merely an IT function but a fundamental capability distributed across physical, digital, and human interfaces.

In summary, cybersecurity has become an integral enabler of innovation and competitiveness in modern supply chains. As Kumar and Mallipeddi (2022) aptly note, the future of supply chain management will be defined by the strategic alignment of digital innovation and cybersecurity maturity. Organizations must not only defend against cyber threats but also design systems that are intrinsically secure, flexible, and transparent. This requires a multidimensional approach—embracing zero trust principles, leveraging secure-by-design methodologies, adopting distributed computing architectures, and cultivating cyber-resilient cultures across the value chain. Ultimately, cybersecurity should no longer be perceived as a constraint on digital supply chain innovation but as a strategic pillar that enables sustained, secure, and scalable transformation.

5. REAL-WORLD APPLICATIONS AND SECTORAL INNOVATIONS

Over the past three years, cyber-enabled technologies have been increasingly embedded in sector-specific supply chain operations to address key vulnerabilities and optimize performance. This transformation is evident in four critical sectors—pharmaceuticals, automotive, retail & e-commerce, and agrifood—where solutions such as blockchain, artificial intelligence (AI), Internet of Things (IoT), and advanced cybersecurity frameworks have been operationalized to improve transparency, resilience, and security. These innovations are no longer confined to theoretical models but are being implemented through robust architectures and yielding measurable benefits. In the pharmaceutical sector, the integration of blockchain with IoT sensors has enabled unprecedented levels of traceability and quality assurance in cold-chain logistics. SkyCell, a logistics provider specializing in temperature-sensitive pharmaceuticals, exemplifies this shift with their deployment of smart containers equipped with tamper-proof sensors and a blockchain backend. These containers record temperature and humidity in real-time, and the data is securely appended to a permissioned blockchain, allowing stakeholders across the supply chain—including manufacturers, transporters, and hospitals—to verify compliance at every handoff point (Softeq, 2023; greaterzuricharea.com, 2023). The effectiveness of this system was demonstrated during intercontinental COVID-19 vaccine shipments, where

SkyCell maintained optimal conditions despite external heat exposure, thereby preventing costly spoilage and ensuring regulatory compliance under frameworks such as the U.S. Drug Supply Chain Security Act (DSCSA). These outcomes—alongside reduced spoilage rates and accelerated incident responses—illustrate how blockchain-led cold-chain systems are reshaping pharmaceutical logistics.

In the automotive sector, firms are leveraging AI to navigate increasingly volatile and complex sourcing environments. Traditional methods of supplier risk evaluation have proved insufficient in the face of dynamic global disruptions such as the semiconductor shortage, port closures, and geopolitical instability. In response, automakers like Volkswagen Mexico have deployed AI-powered platforms such as Prewave, which aggregates multi-source data (e.g., news feeds, social media, supplier financials) and applies natural language processing and machine learning models to generate real-time risk alerts. These alerts enable proactive mitigation strategies such as re-sequencing production lines, rerouting shipments, or identifying alternate suppliers (Capgemini, 2023; Automotive Logistics, 2023). Volkswagen's AI-based digital risk matrix, for example, categorizes and prioritizes supplier threats within a 48-hour time frame, supporting rapid intervention and supply continuity. Beyond operational risk, AI systems are increasingly being applied for environmental, social, and governance (ESG) monitoring in response to due diligence mandates like Germany's Supply Chain Act. Platforms now map multi-tier supplier networks and flag not only logistical but also ethical risks. The results are compelling: improved foresight, reduced downtime, and a stronger capacity to meet regulatory and stakeholder demands. Nonetheless, implementing AI in such contexts is complex. Data standardization, integration with legacy ERP systems, and trust in algorithmic decision-making remain ongoing challenges that organizations must address through process redesign and cross-functional alignment (Capgemini, 2023).

Retail and e-commerce sectors have seen an exponential rise in cybersecurity investment, particularly in securing last-mile delivery systems. These systems encompass a range of digital components—from driver mobile apps to IoT-equipped drop boxes—and are increasingly targeted by cybercriminals exploiting vulnerabilities in routing software, customer databases, and third-party access points. The 2022 DoorDash breach, which compromised data of nearly five million users due to a third-party vulnerability, marked a turning point in how firms manage delivery data security (TechCrunch, 2022). In response, companies have adopted Zero Trust architectures, implemented multi-factor authentication, and enhanced encryption for both data in transit and at rest. UPS, for example, launched "DeliveryDefense," an AI-based risk scoring tool that predicts the likelihood of successful package delivery by analyzing address-level threat factors, indirectly supporting cybersecurity by mitigating physical theft risks associated with digital order systems (IoT World Today, 2023). Similarly, FedEx and DHL are integrating AI-driven anomaly detection into their delivery networks to flag suspicious activity in real-time, while ensuring privacy and data integrity through continuous monitoring and penetration testing (UPS, 2024; DHL, 2024). These measures have fortified operational resilience and safeguarded customer trust, with firms reporting lower breach frequencies and improved compliance with GDPR and other data protection regulations. However, fragmented subcontracting models in last-mile logistics and proliferation of under-secured IoT devices remain vulnerabilities that require systemic interventions, including enhanced third-party risk assessments and industry-wide threat intelligence sharing.

The agrifood sector presents another compelling case of cyber-physical integration, where IoT technologies are enabling continuous environmental monitoring across food production and distribution chains. These systems are particularly impactful in cold-chain logistics, where produce, dairy, and meat must be transported under strict temperature and humidity thresholds. Companies like Wiliot have pioneered battery-free IoT tags ("IoT Pixels") that attach to individual crates and monitor conditions via Bluetooth, transmitting encrypted data to cloud platforms using 128-bit AES encryption (Dairy Reporter, 2023). These solutions provide real-time visibility and alerting, allowing for immediate corrective action and improved traceability. The data is often used to comply with emerging food safety regulations, such as the U.S. FDA's FSMA Rule 204, which requires enhanced traceability for high-risk foods. Moreover, blockchain-IoT hybrids are emerging in this space, enabling not just monitoring but also immutable proof of compliance and provenance. These advancements improve not only operational efficiency and food safety but also customer confidence, as consumers increasingly demand transparency on how food is grown, stored, and transported. Nevertheless, the sector faces barriers in power supply, network infrastructure, and encryption overhead for constrained devices, especially in rural or under-resourced regions. Lightweight cryptographic solutions and standardized interoperability protocols are being developed to address these challenges and scale adoption beyond pilot programs (The Things Network, 2023; AWS, 2023).

Table 1 provides a comparative summary of cyber-enabled innovations across four key supply chain sectors—pharmaceuticals, automotive, retail & e-commerce, and agrifood. Each entry outlines the specific digital technology employed, a real-world implementation example, and the associated operational and strategic benefits.

Table 1. Cyber-enabled innovations in modern supply chains

Sector	Cyber Technology & Use Case	Example Implementation	Key Benefits
Pharmaceuticals	Blockchain + IoT for cold-chain traceability	SkyCell smart containers: IoT sensors record temperature & humidity to a blockchain platform; used by Virgin Atlantic	- End-to-end traceability and compliance - Spoilage reduced to <0.1% vs ~12% - Shared, immutable data improves trust and recall accuracy
Automotive	AI-driven risk forecasting in global sourcing	VW Mexico + Prewave: AI platform analyzes news and supplier data to flag disruption risks	- Early-warning system for delays - Real-time multi-tier supplier visibility - Avoids production halts and enhances ESG compliance
Retail & E-commerce	Cybersecurity in last-mile delivery systems	UPS "DeliveryDefense": AI-based system scores delivery address risk; DoorDash encrypts customer data after breach	- Protects customer PII - Prevents fraud and delivery theft - Strengthens network resilience against outages and cyberattacks
Agrifood	IoT-based monitoring with encrypted transmission	Wiliot "IoT Pixels": sensor tags on food crates send AES-encrypted temp/ humidity data to cloud	- Ensures cold-chain integrity and food safety - Reduces waste and improves compliance - Provides traceability from farm to shelf using secure data

In conclusion, cyber-enabled innovations across pharmaceuticals, automotive, retail, and agrifood sectors are fundamentally reshaping the structure and security of global supply chains. Each case demonstrates how tailored applications of digital technologies—when integrated with cybersecurity best practices—can generate transformative benefits in transparency, compliance, resilience, and trust. Although technical and organizational challenges persist, these sectors collectively illustrate a shift toward cyber-physical resilience as a strategic imperative in modern supply chain management.

6. GOVERNANCE, REGULATION, AND ETHICAL CHALLENGES

As digital transformation accelerates across supply chains, a parallel concern has emerged around the governance, regulatory alignment, and ethical implications of technology integration—especially in relation to cybersecurity, data sovereignty, and algorithmic accountability. The inherently global and decentralized nature of digital supply chains presents a complex regulatory landscape where data flows, cybersecurity standards, and ethical use of artificial intelligence (AI) often transcend national borders and sectoral boundaries. In particular, the development of cybersecurity standards for emerging technologies such as the Internet of Things (IoT) has been reactive and fragmented. Brass et al. (2018) emphasize that IoT security standardization remains a "moving target," where industry bodies, national regulators, and international organizations have yet to agree on a consistent and enforceable framework. This lack of consensus not only slows down technology adoption but also creates compliance uncertainty for supply chain actors who operate across jurisdictions. The tension between innovation speed and standardization complexity becomes more pronounced as supply chains adopt real-time IoT monitoring, edge computing, and autonomous systems, all of which require robust and coordinated governance.

One significant initiative in this domain is the development of cybersecurity certification schemes tailored for supply chains, which aim to establish trust through technical assurance. Michota and Polemi (2022) propose a certification framework grounded in the European Union's Cybersecurity Act, which would provide supply chain service providers with verifiable credentials regarding their cybersecurity readiness. These schemes advocate for the classification of services based on risk exposure and criticality, offering different assurance levels—basic, substantial, and high—to guide regulatory oversight and procurement decisions. Such certification not only helps in benchmarking suppliers but also supports transparent communication across multi-tier networks. However, as Topping et al. (2021) reveal through their comparative analysis of cybersecurity policies in critical infrastructure sectors, many current frameworks either overlook supply chain-specific risks or fail to provide cross-sectoral interoperability. There is often an overemphasis on compliance checklists and insufficient attention to dynamic threat modeling and continuous assessment—factors that are vital in high-risk, real-time supply environments. These gaps signal a pressing need for agile regulatory frameworks that are sector-sensitive, risk-informed, and technology-neutral, capable of evolving alongside cyber-physical innovations.

Ethical considerations further complicate the governance of digitally-enabled supply chains. In particular, the use of artificial intelligence and machine learning in supply chain decision-making raises concerns related to algorithmic bias, data transparency, and accountability. As Singh (2023) and Khoa (2024) discuss, AI is becoming central to tasks such as demand forecasting, supplier evaluation, and inventory optimization. However, without appropriate oversight, these technologies may inadvertently perpetuate discriminatory practices—especially when trained on biased historical datasets or implemented without stakeholder consultation. Hao and Demir (2024) propose a governance model that explicitly integrates Environmental, Social, and Governance (ESG) triggers into AI decision-making frameworks to mitigate ethical risks. Their protocol encourages companies to assess not only the operational efficiency of AI but also its societal and environmental externalities. This model reflects a growing recognition that technological deployment must be coupled with value-driven governance, ensuring that digital transformation supports broader sustainability and equity goals. It also aligns with the emerging principle of "responsible AI," which advocates for transparent algorithmic logic, inclusive data representation, and clear lines of human accountability in automated decision chains.

Beyond AI ethics, the cross-border nature of supply chain data flows presents significant legal and political challenges, particularly regarding data sovereignty. As Bolatbekkyzy (2024) and Chen (2021) articulate, divergent national laws governing data localization, privacy, and cybersecurity often clash in multinational supply chains. For example, while the European Union's General Data Protection Regulation (GDPR) emphasizes strict control over the export of personal data, other jurisdictions adopt more flexible or commercially-driven approaches. This regulatory divergence creates operational uncertainty, especially for firms leveraging cloud services, distributed ledgers, or global IoT platforms. Moreover, the geopolitical implications of data sovereignty have become increasingly salient, with governments using digital regulation as a tool for asserting economic and strategic influence. In response, efforts such as those proposed by Da Silva Carvalho et al. (2023) aim to create interoperable governance models that respect national sovereignty while enabling trusted cross-border data exchange in digital public services. These frameworks advocate for user-centric data controls, decentralized identity verification, and consensus-based regulatory cooperation—a direction that supply chain systems could emulate to balance openness with sovereignty.

Additionally, the integration of cybersecurity into smart manufacturing and cyber-physical systems introduces challenges around operational ethics and labor displacement. Ramya and Srinivasagan (2023) highlight that while smart factories enhance efficiency through real-time data exchange, they may also concentrate decision-making power in algorithmic systems, sidelining human oversight. Furthermore, the deployment of autonomous robots and AI-driven quality control raises issues of transparency and workforce displacement, which must be addressed through ethical labor strategies and retraining programs. Governance frameworks must therefore ensure that smart technologies in supply chains do not exacerbate social inequalities or undermine worker dignity. These considerations necessitate not only technological safeguards but also organizational policies and cultural norms that emphasize digital ethics, inclusive innovation, and stakeholder engagement.

In conclusion, the governance and regulation of cybersecurity in digital supply chains must evolve to match the complexity and velocity of technological change. A future-oriented approach requires harmonized standards, cross-border legal frameworks, AI ethics protocols, and participatory policymaking, all designed to foster trust, transparency, and accountability. As supply chains continue to digitize, the convergence of regulatory clarity and ethical integrity will determine whether cybersecurity remains a reactive burden or transforms into a foundational pillar of responsible innovation and global cooperation.

7. BARRIERS AND STRATEGIC TRADE-OFFS

Despite the considerable potential of digital technologies to revolutionize supply chains, their adoption is often hindered by financial constraints and strategic misalignments between innovation goals and available resources. Many organizations, particularly small and medium-sized enterprises (SMEs), struggle to balance the cost of digital investment with short-term operational demands. Caliskan, Eryilmaz, and Ozturkoglu (2025) observe that limited budgets and uncertainty about return on investment are among the most cited barriers to implementing Logistics 4.0 solutions. Firms often hesitate to invest in cybersecurity tools, blockchain platforms, or AI-driven analytics due to the high upfront costs and the complexity of quantifying long-term benefits. This hesitancy is further compounded when digital projects are not directly linked to immediate efficiency gains or cost savings, making it challenging to justify large-scale innovation within constrained budget cycles. Garg (2023) similarly highlights that without strong leadership commitment and financial planning, digital transformation efforts in logistics firms tend to remain fragmented or stall after initial pilot phases. These dynamics create a critical trade-off between innovation acceleration and financial prudence, where the risk of underinvestment may lead to competitive stagnation, while overinvestment without clear strategic alignment may result in technology misfit or sunk costs.

A major structural barrier to digital transformation is the persistent reliance on legacy systems, which inhibit the integration of new digital technologies and create operational bottlenecks. These systems, often built on outdated software and rigid architecture, lack the interoperability needed to support real-time data exchange, cybersecurity upgrades, or cloud-based applications. Irani et al. (2023), through their multi-case analysis of European public sector transformation, emphasize that legacy infrastructure not only slows down digital transitions but also consumes significant maintenance budgets, reducing the funds available for innovation. Similarly, Abdellatif et al. (2021) propose a taxonomy of service identification approaches to support legacy software modernization, yet highlight the technical and managerial challenges in re-engineering deeply embedded processes. In the supply chain context, legacy systems often lack API compatibility or scalable data frameworks, making it difficult to connect with IoT devices or blockchain networks. This misalignment creates inefficiencies, as organizations must either build expensive middleware or undertake full system overhauls, both of which demand resources and time. Tabim, Ayala, and Frank (2024) further stress that the vertical integration necessary for Industry 4.0 adoption is heavily influenced by legacy system maturity, particularly in terms of data structure uniformity and automation capabilities. Thus, modernizing outdated infrastructure becomes a prerequisite for realizing the full potential of smart supply chain ecosystems.

Beyond technical and financial constraints, organizations frequently face cultural resistance to digital adoption, particularly in traditional logistics environments where operational practices have remained unchanged for decades. Cichosz, Wallenburg, and Knemeyer (2020) find that organizational inertia, low digital literacy, and fear of job displacement contribute to a skeptical attitude toward technological change among logistics personnel. This resistance can manifest in the form of slow adoption of new tools, poor system usage, or outright rejection of digital workflows, even when infrastructure is available. Moreover, top-down digital mandates that overlook employee engagement and training often exacerbate this divide, leading to underutilization of advanced capabilities. Caliskan et al. (2025) note that digital transformation strategies must include change management initiatives that address workforce concerns and build trust in automation. Effective transformation therefore requires not only hardware and software upgrades but also an inclusive and adaptive organizational culture that supports lifelong learning and process reengineering. Without this cultural foundation, digital tools may be introduced but never embedded, and supply chains will fail to reach their desired levels of agility and responsiveness.

One of the most pressing strategic dilemmas in digital supply chains is managing the trade-off between data transparency and confidentiality, particularly as organizations embrace blockchain, big data analytics, and AI. On the one hand, increased data sharing across suppliers, partners, and regulators enhances visibility, traceability, and collaborative decision-making. Lautenschlager et al. (2023), in their blockchain-based delivery invoice case study, show how distributed ledgers can solve documentation inefficiencies and enhance trust in multi-stakeholder supply chains. However, such transparency often comes at the cost of data privacy, intellectual property protection, and cybersecurity risks. Janssen and van den Hoven (2015) describe this as the "transparency–privacy paradox" in digital governance, where openness can inadvertently expose sensitive operational or personal data. This paradox is amplified in AI and IoT ecosystems where continuous data collection and cloud transmission are the norm. Lysaght et al. (2021), in their survey on precision medicine data sharing, found that users are willing to share information only when they feel a high degree of control and security—principles equally applicable in supply chain settings. Taher, Mehrnezhad, and Morisset (2022) further highlight how a perceived loss of control over digital data reduces trust in smart environments. In the supply chain domain, balancing transparency with confidentiality thus requires robust governance mechanisms, including tiered data access, role-based permissions, encrypted transactions, and standardized consent protocols.

Finally, the increased complexity of managing data ecosystems in digital supply chains creates operational and strategic challenges. As Geisler et al. (2021) point out, modern supply chains rely on highly distributed, knowledge-driven data architectures that span multiple jurisdictions and industries. These ecosystems must reconcile conflicting data standards, ensure semantic interoperability, and support real-time analytics without compromising data quality or cybersecurity. Alhija et al. (2024) analyze this complexity in the healthcare IoT context, where blockchain must be optimized to balance scalability, privacy, and efficiency—a triad of goals that often pull in opposite directions. Similar dynamics apply to supply chains, where designing a system that is simultaneously secure, fast, and transparent requires careful architectural trade-offs. Overemphasizing privacy may limit real-time responsiveness; prioritizing speed might weaken encryption; focusing on transparency could create compliance risks. These trade-offs must be actively managed through strategic alignment, cross-functional collaboration, and continuous scenario testing, ensuring that digital infrastructure supports both operational performance and organizational values.

In summary, while digital technologies offer transformative potential for supply chains, they also introduce a range of technical, financial, cultural, and ethical barriers. Overcoming these obstacles requires more than technological upgrades; it demands an integrated strategy that considers budget planning, system modernization, workforce readiness, and data governance. Organizations must navigate these trade-offs thoughtfully, acknowledging that the pursuit of innovation will always involve constraints, compromises, and recalibrations. The most successful supply chains will be those that can balance speed with security, transparency with privacy, and automation with inclusiveness, crafting a digital transformation journey that is both resilient and responsible.

8. STRATEGIC RECOMMENDATIONS

As supply chains become increasingly digitized and globally interconnected, organizations must adopt forward-looking strategies that not only enhance operational efficiency but also embed cybersecurity and sustainability into the core of their supply chain governance. The convergence of these domains is no longer aspirational—it is essential for managing risk, ensuring compliance, and building long-term trust. Based on the cross-sectoral insights explored in this chapter, the following strategic recommendations are proposed to guide supply chain leaders in developing cyber-secure, sustainable, and resilient operations.

First, a unified framework for aligning cybersecurity with sustainability goals should be adopted. Traditionally treated as separate pillars, sustainability and cybersecurity are deeply interlinked in modern supply chains. Secure digital systems are foundational to accurate emissions tracking, ethical sourcing verification, and regulatory reporting. For instance, blockchain platforms used in pharmaceutical cold-chain logistics (e.g., SkyCell) and agrifood IoT monitoring (e.g., Wiliot) demonstrate how data integrity and traceability—enabled by encrypted digital infrastructure—support both product safety and environmental stewardship (Softeq, 2023; Dairy Reporter, 2023). Organizations should ensure that sustainability data, such as carbon footprint or sourcing origin, is protected through secure channels and validated with tamper-proof technologies like blockchain or digitally signed IoT feeds. This not only ensures transparency and regulatory compliance but also enhances stakeholder confidence in sustainability claims, a critical factor in ESG reporting (Rejeb et al., 2021; Esan et al., 2024).

Second, companies must prioritize the development of cyber-aware leadership in supply chain management. As the complexity of digital supply chains grows, decision-makers must be equipped not only with traditional logistics and procurement knowledge but also with a working understanding of cyber risk, data governance, and digital ethics. As shown in the automotive sector, leaders like VW Mexico's logistics team have begun relying on AI-generated risk alerts to shape supplier decisions, emphasizing the strategic value of data literacy and cyber risk interpretation at the executive level (Automotive Logistics, 2023). Leadership buy-in is also crucial to drive cross-functional collaboration between IT, cybersecurity teams, procurement, and sustainability officers. Without a cyber-literate leadership culture, technology adoption risks becoming fragmented or misaligned with business goals.

Third, workforce training and cyber risk literacy programs must be embedded across all tiers of the supply chain. Cybersecurity incidents in e-commerce and logistics, such as the DoorDash breach and Expeditors International ransomware attack, have highlighted that human error and third-party vulnerabilities are frequent points of failure (TechCrunch, 2022; DHL, 2024). To address this, organizations must move beyond compliance-based training toward role-specific, scenario-based education that helps employees—from warehouse staff to delivery drivers—recognize threats and act accordingly. As discussed in the retail and last-mile delivery context, even gig-economy drivers are now receiving phishing awareness and mobile security training as part of a broader effort to reduce systemic cyber exposure (UPS, 2024). Likewise, awareness programs must extend to suppliers and subcontractors, particularly in fragmented or gig-based delivery ecosystems where security standards are inconsistent.

Fourth, the development of adaptive, resilient, and inclusive digital supply chain strategies should be prioritized. As illustrated by AI-based risk forecasting in automotive supply chains and secure IoT monitoring in agrifood logistics, real-time responsiveness, redundancy, and data integration are key to surviving and thriving under uncertainty (Capgemini, 2023; AWS, 2023). However, resilience must be inclusive—meaning it supports small suppliers, rural producers, and lower-tier partners in achieving security and digital maturity. Scalable technologies like lightweight cryptography, standardized APIs, and cloud-based dashboards can help democratize access to secure supply chain platforms, avoiding a digital divide that leaves smaller players behind. Moreover, integrating ethical AI models (e.g., ESG-triggered decision-making in sourcing platforms) ensures that automation enhances sustainability without compromising social values (Hao & Demir, 2024). Strategic investments should focus not only on tools, but also on governance: ensuring that supply chain policies are agile, equity-focused, and aligned with international standards such as GDPR, ISO/IEC 27001, and GRI sustainability reporting frameworks.

To support practical implementation, organizations can apply a Cyber-Sustainability Integration Roadmap, serving as a checklist for transformation:

1. Map cybersecurity and sustainability interdependencies across the supply chain (e.g., traceability systems, ESG reporting platforms).
2. Conduct joint risk assessments that evaluate both cyber threats and sustainability vulnerabilities (e.g., data loss and carbon non-compliance).
3. Standardize secure data architectures for ESG metrics (e.g., encrypted environmental data from IoT sensors).
4. Train staff and partners on both cyber hygiene and digital sustainability tools.
5. Embed cyber resilience into digital sustainability initiatives, such as AI-based energy optimization or blockchain for ethical sourcing.
6. Monitor, evaluate, and adapt, using KPIs that track not just efficiency, but security incidents and sustainability outcomes.

These strategic directions, rooted in sector-specific best practices and technological innovations, aim to equip supply chain organizations with the capabilities to manage growing complexity in a responsible and resilient manner. As shown across all examined sectors, cybersecurity is no longer a peripheral concern but a central enabler of sustainable supply chain transformation.

9. CONCLUSION

The evolution of modern supply chains into smart, secure, and sustainable ecosystems underscores the strategic necessity of integrating cybersecurity into every layer of digital transformation. As demonstrated across the pharmaceutical, automotive, retail, and agrifood sectors, technologies such as blockchain, artificial intelligence, and encrypted IoT are no longer emerging tools—they are operational imperatives driving traceability, risk mitigation, and consumer trust. However, the full potential of these innovations is only realized when cyber resilience is embedded alongside sustainability objectives, supported by informed leadership, cross-functional collaboration, and inclusive digital strategies. The convergence of these domains creates a new paradigm of supply chain management—one that is not only responsive and efficient but also ethically grounded and future-proof. By adopting cyber-sustainability frameworks, building organizational cyber awareness, and investing in adaptive infrastructures, firms can navigate uncertainty while delivering value, compliance, and integrity across global networks. The insights presented in this chapter reaffirm that cybersecurity is not merely a technical safeguard but a foundational enabler of innovation, resilience, and long-term sustainability in the digital supply chain era.

REFERENCES

Aarland, M. (2025). Cybersecurity in digital supply chains in the procurement process: Introducing the digital supply chain management framework. *Information and Computer Security*, *33*(1), 5–24. DOI: 10.1108/ICS-10-2023-0198

Abaku, E. A., Edunjobi, T. E., & Odimarha, A. C. (2024). Theoretical approaches to AI in supply chain optimization: Pathways to efficiency and resilience. *International Journal of Science and Technology Research Archive, 6*(1), 092-107.

Abdellatif, M., Shatnawi, A., Mili, H., Moha, N., El Boussaidi, G., Hecht, G., & Guéhéneuc, Y. G. (2021). A taxonomy of service identification approaches for legacy software systems modernization. *Journal of Systems and Software*, *173*, 110868. DOI: 10.1016/j.jss.2020.110868

Akkartal, G. R., & Mızrak, F. (2024). Operational Efficiency and Competitiveness in the Global Logistics Industry: An Examination of Human Resources Management Strategies. In *Strategic Innovations for Dynamic Supply Chains* (pp. 71-102). IGI Global.

Al-Okaily, M., Younis, H., & Al-Okaily, A. (2024). The impact of management practices and industry 4.0 technologies on supply chain sustainability: A systematic review. *Heliyon*, *10*(17), e36421. DOI: 10.1016/j.heliyon.2024.e36421 PMID: 39263079

Alhija, M. A., Al-Baik, O., Hussein, A., & Abdeljaber, H. (2024). Optimizing blockchain for healthcare IoT: A practical guide to navigating scalability, privacy, and efficiency trade-offs. *Indonesian Journal of Electrical Engineering and Computer Science*, *35*(3), 1773–1785. DOI: 10.11591/ijeecs.v35.i3.pp1773-1785

Automotive Logistics. (2023). How VW Mexico is using AI to improve logistics decision-making. Retrieved from https://www.automotivelogistics.media

AWS. (2023). Cold-chain monitoring with AWS IoT. Retrieved from https://www .aws.amazon.com

Azad, M. A., Abdullah, S., Arshad, J., Lallie, H., & Ahmed, Y. H. (2024). Verify and trust: A multidimensional survey of zero-trust security in the age of IoT. *Internet of Things : Engineering Cyber Physical Human Systems*, *27*, 101227. DOI: 10.1016/j.iot.2024.101227

Bolatbekkyzy, G. (2024). Legal Issues of Cross-Border Data Transfer in the Era of Digital Government. *Journal of Digital Technologies and Law*, *2*(2), 286–307. DOI: 10.21202/jdtl.2024.15

Boyson, S., Corsi, T. M., & Paraskevas, J. P. (2022). Defending digital supply chains: Evidence from a decade-long research program. *Technovation, 118*, 102380. DOI: 10.1016/j.technovation.2021.102380

Brass, I., Tanczer, L., Carr, M., Elsden, M., & Blackstock, J. (2018). Standardising a moving target: The development and evolution of IoT security standards. In *Living in the Internet of Things: Cybersecurity of the IoT-2018* (p. 24). IET. DOI: 10.1049/cp.2018.0024

Caliskan, A., Eryilmaz, S., & Ozturkoglu, Y. (2025). Investigating the effects of barriers and challenges on Logistics 4.0 in the era of evolving digital technology. *Journal of Modelling in Management, 20*(3), 949–973. DOI: 10.1108/JM2-01-2024-0026

Capgemini. (2023). AI in the automotive supply chain: Driving resilience through predictive intelligence. Retrieved from https://www.capgemini.com

Cha, S. Y. (2022). The art of cyber security in the age of the digital supply chain: detecting and defending against vulnerabilities in your supply chain. In *The Digital Supply Chain* (pp. 215–233). Elsevier. DOI: 10.1016/B978-0-323-91614-1.00013-7

Chen, S. (2021). Research on data sovereignty rules in cross-border data flow and Chinese solution. *US-China L.Rev., 18*, 261.

Cichosz, M., Wallenburg, C. M., & Knemeyer, A. M. (2020). Digital transformation at logistics service providers: Barriers, success factors and leading practices. *International Journal of Logistics Management, 31*(2), 209–238. DOI: 10.1108/IJLM-08-2019-0229

Da Silva Carvalho, N., Jabbarpour, J., Temple, L., Belacort, I. M., Barturen, U. I., Kortlander, M., & Mureddu, F. (2023, September). A more inclusive Europe through personal data sovereignty in cross-border digital public services. In *Proceedings of the 16th International Conference on Theory and Practice of Electronic Governance* (pp. 63-71). DOI: 10.1145/3614321.3614329

Dairy Reporter. (2023). Wiliot's ambient IoT tags bring real-time freshness data to retailers. Retrieved from https://www.dairyreporter.com

DHL. (2024). Cybersecurity 2.0 in logistics: Proactive defense in the digital age. Retrieved from https://www.dhl.com

Esan, O., Ajayi, F. A., & Olawale, O. (2024). Supply chain integrating sustainability and ethics: Strategies for modern supply chain management. *World Journal of Advanced Research and Reviews, 22*(1), 1930–1953. DOI: 10.30574/wjarr.2024.22.1.1259

Garg, A. (2023). Factors affecting digital transformation in logistic firms. *Journal of Informatics Education and Research, 3*(2). Advance online publication. DOI: 10.52783/jier.v3i2.326

Gaudenzi, B., & Baldi, B. (2024). Cyber resilience in organisations and supply chains: From perceptions to actions. *International Journal of Logistics Management, 35*(7), 99–122. DOI: 10.1108/IJLM-09-2023-0372

Geisler, S., Vidal, M. E., Cappiello, C., Lóscio, B. F., Gal, A., Jarke, M., Lenzerini, M., Missier, P., Otto, B., Paja, E., Pernici, B., & Rehof, J. (2021). Knowledge-driven data ecosystems toward data transparency. [JDIQ]. *ACM Journal of Data and Information Quality, 14*(1), 1–12. DOI: 10.1145/3467022

Greater Zurich Area. (2023). SkyCell: Pharma shipping with blockchain-backed security. Retrieved from https://www.greaterzuricharea.com

Guo, S., Dai, Y., Xu, S., Qiu, X., & Qi, F. (2019). Trusted cloud-edge network resource management: DRL-driven service function chain orchestration for IoT. *IEEE Internet of Things Journal, 7*(7), 6010–6022. DOI: 10.1109/JIOT.2019.2951593

Hammi, B., Zeadally, S., & Nebhen, J. (2023). Security threats, countermeasures, and challenges of digital supply chains. *ACM Computing Surveys, 55*(14s), 1–40. DOI: 10.1145/3588999

Hao, X., & Demir, E. (2024). Artificial intelligence in supply chain decision-making: An environmental, social, and governance triggering and technological inhibiting protocol. *Journal of Modelling in Management, 19*(2), 605–629. DOI: 10.1108/JM2-01-2023-0009

Hellani, H., Sliman, L., Samhat, A. E., & Exposito, E. (2021). On blockchain integration with supply chain: Overview on data transparency. *Logistics (Basel), 5*(3), 46. DOI: 10.3390/logistics5030046

IoT World Today. (2023). UPS's DeliveryDefense uses AI to reduce package theft. Retrieved from https://www.iotworldtoday.com

Irani, Z., Abril, R. M., Weerakkody, V., Omar, A., & Sivarajah, U. (2023). The impact of legacy systems on digital transformation in European public administration: Lesson learned from a multi case analysis. *Government Information Quarterly, 40*(1), 101784. DOI: 10.1016/j.giq.2022.101784

Ivanov, D., & Dolgui, A. (2022). Stress testing supply chains and creating viable ecosystems. *Operations Management Research : Advancing Practice Through Research, 15*(1), 475–486. DOI: 10.1007/s12063-021-00194-z

Jampani, S., Avancha, S., Mangal, A., Singh, S. P., Jain, S., & Agarwal, R. (2023). Machine learning algorithms for supply chain optimisation. [IJRMEET]. *International Journal of Research in Modern Engineering and Emerging Technology, 11*(4).

Janssen, M., & van den Hoven, J. (2015). Big and Open Linked Data (BOLD) in government: A challenge to transparency and privacy? *Government Information Quarterly, 32*(4), 363–368. DOI: 10.1016/j.giq.2015.11.007

Khan, S. A., Mubarik, M. S., Kusi-Sarpong, S., Gupta, H., Zaman, S. I., & Mubarik, M. (2022). Blockchain technologies as enablers of supply chain mapping for sustainable supply chains. *Business Strategy and the Environment, 31*(8), 3742–3756. DOI: 10.1002/bse.3029

Khoa, B. Q., Nguyen, H.-T., Anh, D. B. H., & Ngoc, N. M. (2024). Impact of Artificial Intelligence's part in supply chain planning and decision making optimization. *International Journal of Multidisciplinary Research and Growth Evaluation, 5*(6), 837–856. DOI: 10.54660/.IJMRGE.2024.5.6.837-856

Kumar, S., & Mallipeddi, R. R. (2022). Impact of cybersecurity on operations and supply chain management: Emerging trends and future research directions. *Production and Operations Management, 31*(12), 4488–4500. DOI: 10.1111/poms.13859

Lautenschlager, J., Stramm, J., Guggenberger, T., Schweizer, A., & Rösch, A. (2023, September). Overcoming the data transparency trade-off: Designing a blockchain-based delivery invoice system for the construction industry. In *International Conference on Wirtschaftsinformatik* (pp. 377-392). Cham: Springer Nature Switzerland.

Lysaght, T., Ballantyne, A., Toh, H. J., Lau, A., Ong, S., Schaefer, O., Shiraishi, M., van den Boom, W., Xafis, V., & Tai, E. S. (2021). Trust and trade-offs in sharing data for precision medicine: A national survey of Singapore. *Journal of Personalized Medicine, 11*(9), 921. DOI: 10.3390/jpm11090921 PMID: 34575698

Michota, A., & Polemi, N. (2022, July). A Supply Chain Service Cybersecurity Certification Scheme based on the Cybersecurity Act. In *2022 IEEE International Conference on Cyber Security and Resilience (CSR)* (pp. 382-387). IEEE. DOI: 10.1109/CSR54599.2022.9850323

Mızrak, F. (2024). *Strategic Innovations for Dynamic Supply Chains*. IGI Global.

Nikookar, E., Stevenson, M., & Varsei, M. (2024). Building an antifragile supply chain: A capability blueprint for resilience and post-disruption growth. *The Journal of Supply Chain Management, 60*(1), 13–31. DOI: 10.1111/jscm.12313

Odimarha, A. C., Ayodeji, S. A., & Abaku, E. A. (2024). Securing the digital supply chain: Cybersecurity best practices for logistics and shipping companies,'. *World Journal of Advanced Science and Technology, 5*(1), 026-030.

Okwuibe, J., Haavisto, J., Kovacevic, I., Harjula, E., Ahmad, I., Islam, J., & Ylianttila, M. (2021). SDN-enabled resource orchestration for industrial IoT in collaborative edge-cloud networks. *IEEE Access : Practical Innovations, Open Solutions, 9*, 115839–115854. DOI: 10.1109/ACCESS.2021.3105944

Onwuegbuzie, I. U., & Alabi, O. A. (2025). A Review of Authentication and Authorization Mechanisms in Zero Trust Architecture: Evolution and Efficiency. *Tech-Sphere Journal for Pure and Applied Sciences, 2*(1).

Oriekhoe, O. I., Oyeyemi, O. P., Bello, B. G., Omotoye, G. B., Daraojimba, A. I., & Adefemi, A. (2024). Blockchain in supply chain management: A review of efficiency, transparency, and innovation. *International Journal of Science and Research Archive, 11*(1), 173–181. DOI: 10.30574/ijsra.2024.11.1.0028

Pan, S., Trentesaux, D., McFarlane, D., Montreuil, B., Ballot, E., & Huang, G. Q. (2021). Digital interoperability in logistics and supply chain management: State-of-the-art and research avenues towards Physical Internet. *Computers in Industry, 128*, 103435. DOI: 10.1016/j.compind.2021.103435

Pandey, S., Singh, R. K., Gunasekaran, A., & Kaushik, A. (2020). Cyber security risks in globalized supply chains: Conceptual framework. *Journal of Global Operations and Strategic Sourcing, 13*(1), 103–128. DOI: 10.1108/JGOSS-05-2019-0042

Patel, A., & Chaudhary, M. (2024). Zero Trust Architecture: A Comprehensive Guide to Modern IT Security. *Baltic Multidisciplinary Research Letters Journal, 1*(3), 44–53.

Ramya, G., & Srinivasagan, K. G. Integrating Cybersecurity Threats into Smart Manufacturing: Best Practices and Frameworks. In *Artificial Intelligence Solutions for Cyber-Physical Systems* (pp. 120-138). Auerbach Publications.

Rejeb, A., Keogh, J. G., Simske, S. J., Stafford, T., & Treiblmaier, H. (2021). Potentials of blockchain technologies for supply chain collaboration: A conceptual framework. *International Journal of Logistics Management, 32*(3), 973–994. DOI: 10.1108/IJLM-02-2020-0098

Rivera, J. J. D., Muhammad, A., & Song, W. C. (2024). Securing digital identity in the zero trust architecture: A blockchain approach to privacy-focused multi-factor authentication. *IEEE Open Journal of the Communications Society*.

Sadeghi, K., Azadegan, A., & Ojha, D. (2023). A path to build supply chain cyber-resilience through absorptive capacity and visibility: Two empirical studies. *Industrial Marketing Management, 111*, 202–215. DOI: 10.1016/j.indmarman.2023.04.001

Sindiramutty, S. R., Tan, C. E., Goh, W. W., Balakrishnan, S., Hamzah, N., & Akbar, R. (2024). Securing the Supply Chain: Cybersecurity Strategies for Logistics Resilience. In *Navigating Cyber Threats and Cybersecurity in the Logistics Industry* (pp. 300-365). IGI Global.

Singh, P. K. (2023). Digital transformation in supply chain management: Artificial Intelligence (AI) and Machine Learning (ML) as Catalysts for Value Creation. *International Journal of Supply Chain Management, 12*(6), 57–63. DOI: 10.59160/ijscm.v12i6.6216

Softeq. (2023). SkyCell: Blockchain and IoT for pharmaceutical cold chain. Retrieved from https://www.softeq.com

Tabim, V. M., Ayala, N. F., & Frank, A. G. (2024). Implementing vertical integration in the industry 4.0 journey: Which factors influence the process of information systems adoption? *Information Systems Frontiers, 26*(5), 1615–1632. DOI: 10.1007/s10796-021-10220-x PMID: 34776762

Taher, R., Mehrnezhad, M., & Morisset, C. (2022, September). "I feel spied on and i don't have any control over my data": user privacy perception, preferences and trade-offs in university smart buildings. In *International Workshop on Socio-Technical Aspects in Security* (pp. 73-92). Cham: Springer Nature Switzerland.

TechCrunch. (2022). DoorDash confirms data breach impacted millions of customers. Retrieved from https://www.techcrunch.com

The Things Network. (2023). LoRaWAN security fundamentals: How AES encryption protects agricultural IoT. https://www.thethingsnetwork.org

Topping, C., Dwyer, A., Michalec, O., Craggs, B., & Rashid, A. (2021). Beware suppliers bearing gifts!: Analysing coverage of supply chain cyber security in critical national infrastructure sectorial and cross-sectorial frameworks. *Computers & Security, 108*, 102324. DOI: 10.1016/j.cose.2021.102324

UPS. (2024). Investor Relations: Cybersecurity risk and resilience. Retrieved from https://investors.ups.com

WJARR. (2023). Security analysis of IoT devices used in agricultural supply chains. *World Journal of Advanced Research and Reviews, 22*(1), 1023–1037.

Wu, Y., Dai, H. N., & Wang, H. (2020). Convergence of blockchain and edge computing for secure and scalable IIoT critical infrastructures in industry 4.0. *IEEE Internet of Things Journal, 8*(4), 2300–2317. DOI: 10.1109/JIOT.2020.3025916

Yang, C., Lan, S., Zhao, Z., Zhang, M., Wu, W., & Huang, G. Q. (2022). Edge-cloud blockchain and IoE-enabled quality management platform for perishable supply chain logistics. *IEEE Internet of Things Journal, 10*(4), 3264–3275. DOI: 10.1109/JIOT.2022.3142095

Chapter 10
Cyber-Resilient Sustainable Airports:
Managing Digital Risks in Green Aviation Initiatives

Umit Kanmaz
https://orcid.org/0000-0003-2186-2737
Istanbul Ticaret University, Turkey

ABSTRACT

The convergence of digital transformation and sustainability in the aviation sector has led to the emergence of smart airport ecosystems that rely heavily on interconnected technologies to achieve environmental goals. While innovations such as IoT-enabled energy systems, AI-driven carbon monitoring, and digital twin simulations enhance operational efficiency and support decarbonization, they also introduce new cybersecurity vulnerabilities. This chapter explores the critical role of cybersecurity as a foundational element of sustainable airport strategies. It examines the threats targeting green digital infrastructures, evaluates the integration of standards such as ISO/IEC 27001 and ISO 14001, and proposes strategic approaches for managing cyber-resilience in smart, sustainable airports. By framing cybersecurity as a strategic enabler rather than a barrier, the chapter provides a roadmap for aligning environmental integrity, operational continuity, and digital trust in the next generation of airport management.

DOI: 10.4018/979-8-3693-6417-8.ch010

1. INTRODUCTION

The global aviation industry stands at a critical juncture, where the dual imperatives of digital transformation and environmental sustainability are reshaping traditional airport operations into interconnected, intelligent ecosystems. As airports pursue aggressive decarbonization targets in alignment with the Sustainable Development Goals (SDGs) and international frameworks such as ICAO's Long-Term Aspirational Goal (LTAG), they are increasingly deploying advanced digital technologies to enable real-time monitoring, automation, and energy optimization. These technologies include Internet of Things (IoT) devices, digital twins, artificial intelligence (AI)-driven energy management systems, and blockchain-based emissions verification platforms—all designed to reduce environmental impact while improving operational efficiency (Dias & Silva, 2024; Zhou, 2022). At the heart of this transition is the evolution of the airport from a carbon-intensive, siloed infrastructure into a smart, sustainable node within a broader urban and energy ecosystem. These innovations, however, come with a parallel increase in complexity, interdependence, and vulnerability—particularly in the form of cybersecurity threats targeting critical systems and environmental data streams.

The reliance on data-rich systems to manage renewable energy integration, sustainable aviation fuel (SAF) logistics, and emissions tracking platforms introduces a new category of operational risk that extends beyond traditional safety and reliability concerns. As digital systems become central to managing the environmental performance of airports, cybersecurity is no longer a peripheral IT issue but a foundational pillar of sustainable infrastructure. Compromised energy systems, falsified carbon accounting data, or ransomware attacks on environmental databases can paralyze operations, disrupt compliance with regulatory frameworks, and damage stakeholder trust. As Mızrak and Akkartal (2024) emphasize, cybersecurity must be strategically integrated into digital transformation plans—not merely as a protective measure, but as an enabler of operational continuity and environmental accountability. This is especially true as airports become key players in smart grid coordination, decentralized renewable energy adoption, and carbon offset verification—domains where cyber-physical system integrity is indispensable to achieving sustainability objectives (Ranawaka et al., 2024; Khalid, 2024).

Despite the growing urgency, many sustainability initiatives continue to overlook the cybersecurity dimension, often underestimating the systemic risks posed by digital dependence in environmental management systems. The need for integrated governance frameworks, secure-by-design engineering, and cyber-aware sustainability teams has become increasingly clear. Effective responses to this challenge require a rethinking of how cyber-resilience is managed across environmental, technical, and organizational boundaries. As Mızrak (2023, 2024) argues, strategic cybersecurity risk management must be embedded into the broader managerial architecture of aviation institutions, with particular attention to human capital, institutional alignment, and proactive resilience building. Similarly, studies by Murat et al. (2024) and Yaseen (2024) support the view that cybersecurity must be addressed at the design stage of green airport infrastructure, rather than as an afterthought.

This chapter aims to explore the evolving intersection of digitalization, cybersecurity, and sustainability within the context of airport management. It begins by examining the core digital technologies driving green airport infrastructure, including smart grids, AI-enabled energy platforms, and carbon data ecosystems. It then explores the emerging cybersecurity threats that target these systems, including attacks on digital ESG platforms, SAF logistics, and smart energy supply chains. Subsequent sections evaluate the global standards and frameworks—such as ISO 14001, ISO/IEC 27001, the NIST Cybersecurity Framework, and ICAO guidelines—that support the integration of cybersecurity into sustainable airport operations. The chapter further presents strategic approaches to airport cyber-resilience, encompassing governance models, secure-by-design methodologies, human resource strategies, and cyber-aware training systems. Ultimately, this chapter positions cybersecurity not as a technical constraint on sustainability innovation, but as a strategic enabler of secure, reliable, and future-ready green transformation in aviation. Through an interdisciplinary synthesis of technical, managerial, and regulatory insights, it offers a roadmap for embedding digital trust into the next generation of sustainable airport systems.

2. GREEN TECHNOLOGIES AND SMART INFRASTRUCTURE IN AIRPORTS

The aviation industry is undergoing a profound transformation driven by the convergence of digitalization and sustainability imperatives. As aviation stakeholders strive to reduce greenhouse gas emissions and improve operational efficiency, airports are emerging as critical nodes for the deployment of integrated green technologies. The concept of the "smart airport" encapsulates this evolution, referring to digitally augmented environments where data-driven systems coordinate various operational functions—passenger processing, airside logistics, energy consumption, and maintenance—with the explicit goal of improving both environmental and service outcomes. Smart airports leverage a suite of interconnected technologies, including the Internet of Things (IoT), artificial intelligence (AI), digital twin simulations, and smart grid systems to enable predictive, responsive, and sustainable operations. Dias and Silva (2024) provide a comprehensive overview of this new paradigm, emphasizing how these technologies are strategically deployed not only to optimize resource use and reduce operational costs, but also to meet escalating regulatory and societal expectations for sustainable development in aviation.

A pivotal element in achieving green transformation is the application of intelligent energy management systems powered by IoT and AI. In modern airports, IoT-enabled sensors are deployed across a range of infrastructures—from terminal buildings and baggage handling systems to lighting arrays and HVAC units—to continuously capture real-time data on environmental conditions, energy usage, and equipment status. This data is then fed into AI-based control systems capable of dynamically adjusting energy loads in response to contextual variables such as occupancy levels, flight schedules, and ambient temperature. This capability reduces waste, prevents overuse, and ensures that energy is deployed only where and when it is needed, significantly reducing the airport's carbon footprint. In advanced models, these systems are supplemented by machine learning algorithms that analyze historical data to predict energy demands with high accuracy, enabling proactive load balancing and integration with renewable energy inputs (Zhou, 2022). These systems are not only efficient but essential to achieving the low-carbon transition of airports into energy-smart hubs, particularly when aligned with hydrogen-based storage and flexible grid configurations that allow airports to operate as prosumers within urban smart grid ecosystems.

Another layer of technological sophistication is added through the use of digital twin technology, which creates dynamic virtual replicas of physical airport systems. These digital twins are synchronized in real time with physical assets via sensors and data acquisition systems and are used to simulate, monitor, and optimize operations. For instance, Sadeghi et al. (2024) describe the application of digital twins in the predictive maintenance of aircraft fleets and support vehicles, allowing maintenance crews to anticipate and address potential failures before they occur. This reduces unplanned downtime, extends equipment life cycles, and ensures optimal performance—all of which contribute to lower emissions and reduced energy consumption. Moreover, digital twins are increasingly used in building management systems to simulate airflow, lighting, and energy consumption in terminal buildings, allowing airport operators to test and implement energy-saving strategies in virtual environments before applying them in the real world. These simulations provide decision-makers with the insights needed to optimize system interactions, identify inefficiencies, and prioritize retrofitting or investments in renewable infrastructure.

A critical technical advancement in the green infrastructure of airports lies in the deployment of AI-integrated smart grid systems, which enable the coordination of diverse and decentralized energy resources. According to Mchirgui et al. (2024), these systems utilize advanced AI algorithms and digital twin simulations to manage the complex flows of energy between renewable generation units (such as solar PV and wind turbines), battery energy storage systems (BESS), and airport loads. The integration of these components into a unified smart grid allows for intelligent load forecasting, automated demand response, and real-time optimization of energy sourcing based on cost, carbon intensity, and system constraints. Khalid (2024) refers to this transformation as Energy 4.0, where digitalization and decentralization redefine traditional energy consumption patterns in critical infrastructure. In airports, this manifests as automated systems that can shift non-essential energy loads to off-peak hours, store surplus energy during low-demand periods, and even sell energy back to the grid during peak generation, thereby reducing the airport's dependence on fossil fuel-based power and enhancing overall energy resilience.

These digital infrastructures are not only internally focused but also impact how airports engage with external sustainability frameworks, particularly through AI-driven carbon accounting and emissions monitoring systems. Emerging blockchain-based platforms are being utilized to collect, verify, and record carbon emissions data from aircraft operations, ground vehicles, and stationary systems in real time. These platforms ensure transparency, auditability, and security of data used in environmental reporting, particularly for compliance with global schemes such as the Carbon Offsetting and Reduction Scheme for International Aviation (CORSIA). Mizrak, Polat, and Tasar (2024) present a case study of Istanbul Airport that demonstrates how strategic sustainability planning, supported by fuzzy multi-criteria decision-making methods, allows airport managers to prioritize investments in technologies that align both with environmental goals and operational demands. Their work highlights how advanced decision-making frameworks can incorporate diverse inputs—environmental impact, cost-effectiveness, operational reliability—to guide sustainability strategies in high-complexity infrastructures such as international airports.

On the passenger services side, smart technologies are also contributing to sustainability through the dematerialization and automation of processes. Digital wayfinding, biometric boarding, mobile check-ins, and smart baggage handling systems reduce the need for physical infrastructure and paper-based processing, while also decreasing waiting times and energy use in terminal operations. Rubio-Andrada et al. (2023) highlight the role of these technologies in improving passenger satisfaction and reducing environmental burdens, noting that passenger acceptance varies by demographic factors such as gender and age. Their findings point to the importance of inclusive and user-sensitive design when implementing digital tools intended to support environmental goals. These systems not only enhance the customer experience but also contribute to sustainability by lowering energy use during peak times, minimizing idle system loads, and reducing resource consumption across the board.

However, as airports become more digitized and interconnected in their pursuit of sustainability, their exposure to cyber threats increases significantly. Mizrak and Akkartal (2024) emphasize the urgent need to integrate cybersecurity measures into sustainability planning, particularly as operational technologies and energy management systems become critical points of vulnerability. Cyber-attacks on smart grids, digital twins, or carbon data repositories could compromise not only operational continuity but also environmental reporting and regulatory compliance. In such contexts, cybersecurity must be embedded into the very design and governance of digital sustainability infrastructures. This includes implementing secure communication protocols, segmenting networks, enforcing real-time monitoring and threat detection, and training personnel across departments—not just IT—in cyber-resilient practices.

Beyond technology alone, the success of green airport transformation depends heavily on organizational values, leadership, and stakeholder coordination. Bamidele et al. (2023) argue that biospheric values and institutional commitment to environmental ethics are essential enablers of green performance. Airports that integrate sustainability into their culture—through green design principles, staff training, and stakeholder collaboration—are more likely to succeed in deploying complex technologies effectively. As airports increasingly serve as flagship examples of sustainability in urban systems, their ability to align digital innovation with ecological responsibility will determine not only their operational success but also their legitimacy in the eyes of regulators, investors, and the public.

Finally, AI and machine learning models are increasingly being used in optimizing ground transportation systems within airports. These models manage autonomous electric buses, monitor fleet energy consumption, and calculate the most carbon-efficient routes for service vehicles. Vashishth et al. (2024) demonstrate how AI-enabled energy optimization in smart vehicle systems can drastically reduce the carbon footprint of ground operations. These advancements, combined with predictive analytics for maintenance and energy usage, enable airports to move beyond reactive sustainability measures and toward a holistic, proactive approach.

In conclusion, the integration of green technologies and smart infrastructure into airport environments constitutes a multi-dimensional strategy encompassing operational, environmental, and cybersecurity components. The effective convergence of digital systems with sustainability objectives relies not only on technological capabilities but also on strategic alignment, stakeholder buy-in, and robust risk management frameworks. As airports evolve into intelligent, energy-optimized ecosystems, they must address the dual imperative of reducing environmental impact while safeguarding the integrity and resilience of their digital infrastructures. This symbiotic relationship between sustainability and cybersecurity will define the next frontier of airport management in the era of climate-conscious innovation.

3. EMERGING CYBERSECURITY THREATS TO SUSTAINABLE AVIATION SYSTEMS

The increasing reliance on digital technologies in pursuit of sustainable aviation goals has simultaneously amplified the vulnerability of airport ecosystems to cybersecurity threats. As airports adopt smart systems for energy management, emissions tracking, and infrastructure optimization, they become increasingly exposed to cyber risks that target the very backbone of their digital sustainability frameworks. One of the most critical areas of concern involves the protection of environmental data and digital ESG (Environmental, Social, and Governance) platforms, which are essential for compliance with global sustainability standards and transparent environmental reporting. These systems often aggregate large volumes of sensitive data from IoT sensors, digital twins, and AI algorithms to monitor carbon emissions, manage energy efficiency, and validate sustainable aviation fuel (SAF) usage. If compromised, these platforms not only risk operational disruption but may also lead to regulatory penalties and reputational damage due to greenwashing accusations or inaccurate environmental disclosures.

Ferdaus et al. (2024) emphasize the integral role of digital technologies—including AI, cloud computing, and edge analytics—in achieving net-zero energy goals across complex infrastructures such as airports. However, these technologies are inherently susceptible to attack vectors such as data tampering, unauthorized access, and ransomware targeting environmental control systems. For example, cyber attackers may exploit machine learning models used for energy demand forecasting, leading to manipulated load balancing decisions and resulting in operational inefficiencies or blackouts. Ranawaka et al. (2024) further highlight how the coupling of digital twins with AI for smart grid control introduces new threat surfaces. A compromised digital twin, if fed falsified or spoofed sensor data, could generate inaccurate simulations that misguide real-time decision-making, thereby destabilizing power distribution and potentially disrupting critical operations such as runway lighting, HVAC systems, or electric vehicle (EV) charging stations. Bhute and Bhute (2025) reinforce this concern by reviewing the vulnerabilities inherent in digital innovations for renewable energy systems, noting that sustainability initiatives often outpace the development of corresponding cyber risk governance structures, leaving critical infrastructure exposed to stealthy but impactful attacks.

Equally significant is the emerging vulnerability within the supply chains that support sustainable aviation technologies, particularly SAF logistics and renewable energy hardware. Unlike traditional jet fuel supply chains, SAF operations depend on decentralized, highly digitalized networks involving biorefineries, carbon accounting systems, and multimodal logistics platforms. These complex digital ecosystems, often dependent on software-defined logistics and just-in-time delivery models, are increasingly targeted by attackers seeking to disrupt critical pathways in fuel distribution and certification. Clavijo Mesa et al. (2024) draw parallels from maritime supply chains, where cyber-attacks have already demonstrated the capacity to paralyze logistics operations, manipulate cargo data, and halt port activity. Airports adopting SAF face similar risks, particularly at the interface of biofuel supply, customs clearance, and quality verification systems. Barbieri and Capoani (2025) highlight how the rapid digitalization of transport systems for green energy integration can backfire when cybersecurity is not embedded into the digital infrastructure from the outset. A disruption in SAF logistics—whether through denial-of-service (DoS) attacks on supplier platforms or falsification of SAF origin and carbon intensity data—could interrupt fueling operations, delay flights, and undermine emissions reduction targets.

The hardware and software components of renewable energy technologies themselves are also increasingly scrutinized as vectors of cyber risk. According to Reichert and Obelheiro (2024), software supply chain attacks are rising in frequency and sophistication, often targeting open-source components embedded in control systems. These attacks can remain undetected for long periods, during which adversaries can inject malicious code or manipulate firmware updates. Airports deploying smart grid technologies, solar PV controllers, or BESS units sourced from multiple vendors face heightened risks from supply chain compromise, particularly when visibility and authentication protocols are weak. This is especially true in EV-to-grid (V2G) systems deployed in airport ground transportation, where insecure charging stations or unverified firmware can provide access points to the broader airport network. Moghadasi et al. (2022) underscore the importance of trust frameworks in securing V2G infrastructure and highlight how a lack of standardization in hardware interfaces can lead to systemic vulnerabilities. Mizrak and Akkartal (2024), focusing specifically on the aviation sector, have demonstrated through fuzzy decision analysis that cybersecurity priorities must be integrated into aviation planning, especially when dealing with interconnected systems like smart fueling operations and sustainability reporting platforms.

Beyond technical vulnerabilities, recent literature has increasingly focused on modeling and understanding actual and hypothetical threat scenarios affecting cyber-physical systems in aviation. Żebrowski et al. (2022) propose a Bayesian framework for assessing and mitigating cyber threats in complex operational systems, illustrating how probabilistic reasoning can inform security investments in aviation contexts. Their approach models cascading failures initiated by cyber intrusions and evaluates the most effective intervention points for reducing systemic impact. Zografopoulos et al. (2021) complement this by offering a comprehensive threat modeling approach tailored for cyber-physical energy systems, many of which are now embedded in airport smart grids. Their findings emphasize that cyber risk assessment must account for not only traditional IT vulnerabilities but also those emerging at the interface of physical systems—such as electricity, fuel, water, and air conditioning—and their corresponding digital controllers.

Real-world incidents—though often underreported in the aviation context due to reputational concerns—highlight the tangible risks associated with these threat vectors. There have been growing concerns about ransomware attacks targeting airport energy management platforms, unauthorized access to sustainability data centers, and deliberate manipulation of emissions monitoring systems to distort regulatory compliance outputs. In hypothetical scenarios, attackers may target carbon offset trading platforms, manipulating credits to cause reputational or financial harm, or breach airport renewable energy SCADA systems to sabotage peak load balancing during critical operational windows. These scenarios are not merely speculative; they are increasingly plausible in light of the aviation industry's aggressive digital transformation and growing dependence on decentralized energy infrastructures.

Ultimately, the cybersecurity threats facing sustainable aviation systems are multifaceted and dynamically evolving. They span from attacks on AI models and digital twins to vulnerabilities in SAF logistics, energy grids, and emissions reporting platforms. What binds them is a common weakness in the current frameworks that govern the convergence of digital innovation and environmental performance. Addressing these gaps requires a proactive, system-wide approach to cybersecurity—one that encompasses technological resilience, supply chain integrity, stakeholder collaboration, and regulatory alignment. As airports continue to lead the push toward sustainable aviation, ensuring the security of the digital foundations supporting these goals must be recognized as not just a technical necessity but a strategic imperative.

4. STANDARDS AND FRAMEWORKS: BRIDGING CYBERSECURITY AND SUSTAINABILITY

The convergence of cybersecurity and environmental sustainability in aviation management necessitates a harmonized approach to standards and regulatory frameworks. As airports embrace digital transformation to enhance sustainability—through smart energy systems, carbon accounting platforms, and digital twin simulations—the integration of internationally recognized management system standards becomes essential to ensure both operational resilience and regulatory compliance. A compelling foundation for this integration lies in the joint application of ISO 14001, which provides a framework for effective environmental management systems (EMS), and ISO/IEC 27001, the globally recognized standard for information security management systems (ISMS). While ISO 14001 focuses on minimizing environmental impact and promoting sustainability through structured environmental governance, ISO/IEC 27001 addresses the confidentiality, integrity, and availability of information assets, including the protection of digital infrastructure critical to sustainability operations.

The integration of these two standards provides a systematic mechanism to embed cybersecurity within the architecture of environmentally sustainable airport systems. Podrecca et al. (2022) demonstrate that the adoption of ISO/IEC 27001 not only improves information security but also drives broader organizational value creation, particularly in industries undergoing digitalization. In the context of smart airports, this translates into increased trust in automated energy management systems, secure reporting of emissions data, and protection of AI models used for predictive maintenance and load forecasting. Mohammed and Jasim (2022) emphasize that designing protection models for documented information by aligning ISO 27001 with complementary standards (e.g., ISO 10013:2021) enhances the integrity of environmental documentation and audit trails—critical for verifying sustainability performance in line with international and EU green finance frameworks. Similarly, Majerník et al. (2023) provide insights from the energy sector, showing how integrated management systems that combine environmental and safety standards help identify and mitigate cascading risks across digital and physical domains—an increasingly relevant concern for smart aviation ecosystems that depend on cyber-physical systems for operational efficiency and carbon reduction.

The adoption rate of ISO/IEC 27001 in aviation and other critical infrastructure sectors reflects a growing recognition of its strategic value. Mirtsch (2023) conducted a cross-sectoral analysis in Germany and found that organizations with a higher level of digital maturity are more likely to adopt ISO/IEC 27001 as a proactive measure for resilience building. In airports, where digital twin models, autonomous systems, and interconnected grids are deployed to support sustainability objectives, such proactive adoption is particularly vital. The standard enables risk-based decision-making and the implementation of control measures that are flexible enough to address evolving cyber threats to both IT and OT (operational technology) systems. Alrehili and Alhazmi (2023) offer an analytical comparison of ISO/IEC 27001's framework components, confirming its compatibility with a wide range of sector-specific cybersecurity needs, while Nugraha and Nasyuha (2024) demonstrate how ISO 27001 can be integrated with national data protection regulations to create tailored compliance architectures—a concept increasingly important as airports handle personal and environmental data under multiple overlapping jurisdictions.

Complementing these ISO-based approaches are broader international frameworks such as the NIST Cybersecurity Framework (CSF), which offers a flexible, risk-based methodology for identifying, protecting, detecting, responding to, and recovering from cyber incidents. While originally developed for critical infrastructure protection in the United States, NIST CSF is widely recognized as a global best practice, and it offers modular compatibility with ISO/IEC 27001. Its relevance to smart and sustainable aviation lies in its adaptability to diverse threat environments and its ability to integrate sector-specific controls. Marchiafava (2022) draws parallels between cybersecurity in shipping and aviation, emphasizing the need for cross-domain applicability of standards such as NIST CSF in protecting digital logistics systems and sustainability platforms. Johnson (2014) adds to this by outlining tools and techniques for cyber incident analysis in safety-critical environments, highlighting that the aviation sector's unique safety imperatives require incident response mechanisms that account for both technological failures and environmental risks. As airports incorporate sustainability data into their critical systems—whether in the form of carbon tracking, energy efficiency metrics, or emissions certification—NIST-aligned controls become indispensable for ensuring traceability, accountability, and response readiness in the face of cyber disruptions.

In the aviation-specific context, the International Civil Aviation Organization (ICAO) provides a complementary cyber-safety framework focused on the protection of civil aviation's digital infrastructure, particularly in light of increasing reliance on data-driven operations. Svanadze (2020) discusses the challenges facing civil aviation in building a cybersecurity culture, noting the absence of enforceable global standards and the inconsistent implementation of existing guidelines across regions. The ICAO Aviation Cybersecurity Strategy calls for harmonization of national regulatory efforts, integration of cyber risk into safety management systems, and capacity-building to support secure digital transformation. For airports engaged in sustainability transitions—such as the implementation of digital emissions monitoring or electrification of ground support—compliance with ICAO's guidance ensures that these innovations do not inadvertently introduce systemic vulnerabilities.

An emerging dimension of this convergence is the alignment of cybersecurity governance with sustainable development goals (SDGs) and green investment criteria, particularly under frameworks such as the EU Taxonomy for Sustainable Activities. The EU Taxonomy requires organizations to meet strict criteria for environmental performance, including climate change mitigation and adaptation, while also ensuring that no significant harm is done to other sustainability objectives—including digital governance and data protection. In this context, robust cybersecurity measures serve not just as technical safeguards but as enablers of green finance eligibility. A secure, verifiable carbon accounting system, for instance, ensures the credibility of emissions reductions claims, enabling airports to access sustainability-linked bonds or environmental performance-based funding mechanisms. Furthermore, as financial institutions increasingly incorporate ESG risk ratings into lending and investment decisions, airports that demonstrate alignment with cybersecurity and sustainability standards are likely to enjoy more favorable financing conditions.

In sum, bridging cybersecurity and sustainability in aviation management requires more than isolated technical solutions; it demands the deliberate integration of internationally recognized standards, sector-specific frameworks, and ESG-aligned compliance tools. By embedding cybersecurity into environmental governance systems—through ISO 14001 and ISO/IEC 27001, the NIST Cybersecurity Framework, and ICAO's cyber-safety strategies—airports can enhance both their digital resilience and their environmental credibility. This integrated approach not only supports operational continuity in the face of cyber threats but also strengthens the legitimacy of sustainability claims, positioning airports to lead in the emerging landscape of responsible, secure, and data-driven green transformation.

5. STRATEGIC MANAGEMENT OF AIRPORT CYBER-RESILIENCE

As the aviation industry accelerates its digital and environmental transformation, the imperative to develop strategic frameworks for managing cybersecurity risks becomes increasingly critical. The complexity of airport ecosystems—characterized by high passenger volumes, interconnected cyber-physical systems, digital energy platforms, and sustainability data flows—necessitates a comprehensive approach to cyber-resilience that is both technical and organizational. Cybersecurity can no longer be confined to isolated IT departments; instead, it must be embedded into the broader strategic management architecture of airports, with close alignment to operational continuity, safety, environmental compliance, and human capital development. Mızrak (2023) emphasizes this shift in her extensive literature review, arguing that cybersecurity risk management should be seen as a core pillar of strategic management rather than a reactive set of protective controls. Particularly in airport environments, where vulnerabilities may propagate across infrastructure, operational technology (OT), and environmental data systems, a multi-layered and forward-looking cyber-resilience strategy is essential for ensuring sustainable and secure operations.

A foundational element of this strategic orientation is the integration of cybersecurity into airport design and digital transformation planning, especially as airports invest in smart infrastructure, renewable energy systems, and digital emissions tracking. Embedding security into the planning phase—often referred to as a "secure-by-design" approach—ensures that digital sustainability systems are architected with threat modeling, access control, and system resilience as primary design parameters, not afterthoughts. Murat et al. (2024) elaborate on this methodology, highlighting how systems security engineering and proactive threat identification during early design phases lead to robust, resilient infrastructures capable of withstanding both conventional cyber-attacks and emergent, sophisticated threats such as AI-generated malware or cross-domain ransomware targeting SCADA systems. This is particularly relevant to airports as they modernize HVAC, baggage handling, and energy management systems with interconnected digital controls, many of which interface directly with external suppliers and government regulators.

Governance models play an equally critical role in managing cybersecurity at the strategic level. Effective cyber-resilience in airport ecosystems depends on cross-functional collaboration between IT, operations, environmental management, and sustainability teams, ensuring that cybersecurity is not siloed but embedded throughout the organization's culture and workflows. Mızrak (2024) proposes a governance model that merges cybersecurity and HRM strategies to support digital resilience by formalizing communication flows, incident response protocols, and internal risk awareness campaigns. She argues that in aviation organizations, the collaboration between Chief Information Security Officers (CISOs), Chief Sustainability Officers (CSOs), and HR leaders can create an ecosystem where threat intelligence, environmental performance, and organizational behavior are monitored and governed in a harmonized fashion. Furthermore, Yaseen (2024) demonstrates how automated infrastructure management systems, including AI-powered network configuration tools and anomaly detection platforms, can streamline cybersecurity governance by reducing reliance on manual interventions, increasing accuracy in threat identification, and allowing for adaptive reconfiguration of digital assets in response to emerging attack vectors.

Human capital is also a strategic enabler of cyber-resilience, especially as employee behavior remains one of the most common entry points for cyber breaches in complex organizations. As noted by Mızrak, Demirel, Yaşar, and Karakaya (2025), cybersecurity fatigue among employees—especially those operating in hybrid or digitally dense environments such as airport sustainability teams—can result in elevated vulnerability to phishing, misconfigurations, and policy non-compliance. Addressing this challenge requires a holistic approach to human resource management, including the development of training programs that enhance cybersecurity awareness while simultaneously addressing stress and burnout. Mızrak (2024) argues that the integration of AI tools in aviation cybersecurity not only supports threat detection but can also enhance personnel workflows, reduce cognitive overload, and provide HR teams with real-time insights into behavioral patterns that may signal security fatigue or disengagement. Strategic HRM thus becomes a critical defense layer in airport cybersecurity architectures, particularly when AI is used not only to detect threats but also to promote well-being and retention among cyber-relevant personnel.

Cybersecurity awareness training tailored to the unique context of sustainability-focused airport staff is another strategic priority. As Forouzan, Hosseinian-Far, and Sarwar (2023) point out, even small and medium-sized enterprises struggle with ensuring cyber awareness among non-technical teams, and large-scale aviation enterprises are no exception. Effective training must go beyond general compliance and instead incorporate context-specific scenarios, simulations, and decision-making exercises relevant to airport energy systems, emissions data handling, and green procurement systems. Salman et al. (2023) introduce a gamified cybersecurity training platform, "CyberSafe," that demonstrates promising results in engaging diverse audiences and reinforcing secure behavior through interactive, real-time challenges. Such methods are especially applicable in environments like airports, where personnel span a broad spectrum of technical proficiency and operational roles. Furthermore, as Loevenich et al. (2024) explain in the context of military networks, the development of autonomous cyber defense agents requires parallel investments in human training and decision-making protocols. Airports aiming to incorporate autonomous cybersecurity tools—such as AI-based threat detection or self-healing networks—must also invest in upskilling personnel who can effectively interpret alerts, manage responses, and ensure system accountability.

Ultimately, strategic management of airport cyber-resilience demands an integrated approach that spans infrastructure design, organizational governance, human resource management, and operational training. The aviation sector's move toward digital sustainability increases the complexity of its cyber threat landscape, but also presents an opportunity to build resilient systems that are secure by default, adaptive by design, and governed by a cross-disciplinary understanding of risks and responsibilities. As digital infrastructure becomes central to achieving sustainability goals in areas such as energy efficiency, emissions compliance, and green finance eligibility, the failure to invest in robust cybersecurity measures could undermine not only operational reliability but also environmental credibility. Strategic foresight, therefore, must include cybersecurity as a core competency of sustainable airport management—one that is managed not only through technical safeguards but through inclusive, proactive, and well-coordinated strategic leadership.

6. CONCLUSION

The transformation of airport infrastructure into smart, sustainable ecosystems presents an unprecedented opportunity for the aviation industry to align its operations with global climate and digitalization objectives. However, this transition is not without its risks. As demonstrated throughout this chapter, the increasing reliance on digital technologies—such as artificial intelligence, IoT, digital twins, and blockchain-enabled carbon tracking systems—has significantly expanded the attack surface of modern airport ecosystems. Cyber threats that once targeted traditional IT systems now extend to operational technology (OT), energy management platforms, emissions reporting tools, and supply chains for sustainable aviation fuel (SAF). Consequently, cybersecurity has emerged not only as a technical concern but as a strategic imperative—integral to the environmental integrity, operational reliability, and stakeholder trustworthiness of sustainable airport systems (Mızrak & Akkartal, 2024; Ferdaus et al., 2024; Sadeghi et al., 2024).

This chapter has shown that cybersecurity and sustainability are not independent domains but deeply interdependent pillars of contemporary airport management. Effective environmental performance—whether in the form of reduced emissions, optimized energy usage, or compliance with ESG reporting standards—depends on the confidentiality, integrity, and availability of digital infrastructure. Simultaneously, the credibility of sustainability claims rests on the resilience of the systems that collect, analyze, and report environmental data. Thus, the digital-sustainability nexus in aviation cannot be fully realized unless cybersecurity is embedded into the design, governance, and operation of green airport technologies (Dias & Silva, 2024; Khalid, 2024; Mirtsch, 2023). The integration of ISO/IEC 27001 with ISO 14001, as discussed in this chapter, provides one such pathway to achieve operational synergy between environmental management and information security. Similarly, alignment with frameworks like the NIST Cybersecurity Framework and ICAO's Aviation Cybersecurity Strategy reinforces the need for a structured and internationally harmonized approach.

Strategic management of airport cyber-resilience requires more than technical upgrades; it calls for institutional realignment, workforce development, and anticipatory governance. As highlighted by Mızrak (2023, 2024), embedding cybersecurity risk management into broader strategic planning—particularly in the context of human resources and sustainability—is critical for long-term resilience. Training programs tailored to sustainability teams, as well as gamified and role-specific cybersecurity education, must become routine components of organizational culture (Salman et al., 2023; Forouzan et al., 2023). Moreover, secure-by-design methodologies, coupled with automated infrastructure management systems and AI-based anomaly detection tools, are essential for managing complex and decentralized airport systems (Murat et al., 2024; Yaseen, 2024). Equally important is the strategic alignment of IT, operational, and sustainability functions under a unified governance framework—enabling cross-functional coordination, rapid incident response, and system-wide resilience.

As illustrated in Figure 1, the pursuit of sustainability goals in smart airports cannot be separated from the cybersecurity and digital transformation frameworks that enable them. The overlapping demands of real-time data processing, secure emissions tracking, and intelligent infrastructure management highlight the need for an integrated approach—one where digital innovation, environmental responsibility, and cyber-resilience function as a unified system.

Figure 1. The digital–sustainability–cybersecurity nexus in smart airport operations

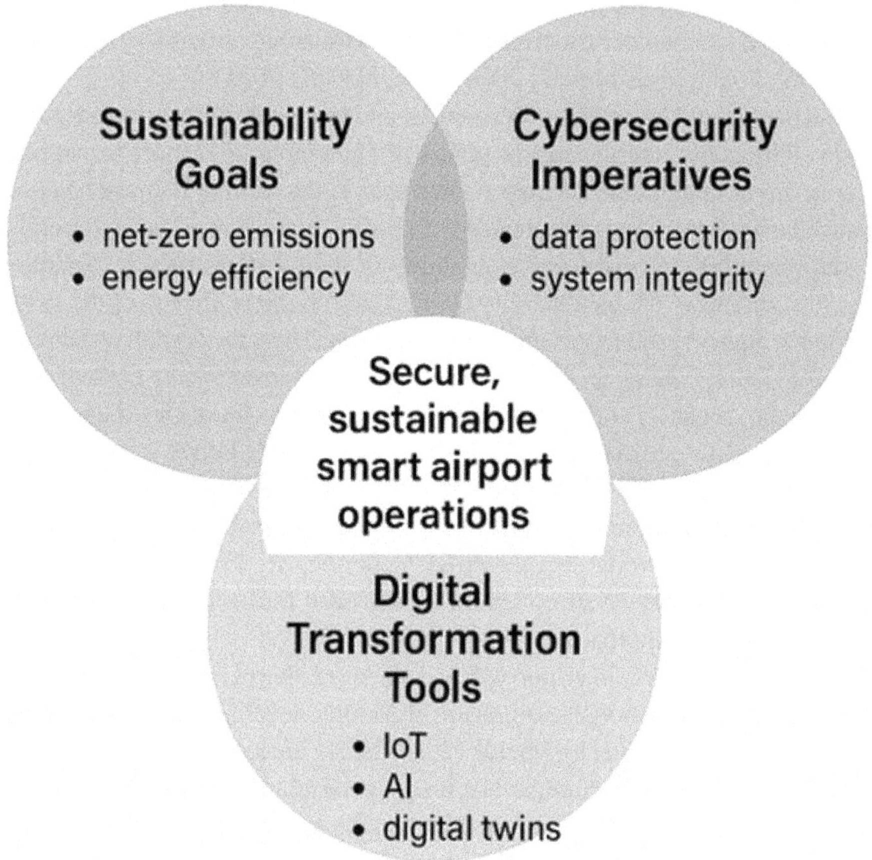

Based on the findings and discussions presented, the following recommendations are offered to aviation stakeholders, airport authorities, policymakers, and researchers aiming to enhance cybersecurity within sustainable airport infrastructures:

- Airports should systematically implement both ISO/IEC 27001 for information security and ISO 14001 for environmental management. This dual adoption ensures that sustainability objectives are supported by secure data systems and risk-based controls across both digital and ecological domains.
- All green infrastructure investments—whether in digital energy management, SAF supply chains, or emissions monitoring—must incorporate security engineering and threat modeling from inception. Secure-by-design practices re-

duce vulnerabilities, increase interoperability, and enhance long-term system resilience.

- Establish formal coordination between IT, sustainability, operations, and HR functions. A centralized cyber-resilience unit that spans these domains can ensure that sustainability innovations do not unintentionally introduce unmanaged cyber risks.
- Provide role-specific training for non-technical staff involved in sustainability and operations, using simulations, gamified platforms, and scenario-based learning modules. Recognize cybersecurity fatigue as an occupational risk and manage it proactively through workload balancing and digital wellness initiatives (Mızrak et al., 2025).
- SAF logistics, energy procurement, and emissions trading platforms must be assessed for software and hardware vulnerabilities. Apply vendor risk assessments, contractually mandate cybersecurity standards, and monitor third-party access continuously.
- As the EU Taxonomy and other frameworks begin to consider data governance and digital resilience in sustainability assessments, airport management should proactively align cybersecurity reporting with environmental disclosures to strengthen investor confidence and financial positioning.
- Engage with global aviation bodies such as ICAO and IATA to contribute to the development of aviation-specific cybersecurity guidelines that explicitly address the environmental dimension of digital infrastructures.

In conclusion, the successful realization of smart, sustainable, and secure airports depends on the seamless integration of cybersecurity into every layer of digital and environmental strategy. By treating cybersecurity not as a constraint but as a foundational enabler of sustainable innovation, airport leaders can safeguard their digital infrastructure, protect public trust, and lead the aviation sector toward a resilient and climate-aligned future.

REFERENCES

Alrehili, A. A., & Alhazmi, O. H. (2023, September). ISO/IEC 27001 Standard: Analytical and Comparative Overview. In International Conference on Advances in Data-driven Computing and Intelligent Systems (pp. 143-156). Singapore: Springer Nature Singapore.

Bamidele, R. O., Ozturen, A., Haktanir, M., & Ogunmokun, O. A. (2023). Realizing green airport performance through green management intransigence, airport reputation, biospheric value, and eco-design. *Sustainability (Basel), 15*(3), 2475. DOI: 10.3390/su15032475

Barbieri, E., & Capoani, L. (2025). Renewable Energy, Resilience, Digitalization, and Industrial Policies in Seaborne Transport. *Energies, 18*(5), 1089. DOI: 10.3390/en18051089

Bhute, A., & Bhute, H. (2025). A Comprehensive Review on Digital Innovations for Renewable Energy and Conservation. Digital Innovations for Renewable Energy and Conservation, 1-20.

Clavijo Mesa, M. V., Patino-Rodriguez, C. E., & Guevara Carazas, F. J. (2024). Cybersecurity at Sea: A Literature Review of Cyber-Attack Impacts and Defenses in Maritime Supply Chains. *Information (Basel), 15*(11), 710. DOI: 10.3390/info15110710

Dias, C., & Silva, J. (2024). Unveiling the future: Smart airports-applications, advantages, strategies and technological challenges. *Journal of Airline and Airport Management, 14*(2), 38–56. DOI: 10.3926/jairm.419

Ferdaus, M. M., Dam, T., Anavatti, S., & Das, S. (2024). Digital technologies for a net-zero energy future: A comprehensive review. *Renewable & Sustainable Energy Reviews, 202*, 114681. DOI: 10.1016/j.rser.2024.114681

Forouzan, H., Hosseinian-Far, A., & Sarwar, D. (2023, January). Are Small Medium Enterprises Cyber Aware? In Cybersecurity in the Age of Smart Societies: Proceedings of the 14th International Conference on Global Security, Safety and Sustainability, London, September 2022 (pp. 385-397). Cham: Springer International Publishing.

Jaganraja, V., Seidakhmet, N., Guhan, T., Revathy, N., & Premkumar, R. (2024). Harnessing Advanced Digital (AI) Technologies for Environmental Applications: Carbon-Based Materials. In Environmental Applications of Carbon-Based Materials (pp. 30-56). IGI Global.

Khalid, M. (2024). Energy 4.0: AI-enabled digital transformation for sustainable power networks. *Computers & Industrial Engineering*, *193*, 110253. DOI: 10.1016/j.cie.2024.110253

Loevenich, J. F., Adler, E., Bécue, A., Velazquez, A., Wrona, K., Boshnakov, V., . . . Lopes, F. (2024, October). Training Autonomous Cyber Defense Agents: Challenges & Opportunities in Military Networks. In MILCOM 2024-2024 IEEE Military Communications Conference (MILCOM) (pp. 158-163). IEEE.

Majerník, M., Daneshjo, N., Malega, P., Drábik, P., Ševčíková, R., & Vravec, J. (2023). Integrated Management of the Environment-Safety Risks in the Thermal Power Station. *Polish Journal of Environmental Studies*, *32*(5), 4725–4738. DOI: 10.15244/pjoes/168290

MARCHIAFAVA., G. (2022). Cybercrime and cybersecurity in shipping. Rivista di Studi Politici Internazionali, 89(2 (354), 239-258. Johnson, C. W. (2014, October). Tools and techniques for reporting and analysing the causes of cyber-security incidents in safety-critical systems. In *9th IET International Conference on System Safety and Cyber Security* (2014) (pp. 3-2).

Mchirgui, N., Quadar, N., Kraiem, H., & Lakhssassi, A. (2024). The applications and challenges of digital twin technology in smart grids: A comprehensive review. *Applied Sciences (Basel, Switzerland)*, *14*(23), 10933. DOI: 10.3390/app142310933

Mirtsch, M. (2023). Adoption of the information security management system standard ISO/IEC 27001-A study among German organizations. *International Journal of Qualitative Research*, *17*(3), 747–768. DOI: 10.24874/IJQR17.03-08

Mızrak, F. (2023). Integrating cybersecurity risk management into strategic management: A comprehensive literature review. *Research Journal of Business and Management*, *10*(3), 98–108. DOI: 10.17261/Pressacademia.2023.1807

Mızrak, F. (2024). Enhancing Cybersecurity risk management through conceptual analysis of Hrm integration. *Yönetim Bilimleri Dergisi*, *22*(51), 96–118. DOI: 10.35408/comuybd.1342408

Mızrak, F. (2024). Integrating AI with aviation cybersecurity: The strategic role of human resources. *Business & Management Studies: An International Journal*, *12*(3), 610–628. DOI: 10.15295/bmij.v12i3.2396

Mizrak, F., & Akkartal, G. R. (2024). Prioritizing cybersecurity initiatives in aviation: A dematel-QSFS methodology. *Heliyon*, *10*(16), e35487. DOI: 10.1016/j.heliyon.2024.e35487 PMID: 39687858

Mizrak, F., Demirel, H. G., Yaşar, O., & Karakaya, T. (2025). Digital detox: Exploring the impact of cybersecurity fatigue on employee productivity and mental health. *Discover Mental Health*, *5*(1), 1–21. DOI: 10.1007/s44192-025-00149-x PMID: 39998759

Mizrak, F., Polat, L., & Tasar, S. A. (2024). Applying Entropy Weighting and 2-Tuple Linguistic T-Spherical Fuzzy MCDM: A Case Study of Developing a Strategic Sustainability Plan for Istanbul Airport. *Sustainability (Basel)*, *16*(24), 11104. DOI: 10.3390/su162411104

Moghadasi, N., Collier, Z. A., Koch, A., Slutzky, D. L., Polmateer, T. L., Manasco, M. C., & Lambert, J. H. (2022). Trust and security of electric vehicle-to-grid systems and hardware supply chains. *Reliability Engineering & System Safety*, *225*, 108565. DOI: 10.1016/j.ress.2022.108565

Mohammed, T. J., & Jasim, N. A. (2022). Designing a model to protect documented information according to the integration of some international standards (ISO 27001: 2013)(ISO 10013: 2021): A case study. *International Journal of Health Sciences*, (III), 431069. DOI: 10.53730/ijhs.v6nS3.8376

Murat, D., Berkan, U., & Ali, I. (2024, October). An Overview of Secure by Design: Enhancing Systems Security through Systems Security Engineering and Threat Modeling. In 2024 17th International Conference on Information Security and Cryptology (ISCTürkiye) (pp. 1-6). IEEE.

Nugraha, A. A., & Nasyuha, A. H. (2024). Integrating ISO 27001 and Indonesia's Personal Data Protection Law for Data Protection Requirement Model. *Journal of Information Systems and Informatics*, *6*(2), 1052–1069. DOI: 10.51519/journalisi.v6i2.754

Podrecca, M., Culot, G., Nassimbeni, G., & Sartor, M. (2022). Information security and value creation: The performance implications of ISO/IEC 27001. *Computers in Industry*, *142*, 103744. DOI: 10.1016/j.compind.2022.103744

Raimundo, R. J., Baltazar, M. E., & Cruz, S. P. (2023). Sustainability in the airports ecosystem: A literature review. *Sustainability (Basel)*, *15*(16), 12325. DOI: 10.3390/su151612325

Ranawaka, A., Alahakoon, D., Sun, Y., & Hewapathirana, K. (2024). Leveraging the Synergy of Digital Twins and Artificial Intelligence for Sustainable Power Grids: A Scoping Review. *Energies*, *17*(21), 5342. DOI: 10.3390/en17215342

Reichert, B. M., & Obelheiro, R. R. (2024). Software supply chain security: A systematic literature review. *International Journal of Computers and Applications*, *46*(10), 853–867. DOI: 10.1080/1206212X.2024.2390978

Rubio-Andrada, L., Celemín-Pedroche, M. S., Escat-Cortés, M. D., & Jiménez-Crisóstomo, A. (2023). Passengers satisfaction with the technologies used in smart airports: An empirical study from a gender perspective. *Journal of Air Transport Management*, *107*, 102347. DOI: 10.1016/j.jairtraman.2022.102347

Sabet, S., & Farooq, B. (2023). Energy-smart transportation systems: Role of connectivity, automation, big data, and machine learning. In *Handbook of Smart Energy Systems* (pp. 2003–2023). Springer International Publishing. DOI: 10.1007/978-3-030-97940-9_126

Sadeghi, A., Bellavista, P., Song, W., & Yazdani-Asrami, M. (2024). Digital twins for condition and fleet monitoring of aircraft: Towards more-intelligent electrified aviation systems. *IEEE Access : Practical Innovations, Open Solutions*, *12*, 99806–99832. DOI: 10.1109/ACCESS.2024.3371902

Salman, O. H., Alawida, M., Hazeem, R. M. A., Zeyadeh, M. S., & Alameri, M. R. (2023, December). CyberSafe: A Gamified Cyber Security Training Method. In *2023 International Conference on Electrical, Communication and Computer Engineering (ICECCE)* (pp. 1-6). IEEE. DOI: 10.1109/ICECCE61019.2023.10442243

Stevenage UK: IET. Svanadze, V. (2020). Cybersecurity in the civil aviation and existing challenges. Юридичний вісник. Повітряне і космічне право, (4), 27-33.

Vashishth, T. K., Sharma, V., Sharma, K. K., Kumar, B., Chaudhary, S., & Panwar, R. (2024). Environmental sustainability and carbon footprint reduction through artificial intelligence-enabled energy management in electric vehicles. In *Artificial Intelligence-Empowered Modern Electric Vehicles in Smart Grid Systems* (pp. 477–502). Elsevier. DOI: 10.1016/B978-0-443-23814-7.00017-1

Yaseen, A. (2024). Enhancing Cybersecurity through Automated Infrastructure Management: A Comprehensive Study on Optimizing Security Measures. *Quarterly Journal of Emerging Technologies and Innovations*, *9*(1), 38–60.

Żebrowski, P., Couce-Vieira, A., & Mancuso, A. (2022). A Bayesian framework for the analysis and optimal mitigation of cyber threats to cyber-physical systems. *Risk Analysis*, *42*(10), 2275–2290. DOI: 10.1111/risa.13900 PMID: 35229333

Zhou, Y. (2022). Low-carbon transition in smart city with sustainable airport energy ecosystems and hydrogen-based renewable-grid-storage-flexibility. *Energy Reviews*, *1*(1), 100001. DOI: 10.1016/j.enrev.2022.100001

Zografopoulos, I., Ospina, J., Liu, X., & Konstantinou, C. (2021). Cyber-physical energy systems security: Threat modeling, risk assessment, resources, metrics, and case studies. *IEEE Access : Practical Innovations, Open Solutions*, *9*, 29775–29818. DOI: 10.1109/ACCESS.2021.3058403

Chapter 11
Securing the Digital Twin: Cybersecurity Strategies for Virtual Replicas in Aviation Management

Cengiz Kerem Kutahya
https://orcid.org/0000-0002-7222-0921
Australian University, Kuwait

ABSTRACT

This chapter explores the integration of cybersecurity strategies into the design and operation of digital twin technologies within the aviation industry. As digital twins become central to predictive maintenance, real-time simulation, and intelligent automation, they also introduce new cyber-physical vulnerabilities that can compromise safety and operational continuity. The chapter examines key threats across the digital twin lifecycle, from data acquisition to control systems, and proposes a layered security architecture tailored for aviation contexts. It emphasizes the need for proactive, strategic approaches that align cybersecurity with organizational structures, human resource management, and emerging technologies such as AI. By offering both conceptual frameworks and applied insights, the chapter contributes to a more resilient and secure digital transformation in aviation.

1. INTRODUCTION

The aviation industry has entered an era defined by rapid digital evolution, marked by the convergence of physical assets with real-time data-driven systems. Among the most transformative advancements is the deployment of digital twin technologies, which enable virtual replicas of aircraft systems, air traffic infrastructures, and

DOI: 10.4018/979-8-3693-6417-8.ch011

entire airport environments to operate in synchronized tandem with their physical counterparts. These digital twins provide the aviation sector with powerful tools for predictive maintenance, real-time simulation, and operational optimization, ultimately supporting more efficient, safer, and sustainable aviation systems (Xiong & Wang, 2022; Chia et al., 2024). As the use of digital twins becomes increasingly sophisticated, their reliance on continuous data exchange, algorithmic control, and AI integration also introduces significant cybersecurity vulnerabilities.

At the core of this transformation lies a critical and often underexamined intersection: the link between digital twin technologies and cybersecurity risk management. Unlike traditional IT systems, digital twins exist within cyber-physical ecosystems, where threats in the digital realm can lead to real-world operational disruptions, safety hazards, or service failures (Alcaraz & Lopez, 2022; Holmes et al., 2021). This is particularly relevant in aviation, where even minor system anomalies can have cascading impacts on safety, reliability, and regulatory compliance. Mızrak (2023) emphasizes that cybersecurity is no longer a stand-alone technical domain but a strategic imperative that must be embedded across organizational layers, including operations, design, human resources, and AI governance. The integration of cybersecurity into digital twin systems is thus not only a technical challenge but also an organizational one—requiring strategic alignment, interdisciplinary collaboration, and regulatory coherence.

This chapter aims to explore the evolving landscape of cybersecurity in aviation through the lens of digital twin technologies. It begins by mapping the structure and strategic role of digital twins in modern aviation systems, identifying how they enhance predictive capabilities and operational agility (Sadeghi et al., 2024; Laukotka & Krause, 2023). It then delves into the cybersecurity risks that emerge from the multilayered architecture of digital twins, including threats at the data acquisition, transmission, and processing levels (de Azambuja et al., 2024; Faleiro et al., 2021). The chapter proceeds by examining technical and strategic approaches to securing these systems, with a particular focus on AI integration, blockchain applications, compliance with international standards, and the essential role of human resource managementin cultivating cybersecurity resilience (Mızrak, 2024; Mizrak & Akkartal, 2024). A foundational section is also dedicated to understanding the broader state of cybersecurity in aviation, establishing the sectoral context in which digital twin vulnerabilities and defenses must be situated.

By synthesizing these dimensions, the chapter contributes a multidisciplinary perspective to an increasingly urgent topic in aviation management—highlighting the interplay between digital innovation, systemic vulnerability, and organizational strategy. Ultimately, it positions cybersecurity as a cornerstone of digital twin deployment, offering insights for aviation professionals, researchers, and policymakers committed to advancing secure, intelligent, and resilient air transport systems.

2. DIGITAL TWINS IN AVIATION: STRUCTURE AND STRATEGIC ROLE

Digital twin technology, originally rooted in the manufacturing and automotive industries, has rapidly emerged as a foundational element in the digital transformation of aviation. A digital twin is broadly defined as a dynamic virtual replica of a physical object, system, or process, integrated with real-time data and capable of simulating, monitoring, and predicting operational behavior (Xiong & Wang, 2022). In aviation, this concept has been adapted to encompass aircraft structures, propulsion systems, air traffic management platforms, and even entire airport environments. The architecture of digital twins consists of four primary components: the physical asset, its digital counterpart, a data connection that enables real-time synchronization, and a service layer that supports analytics and decision-making (Laukotka, Hanna, & Krause, 2021). Model-Based Systems Engineering (MBSE) plays a critical role in ensuring data traceability and lifecycle integration across these layers, especially in the complex design and maintenance ecosystems of aviation platforms (Bickford et al., 2020).

One of the most significant applications of digital twins in aviation is in aircraft health monitoring and predictive maintenance. Traditional time-based maintenance strategies are increasingly being replaced by condition-based monitoring systems that use sensor data to assess the real-time status of components, anticipate potential failures, and schedule maintenance activities proactively. This approach not only improves aircraft availability and safety but also significantly reduces costs related to unplanned repairs and component overhauls (Sadeghi et al., 2024). Airframe digital twins have been used to model structural fatigue, stress distribution, and material degradation under varied operational conditions, which in turn enables enhanced structural prognostics and lifecycle extension strategies (Chia et al., 2024). These capabilities are particularly vital in high-utilization environments, such as commercial aviation fleets and military operations, where equipment longevity and readiness are mission-critical.

Beyond individual aircraft, digital twins are being applied at the fleet level to optimize system-wide performance. Fleet-level digital twin platforms enable operators to perform comparative diagnostics across multiple aircraft, integrate data from diverse sensors and maintenance logs, and generate predictive models for operational risk and maintenance planning (Sadeghi et al., 2024). In electrified aviation systems, these models are especially useful in managing battery health, propulsion efficiency, and thermal conditions, which require real-time adjustments to maintain operational integrity (Abro & Abdallah, 2024). This capability has become increasingly relevant with the growth of urban air mobility and hybrid-electric aircraft, where real-time cyber-physical monitoring is essential for both safety and regulatory compliance.

Digital twins also contribute significantly to smart airport management systems. Airports have become increasingly digitized, relying on IoT-connected systems for baggage handling, energy optimization, HVAC management, and crowd control. Digital twins of airport infrastructure enable operators to simulate passenger flows, monitor building energy consumption, and manage terminal logistics in real time, thereby increasing operational efficiency and enhancing the passenger experience (Cheung, Li, & Lei, 2023). For instance, a spatial digital twin can simulate emergency evacuations, optimize gate assignments, or reroute resources based on predicted congestion patterns (Wang et al., 2021). Such simulations help airport authorities develop adaptive strategies that enhance operational responsiveness while minimizing disruptions.

Another emerging area of digital twin implementation lies in unmanned aircraft systems (UAS) and autonomous aviation. The integration of spatial digital twins into UAS airspace management supports enhanced situational awareness, collision avoidance, and autonomous path planning (Fakhraian et al., 2023). These models use real-time data streams from onboard sensors and external sources, such as weather and traffic systems, to simulate future scenarios and inform autonomous decision-making processes. Additionally, UAS operations benefit from digital twin environments that allow testing of control algorithms and regulatory compliance strategies in a risk-free virtual environment before deployment in physical airspace (Wang et al., 2021).

Digital twins are also being incorporated into the training and education of aviation professionals. Simulated environments provide a safe and cost-effective platform for training engineers, pilots, and maintenance technicians. For instance, digital twins of aircraft engines or flight decks allow for immersive, scenario-based learning that replicates real operational conditions without the associated safety risks (Kairat et al., 2023). These tools are increasingly embedded into aviation education curricula and technical certifications, contributing to workforce readiness in digitally advanced environments.

From a systems engineering perspective, digital twins bridge the gap between the design, operation, and continuous improvement of aviation systems. By enabling seamless data flow across the product lifecycle, digital twins support the iterative refinement of both physical and digital components. This integration is especially important for retrofit programs, where legacy systems must be updated to comply with evolving operational and regulatory demands. In such contexts, digital twins facilitate model-driven data handling and system reengineering without disrupting ongoing operations (Laukotka & Krause, 2023).

Finally, the strategic importance of digital twins in aviation management cannot be overstated. As cyber-physical systems become more deeply embedded in aviation operations, digital twins offer a comprehensive framework for risk-informed decision-making, operational resilience, and long-term system optimization (Sycheva & Shpak, 2022). The convergence of digital twins with AI, blockchain, and cybersecurity frameworks further enhances their utility, making them indispensable tools for achieving safety, efficiency, and sustainability goals in the aviation sector (Mao et al., 2025).

3. CYBERSECURITY IN AVIATION: EVOLVING THREATS AND STRATEGIC PRIORITIES

The rapid digitalization of the aviation industry has transformed it into one of the most technologically advanced sectors globally, relying on complex, real-time cyber-physical systems to manage everything from aircraft control and maintenance to airport logistics and passenger services. This transformation has not only enhanced operational efficiency but also introduced an unprecedented level of cyber dependency, which in turn exposes aviation systems to a broad array of cybersecurity threats. As Alcaraz and Lopez (2022) emphasize, aviation's digital infrastructure now encompasses high-value targets such as avionics networks, flight management systems, unmanned aircraft traffic control, and AI-based decision platforms. The criticality of these systems, combined with their real-time and interconnected nature, makes them susceptible to sophisticated cyberattacks with direct consequences for safety, financial stability, and public trust.

Historically, cybersecurity efforts in aviation concentrated on protecting IT assets like ticketing systems, customer databases, and corporate servers. However, this narrow focus has expanded significantly in recent years to encompass Operational Technologies (OT)—including aircraft navigation systems, remote diagnostics, maintenance platforms, and airport automation tools. These OT systems are often embedded, heterogeneous, and designed for long life cycles, which creates difficulties in implementing real-time patches or security upgrades. Recent incidents involving GPS spoofing, ransomware on flight scheduling networks, or breaches in aircraft telemetry have highlighted the urgent need for aviation-specific cybersecurity protocols (Holmes et al., 2021; Faleiro et al., 2021). Mızrak (2023) stresses that these challenges cannot be tackled using isolated, reactive strategies; instead, they must be addressed through strategic risk integration at the organizational level, where cybersecurity is embedded into core business and operational decision-making.

A central theme in addressing these threats is the strategic alignment of cybersecurity with organizational structures and decision frameworks. Cybersecurity should no longer be siloed within IT departments but must be incorporated into enterprise-wide strategic planning. Mızrak (2024) argues that cybersecurity, when embedded into strategic management processes, enables aviation organizations to better align their risk posture with long-term resilience objectives. This involves assessing cyber threats not only in terms of technical vulnerability but also in terms of their impact on operational continuity, service quality, and regulatory compliance. Influence-based decision models such as DEMATEL-QSFS, when applied in aviation contexts, provide a method for prioritizing cybersecurity initiatives by quantifying their impact across interconnected functions (Mızrak & Akkartal, 2024). This allows decision-makers to identify the most critical cybersecurity touchpoints in systems like digital twins, AI platforms, and automated control infrastructures.

The human element of cybersecurity, often overlooked in technical frameworks, is increasingly recognized as pivotal. Aviation organizations operate in environments where human error, lack of awareness, and social engineering attacks can undermine even the most advanced security systems. In this context, Human Resource Management (HRM) emerges as a strategic enabler of cyber resilience. According to Mızrak (2024, *Business & Management Studies: An International Journal*), HRM practices such as employee onboarding protocols, cybersecurity training programs, ethical guidelines, and psychological well-being monitoring are crucial in reducing human-related vulnerabilities. For instance, secure onboarding and offboarding procedures minimize the risk of credential leakage or unauthorized system access. Ongoing cybersecurity training—customized to different employee roles—ensures that staff remain vigilant against phishing, identity spoofing, and other human-targeted threats. Furthermore, HR departments can serve as mediators between technical teams and executive management, helping to translate cybersecurity needs into accessible policy language and enterprise-wide best practices.

The role of Artificial Intelligence (AI) in aviation cybersecurity is both promising and complex. AI-powered systems offer advanced capabilities in monitoring, detecting, and responding to cyber threats in real time. These include anomaly detection systems that identify unusual patterns in aircraft telemetry, predictive analytics for threat anticipation, and automated incident response mechanisms. However, AI systems are also targets of emerging threats such as adversarial machine learning, where attackers subtly manipulate input data to deceive AI models. Mızrak (2024) emphasizes that aviation HR teams must develop AI-literate cybersecurity talent pipelines—professionals who not only understand technical systems but also the ethical and organizational implications of AI deployment. This includes training employees to recognize adversarial attacks, developing oversight mechanisms for AI-driven decisions, and implementing ethical review processes for AI model development. In highly automated aviation environments where AI controls critical infrastructure, the failure to manage AI-related risks can have operational and reputational consequences that far exceed those of traditional IT breaches.

On a regulatory level, aviation cybersecurity is governed by a patchwork of national and international standards, with increasing pressure for global harmonization. Organizations such as ICAO, EASA, and IATA have issued cybersecurity frameworks and guidelines, encouraging states and operators to integrate security considerations across design, operation, and maintenance stages. EASA's Part-IS regulations require manufacturers and operators to consider cyber risks as part of their Safety Management Systems (SMS), while standards like ISO/IEC 27001 and ISO 23247 (focused on digital twins) offer foundational structures for cybersecurity implementation. However, as Mızrak (2024, *Yönetim Bilimleri Dergisi*) points out, mere compliance with external standards is insufficient unless organizations embed these guidelines into internal governance systems. Conceptual models that link cybersecurity protocols with HR strategy, leadership commitment, and corporate culture are essential to ensure that regulations translate into actionable, context-specific practices.

Furthermore, the implementation of cybersecurity strategies must consider the interdependencies between technology, people, and process. Aviation systems function as complex socio-technical ecosystems, where the failure of one component—technical or human—can affect system-wide performance. Mızrak (2024) highlights the need for integrated governance structures that facilitate collaboration between IT, OT, and HR departments, breaking down silos and promoting a shared responsibility model. This collaboration enables holistic cybersecurity planning, where decisions around procurement, system architecture, user behavior, and threat modeling are aligned under a unified risk management approach. Aviation organizations should also conduct regular simulations, tabletop exercises, and internal audits to assess their cybersecurity readiness and response capabilities in realistic threat scenarios.

In conclusion, the evolving threat landscape in aviation requires a shift from reactive, compliance-based cybersecurity approaches to proactive, integrated, and strategically aligned models. As aircraft and airports become more digital, autonomous, and data-reliant, cybersecurity must be recognized not as a peripheral technical concern but as a core organizational competency. This shift necessitates investment in advanced technologies, regulatory alignment, strategic risk modeling, and perhaps most critically, a transformation in how aviation organizations manage human capital. HR departments are no longer passive administrative units but strategic actors in building a cyber-resilient culture. Their role in training, ethical oversight, AI governance, and interdepartmental coordination will be pivotal in securing the digital aviation landscape. Only through this multidisciplinary, multi-layered approach can the aviation industry ensure the safe and sustainable evolution of its digital future.

4. CYBERSECURITY RISKS AND VULNERABILITIES IN DIGITAL TWIN SYSTEMS

As digital twin technologies continue to evolve and integrate into aviation infrastructures, their exposure to cybersecurity risks has become increasingly critical. Digital twins operate at the intersection of the physical and virtual realms, forming complex cyber-physical systems that rely on uninterrupted data flows and real-time synchronization. This inherent connectivity—across sensor networks, communication protocols, data analytics engines, and control systems—creates multiple attack surfaces that adversaries can exploit. According to Alcaraz and Lopez (2022), the unique architecture of digital twins introduces novel vulnerabilities that differ from traditional IT systems, particularly in their dynamic and interdependent nature. Cyber threats targeting digital twins are often multi-stage and multi-vector, affecting not only the digital components but also the physical assets they control. In aviation, where safety and continuity are paramount, any breach in a digital twin system could cascade into real-world disruptions, compromised aircraft functionality, or unsafe operating environments.

One of the most vulnerable layers in digital twin ecosystems is the data acquisition stage, which includes IoT sensors and embedded systems responsible for collecting operational parameters such as engine temperature, vibration, structural load, or spatial position. These sensors are typically distributed across aircraft systems and ground infrastructures and are often deployed in low-resource environments with minimal encryption or authentication protocols. As highlighted by Karaarslan and Babiker (2021), attackers can exploit these weaknesses to conduct sensor spoofing, inject false data, or manipulate telemetry streams, leading to corrupted digital replicas and inaccurate predictive maintenance outcomes. Additionally, these compromised signals can mislead anomaly detection systems, allowing hidden malfunctions or malicious activities to persist undetected.

The data transmission layer introduces another critical risk point due to its reliance on wireless and networked communication channels. Digital twins depend on constant bidirectional data exchange between physical and virtual systems—via Wi-Fi, satellite links, or 5G networks—making them vulnerable to man-in-the-middle attacks, packet sniffing, and protocol spoofing (de Azambuja et al., 2024). In aviation, the impact of such intrusions is exacerbated by the real-time decision-making requirements in flight operations and air traffic control. Holmes et al. (2021) stress that insecure communication protocols can be exploited to delay, distort, or block essential control messages, potentially compromising the integrity of automated systems such as trajectory optimization or engine health management. The aviation sector's increased adoption of cloud-based digital twin services further compounds these vulnerabilities, as third-party integrations and multi-tenant environments broaden the attack surface.

Perhaps the most insidious risks reside in the data processing and actuation layers, where analytics engines, machine learning models, and automation systems convert raw data into actionable insights or commands. Malicious actors can target these layers by introducing adversarial inputs that manipulate algorithmic outputs or corrupt AI-based diagnostic models. Jiang et al. (2024) describe how attackers can alter control logic or simulation results, resulting in incorrect maintenance scheduling or unsafe system responses. In cyber-physical contexts, this manipulation can directly affect physical outcomes—for example, triggering false alarms, halting critical systems, or initiating unsafe mechanical adjustments in aircraft components. As Otoom (2025) explains, the feedback loop between a corrupted model and its real-world asset can create self-reinforcing errors, where each subsequent actuation reinforces the attacker's intended misbehavior.

Specific to the aviation industry, spoofing, data poisoning, and system hijacking are among the most pressing threats. Spoofing attacks, particularly GPS spoofing, can deceive location-tracking systems, which are essential for both flight navigation and ground logistics (Zheng et al., 2022). Data poisoning involves the insertion of subtle but harmful data during model training phases, which can cause predictive systems to make faulty inferences without immediate detection (Shaikh et al., 2023). System hijacking, a more aggressive threat, involves gaining unauthorized access to the entire digital twin platform, potentially enabling full control over aircraft systems or airport infrastructure simulations. As highlighted by Faleiro et al. (2021), these attacks are not hypothetical; they have been simulated in testbeds where adversaries successfully disrupted air traffic flows and manipulated aircraft system diagnostics.

The consequences of these threats are not limited to digital distortions—they can manifest in physical harm and operational breakdowns, especially in high-stakes environments like aviation. Alhumam, Rahman, and Aljughaiman (2025) point out that a well-coordinated cyberattack on a digital twin system can lead to grounded fleets, delayed operations, or even catastrophic system failures. In such cyber-physical systems, resilience cannot rely solely on IT-based firewalls or antivirus tools; instead, it demands embedded security at every layer of the digital twin lifecycle. This includes real-time monitoring, integrity verification, anomaly detection powered by AI, and role-based access control to minimize human-error-driven vulnerabilities (Balta et al., 2023).

Moreover, adversaries are increasingly leveraging game-theoretic approaches to exploit digital twin systems strategically, simulating defender behaviors and optimizing attack vectors over time (Feng et al., 2024). As attackers adopt more sophisticated methods, traditional perimeter-based security models are proving insufficient. The adoption of risk-aware digital twin design, continuous risk auditing, and probabilistic model checking techniques has become essential to ensure systemic cyber resilience (Guo, Yan, & Wang, 2021; Shaikh et al., 2023).

Altogether, the security of digital twin systems in aviation demands a multidimensional defense strategy. These systems must be protected not only through encryption and network segmentation but also through context-aware defense mechanisms that understand the operational semantics of aviation processes. As digital twins continue to evolve into indispensable tools for managing complex aviation systems, ensuring their security will be essential to safeguarding the reliability, safety, and sustainability of the entire air transport ecosystem.

To consolidate the discussion of risks across digital twin systems, Table 1 presents a lifecycle-based threat mapping that highlights critical system components, associated cybersecurity vulnerabilities, their operational impacts, and relevant scholarly sources. This structured view enables aviation stakeholders to visualize the multidimensional nature of threats and prioritize mitigation strategies accordingly.

Table 1. Threat mapping across the digital twin lifecycle in aviation

Lifecycle Stage	Key Components	Cybersecurity Threats	Impact on Aviation Operations	Selected Sources
1. Data Acquisition	IoT sensors, telemetry devices, onboard diagnostics, environmental monitors	Sensor spoofing, data injection, firmware manipulation	Inaccurate operational data, false maintenance triggers, compromised flight system integrity	Karaarslan & Babiker (2021); Alcaraz & Lopez (2022)
2. Data Transmission	Wireless networks, satellite links, 5G infrastructure, cloud gateways	Man-in-the-middle attacks, packet sniffing, DoS attacks, protocol spoofing	Communication loss between aircraft and control centers, delay in real-time decision-making	de Azambuja et al. (2024); Holmes et al. (2021)
3. Data Processing	AI/ML analytics, digital twin model simulations, decision engines	Data poisoning, adversarial machine learning, algorithm manipulation	Misleading diagnostics, flawed performance predictions, unsafe automation outcomes	Jiang et al. (2024); Shaikh et al. (2023)
4. Storage and Archiving	Cloud storage, maintenance logs, simulation history, digital flight records	Unauthorized access, ransomware, data exfiltration	Disclosure of sensitive flight data, regulatory breaches, data availability issues	Otoom (2025); Alhumam et al. (2025)
5. Feedback and Control	Actuation systems, command interfaces, autopilot systems, cockpit-digital twin link	Command spoofing, system hijacking, control override, privilege escalation	Unstable flight control, system misbehavior, safety-critical response failures	Faleiro et al. (2021); Balta et al. (2023)

continued on following page

Table 1. Continued

Lifecycle Stage	Key Components	Cybersecurity Threats	Impact on Aviation Operations	Selected Sources
6. Human-System Interaction	Pilot dashboards, technician terminals, maintenance crew UIs	Social engineering, phishing, credential theft	Unauthorized access, alteration of control inputs, increased insider threat vulnerability	Mızrak (2024); Holmes et al. (2021)
7. Cross-Lifecycle Risks	Software APIs, vendor platforms, firmware updates, integration layers	Supply chain attacks, insider threats, patch manipulation	Persistent system compromise, lateral threat propagation, long-term vulnerabilities	Suhail et al. (2022); Guo et al. (2021)

5. CYBERSECURITY STRATEGIES FOR SECURING AVIATION DIGITAL TWINS

Ensuring the cybersecurity of digital twin systems in aviation requires a comprehensive strategy that integrates both technical safeguards and organizational practices, tailored to the unique characteristics of cyber-physical systems. Digital twins in aviation operate within a layered architecture that simultaneously supports real-time monitoring, predictive analytics, control systems, and system optimization. As such, their security posture must evolve beyond traditional IT boundaries to address system complexity, dynamic interactions, and operational dependencies. Recent literature emphasizes that mitigating threats to these systems demands a multi-pronged approach—one that fuses technical interventions such as secure architecture design with strategic governance frameworks and cultural transformation across aviation organizations (de Azambuja et al., 2024; Mizrak & Akkartal, 2024).

From a technical standpoint, one of the most effective cybersecurity foundations for digital twins is the implementation of a zero trust architecture, which assumes no inherent trust in any network component, whether internal or external. Zero trust principles, combined with network segmentation and sandboxing, can help isolate sensitive simulation models, telemetry feeds, and feedback control systems to prevent lateral movement during a breach (Sneps-Sneppe & Namiot, 2022). This approach is particularly critical in aviation, where interconnected systems—ranging from avionics to smart terminal platforms—operate under strict availability requirements and cannot afford downtime due to cyber incidents. Furthermore, AI-based intrusion detection systems (IDS) and anomaly detection algorithms are increasingly deployed to monitor operational deviations and detect sophisticated threats such as adversarial inputs, model poisoning, or replay attacks (Kuleshov et al., 2024).

These tools leverage machine learning techniques to identify behavioral anomalies across the digital twin lifecycle, enabling faster incident response and predictive cyber risk mitigation.

Another vital layer of defense is the integration of blockchain technologies, particularly for ensuring data integrity and maintaining immutable audit trails in digital twin ecosystems. In aviation, blockchain-based systems have been proposed to authenticate digital records associated with component usage history, maintenance activities, and simulation outcomes (Cheung, Li, & Lei, 2023; Suhail et al., 2022). These distributed ledger technologies reduce the risk of data tampering and provide verifiable transparency in critical systems such as aircraft part tracking or flight condition logs. Additionally, blockchain supports secure multi-party collaboration across manufacturers, airlines, maintenance operators, and regulators without the need for centralized trust mechanisms.

Beyond technical countermeasures, strategic and managerial actions are equally essential in fostering a secure digital twin environment. Cybersecurity must be embedded into the design and development of digital twin systems from the outset—a principle known as cybersecurity-by-design. This includes conducting threat modeling during system development, integrating cybersecurity impact assessments into digital twin life cycle stages, and ensuring modular system designs that can be patched and upgraded without full system downtime (Sellitto et al., 2021; Mizrak, Polat, & Tasar, 2024). Regulatory alignment also plays a critical role. Compliance with frameworks such as the NIST Cybersecurity Framework, ISO/IEC 27001, ISO 23247, and EASA cybersecurity regulations ensures that aviation stakeholders adopt internationally recognized practices and maintain accountability through standardized procedures (Dihan et al., 2024).

Workforce capacity and cross-functional alignment are also central to sustainable cybersecurity. Digital twin security cannot be managed solely by IT departments—it requires collaboration between information technology (IT), operational technology (OT), and engineering teams, each of which manages distinct elements of the digital twin system. Dimitrov (2024) highlights how digital twin systems in building and facility operations have necessitated new forms of organizational coordination, which can be directly extended to aviation. Workforce training programs, simulation-based cybersecurity drills, and shared governance frameworks are needed to ensure operational personnel understand the security dynamics of the systems they interact with. Organizational readiness for cyber threats must be reinforced through continuous learning and shared accountability across all levels of aviation management (Zhan, Hwang, & Krishnankutty, 2023).

Moreover, aviation organizations must prioritize risk-based decision-making to strategically allocate cybersecurity resources in digital twin environments. Using hybrid multi-criteria decision-making models, such as DEMATEL-QSFS or entropy-based fuzzy evaluations, decision-makers can assess the influence, urgency, and interdependence of cybersecurity criteria specific to their infrastructure and operations (Mizrak & Akkartal, 2024; Mizrak, Polat, & Tasar, 2024). These analytical frameworks enable aviation managers to identify critical control points in the digital twin ecosystem—whether at the sensor, processing, or actuation level—and develop targeted security protocols based on quantified priorities.

Figure 1. Secure digital twin architecture in aviation

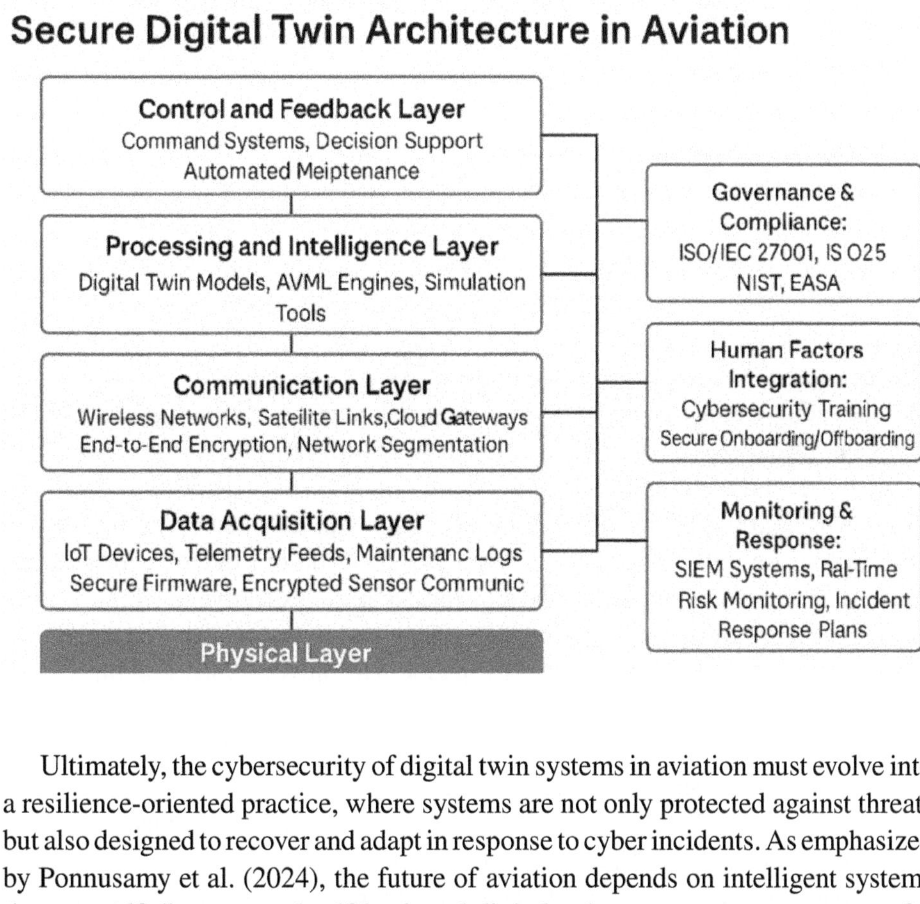

Ultimately, the cybersecurity of digital twin systems in aviation must evolve into a resilience-oriented practice, where systems are not only protected against threats but also designed to recover and adapt in response to cyber incidents. As emphasized by Ponnusamy et al. (2024), the future of aviation depends on intelligent systems that can self-diagnose and self-heal, and digital twins represent a cornerstone for building such resilience. The integration of cybersecurity into every layer—from architecture and data governance to training and policy—will determine the long-term success and safety of aviation's digital transformation journey.

5. CONCLUSION

The growing adoption of digital twin technologies in aviation marks a significant advancement in how the industry monitors, manages, and optimizes its operations. These virtual counterparts of physical assets have revolutionized predictive maintenance, real-time performance monitoring, and strategic planning in both aircraft systems and airport infrastructure. However, their integration into aviation ecosystems also introduces substantial cybersecurity concerns. As aviation systems become more digitized and interconnected, the risks associated with data breaches, system manipulation, and cyber-physical attacks increase exponentially. The inherent complexity of digital twin ecosystems—spanning sensors, AI models, cloud services, and automated feedback loops—necessitates a cybersecurity strategy that is as layered and dynamic as the systems themselves.

Throughout this chapter, it has been demonstrated that digital twin environments are vulnerable at multiple points, including data acquisition, communication, processing, and control. These vulnerabilities expose critical systems to a wide range of threats, from sensor spoofing and data poisoning to the manipulation of machine learning algorithms and unauthorized control of aircraft components. Such threats have the potential to compromise operational safety, disrupt continuity, and erode trust in aviation technologies. Addressing these risks requires moving beyond isolated technical fixes toward integrated and proactive security models that are embedded across the digital twin lifecycle.

A key insight from this analysis is the necessity of positioning cybersecurity as a strategic function rather than merely a technical responsibility. Effective cybersecurity for digital twins must be planned and governed at the executive level, embedded in long-term organizational objectives, and aligned with broader frameworks of operational resilience and digital transformation. This involves incorporating cybersecurity considerations at the design stage of digital systems, applying structured decision-making tools to prioritize areas of greatest vulnerability, and establishing governance mechanisms that ensure accountability across departments.

Another critical dimension involves the human factor. The resilience of digital twin systems is directly influenced by the behavior, awareness, and capabilities of the people who interact with them. Human resource management plays a pivotal role in this process, from implementing secure access protocols and ongoing training programs to fostering a culture that values cybersecurity as a shared responsibility. As technologies such as artificial intelligence become more integrated into digital twin applications, the need for a workforce that is not only technologically competent but also security-conscious becomes even more essential. Employees across all operational levels must be prepared to recognize potential cyber risks, respond effectively to incidents, and uphold digital ethics in an increasingly automated environment.

In addition to organizational efforts, the aviation sector must also maintain alignment with international cybersecurity standards and regulatory frameworks. Compliance alone is not sufficient; what is needed is the internalization of these standards into everyday practices and strategic planning processes. Aviation organizations should view compliance as a baseline rather than an endpoint, and work to build systems that are adaptable, continuously monitored, and capable of learning from past incidents.

To achieve secure and sustainable implementation of digital twin technologies, aviation organizations must adopt a mindset of continuous improvement. This means regularly assessing risk exposure, updating defense mechanisms, and investing in both technological and human capacities. Building cross-functional teams that integrate expertise from IT, operations, engineering, and HR will support a more resilient and responsive cybersecurity posture. Simulation-based scenario testing, incident drills, and system audits should become standard practices to ensure preparedness for a wide range of cyber threats.

In conclusion, the future of aviation's digital transformation depends on how effectively cybersecurity can be woven into the fabric of technological innovation. Digital twins offer immense value in optimizing aviation operations, but this value can only be fully realized if security is treated as a foundational element of their development and deployment. A secure digital twin is not only a technical construct but a reflection of strategic foresight, organizational discipline, and cultural readiness. As the aviation industry continues to advance toward more intelligent and automated systems, cybersecurity must remain central to its vision of safety, sustainability, and global reliability.

REFERENCES

Abro, G. E. M., & Abdallah, A. M. (2024). Digital twins and control theory: A critical review on revolutionizing quadrotor UAVs. *IEEE Access : Practical Innovations, Open Solutions*, *12*, 43291–43307. DOI: 10.1109/ACCESS.2024.3376589

Alcaraz, C., & Lopez, J. (2022). Digital twin: A comprehensive survey of security threats. *IEEE Communications Surveys and Tutorials*, *24*(3), 1475–1503. DOI: 10.1109/COMST.2022.3171465

Alhumam, N., Rahman, M. H., & Aljughaiman, A. (2025). A Comprehensive Review on Cybersecurity of Digital Twins Issues, Challenges, and Future Research Directions. *IEEE Access : Practical Innovations, Open Solutions*, *13*, 45106–45124. DOI: 10.1109/ACCESS.2025.3545004

Balta, E. C., Pease, M., Moyne, J., Barton, K., & Tilbury, D. M. (2023). Digital twin-based cyber-attack detection framework for cyber-physical manufacturing systems. *IEEE Transactions on Automation Science and Engineering*, *21*(2), 1695–1712. DOI: 10.1109/TASE.2023.3243147

Bickford, J., Van Bossuyt, D. L., Beery, P., & Pollman, A. (2020). Operationalizing digital twins through model-based systems engineering methods. *Systems Engineering*, *23*(6), 724–750. DOI: 10.1002/sys.21559

Cheung, T., Li, B., & Lei, Z. (2023). A paradigm shift in the aviation industry with digital twin, blockchain, and AI technologies. In *Handbook on Artificial Intelligence and Transport* (pp. 323–346). Edward Elgar Publishing. DOI: 10.4337/9781803929545.00020

Cheung, T., Li, B., & Lei, Z. (2023). A paradigm shift in the aviation industry with digital twin, blockchain, and AI technologies. In *Handbook on Artificial Intelligence and Transport* (pp. 323–346). Edward Elgar Publishing. DOI: 10.4337/9781803929545.00020

Chia, J. W., Verhagen, W. J., Silva, J. M., & Cole, I. S. (2024). A review and outlook of airframe digital twins for structural prognostics and health management in the aviation industry. *Journal of Manufacturing Systems*, *77*, 398–417. DOI: 10.1016/j.jmsy.2024.09.024

de Azambuja, A. J. G., Giese, T., Schützer, K., Anderl, R., Schleich, B., & Almeida, V. R. (2024). Digital Twins in Industry 4.0–Opportunities and challenges related to cyber security. *Procedia CIRP*, *121*, 25–30. DOI: 10.1016/j.procir.2023.09.225

de Azambuja, A. J. G., Giese, T., Schützer, K., Anderl, R., Schleich, B., & Almeida, V. R. (2024). Digital Twins in Industry 4.0–Opportunities and challenges related to cyber security. *Procedia CIRP*, *121*, 25–30. DOI: 10.1016/j.procir.2023.09.225

Dihan, M. S., Akash, A. I., Tasneem, Z., Das, P., Das, S. K., Islam, M. R., Islam, M. M., Badal, F. R., Ali, M. F., Ahamed, M. H., Abhi, S. H., Sarker, S. K., & Hasan, M. M. (2024). Digital twin: Data exploration, architecture, implementation and future. *Heliyon*, *10*(5), e26503. DOI: 10.1016/j.heliyon.2024.e26503 PMID: 38444502

Dimitrov, D. S. (2024). *The New Work of Building Operations in the Digital Age: The Impact of IoT and Digital Twins on Facility Management and Operational Practices* (Doctoral dissertation, University of Washington).

Fakhraian, E., Semanjski, I., Semanjski, S., & Aghezzaf, E. H. (2023). Towards safe and efficient unmanned aircraft system operations: Literature review of digital twins' applications and european union regulatory compliance. *Drones (Basel)*, *7*(7), 478. DOI: 10.3390/drones7070478

Faleiro, R., Pan, L., Pokhrel, S. R., & Doss, R. (2021, October). Digital twin for cybersecurity: Towards enhancing cyber resilience. In *International Conference on Broadband Communications, Networks and Systems* (pp. 57-76). Cham: Springer International Publishing.

Feng, H., Chen, D., Lv, H., & Lv, Z. (2024). Game theory in network security for digital twins in industry. *Digital Communications and Networks*, *10*(4), 1068–1078. DOI: 10.1016/j.dcan.2023.01.004

Guo, Y., Yan, A., & Wang, J. (2021, December). Cyber security risk analysis of physical protection systems of nuclear power plants and research on the cyber security test platform using digital twin technology. In *2021 International Conference on Power System Technology (POWERCON)* (pp. 1889-1892). IEEE. DOI: 10.1109/POWERCON53785.2021.9697764

Holmes, D., Papathanasaki, M., Maglaras, L., Ferrag, M. A., Nepal, S., & Janicke, H. (2021, September). Digital twins and cyber security–solution or challenge? In *2021 6th South-East Europe Design Automation, Computer Engineering, Computer Networks and Social Media Conference (SEEDA-CECNSM)* (pp. 1-8). IEEE. DOI: 10.1109/SEEDA-CECNSM53056.2021.9566277

Jiang, Y., Wang, W., Ding, J., Lu, X., & Jing, Y. (2024). Leveraging Digital Twin Technology for Enhanced Cybersecurity in Cyber–Physical Production Systems. *Future Internet*, *16*(4), 134. DOI: 10.3390/fi16040134

Kairat, K., Ildar, P., Karygash, A., Saule, B., Indira, K., Markhaba, K., & Aizhan, B. (2023). Digital Twins Technology in the Educational Process of the Aviation Equipment Repair. *Indonesian Journal of Electrical Engineering and Computer Science*, *32*(2), 752–762. DOI: 10.11591/ijeecs.v32.i2.pp752-762

Karaarslan, E., & Babiker, M. (2021, December). Digital twin security threats and countermeasures: An introduction. In *2021 International Conference on Information Security and Cryptology (ISCTURKEY)* (pp. 7-11). IEEE. DOI: 10.1109/ISCTURKEY53027.2021.9654360

Kuleshov, Y. A., Nagpal, K., Ucpinar, K., Gadaginmath, A., Gadaginmath, S., O'Daniel, K., . . . Monangi, H. (2024). Cyber attacks on avionics networks in digital twin environment: detection and defense. In *AIAA SCITECH 2024 Forum* (p. 0277). DOI: 10.2514/6.2024-0277

Laukotka, F., Hanna, M., & Krause, D. (2021). Digital twins of product families in aviation based on an MBSE-assisted approach. *Procedia CIRP*, *100*, 684–689. DOI: 10.1016/j.procir.2021.05.144

Laukotka, F. N., & Krause, D. (2023). Supporting digital twins for the retrofit in aviation by a model-driven data handling. *Systems*, *11*(3), 142. DOI: 10.3390/systems11030142

Mao, R., Li, Y., Li, G., Hildre, H. P., & Zhang, H. (2025). A Systematic Survey of Digital Twin Applications: Transferring Knowledge From Automotive and Aviation to Maritime Industry. *IEEE Transactions on Intelligent Transportation Systems*, *26*(4), 4240–4259. DOI: 10.1109/TITS.2025.3535593

Mızrak, F. (2023). Integrating cybersecurity risk management into strategic management: A comprehensive literature review. *Research Journal of Business and Management*, *10*(3), 98–108. DOI: 10.17261/Pressacademia.2023.1807

Mızrak, F. (2024). Integrating AI with aviation cybersecurity: The strategic role of human resources. *Business & Management Studies: An International Journal*, *12*(3), 610–628. DOI: 10.15295/bmij.v12i3.2396

Mızrak, F. (2024). Integrating AI with aviation cybersecurity: The strategic role of human resources. *Business & Management Studies: An International Journal*, *12*(3), 610–628. DOI: 10.15295/bmij.v12i3.2396

Mızrak, F. (2024). Enhancing Cybersecurity risk management through conceptual analysis of Hrm integration. *Yönetim Bilimleri Dergisi*, *22*(51), 96–118. DOI: 10.35408/comuybd.1342408

Mizrak, F., & Akkartal, G. R. (2024). Prioritizing cybersecurity initiatives in aviation: A dematel-QSFS methodology. *Heliyon, 10*(16), e35487. DOI: 10.1016/j.heliyon.2024.e35487 PMID: 39687858

Mizrak, F., Polat, L., & Tasar, S. A. (2024). Applying Entropy Weighting and 2-Tuple Linguistic T-Spherical Fuzzy MCDM: A Case Study of Developing a Strategic Sustainability Plan for Istanbul Airport. *Sustainability (Basel), 16*(24), 11104. DOI: 10.3390/su162411104

Otoom, S. (2025). Risk auditing for Digital Twins in cyber physical systems: A systematic review. *Journal of Cyber Security and Risk Auditing, 2025*(1), 22–35. DOI: 10.63180/jcsra.thestap.2025.1.3

Ponnusamy, S., Assaf, M., Antari, J., Singh, S., & Kalyanaraman, S. (Eds.). (2024). *Digital twin technology and AI implementations in future-focused businesses*. IGI Global. DOI: 10.4018/979-8-3693-1818-8

Sadeghi, A., Bellavista, P., Song, W., & Yazdani-Asrami, M. (2024). Digital twins for condition and fleet monitoring of aircraft: Towards more-intelligent electrified aviation systems. *IEEE Access : Practical Innovations, Open Solutions, 12*, 99806–99832. DOI: 10.1109/ACCESS.2024.3371902

Sadeghi, A., Bellavista, P., Song, W., & Yazdani-Asrami, M. (2024). Digital twins for condition and fleet monitoring of aircraft: Towards more-intelligent electrified aviation systems. *IEEE Access : Practical Innovations, Open Solutions, 12*, 99806–99832. DOI: 10.1109/ACCESS.2024.3371902

Sellitto, G. P., Masi, M., Pavleska, T., & Aranha, H. (2021, November). A cyber security digital twin for critical infrastructure protection: The intelligent transport system use case. In *IFIP Working Conference on The Practice of Enterprise Modeling* (pp. 230-244). Cham: Springer International Publishing. DOI: 10.1007/978-3-030-91279-6_16

Shaikh, E., Al-Ali, A. R., Muhammad, S., Mohammad, N., & Aloul, F. (2023). Security analysis of a digital twin framework using probabilistic model checking. *IEEE Access : Practical Innovations, Open Solutions, 11*, 26358–26374. DOI: 10.1109/ACCESS.2023.3257171

Sneps-Sneppe, M., & Namiot, D. (2022, December). On Digital Twin Software and Cyber Threats. In *International Conference on Next Generation Wired/Wireless Networking* (pp. 481-493). Cham: Springer Nature Switzerland.

Suhail, S., Hussain, R., Jurdak, R., Oracevic, A., Salah, K., Hong, C. S., & Matulevičius, R. (2022). Blockchain-based digital twins: Research trends, issues, and future challenges. *ACM Computing Surveys, 54*(11s), 1–34. DOI: 10.1145/3517189

Sycheva, E., & Shpak, P. (2022). Practical application of the concept of digital twins in the aviation sector. In *Digital Transformation in Industry: Digital Twins and New Business Models* (pp. 29–42). Springer International Publishing. DOI: 10.1007/978-3-030-94617-3_3

Wang, W., Li, X., Xie, L., Lv, H., & Lv, Z. (2021). Unmanned aircraft system airspace structure and safety measures based on spatial digital twins. *IEEE Transactions on Intelligent Transportation Systems, 23*(3), 2809–2818. DOI: 10.1109/TITS.2021.3108995

Xiong, M., & Wang, H. (2022). Digital twin applications in aviation industry: A review. *International Journal of Advanced Manufacturing Technology, 121*(9), 5677–5692. DOI: 10.1007/s00170-022-09717-9

Zhan, H., Hwang, B. G., & Krishnankutty, P. (2023). Embracing digital transformation for sustainable development: Barriers to adopting digital twin in asset management within Singapore's energy and chemicals industry. *Sustainable Development.*

Zheng, T., Liu, M., Puthal, D., Yi, P., Wu, Y., & He, X. (2022). Smart grid: Cyber attacks, critical defense approaches, and digital twin. *arXiv preprint arXiv:2205.11783.*

Compilation of References

Aarland, M. (2025). Cybersecurity in digital supply chains in the procurement process: Introducing the digital supply chain management framework. *Information and Computer Security*, *33*(1), 5–24. DOI: 10.1108/ICS-10-2023-0198

Abaku, E. A., Edunjobi, T. E., & Odimarha, A. C. (2024). Theoretical approaches to AI in supply chain optimization: Pathways to efficiency and resilience. *International Journal of Science and Technology Research Archive, 6*(1), 092-107.

Abdalla, H. B. (2022). A brief survey on big data: Technologies, terminologies, and data-intensive applications. *Journal of Big Data*, *9*(1), 107. Advance online publication. DOI: 10.1186/s40537-022-00659-3

Abdellatif, M., Shatnawi, A., Mili, H., Moha, N., El Boussaidi, G., Hecht, G., & Guéhéneuc, Y. G. (2021). A taxonomy of service identification approaches for legacy software systems modernization. *Journal of Systems and Software*, *173*, 110868. DOI: 10.1016/j.jss.2020.110868

Abdulsalam, Y. S., & Hedabou, M. (2022). Security and privacy in cloud computing: Technical review. *Future Internet*, *14*(1), 11. DOI: 10.3390/fi14010011

Aboobaker, N., & Shanujas, V. (2025). Towards a sustainable workplace: Investigating workplace cyberbullying and its relationship with employee wellbeing and intention to stay in remote and hybrid work settings. *International Journal of Productivity and Performance Management*, *74*(2), 453–470. DOI: 10.1108/IJPPM-12-2023-0662

Abrahams, T. O., Farayola, O. A., Kaggwa, S., Uwaoma, P. U., Hassan, A. O., & Dawodu, S. O. (2024). Cybersecurity awareness and education programs: A review of employee engagement and accountability. *Computer Science & IT Research Journal*, *5*(1), 100–119. DOI: 10.51594/csitrj.v5i1.708

Abro, G. E. M., & Abdallah, A. M. (2024). Digital twins and control theory: A critical review on revolutionizing quadrotor UAVs. *IEEE Access : Practical Innovations, Open Solutions*, *12*, 43291–43307. DOI: 10.1109/ACCESS.2024.3376589

Abto Software. (2021). *Zoom end-to-end encryption: How it works and why it matters*. Retrieved from https://www.abtosoftware.com

Adams, E. (2024). *See Yourself in Cyber: Security Careers Beyond Hacking*. John Wiley & Sons.

Agarkar, A. A., Karyakarte, M., Chavhan, G., Patil, M., Talware, R., & Kulkarni, L. (2024). Blockchain aware decentralized identity management and access control system. *Measurement. Sensors*, *31*, 101032. DOI: 10.1016/j.measen.2024.101032

Agozie, D. Q., Edu, A. S., & Nat, M. (2022). Toward building organizational resilience to social engineering among higher educational institution professionals. In *Delivering distinctive value in emerging economies* (pp. 347–367). Productivity Press. DOI: 10.4324/9781003152217-29

Agyemang, E. F. (2024). Anomaly detection using unsupervised machine learning algorithms: A simulation study.

Ahmad, A. N., Raffei, A. F. M., Razak, M. F. A., & Ahmad, A. (2024). Distributed denial of service attack detection in IoT networks using deep learning and feature fusion: A review. *Mesopotamian Journal of Cybersecurity*, *4*(1), 47–70.

Ahmad, A., Hadgkiss, J., & Ruighaver, A. B. (2021). Incident response teams–Challenges in supporting the organizational security function. *Computers & Security*, *92*, 101768.

Ahmad, I. A., Osasona, F., Dawodu, S. O., Obi, O. C., Anyanwu, A. C., & Onwusinkwue, S. (2024, January 26). Emerging 5G technology: A review of its far-reaching implications for communication. *World Journal of Advanced Research and Reviews*, *21*(01), 2474–2486. DOI: 10.30574/wjarr.2024.21.1.0346

Ahmadi, S. (2024). Ocak 2). Next Generation AI-Based Firewalls: A Comparative. International. *Journal of Computers*, •••, 245–262.

Ahsan, M. J. (2025). Cultivating a culture of learning: The role of leadership in fostering lifelong development. *The Learning Organization*, *32*(2), 282–306. DOI: 10.1108/TLO-03-2024-0099

Ahsan, M., Nygard, K. E., Gomes, R., Chowdhury, M. M., Rifat, N., & Connolly, J. F. (2022). Cybersecurity threats and their mitigation approaches using machine learning- A review. *Journal of Cybersecurity and Privacy*, *2*(3), 527–555. DOI: 10.3390/jcp2030027

Ajah, I. A., & Nweke, H. F. (2019). Big data and business analytics: Trends, platforms, success factors, and applications. *Big Data and Cognitive Computing*, *3*(2), 32. DOI: 10.3390/bdcc3020032

Aji, G. G., Widodo, S., Aji, G. N., Aji, G. G., & Prawitasari, D. (2023). Building trust in digital age: How HRM and cybersecurity collaborate for effective stakeholder relations. *Management Analysis Journal*, *12*(2), 254–260.

Ajunwa, I. (2023). *The quantified worker*. Cambridge University Press. DOI: 10.1017/9781316888681

Ajzen, I. (1991). The theory of planned behavior. *Organizational Behavior and Human Decision Processes*, *50*(2), 179–211. DOI: 10.1016/0749-5978(91)90020-T

Akhtar, Z. B., & Rawol, A. T. (2024, August). Enhancing Cybersecurity through Artificial Intelligence (AI)-Powered Security Mechanisms. *IT Journal Research and Development*, *9*(1), 50–67. DOI: 10.25299/itjrd.2024.16852

Akintoye, R., Ogunode, O., Ajayi, M., & Joshua, A. A. (2022). Cyber security and financial innovation of selected deposit money banks in Nigeria. *universal Journal of Accounting and Finance, 10*(3), 643-652.

Akkartal, G. R., & Mızrak, F. (2024). Operational Efficiency and Competitiveness in the Global Logistics Industry: An Examination of Human Resources Management Strategies. In *Strategic Innovations for Dynamic Supply Chains* (pp. 71-102). IGI Global.

Alamri, B., Crowley, K., & Richardson, I. (2022). Cybersecurity risk management framework for blockchain identity management systems in health IoT. *Sensors (Basel)*, *23*(1), 218. DOI: 10.3390/s23010218 PMID: 36616816

Alawida, M., Mejri, S., Mehmood, A., Chikhaoui, B., & Isaac Abiodun, O. (2023). A comprehensive study of ChatGPT: Advancements, limitations, and ethical considerations in natural language processing and cybersecurity. *Information (Basel)*, *14*(8), 462. DOI: 10.3390/info14080462

Alcaraz, C., & Lopez, J. (2022). Digital twin: A comprehensive survey of security threats. *IEEE Communications Surveys and Tutorials*, *24*(3), 1475–1503. DOI: 10.1109/COMST.2022.3171465

Alcaraz, C., & Zeadally, S. (2015). Ocak). Critical Infrastructure Protection: Requirements and Challenges for the 21st Century. *International Journal of Critical Infrastructure Protection*, *8*, 53–66. DOI: 10.1016/j.ijcip.2014.12.002

AlDaajeh, S., & Alrabaee, S. (2024). Strategic cybersecurity. *Computers & Security, 141*, 103845. DOI: 10.1016/j.cose.2024.103845

AlDaajeh, S., Saleous, H., Alrabaee, S., Barka, E., Breitinger, F., & Choo, K. K. R. (2022). The role of national cybersecurity strategies on the improvement of cybersecurity education. *Computers & Security, 119*, 102754. DOI: 10.1016/j.cose.2022.102754

Alevizos, L., Bhakuni, L., & Jäschke, S. (2025). A value driven framework for cybersecurity innovation in transportation and infrastructure. *International Journal of Information Technology : an Official Journal of Bharati Vidyapeeth's Institute of Computer Applications and Management, 17*(1), 321–331. DOI: 10.1007/s41870-024-02288-w

Alhidaifi, S. M., Asghar, M. R., & Ansari, I. S. (2024). A survey on cyber resilience: Key strategies, research challenges, and future directions. *ACM Computing Surveys, 56*(8), 1–48. DOI: 10.1145/3649218

Alhija, M. A., Al-Baik, O., Hussein, A., & Abdeljaber, H. (2024). Optimizing blockchain for healthcare IoT: A practical guide to navigating scalability, privacy, and efficiency trade-offs. *Indonesian Journal of Electrical Engineering and Computer Science, 35*(3), 1773–1785. DOI: 10.11591/ijeecs.v35.i3.pp1773-1785

AlHogail, A. (2015). *Design and validation of information security culture framework*. Computer Human Behaviour. DOI: 10.1016/j.chb.2015.03.054

Alhumam, N., Rahman, M. H., & Aljughaiman, A. (2025). A Comprehensive Review on Cybersecurity of Digital Twins Issues, Challenges, and Future Research Directions. *IEEE Access : Practical Innovations, Open Solutions, 13*, 45106–45124. DOI: 10.1109/ACCESS.2025.3545004

Ali, H. A., Abid, A., Ammar, M., Qamar, A., Khalid, R., & Shahid, A. R. (2024). Ethereum based electronic health record management system for secure and controlled access. *arXiv preprint arXiv:2412.02851*. Retrieved from https://arxiv.org/abs/2412.02851

Ali, M. H., Jaber, M. M., Abd, S. K., Rehman, A., Awan, M. J., Damaševicius, R., & Bahaj, S. A. (2022). Threat Analysis and Distributed Denial of Service (DDoS) Attack Recognition in the Internet of Things (IoT). Electronics MDPI.

Aljumaiah, O., Jiang, W., Addula, S. R., & Almaiah, M. A. (2025). Analyzing cybersecurity risks and threats in IT infrastructure based on NIST framework. *Journal of Cyber Security and Risk Auditing, 2*(2), 12–26. DOI: 10.63180/jcsra.thestap.2025.2.2

Alkhalil, Z., Hewage, C., Nawaf, L., & Khan, I. (2021). Phishing attacks: A recent comprehensive study and a new anatomy. *Frontiers of Computer Science*, *3*(6), 563060. DOI: 10.3389/fcomp.2021.563060

Alkhazi, B., Alshaikh, M., Alkhezi, S., & Labbaci, H. (2022). Assessment of the impact of information security awareness training methods on knowledge, attitude, and behavior. *IEEE Access: Practical Innovations, Open Solutions*, *10*, 132132–132143. DOI: 10.1109/ACCESS.2022.3230286

Allahrakha, N. (2023). Balancing cyber-security and privacy: Legal and ethical considerations in the digital age. *Legal Issues in the digital. The Age (Melbourne, Vic.)*, (2), 78–121.

Al-ma'aitah, M. A. (2022). Investigating the drivers of cybersecurity enhancement in public organizations: The case of Jordan. *The Electronic Journal on Information Systems in Developing Countries*, *88*(5), e12223. DOI: 10.1002/isd2.12223

Almomani, A., Alauthman, M., Shatnawi, M. T., Alweshah, M., Alrosan, A., Alomoush, W., Gupta, B. B., Gupta, B. B., & Gupta, B. B. (2022). Phishing website detection with semantic features based on machine learning classifiers: A comparative study. *International Journal on Semantic Web and Information Systems*, *18*(1), 1–24. DOI: 10.4018/IJSWIS.297032

Alnafessah, A., & Casale, G. (2020). Artificial neural networks based techniques for anomaly detection in Apache Spark. *Cluster Computing*, *23*(2), 1345–1360. DOI: 10.1007/s10586-019-02998-y

Al-Okaily, M., Younis, H., & Al-Okaily, A. (2024). The impact of management practices and industry 4.0 technologies on supply chain sustainability: A systematic review. *Heliyon*, *10*(17), e36421. DOI: 10.1016/j.heliyon.2024.e36421 PMID: 39263079

Alrehili, A. A., & Alhazmi, O. H. (2023, September). ISO/IEC 27001 Standard: Analytical and Comparative Overview. In International Conference on Advances in Data-driven Computing and Intelligent Systems (pp. 143-156). Singapore: Springer Nature Singapore.

Alshaikh, M. (2020, August 21). Developing cybersecurity culture to influence employee behavior: A practice perspective. *Computers & Security*, *98*, 2–10. DOI: 10.1016/j.cose.2020.102003

Al-Somali, S. A., Saqr, R. R., Asiri, A. M., & Al-Somali, N. A. (2024). Organizational cybersecurity systems and sustainable business performance of small and medium enterprises (SMEs) in Saudi Arabia: The mediating and moderating role of cybersecurity resilience and organizational culture. *Sustainability (Basel)*, *16*(5), 1880. DOI: 10.3390/su16051880

Altulaihan, E., Almaiah, M. A., & Aljughaiman, A. (2022). Cybersecurity threats, countermeasures and mitigation techniques on the IoT: Future research directions. *Electronics (Basel)*, *11*(20), 3330. DOI: 10.3390/electronics11203330

Aluvalu, R., & Muddana, L. (2015). A survey on access control models in cloud computing. In S. Satapathy, A. Govardhan, K. Raju, & J. Mandal (Eds.), Emerging ICT for bridging the future – Proceedings of the 49th Annual Convention of the Computer Society of India (CSI) Volume 1 (Vol. 337, pp. 611–619). Springer. DOI: 10.1007/978-3-319-13728-5_73

Amin, Z. (2019). A practical road map for assessing cyber risk. *Journal of Risk Research*, *22*(1), 32–43. DOI: 10.1080/13669877.2017.1351467

Amoo, O. O., Osasona, F., Atadoga, A., Ayinla, B. S., Farayola, O. A., & Abrahams, T. O. (2024). Cybersecurity threats in the age of IoT: A review of protective measures. *International Journal of Science and Research Archive*, *11*(1), 1304–1310. DOI: 10.30574/ijsra.2024.11.1.0217

Anand, N., Saifulla, M. A., Ponnuru, R. B., Alavalapati, G. R., Patan, R., & Gandomi, A. H. (2024). Securing Software Defined Networks: A Comprehensive Analysis of Approaches, Applications, and Future Strategies against DoS Attacks. *IEEE Access : Practical Innovations, Open Solutions*.

Andersen, R., Barton, C., Böhme, R., Clayton, R., Ganan, C., Grasso, T., Levi, M., Moore, T., & Vasek, M. (2019). *Measuring the changing cost of cybercrime*. Conference Paper, The 2019 Workshop on the Economics of Information Security, Boston.

Andrejevic, M. (2025). Labor and surveillance: The productivity of being watched. In *The handbook of digital labor* (pp. 119–131). Cambridge University Press. DOI: 10.1002/9781119981831.ch7

Andrew, J., & Baker, M. (2021). The general data protection regulation in the age of surveillance capitalism. *Journal of Business Ethics*, *168*(3), 565–578. DOI: 10.1007/s10551-019-04239-z

Annarelli, A., & Palombi, G. (2021). Digitalization capabilities for sustainable cyber resilience: A conceptual framework. *Sustainability (Basel)*, *13*(23), 13065. DOI: 10.3390/su132313065

ANSI. (2023). *Digital twins and cybersecurity in Industry 4.0: Standardization trends and recommendations*. American National Standards Institute. Retrieved from https://www.ansi.org

Antonakakis, M., April, T., Bailey, M., Bernhard, M., Bursztein, E., Cochran, J., Durumeric, Z., Halderman, J. A., Invernizzi, L., Kallitsis, M., Kumar, D., Lever, C., Ma, Z., Mason, J., Menscher, D., Seaman, C., Sullivan, N., Thomas, K., & Zhou, Y. (2017). Understanding the Mirai botnet. In *Proceedings of the 26th USENIX Security Symposium* (pp. 1093-1110). (Proceedings of the 26th USENIX Security Symposium). USENIX Association.

Aposporis, P. (2024). A review of global and regional frameworks for the integration of an unmanned aircraft system in air traffic management. *Transportation Research Interdisciplinary Perspectives*, *24*, 101064. DOI: 10.1016/j.trip.2024.101064

Arabo, A. (2015). Cyber security challenges within the connected home ecosystem futures. *Procedia Computer Science*, *61*, 227–232. DOI: 10.1016/j.procs.2015.09.201

Argaw, S. T., Troncoso-Pastoriza, J. R., Lacey, D., Florin, M., Calcavecchia, F., Andersen, D., Burleson, W., Vogel, J., O'Leary, C., Eshaya-Chauvin, B., & Antoine, F. (2020). Cybersecurity of hospitals: Discussing the challenges and working towards mitigating the risks. *BMC Medical Informatics and Decision Making*, *20*(1), 146. DOI: 10.1186/s12911-020-01161-7 PMID: 32620167

Asghar, M. R., Hu, Q., & Zeadally, S. (2019, December 24). Cybersecurity in industrial control systems: Issues, technologies, and challenges. *Computer Networks*, *165*, 165. DOI: 10.1016/j.comnet.2019.106946

Aslan, Ö., Aktuğ, S. S., Ozkan-Okay, M., Yilmaz, A. A., & Akin, E. (2023). A comprehensive review of cyber security vulnerabilities, threats, attacks, and solutions. *Electronics (Basel)*, *12*(6), 1333. DOI: 10.3390/electronics12061333

Aslay, F. (2017). Siber saldırı yöntemleri ve Türkiye'nin siber güvenlik mevcut durum analizi. *International Journal of Multidisciplinary Studies and Innovative Technologies*, *1*(1), 24–28.

Attkan, A., & Ranga, V. (2022). Cyber-physical security for IoT networks: A comprehensive review on traditional, blockchain and artificial intelligence based key-security. *Complex & Intelligent Systems*, *8*(4), 3559–3591. DOI: 10.1007/s40747-022-00667-z

Aurigemma, S., & Panko, R. (2012). A composite framework for behavioralcompliance with information security policies. In 45th HawaiiInternational Conference on Systems Sciences. Maui, Hawaii.

Automotive Logistics. (2023). How VW Mexico is using AI to improve logistics decision-making. Retrieved from https://www.automotivelogistics.media

Avcı, İ. (2022). Akıllı Evlerde IoT Teknolojileri ve Siber Güvenlik. *Avrupa Bilim ve Teknoloji Dergisi*, (34), 226–233. DOI: 10.31590/ejosat.1080228

Avolution. (2024). *Case Study: Sophos and Cybersecurity Architecture*. Retrieved from https://www.avolutionsoftware.com/our-resources/sophos/

AWS. (2023). Cold-chain monitoring with AWS IoT. Retrieved from https://www.aws.amazon.com

Aydın, H., Barışkan, M. A., & Çetinkaya, A. (2021). Mayıs). *Güvenlik Bilimleri Dergisi, 10*(1), 151–174. DOI: 10.28956/gbd.941801

Azad, M. A., Abdullah, S., Arshad, J., Lallie, H., & Ahmed, Y. H. (2024). Verify and trust: A multidimensional survey of zero-trust security in the age of IoT. *Internet of Things : Engineering Cyber Physical Human Systems*, *27*, 101227. DOI: 10.1016/j.iot.2024.101227

Badawy, M., Sherief, N. H., & Abdel-Hamid, A. A. (2024). Legacy ICS cybersecurity assessment using hybrid threat modeling—An oil and gas sector case study. *Applied Sciences (Basel, Switzerland)*, *14*(18), 8398. DOI: 10.3390/app14188398

Badshah, A., Daud, A., Alharbey, R., Banjar, A., Bukhari, A., & Alshemaimri, B. (2024). Big data applications: Overview, challenges and future. *Artificial Intelligence Review*, *57*(11), 290. DOI: 10.1007/s10462-024-10938-5

Bahyan, H., Ajmal, M. M., & Saber, H. (2024). Going resilient with digital transformation, human capabilities and innovation readiness: Empirical evidence from the energy sector. *Benchmarking*. Advance online publication. DOI: 10.1108/BIJ-10-2023-0699

Bakyt, M., La Spada, L., Zeeshan, N., Moldamurat, K., Atanov, S., Konyrkhanova, A., & Tilenbayev, A. (2025). Advanced Cybersecurity Framework for LEO Aerospace: Integrating Quantum Cryptography, Artificial Intelligence Anomaly Detection, and Blockchain Technology. [JRC]. *Journal of Robotics and Control*, *6*(2), 695–714.

Bala, B., & Behal, S. (2024, May). AI techniques for IoT-based DDoS attack detection: Taxonomies, comprehensive review and research challenges. *Computer Science Review*, *52*, 52. DOI: 10.1016/j.cosrev.2024.100631

Ball, K. (2010). Workplace surveillance: An overview. *Labor History*, *51*(1), 87–106. DOI: 10.1080/00236561003654776

Ball, K. (2014). Electronic surveillance at work: An ethical analysis. *Public Administration Review, 74*(3), 348–359.

Ball, K. (2022). Surveillance in the workplace: Past, present, and future. *Surveillance & Society, 20*(4), 455–461. DOI: 10.24908/ss.v20i4.15805

Balta, E. C., Pease, M., Moyne, J., Barton, K., & Tilbury, D. M. (2023). Digital twin-based cyber-attack detection framework for cyber-physical manufacturing systems. *IEEE Transactions on Automation Science and Engineering, 21*(2), 1695–1712. DOI: 10.1109/TASE.2023.3243147

Bamidele, R. O., Ozturen, A., Haktanir, M., & Ogunmokun, O. A. (2023). Realizing green airport performance through green management intransigence, airport reputation, biospheric value, and eco-design. *Sustainability (Basel), 15*(3), 2475. DOI: 10.3390/su15032475

Banger, G. (2018). *Endüstri 4.0 ve akıllı işletme* [Industry 4.0 and the smart enterprise]. Dorlion Yayınları.

Barbieri, E., & Capoani, L. (2025). Renewable Energy, Resilience, Digitalization, and Industrial Policies in Seaborne Transport. *Energies, 18*(5), 1089. DOI: 10.3390/en18051089

Becker, G. (1968). Crime and punishment: An economic approach. *Journal of Political Economy, 76*(2), 169–217. DOI: 10.1086/259394

Bendiab, G., Hameurlaine, A., Germanos, G., Kolokotronis, N., & Shiaeles, S. (2023). Autonomous vehicles security: Challenges and solutions using blockchain and artificial intelligence. *IEEE Transactions on Intelligent Transportation Systems, 24*(4), 3614–3637. DOI: 10.1109/TITS.2023.3236274

Bennett, C. J., & Raab, C. D. (2020). *The governance of privacy: Policy instruments in global perspective* (3rd ed.). MIT Press.

Bernstein, E., Shore, J., & Lazer, D. (2022). How intermittent breaks improve productivity. *Harvard Business Review, 100*(1), 94–101.

Bhute, A., & Bhute, H. (2025). A Comprehensive Review on Digital Innovations for Renewable Energy and Conservation. Digital Innovations for Renewable Energy and Conservation, 1-20.

Bickford, J., Van Bossuyt, D. L., Beery, P., & Pollman, A. (2020). Operationalizing digital twins through model-based systems engineering methods. *Systems Engineering, 23*(6), 724–750. DOI: 10.1002/sys.21559

Binns, R., Veale, M., Van Kleek, M., & Shadbolt, N. (2018). "It's reducing a human being to a percentage": Perceptions of justice in algorithmic decisions. In Proceedings of the 2018 CHI Conference on Human Factors in Computing Systems (pp. 1–14). ACM. DOI: 10.1145/3173574.3173951

Blin, P. F., Aditya, T., Claramunt, C., Kermarrec, Y., & Santosa, P. B. (2022). Cybersecurity Risk-Management to Maintain Integrity Land Data Transactions: Application to Indonesian and French Land Administration Systems. *The International Archives of the Photogrammetry, Remote Sensing and Spatial Information Sciences*, *48*, 29–31. DOI: 10.5194/isprs-archives-XLVIII-4-W3-2022-29-2022

Bolatbekkyzy, G. (2024). Legal Issues of Cross-Border Data Transfer in the Era of Digital Government. *Journal of Digital Technologies and Law*, *2*(2), 286–307. DOI: 10.21202/jdtl.2024.15

Boyson, S., Corsi, T. M., & Paraskevas, J. P. (2022). Defending digital supply chains: Evidence from a decade-long research program. *Technovation*, *118*, 102380. DOI: 10.1016/j.technovation.2021.102380

Brass, I., Tanczer, L., Carr, M., Elsden, M., & Blackstock, J. (2018). Standardising a moving target: The development and evolution of IoT security standards. In *Living in the Internet of Things: Cybersecurity of the IoT-2018* (p. 24). IET. DOI: 10.1049/cp.2018.0024

Brezavšček, A., & Baggia, A. (2025). Recent Trends in Information and Cyber Security Maturity Assessment: A Systematic Literature Review. *Systems*, *13*(1), 52. DOI: 10.3390/systems13010052

Brilingaitė, A., Bukauskas, L., Domarkienė, I., Rančelis, T., Ambrozaitytė, L., Pirta, R., & Knox, B. J. (2025). Towards projection of the individualised risk assessment for the cybersecurity workforce. *Computer Standards & Interfaces*, *93*, 103962.

Brilingaitė, A., Bukauskas, L., & Juozapavičius, A. (2020). A framework for competence development and assessment in hybrid cybersecurity exercises. *Computers & Security*, *88*, 101607. DOI: 10.1016/j.cose.2019.101607

Brougham, D., & Haar, J. (2018). Smart technology, artificial intelligence, robotics, and algorithms (STARA): Employees' perceptions of future workplaces. *Journal of Management & Organization*, *24*(2), 239–257. DOI: 10.1017/jmo.2016.55

Brynjolfsson, E., & McAfee, A. (2014). *The second machine age: Work, progress, and prosperity in a time of brilliant technologies*. W.W. Norton & Co.

Buchta, R., Gkoktsis, G., Heine, F., & Kleiner, C. (2024). Advanced persistent threat attack detection systems: A review of approaches, challenges, and trends. *Digital Threats : Research and Practice*, *5*(4), 1–37. DOI: 10.1145/3696014

Burns, S., & Roberts, L. (2013). Applying the theory of planned behaviour to predicting online safety behaviour. *Crime Prevention and Community Safety*, *15*, 48–64.

Calder, A., (2018). NIST Cybersecurity Framework: A pocket Guide. Ely, IT Governance Publishing, 5–78.

Caliskan, A., Eryilmaz, S., & Ozturkoglu, Y. (2025). Investigating the effects of barriers and challenges on Logistics 4.0 in the era of evolving digital technology. *Journal of Modelling in Management*, *20*(3), 949–973. DOI: 10.1108/JM2-01-2024-0026

Calvard, T. S., & Jeske, D. (2018). Developing human resource data risk management in the age of big data. *International Journal of Information Management*, *43*, 159–164. DOI: 10.1016/j.ijinfomgt.2018.07.011

Camacho, N. G. (2024). The role of AI in cybersecurity: Addressing threats in the digital age. *Journal of Artificial Intelligence General science (JAIGS) ISSN: 3006-4023, 3*(1), 143-154.

Capgemini. (2023). AI in the automotive supply chain: Driving resilience through predictive intelligence. Retrieved from https://www.capgemini.com

Carayannis, E. G., Dezi, L., Gregori, G., & Calo, E. (2022). Smart environments and techno-centric and human-centric innovations for Industry and Society 5.0: A quintuple helix innovation system view towards smart, sustainable, and inclusive solutions. *Journal of the Knowledge Economy*, *13*(2), 926–955. DOI: 10.1007/s13132-021-00763-4

Çelik, K. (2021). Bulut bilişim teknolojileri [Cloud computing technologies]. *Bartın Üniversitesi İktisadi ve İdari Bilimler Fakültesi Dergisi*, *12*(24), 436–450. DOI: 10.47129/bartiniibf.1019898

Cevher, M. F. (2023). Bibliometric analysis of the internet of things from a marketing perspective. *Journal of Research in Business*, *8*(1), 153–170. DOI: 10.54452/jrb.1181367

Chalkbeat. (2020, May 6). *NYC lifts Zoom ban after security improvements*. Retrieved from https://www.chalkbeat.org/newyork/2020/05/06/nyc-lifts-zoom-ban-after-security-improvements

Chang, C. H., Wenming, S., Wei, Z., Changki, P., & Kontovas, C. A. (2019). Evaluating cybersecurity risks in the maritime industry: a literature review. In: Proceedings of the International Association of Maritime Universities (IAMU) Conference. (International Association of Maritime Universities (IAMU), 29 October 2019 - 01 November 2019, Tokyo).

Chang, K. Y., Chen, C. D., & Ku, E. C. (2024). Enhancing smart tourism and smart city development: Evidence from Taoyuan smart aviation city in Taiwan. *International Journal of Tourism Cities, 10*(1), 146–165. DOI: 10.1108/IJTC-05-2023-0088

Cha, S. Y. (2022). The art of cyber security in the age of the digital supply chain: detecting and defending against vulnerabilities in your supply chain. In *The Digital Supply Chain* (pp. 215–233). Elsevier. DOI: 10.1016/B978-0-323-91614-1.00013-7

Chaudhary, S. (2024). Driving behaviour change with cybersecurity awareness. *Computers & Security, 142*, 103858. DOI: 10.1016/j.cose.2024.103858

Chen, J., Zheng, X., & Rong, C. (2015). Survey on software-defined networking. In *Proceedings of the Second International Conference on Cloud Computing and Big Data in Asia*, Huangshan, China, 17–19 June 2015; Springer: Cham, Switzerland, 115–124.

Chen, S. (2021). Research on data sovereignty rules in cross-border data flow and Chinese solution. *US-China L.Rev., 18*, 261.

Chen, Y., Wang, W., Yang, Z., Deveci, M., & Delen, D. (2024). Evaluating risk of IoT adoption in the food supply chain using an integrated interval-valued spherical fuzzy generalised TODIM method. *International Journal of Production Economics, 277*, 109386. DOI: 10.1016/j.ijpe.2024.109386

Cheung, T., Li, B., & Lei, Z. (2023). A paradigm shift in the aviation industry with digital twin, blockchain, and AI technologies. In *Handbook on Artificial Intelligence and Transport* (pp. 323–346). Edward Elgar Publishing. DOI: 10.4337/9781803929545.00020

Chia, J. W., Verhagen, W. J., Silva, J. M., & Cole, I. S. (2024). A review and outlook of airframe digital twins for structural prognostics and health management in the aviation industry. *Journal of Manufacturing Systems, 77*, 398–417. DOI: 10.1016/j.jmsy.2024.09.024

Chidukwani, A., Zander, S., & Koutsakis, P. (2024). Cybersecurity preparedness of small-to-medium businesses: A Western Australia study with broader implications. *Computers & Security, 145*, 104026. DOI: 10.1016/j.cose.2024.104026

Cichosz, M., Wallenburg, C. M., & Knemeyer, A. M. (2020). Digital transformation at logistics service providers: Barriers, success factors and leading practices. *International Journal of Logistics Management, 31*(2), 209–238. DOI: 10.1108/IJLM-08-2019-0229

Cindric, I., Jurcevic, M., & Hadjina, T. (2025). *Mapping of Industrial IoT to IEC 62443 Standards*. MDPI. DOI: 10.3390/s25030728

CISA. (2021). *Unmanned Aircraft Systems: Cybersecurity Risks and Mitigation Approaches*. Retrieved from https://www.cisa.gov

Claudia Greco, G. F., & Choo, K.-K. R. (2023). AI-enabled IoT penetration testing: State-of-the-art and research challenges. *Enterprise Information Systems, 17*(9), 1223–1247.

Clavijo Mesa, M. V., Patino-Rodriguez, C. E., & Guevara Carazas, F. J. (2024). Cybersecurity at Sea: A Literature Review of Cyber-Attack Impacts and Defenses in Maritime Supply Chains. *Information (Basel), 15*(11), 710. DOI: 10.3390/info15110710

Cofense, (2022). Keeping up with phishing. https://get.cofense.com/CRA-Keeping - Up- With- Phishing.html

Colbert, A., Yee, N., & George, G. (2016). The digital workforce and the workplace of the future. *Academy of Management Journal, 59*(3), 731–739. DOI: 10.5465/amj.2016.4003

Conti, M., Dehghantanha, A., & Franke, K. (2018). Cyber threat intelligence: Challenges and opportunities. *Computer Fraud & Security, 2018*(9), 14–17.

Coutinho, B., Ferreira, J., Yevseyeva, I., & Basto-Fernandes, V. (2023). Integrated cybersecurity methodology and supporting tools for healthcare operational information systems. *Computers & Security, 129*, 103189. DOI: 10.1016/j.cose.2023.103189

Da Silva Carvalho, N., Jabbarpour, J., Temple, L., Belacort, I. M., Barturen, U. I., Kortlander, M., & Mureddu, F. (2023, September). A more inclusive Europe through personal data sovereignty in cross-border digital public services. In *Proceedings of the 16th International Conference on Theory and Practice of Electronic Governance* (pp. 63-71). DOI: 10.1145/3614321.3614329

Da Veiga, A., Astakhova, L., Botha, A., & Herselman, H. (2020, May 30). Defining organisational information security culture—Perspectives from academia and industry. *Computers & Security, 92*, 101713. DOI: 10.1016/j.cose.2020.101713

Da Veiga, A., & Eloff, J. (2010, March 1). A framework and assessment instrument for information security culture. *Computers & Security*, *29*(2), 196–207. DOI: 10.1016/j.cose.2009.09.002

Dabke, V., Dabke, Y., & Gadgil, G. (2023). Social engineering as a driving force for innovation in cybersecurity. *Authorea Preprints*.

Dairy Reporter. (2023). Wiliot's ambient IoT tags bring real-time freshness data to retailers. Retrieved from https://www.dairyreporter.com

Dangheralou, A., & Jahankhani, H. (2022). The Impact of GDPR Regulations on Cyber Security Effectiveness Whilst Working Remotely. In *Artificial Intelligence in Cyber Security: Impact and Implications: Security Challenges, Technical and Ethical Issues, Forensic Investigative Challenges* (pp. 253–279). Springer International Publishing.

Dave, G., Choudhary, G., Sihag, V., You, I., & Choo, K. K. R. (2022). Cyber security challenges in aviation communication, navigation, and surveillance. *Computers & Security*, *112*, 102516. DOI: 10.1016/j.cose.2021.102516

Dawood, M., Tu, S., Xiao, C., Alasmary, H., Waqas, M., & Rehman, S. U. (2023). Cyberattacks and security of cloud computing: A complete guideline. *Symmetry*, *15*(11), 1981. DOI: 10.3390/sym15111981

DBIR. (2023) Data Breach Investigations Report Public Sector Snapshot, Verizon. https://www.verizon.com/business/resources/Te46/reports/2023-dbir-public-sector-snapshot.pdf

de Azambuja, A. J. G., Giese, T., Schützer, K., Anderl, R., Schleich, B., & Almeida, V. R. (2024). Digital Twins in Industry 4.0–Opportunities and challenges related to cyber security. *Procedia CIRP*, *121*, 25–30. DOI: 10.1016/j.procir.2023.09.225

Decta. (2021). *Blockchain in banking: Transforming trade finance with digital trust*. Retrieved from https://www.decta.com/blog/blockchain-in-banking/

Dehghantanha, A., Yazdinejad, A., & Parizi, R. M. (2024). Autonomous Cybersecurity: Evolving Challenges, Emerging Opportunities, and Future Research Trajectories. CCS '24: ACM SIGSAC Conference on Computer and Communications Security. Salt Lake City, U.S.A.: ACM CCS.

Deloitte University Press. (n.d.). Industry 4.0 – Is your ERP system ready for the digital era? (p. 8). Retrieved from https://www2.deloitte.com/content/dam/Deloitte/de/Documents/technology/Deloitte _ERP_ Industrie-4-0_Whitepaper.pdf as cited in Eğilmez, M. (2018). Industry 4.0. Journal of Accounting and Financial History Research, 15, 268. https://dergipark.org.tr/tr/download/issue-full-file/37137

Demirçi, Z. Ö. (2025). Şubat). Karakuri Kaizen: Yalın Üretimde Sürekli İyileştirmenin Mekanik Uygulmaları. *Anahtar Makale*, *434*, 30–32.

Demir, S., & Paksoy, T. (2025). A Conceptual Framework for Smart and Sustainable Operations in the Aviation Industry. In *Smart and Sustainable Operations Management in the Aviation Industry* (pp. 1–14). CRC Press.

Denis, A., Thomas, A., Robert, W., Samuel, A., Kabiito, S. P., Morish, Z., Sallam, M., Ali, G., & Mijwil, M. M. (2025). A Survey on Artificial Intelligence and Blockchain Applications in Cybersecurity for Smart Cities. *SHIFRA*, *2025*, 1–45. DOI: 10.70470/SHIFRA/2025/001

Dentoni, D., Pinkse, J., & Lubberink, R. (2021). Linking sustainable business models to socio-ecological resilience through cross-sector partnerships: A complex adaptive systems view. *Business & Society*, *60*(5), 1216–1252. DOI: 10.1177/0007650320935015

Destriani, R., Adhitama, R. Y., Sensuse, D. I., Hidayat, D. S., & Purwaningsih, E. H. (2024). Challenges and technology trends in implementing a human resource management system: A systematic literature review. *Journal of Information Systems Engineering and Business Intelligence*, *10*(3), 355–367. DOI: 10.20473/jisebi.10.3.355-367

Dhirani, L. L., Mukhtiar, N., Chowdhry, B. S., & Newe, T. (2023). Ethical dilemmas and privacy issues in emerging technologies: A review. *Sensors (Basel)*, *23*(3), 1151. DOI: 10.3390/s23031151 PMID: 36772190

DHL. (2024). Cybersecurity 2.0 in logistics: Proactive defense in the digital age. Retrieved from https://www.dhl.com

Dias, C., & Silva, J. (2024). Unveiling the future: Smart airports-applications, advantages, strategies and technological challenges. *Journal of Airline and Airport Management*, *14*(2), 38–56. DOI: 10.3926/jairm.419

Dihan, M. S., Akash, A. I., Tasneem, Z., Das, P., Das, S. K., Islam, M. R., Islam, M. M., Badal, F. R., Ali, M. F., Ahamed, M. H., Abhi, S. H., Sarker, S. K., & Hasan, M. M. (2024). Digital twin: Data exploration, architecture, implementation and future. *Heliyon*, *10*(5), e26503. DOI: 10.1016/j.heliyon.2024.e26503 PMID: 38444502

Dimitrov, D. S. (2024). *The New Work of Building Operations in the Digital Age: The Impact of IoT and Digital Twins on Facility Management and Operational Practices* (Doctoral dissertation, University of Washington).

Doargajudhur, M. S., & Dell, P. (2018). The effect of bring your own device (BYOD) adoption on work performance and motivation. *Journal of Computer Information Systems*, *60*(6), 518–529. DOI: 10.1080/08874417.2018.1543001

Downer, K., & Bhattacharya, M. (2022). BYOD security: A study of human dimensions. *Informatics (MDPI)*, *9*(1), 16. DOI: 10.3390/informatics9010016

Dreyer, P., Jones, T., Klima, K., Oberholtzer, J., Strong, A., Welburn, J. W., & Winkelman, Z. (2018). Estimating the global cost of cyber risk. [*-WFHF, Rand Corporation.*]. *Research Reports (Montgomery)*, ●●●, RR-2299.

Dua, A., Barpanda, S. S., Kumar, N., & Tanwar, S. (2020, December). Trustful: A decentralized public key infrastructure and identity management system. In *2020 IEEE Globecom Workshops (GC Wkshps* (pp. 1-6). IEEE. DOI: 10.1109/GCWkshps50303.2020.9367444

Dubois, E., Heymans, P., Mayer, N., & Matulevicius, R. (2010). A systematic approach to define the domain of information system security risk management. In Nurcan, S., Salinesi, C., Souveyet, C., & Ralyté, J. (Eds.), *Intentional Perspectives on Information Systems Engineering*. Springer. DOI: 10.1007/978-3-642-12544-7_16

Dudorov, D., Stupples, D., & Newby, M. (2013), "Probability analysis of cyber attack paths against business and commercial enterprise systems", *European Intelligence and Security Informatics Conference (EISIC)*, Uppsala. DOI: 10.1109/EISIC.2013.13

Dupont, B., Shearing, C., Bernier, M., & Leukfeldt, R. (2023, June 29). The tensions of cyber-resilience: From sensemaking to practice. *Computers & Security*, *132*, 103372. DOI: 10.1016/j.cose.2023.103372

Echeverría, A., Cevallos, C., Ortiz-Garces, I., & Andrade, R. O. (2021). Cybersecurity model based on hardening for secure internet of things implementation. *Applied Sciences (Basel, Switzerland)*, *11*(7), 3260. DOI: 10.3390/app11073260

Efe, A. (2021). Yapay Zekâ Odaklı Siber Risk ve Güvenlik Yönetimi. *Uluslararası Yönetim Bilişim Sistemleri ve Bilgisayar Bilimleri Dergisi*, *5*(2), 144–165. DOI: 10.33461/uybisbbd.972206

Efe, A. (2021). Yapay zekâ ve Endüstri 4.0 ilişkisinin siber güvenlik perspektifinden analizi [Analysis of the relationship between artificial intelligence and Industry 4.0 from a cybersecurity perspective]. *Aydın Adnan Menderes Üniversitesi Sosyal Bilimler Enstitüsü Dergisi*, *8*(1), 123–143. DOI: 10.30803/adusobed.936426

Eldem, M. O. (2017). Endüstri 4.0. TMMOB EMO Ankara Şubesi Haber Bülteni, 2017(3), 10. Retrieved from https://www.emo.org.tr/ekler/09287020c96f18a_ek.pdf?dergi=1111

Elendu, C., Omeludike, E. K., Oloyede, P. O., Obidigbo, B. T., & Omeludike, J. C. (2024). Legal implications for clinicians in cybersecurity incidents. *Revista de Medicina (São Paulo)*, *103*(39), e39887. PMID: 39331908

Elmarady, A. A., & Rahouma, K. (2021). Studying cybersecurity in civil aviation, including developing and applying aviation cybersecurity risk assessment. *IEEE Access : Practical Innovations, Open Solutions, 9*, 143997–144016. DOI: 10.1109/ACCESS.2021.3121230

Elmisery, A. M., Sertovic, M., Zayin, A., & Watson, P. (2025). Cyber Threats in Financial Transactions—Addressing the Dual Challenge of AI and Quantum Computing. *arXiv preprint arXiv:2503.15678.*

Eltayeb, O. (2024). Cyber Defense Using Cyber Threat Intelligence to Anticipate and Avoid Future Cyber Attacks. *Journal of Ecohumanism, 3*(4), 2435–2455. DOI: 10.62754/joe.v3i4.3766

Enisa, (2024). ENISA threat landscape 2024. European Union Agency for Cybersecurity June 2023 to June 2024 Report, https://www.enisa.europa.eu/sites/default/files/2024-11/ENISA%20Threat%20Landscape%202024_0.pdf

Erbey, A. (2024). Internet of Things (IoT). In Karaca, M. F. (Ed.), *Current Topics in Management Information Systems* (pp. 15–32). Özgür Yayınları., DOI: 10.58830/ozgur.pub498.c2090

Esan, O., Ajayi, F. A., & Olawale, O. (2024). Supply chain integrating sustainability and ethics: Strategies for modern supply chain management. *World Journal of Advanced Research and Reviews, 22*(1), 1930–1953. DOI: 10.30574/wjarr.2024.22.1.1259

European Union Agency for Cybersecurity. Lella, I., Theocharidou, M., Magonara, E., Malatras, A., Svetozarov Naydenov, R., Ciobanu, C., & Chatzichristos, G. (2024). ENISA threat landscape 2024 : July 2023 to June 2024. https://data.europa.eu/doi/10.2824/0710888

Evren, A. G. (2023). Comparative analysis of the European Union and Turkish personal data protection laws: Basic principles, legal grounds, and rights of data subjects. *Kişisel Verileri Koruma Dergisi, 5*(2), 39–64.

Evren, A. G. (2023, December 25). Avrupa Birliği ve Türkiye Kişisel Verilerin Korunması Kanunlarının Karşılaştırmalı Analizi: Temel İlkeler, Yasal Dayanaklar ve İlgili Kişi Hakları. *Kişisel Verileri Koruma Dergisi, 5*(2), 39–64.

FAA. (2024). *BFDI-AP Test Report: Enhancing Cybersecurity in Public Safety UAS Operations*. Federal Aviation Administration. Retrieved from https://www.faa.gov

Fakhraian, E., Semanjski, I., Semanjski, S., & Aghezzaf, E. H. (2023). Towards safe and efficient unmanned aircraft system operations: Literature review of digital twins' applications and european union regulatory compliance. *Drones (Basel), 7*(7), 478. DOI: 10.3390/drones7070478

Faleiro, R., Pan, L., Pokhrel, S. R., & Doss, R. (2021, October). Digital twin for cybersecurity: Towards enhancing cyber resilience. In *International Conference on Broadband Communications, Networks and Systems* (pp. 57-76). Cham: Springer International Publishing.

Feng, H., Chen, D., Lv, H., & Lv, Z. (2024). Game theory in network security for digital twins in industry. *Digital Communications and Networks, 10*(4), 1068–1078. DOI: 10.1016/j.dcan.2023.01.004

Ferdaus, M. M., Dam, T., Anavatti, S., & Das, S. (2024). Digital technologies for a net-zero energy future: A comprehensive review. *Renewable & Sustainable Energy Reviews, 202*, 114681. DOI: 10.1016/j.rser.2024.114681

Ferdousi, B. J. (2022). Cyber security risks of bring your own device (BYOD) practice in workplace and strategies to address the risks. *International Journal of Science Academic Research, 3*(10), 4554–4558.

Ferrara, E. (2023). Fairness and bias in artificial intelligence: A brief survey of sources, impacts, and mitigation strategies. *Sci, 6*(1), 3. DOI: 10.3390/sci6010003

Fiorentino, R., Grimaldi, F., Lamboglia, R., & Merendino, A. (2020). How smart technologies can support sustainable business models: Insights from an air navigation service provider. *Management Decision, 58*(8), 1715–1736. DOI: 10.1108/MD-09-2019-1327

Firmansyah, W. D., & Turmudi, A. (2024). Comprehensive review and future directions in mitigating flooding Distributed Denial of Services (DDoS) attacks. *Novice Research Exploration, 1*(2), 46–54.

Fisher, R., Porod, C., & Peterson, S. (2021). Motivating employees and organizations to adopt a cybersecurity-focused culture. *Journal of Organizational Psychology, 21*(1), 114–131.

Flores, C., Gonzalez, J., Kajtazi, M., Bugeja, J., & Vogel, B. (2023). Human Factors for Cybersecurity Awareness in a Remote Work Environment. In *9th International Conference on Information Systems Security and Privacy (ICISSP 2023)*, Lisbon, Portugal, 22–24 February 2023 (Vol. 1, pp. 608-616). SciTePress. DOI: 10.5220/0011746000003405

Folorunso, A., Mohammed, V., Wada, I., & Samuel, B. (2024). Ekim 21). The impact of ISO security standards on enhancing cybersecurity posture in organizations. *World Journal of Advanced Research and Reviews, 24*(01), 2582–2595. DOI: 10.30574/wjarr.2024.24.1.3169

Forouzan, H., Hosseinian-Far, A., & Sarwar, D. (2023, January). Are Small Medium Enterprises Cyber Aware? In Cybersecurity in the Age of Smart Societies: Proceedings of the 14th International Conference on Global Security, Safety and Sustainability, London, September 2022 (pp. 385-397). Cham: Springer International Publishing.

Fotis, F. (2024). Economic impact of cyber attacks and effective cyber risk management strategies: A light literature review and case study analysis. *Procedia Computer Science*, *251*, 471–478. DOI: 10.1016/j.procs.2024.11.135

Furnell, S., & Clarke, N. (2012). Power to the people? The evolving recognition of human aspects of security. *Computers & Security*, *31*(8), 983–988. DOI: 10.1016/j.cose.2012.08.004

Galandarli, A. (2025). Mitigating AI risks: A comparative analysis of Data Protection Impact Assessments under GDPR and KVKK. *Journal of Data Protection & Privacy*, *7*(3), 252–273. DOI: 10.69554/ATTT2755

Gan, C. L., Lee, Y. Y., & Liew, T. W. (2024). Fishing for phishy messages: Predicting phishing susceptibility through the lens of cyber-routine activities theory and heuristic-systematic model. *Humanities & Social Sciences Communications*, *11*(1), 1–17. DOI: 10.1057/s41599-024-04083-1

Gao, S., Jia, Y., Liu, B., & Mu, W. (2024). Algorithmic monitoring increases unethical behavior in gig workers: The mediating role of moral disengagement. *Information Technology & People*. Advance online publication. DOI: 10.1108/ITP-07-2023-0693

Garcia, A. B., Babiceanu, R. F., & Seker, R. (2021, April). Artificial intelligence and machine learning approaches for aviation cybersecurity: An overview. In *2021 integrated communications navigation and surveillance conference (ICNS)*(pp. 1-8). IEEE.

Garg, A. (2023). Factors affecting digital transformation in logistic firms. *Journal of Informatics Education and Research*, *3*(2). Advance online publication. DOI: 10.52783/jier.v3i2.326

Gaudenzi, B., & Baldi, B. (2024). Cyber resilience in organisations and supply chains: From perceptions to actions. *International Journal of Logistics Management*, *35*(7), 99–122. DOI: 10.1108/IJLM-09-2023-0372

Gaur, P., & Kaushik, M. A. (2021, December). AES Image Encryption (Advanced Encryption Standard). [IJRASET]. *International Journal for Research in Applied Science and Engineering Technology*, *9*(12), 1357–1363. DOI: 10.22214/ijraset.2021.39542

Gcaza, N., Solms, R., Grobler, M., & Jansen van Vuuren, J. (2017). A general morphological analysis: Delineating a cyber-security culture. *Information and Computer Security*, *25*(3), 259–278. DOI: 10.1108/ICS-12-2015-0046

Gebremichael, T., Ledwaba, L. P., Eldefrawy, M. H., Hancke, G. P., Pereira, N., Gidlund, M., & Akerberg, J. (2020). Ağustos 28). Security and Privacy in the Industrial Internet of Things: Current Standards and Future Challenges. *IEEE Access : Practical Innovations, Open Solutions*, *8*, 152351–152366. DOI: 10.1109/ACCESS.2020.3016937

Geisler, S., Vidal, M. E., Cappiello, C., Lóscio, B. F., Gal, A., Jarke, M., Lenzerini, M., Missier, P., Otto, B., Paja, E., Pernici, B., & Rehof, J. (2021). Knowledge-driven data ecosystems toward data transparency. [JDIQ]. *ACM Journal of Data and Information Quality*, *14*(1), 1–12. DOI: 10.1145/3467022

Genç, S. (2022). Aralık 19). Bilişim Teknolojilerinde Blok Zincir ve Kuantum Hesaplamanın Ortak Geleceği: Kuantum Blok Zinciri. *Veri Bilimi Dergisi*, *5*(2), 53–63.

Georgiadou, A., Mouzakitis, S., & Askounis, D. (2022). Working from home during COVID-19 crisis: A cyber security culture assessment survey. *Security Journal*, *35*(2), 486–505. DOI: 10.1057/s41284-021-00286-2

Georgiadou, A., Mouzakitis, S., Boun, K., & Askounis, D. (2022). A Cyber-Security Culture Framework for Assessing Organization Readiness. *Journal of Computer Information Systems*, *62*(3), 452–462. DOI: 10.1080/08874417.2020.1845583

Georgieva, K., Farooq, A., & Dumke, R. R. (2009). Analysis of the risk assessment methods- A survey. In *International Workshop on Software Measurement*, Springer: Berlin, Germany. DOI: 10.1007/978-3-642-05415-0_6

Giacotto, A., Costa Marques, H., Pereira Barreto, E. A., & Martinetti, A. (2021). The need for ecosystem 4.0 to support maintenance 4.0: An aviation assembly line case. *Applied Sciences (Basel, Switzerland)*, *11*(8), 3333. DOI: 10.3390/app11083333

Gibbs, J. P., & Poston, D. L.Jr. (1975). The Division of Labor: Conceptualization and Related Measures. *Social Forces*, *53*(3), 468–476. DOI: 10.2307/2576589

Golubock, D. G. (2024). Remote Workers, Ever-Present Risk: Employer Liability for Data Breaches in the Era of Hybrid Workplaces. *Case W. Res. JL Tech. & Internet*, *15*, 305.

Gönen, S., Yılmaz, E. N., Şanoğlu, S., Karacayılmaz, G., & Özbirinci, Ö. (2021). Endüstri 4.0'ın gelişim sürecinde unutulan bileşen: Siber güvenlik [The forgotten component in the development process of Industry 4.0: Cybersecurity]. *Düzce Üniversitesi Bilim ve Teknoloji Dergisi*, *9*(4), 1152–1171. DOI: 10.29130/dubited.905340

Graham, S., & Wood, D. (2017). Digitizing surveillance: Categorization, space, inequality. In *Surveillance, crime and social control* (pp. 537–558). Routledge. DOI: 10.4324/9781315242002-25

Greater Zurich Area. (2023). SkyCell: Pharma shipping with blockchain-backed security. Retrieved from https://www.greaterzuricharea.com

Gregory, J. (2020), Wannacry: how the widespread ransomware changed cyber-security, IBM, https://www.ibm.com/think/x-force/wannacry-worm-ransomware-changed-cybersecurity

Grima, S., Thalassinos, E., Cristea, M., Kadłubek, M., Maditinos, D., & Peiseniece, L. (Eds.). (2023). *Digital transformation, strategic resilience, cyber security and risk management.* Emerald Publishing Limited.

Gritzalis, D., Kandias, M., Stavrou, V., & Mitrou, L. (2019). History of information: From the Stone Age to the Digital Age. *Journal of Information and Communication Technology, 13*(2), 128–145.

Guo, S., Dai, Y., Xu, S., Qiu, X., & Qi, F. (2019). Trusted cloud-edge network resource management: DRL-driven service function chain orchestration for IoT. *IEEE Internet of Things Journal, 7*(7), 6010–6022. DOI: 10.1109/JIOT.2019.2951593

Guo, Y., Yan, A., & Wang, J. (2021, December). Cyber security risk analysis of physical protection systems of nuclear power plants and research on the cyber security test platform using digital twin technology. In *2021 International Conference on Power System Technology (POWERCON)* (pp. 1889-1892). IEEE. DOI: 10.1109/POWERCON53785.2021.9697764

Hadnagy, C. (2018). *Social engineering: The science of human hacking* (2nd ed.). Wiley. DOI: 10.1002/9781119433729

Hafeez, I., Ding, A. Y., Antikainen, M., & Tarkoma, S. (2018, August). Real-time IoT device activity detection in edge networks. In *International Conference on Network and System Security* (pp. 221-236). Cham: Springer International Publishing. DOI: 10.1007/978-3-030-02744-5_17

Hajnić, M., & Boshkoska, B. M. (2022). Integration of the decision support system with the human resources management and identity and access management systems in an enterprise. In *Rational decisions in organisations* (pp. 203–222). Auerbach Publications. DOI: 10.1201/9781003030966-15

Hamissi, A., & Dhraief, A. (2023). A survey on the unmanned aircraft system traffic management. *ACM Computing Surveys, 56*(3), 1–37. DOI: 10.1145/3617992

Hammi, B., Zeadally, S., & Nebhen, J. (2023). Security threats, countermeasures, and challenges of digital supply chains. *ACM Computing Surveys*, *55*(14s), 1–40. DOI: 10.1145/3588999

Hanandeh, R., Alkhazali, Z., Alhyasat, K. M., Mistarihi, A. M., & Kilani, Q. A. (2025). The impact of data-driven decision-making, real-time analytics, and ethical data practices on HR performance and employee satisfaction

Hao, X., & Demir, E. (2024). Artificial intelligence in supply chain decision-making: An environmental, social, and governance triggering and technological inhibiting protocol. *Journal of Modelling in Management*, *19*(2), 605–629. DOI: 10.1108/JM2-01-2023-0009

Healey, J. (2013). *A Fierce Domain: Conflict in Cyberspace, 1986 to 2012*. Cyber Conflict Studies.

Healthcare, I. T. Today. (2021). *How cybersecurity is shaping the future of telehealth platforms*. Retrieved from https://www.healthcareittoday.com

Heaven, W. D. (2021, June 24). Facebook's "Red Team" is hunting for bias in its AI. *WIRED*. Retrieved from https://www.wired.com/story/facebooks-red-team-hacks-ai-programs/

Hellani, H., Sliman, L., Samhat, A. E., & Exposito, E. (2021). On blockchain integration with supply chain: Overview on data transparency. *Logistics (Basel)*, *5*(3), 46. DOI: 10.3390/logistics5030046

Henrichsen, J. R. (2024). Understanding Nascent Newsroom Security and Safety Cultures: The Emergence of the "Security Champion". In *Journalism and Safety* (pp. 278-297). Routledge.

Henrie, M. (2013). Cybersecurity risk management in the SCADA critical infrastructure environment. *Engineering Management Journal*, *25*(2), 38–45. DOI: 10.1080/10429247.2013.11431973

Hermann, M., Pentek, T., & Otto, B. (2016, January). Design principles for industrie 4.0 scenarios. In 2016 49th Hawaii international conference on system sciences (HICSS) (pp. 3928-3937). IEEE.

Hijji, M., & Alam, G. (2022). Cybersecurity awareness and training (CAT) framework for remote working employees. *Sensors (Basel)*, *22*(22), 8663. DOI: 10.3390/s22228663 PMID: 36433259

Hokmabadi, H., Rezvani, S. M., & de Matos, C. A. (2024). Business resilience for small and medium enterprises and startups by digital transformation and the role of marketing capabilities—A systematic review. *Systems*, *12*(6), 220. DOI: 10.3390/systems12060220

Holmes, D., Papathanasaki, M., Maglaras, L., Ferrag, M. A., Nepal, S., & Janicke, H. (2021, September). Digital twins and cyber security–solution or challenge? In *2021 6th South-East Europe Design Automation, Computer Engineering, Computer Networks and Social Media Conference (SEEDA-CECNSM)* (pp. 1-8). IEEE. DOI: 10.1109/SEEDA-CECNSM53056.2021.9566277

Hossain, M. A., Raza, M. A., & Rahman, T. Y. (2023). Resource allocation and budgetary constraints for cybersecurity projects in small to medium sized banks. *Journal of Multidisciplinary Research*, *9*(01), 135–157.

Hossain, N. U. I., Fazio, S. A., Lezzi, M., & Islam, M. S. (2024). A decision support model for assessing and prioritization of industry 5.0 cybersecurity challenges. *Sustainable Manufacturing and Service Economics*, *100018*, 100018. Advance online publication. DOI: 10.1016/j.smse.2024.100018

Humayun, M., Tariq, N., Alfayad, M., Zakwan, M., Alwakid, G., & Assiri, M. (2024). Securing the Internet of Things in artificial intelligence era: A comprehensive survey. *IEEE Access : Practical Innovations, Open Solutions*, *12*, 25469–25490. DOI: 10.1109/ACCESS.2024.3365634

Hu, S., Hsu, C., & Zhou, Z. (2022). Security education, training, and awareness programs: Literature review. *Journal of Computer Information Systems*, *62*(4), 752–764. DOI: 10.1080/08874417.2021.1913671

Hwang, I., Wakefield, R., Kim, S., & Kim, T. (2021). Security awareness: The first step in information security compliance behavior. *Journal of Computer Information Systems*, *61*(4), 345–356. DOI: 10.1080/08874417.2019.1650676

IBM. (2024). Cost of a Data Breach Report 2024. NewYork: July.

Ibrahim, N., & Kashef, R. (2025). Exploring the emerging role of large language models in smart grid cybersecurity: A survey of attacks, detection mechanisms, and mitigation strategies. *Frontiers in Energy Research*, •••, 13.

Inspira Enterprise. (2024). *Banking and financial case study: Next-gen network access control and identity governance.* Retrieved from https://inspiraenterprise.com/case-studies/

International Electrotechnical Commission. (2013). IEC 62443-3-3. Şubat 9, 2025 tarihinde International Electrotechnical Commission: https://webstore.iec.ch/en/iec_catalog/product/preview/?id=L3B1Yi9wZGYvcHJldmlldy9pbmZvX2llYzYyNDQzLTMtM3tlZDEuMH1iLnBkZg== adresinden alındı

International Organization for Standardization. (2018). *ISO/IEC 27005:2018 Information technology — Security techniques — Information security risk management*. ISO.

IoT World Today. (2023). UPS's DeliveryDefense uses AI to reduce package theft. Retrieved from https://www.iotworldtoday.com

Irani, Z., Abril, R. M., Weerakkody, V., Omar, A., & Sivarajah, U. (2023). The impact of legacy systems on digital transformation in European public administration: Lesson learned from a multi case analysis. *Government Information Quarterly*, *40*(1), 101784. DOI: 10.1016/j.giq.2022.101784

ISACA. (2019). *State of Enterprise Risk Management 2020 Enterprise Risk Research Brief*. ISACA.

ITU. (2014). Fınal Report Itu-D Study Group 1. Geneva: International Telecommunication Union(ITU) Telecommunication Development Bureau (BDT).

Iturbe, E., Mansell, J., Rios, E., & Toledo, N. (2023). Information security risk assessment methodology for industrial systems supporting ISA/IEC 62443 compliance. III. International Conference on Electrical, Computer and Energy Technologies (ICECET 2023). South Africa: IEEE Xplore.

Ivanov, D., & Dolgui, A. (2022). Stress testing supply chains and creating viable ecosystems. *Operations Management Research : Advancing Practice Through Research*, *15*(1), 475–486. DOI: 10.1007/s12063-021-00194-z

Jaganraja, V., Seidakhmet, N., Guhan, T., Revathy, N., & Premkumar, R. (2024). Harnessing Advanced Digital (AI) Technologies for Environmental Applications: Carbon-Based Materials. In Environmental Applications of Carbon-Based Materials (pp. 30-56). IGI Global.

Jampani, S., Avancha, S., Mangal, A., Singh, S. P., Jain, S., & Agarwal, R. (2023). Machine learning algorithms for supply chain optimisation. [IJRMEET]. *International Journal of Research in Modern Engineering and Emerging Technology*, *11*(4).

Janssen, M., & van den Hoven, J. (2015). Big and Open Linked Data (BOLD) in government: A challenge to transparency and privacy? *Government Information Quarterly*, *32*(4), 363–368. DOI: 10.1016/j.giq.2015.11.007

Jeske, D., & Santuzzi, A. M. (2015). Monitoring what and how: Psychological implications of electronic performance monitoring. *New Technology, Work and Employment*, *30*(1), 62–78. DOI: 10.1111/ntwe.12039

Jiang, Y., Tran, T. H., & Williams, L. (2023). Machine learning and mixed reality for smart aviation: Applications and challenges. *Journal of Air Transport Management*, *111*, 102437. DOI: 10.1016/j.jairtraman.2023.102437

Jiang, Y., Wang, W., Ding, J., Lu, X., & Jing, Y. (2024). Leveraging Digital Twin Technology for Enhanced Cybersecurity in Cyber–Physical Production Systems. *Future Internet*, *16*(4), 134. DOI: 10.3390/fi16040134

Joint Technical Committee ISO/IEC JTC 1. (2013). ISO/IEC 27001:2013(en). Şubat 9, 2025 tarihinde Online Browsing Platform (OBP): https://www.iso.org/obp/ui/#iso:std:iso-iec:27001:ed-2:v1:en adresinden alındı

Jones, N. (2019). Innovation as a Driver of Cyber Security. *Cyber Security: Threats and Responses for Government and Business*, 157.

Kabashkin, I. (2024). Unified Aviation Maintenance Ecosystem on the Basis of 6G Technology. *Electronics (Basel)*, *13*(19), 3824. DOI: 10.3390/electronics13193824

Kabashkin, I., & Perekrestov, V. (2024). Ecosystem of aviation maintenance: Transition from aircraft health monitoring to health management based on IoT and AI synergy. *Applied Sciences (Basel, Switzerland)*, *14*(11), 4394. DOI: 10.3390/app14114394

Kagalwalla, N., & Churi, P. P. (2019, September). Cybersecurity in aviation: An intrinsic review. In *2019 5th international conference on computing, communication, control and automation (ICCUBEA)* (pp. 1-6). IEEE.

Kairat, K., Ildar, P., Karygash, A., Saule, B., Indira, K., Markhaba, K., & Aizhan, B. (2023). Digital Twins Technology in the Educational Process of the Aviation Equipment Repair. *Indonesian Journal of Electrical Engineering and Computer Science*, *32*(2), 752–762. DOI: 10.11591/ijeecs.v32.i2.pp752-762

Karaarslan, E., & Babiker, M. (2021, December). Digital twin security threats and countermeasures: An introduction. In *2021 International Conference on Information Security and Cryptology (ISCTURKEY)* (pp. 7-11). IEEE. DOI: 10.1109/ISCTURKEY53027.2021.9654360

Karacı, A., Akyüz, H. İ., & Bilgici, G. (2017). Üniversite öğrencilerinin siber güvenlik davranışlarının incelenmesi. *Kastamonu Eğitim Dergisi*, *25*(4), 1537–1552.

Karayel, T., & Akbıyık, A. (2023, July). Siber Güvenlik Araştırmalarına Küresel Bir Bakış: Yayın Trendleri ve Araştırma Yönelimleri. Bilişim Teknolojileri Dergisi, s. 221-235.

Karayel, T., Aktaş, B., & Akbıyık, A. (2025). Human factors in remote work: Examining cyber hygiene practices. *Information and Computer Security*, *33*(1), 96–116. DOI: 10.1108/ICS-11-2023-0215

Kari, R., & Steinert, M. (2021). Human factor issues in remote ship operations: Lesson learned by studying different domains. *Journal of Marine Science and Engineering*, *9*(4), 385. DOI: 10.3390/jmse9040385

Kaushik, K., Khan, A., Kumari, A., Sharma, I., & Dubey, R. (2024). Ethical considerations in AI-based cybersecurity. In *Next generation cybersecurity: AI, ML, and Blockchain* (pp. 437–470). Springer Nature Singapore. DOI: 10.1007/978-981-97-1249-6_19

Kavak, H., Padilla, J. J., Vernon-Bido, D., Diallo, S., Gore, R., & Shetty, S. (2021). Simulation for cybersecurity: State of the art and future directions. *Journal of Cybersecurity*, *7*(1), 1–13. DOI: 10.1093/cybsec/tyab005

Kavallieratos, G., Spathoulas, G., & Katsikas, S. (2021). Cyber risk propagation and optimal selection of cybersecurity controls for complex cyberphysical systems. *Sensors (Basel)*, *21*(5), 1691. DOI: 10.3390/s21051691 PMID: 33804503

Kavitha, D., & Thejas, S. (2024). Ai enabled threat detection: Leveraging artificial intelligence for advanced security and cyber threat mitigation. *IEEE Access : Practical Innovations, Open Solutions*.

Kaya, M. (2023). ISO 27001, KVKK, and GDPR: A comparison of information security standards and regulations. *Journal of Emerging Technologies*, *5*(1), 15–30.

Kaygin, E., Zengin, Y., & Topçuoğlu, E. (2019). Endüstri 4.0'a akademik bakış. DergiPark. Retrieved from https://dergipark.org.tr/tr/download/article-file/840401

Kelley, D., & Moyle, E. (2023). *Practical Cybersecurity Architecture: A guide to creating and implementing robust designs for cybersecurity architects*. Packt Publishing Ltd.

Khalid, M. (2024). Energy 4.0: AI-enabled digital transformation for sustainable power networks. *Computers & Industrial Engineering*, *193*, 110253. DOI: 10.1016/j.cie.2024.110253

Khan, M. A., Javaid, S., Mohsan, S. A. H., Tanveer, M., & Ullah, I. (2024). Future-proofing security for UAVs with post-quantum cryptography: A review. *IEEE Open Journal of the Communications Society*, *5*, 6849–6871. DOI: 10.1109/OJCOMS.2024.3486649

Khan, S. A., Mubarik, M. S., Kusi-Sarpong, S., Gupta, H., Zaman, S. I., & Mubarik, M. (2022). Blockchain technologies as enablers of supply chain mapping for sustainable supply chains. *Business Strategy and the Environment*, *31*(8), 3742–3756. DOI: 10.1002/bse.3029

Khoa, B. Q., Nguyen, H.-T., Anh, D. B. H., & Ngoc, N. M. (2024). Impact of Artificial Intelligence's part in supply chain planning and decision making optimization. *International Journal of Multidisciplinary Research and Growth Evaluation*, *5*(6), 837–856. DOI: 10.54660/.IJMRGE.2024.5.6.837-856

Kioskli, K., Seralidou, E., & Polemi, N. (2025). A practical human-centric risk management (HRM) methodology. *Electronics (Basel)*, *14*(3), 486. DOI: 10.3390/electronics14030486

Kişisel Verileri Koruma Kurumu, T. C. (2016, 24 3). 6698 Sayılı Kişisel Verilerin Korunması Kanunu. Ankara, Türkiye. Mart 18, 2025 tarihinde https://www.mevzuat.gov.tr/mevzuat?MevzuatNo=6698&MevzuatTur=1&MevzuatTertip=5 adresinden alındı

Kitsios, F., Chatzidimitriou, E., & Kamariotou, M. (2023, Mart 27). The ISO/IEC 27001 Information Security Management Standard: How to Extract Value from Data in the IT Sector. *MDPI.*

Kitsiou, A., Pantelelis, M., Mazarakis, P.-A., Mavroeidi, A.-G., Simou, S., Tzortzaki, E., Stavridis, S., Koutzamanis, G., & Kalloniatis, C. (2025). Self-adaptive privacy in cloud computing environments: Developing an integrated framework and a beta tool for social media platforms. *Electronics (Basel)*, *14*(7), 1412. DOI: 10.3390/electronics14071412

Ko, R. K. L., Lee, B. S., & Pearson, S. (2011). Towards achieving accountability, auditability and trust in cloud computing. In Hemanth, D. J., Guru, D. S., & Mohapatra, D. P. (Eds.), *Advances in computing and communications* (Vol. 193, pp. 432–444). Springer., DOI: 10.1007/978-3-642-22726-4_45

Koroniotis, N., Moustafa, N., & Sitnikova, E. (2019). Mayıs 23). Forensics and Deep Learning Mechanisms for Botnets in Internet of Things: A Survey of Challenges and Solutions. *IEEE Access : Practical Innovations, Open Solutions*, *7*, 61764–61785. DOI: 10.1109/ACCESS.2019.2916717

Kosub, T. (2015). Components and challenges of integrated cyber risk management. *Zeitschrift für die gesamte Versicherungswissenschaft,* 104, 615-634.

Kosutic, D., & Pigni, F. (2022). Cybersecurity: Investing for competitive outcomes. *The Journal of Business Strategy*, *43*(1), 28–36. DOI: 10.1108/JBS-06-2020-0116

Kotila, B., Drezner, J. A., Bartels, E. M., Hill, D., Hodgson, Q. E., Huilgol, S. S., & Wong, J. P. (2023). *Strengthening the defense innovation ecosystem*. RAND Corporation.

Krumay, B., Bernroider, E. W. N., & Walser, R. (2018). Evaluation of Cybersecurity Management Controls and Metrics of Critical Infrastructures: A Literature Review Considering the NIST Cybersecurity Framework. In Gruschka, N. (Ed.), Lecture Notes in Computer Science: Vol. 11252. *Secure IT Systems. NordSec 2018*. Springer. DOI: 10.1007/978-3-030-03638-6_23

Kuleshov, Y. A., Nagpal, K., Ucpinar, K., Gadaginmath, A., Gadaginmath, S., O'Daniel, K., . . . Monangi, H. (2024). Cyber attacks on avionics networks in digital twin environment: detection and defense. In *AIAA SCITECH 2024 Forum* (p. 0277). DOI: 10.2514/6.2024-0277

Kumar, P., Gupta, G. P., & Tripathi, R. (2021). Toward design of an intelligent cyber attack detection system using hybrid feature reduced approach for IoT networks. *Arabian Journal for Science and Engineering*, *46*(4), 3749–3778. DOI: 10.1007/s13369-020-05181-3

Kumar, R., Kumar, P., Tripathi, R., Gupta, G. P., Garg, S., & Hassan, M. M. (2022). A distributed intrusion detection system to detect DDoS attacks in blockchain-enabled IoT network. *Journal of Parallel and Distributed Computing*, *164*, 55–68. DOI: 10.1016/j.jpdc.2022.01.030

Kumar, S., & Mallipeddi, R. R. (2022). Impact of cybersecurity on operations and supply chain management: Emerging trends and future research directions. *Production and Operations Management*, *31*(12), 4488–4500. DOI: 10.1111/poms.13859

Kumar, V. A., Bhardwaj, S., & Lather, M. (2024). Cybersecurity and Safeguarding Digital Assets: An Analysis of Regulatory Frameworks, Legal Liability and Enforcement Mechanisms. *Productivity*, *65*(1), 1–10. DOI: 10.32381/PROD.2024.65.01.1

Kumar, V., Sindhwani, R., Behl, A., Kaur, A., & Pereira, V. (2024). Modelling and analysing the enablers of digital resilience for small and medium enterprises. *Journal of Enterprise Information Management*, *37*(5), 1677–1708. DOI: 10.1108/JEIM-01-2023-0002

Kure, H. I., Islam, S., & Mouratidis, H. (2022). An integrated cyber security risk management framework and risk prediction for the critical infrastructure protection. *Neural Computing & Applications*, *34*(18), 15241–15271. DOI: 10.1007/s00521-022-06959-2

Lam, H., Beckman, T., Harcourt, M., & Shanmugam, S. (2024). Bring your own device (BYOD): Organizational control and justice perspectives. *Employee Responsibilities and Rights Journal*, **•••**, 1–19. DOI: 10.1007/s10672-024-09498-1

Lau, F., Rubin, S. H., Smith, M. H., & Trajkovic, L. (2000). Distributed denial of service attacks. 2000 IEEE International Conference on Systems, Man, and Cybernetics -Cybernetics Evolving to Systems, Humans, Organizations, and Their Complex Interactions, 3, 2275–2280

Laukotka, F. N., & Krause, D. (2023). Supporting digital twins for the retrofit in aviation by a model-driven data handling. *Systems*, *11*(3), 142. DOI: 10.3390/systems11030142

Laukotka, F., Hanna, M., & Krause, D. (2021). Digital twins of product families in aviation based on an MBSE-assisted approach. *Procedia CIRP*, *100*, 684–689. DOI: 10.1016/j.procir.2021.05.144

Lautenschlager, J., Stramm, J., Guggenberger, T., Schweizer, A., & Rösch, A. (2023, September). Overcoming the data transparency trade-off: Designing a blockchain-based delivery invoice system for the construction industry. In *International Conference on Wirtschaftsinformatik* (pp. 377-392). Cham: Springer Nature Switzerland.

Lee, I. (2021). Cybersecurity: Risk management framework and investment cost analysis. *Business Horizons*, *64*(5), 659–671. DOI: 10.1016/j.bushor.2021.02.022

Le, K. H., Nguyen, M. H., Tran, T. D., & Tran, N. D. (2022). IMIDS: An intelligent intrusion detection system against cyber threats in IoT. *Electronics (Basel)*, *11*(4), 524. DOI: 10.3390/electronics11040524

Lekkala, S., & Gurijala, P. (2024). *Security and privacy for modern networks: Strategies and insights for safeguarding digital infrastructures*. Springer., DOI: 10.1007/979-8-8688-0823-4

Leszczyna, R. (2021). Review of cybersecurity assessment methods: Applicability perspective. *Computers & Security*, *108*, 102376.

Lezzi, M., Lazoi, M., & Corallo, A. (2018). Cybersecurity for Industry 4.0 in the current literature: A reference framework. *Computers in Industry*, *103*, 97–110. DOI: 10.1016/j.compind.2018.09.004

Li, B., Zhou, X., Ning, Z., Guan, X., & Yiu, K. F. C. (2022). Dynamic event-triggered security control for networked control systems with cyber-attacks: A model predictive control approach. *Information Sciences*, *612*, 384–398. DOI: 10.1016/j.ins.2022.08.093

Livingston, J. (2022). NERC CIP Standarts: Safeguarding North America's Power Grid. Verve Industrial: https://verveindustrial.com/resources/blog/what-are-the-nerc-cip-standards-in-ics-security/ adresinden alındı

Li, X., Chen, T., Cheng, Q., Ma, S., & Ma, J. (2020). Smart applications in edge computing: Overview on authentication and data security. *IEEE Internet of Things Journal*, *8*(6), 4063–4080. DOI: 10.1109/JIOT.2020.3019297

Li, X., Hu, Z., & Zhang, Q. (2021). Environmental regulation, economic policy uncertainty, and green technology innovation. *Clean Technologies and Environmental Policy*, *23*(10), 2975–2988. DOI: 10.1007/s10098-021-02219-4

Llorens, J. J. (2023). The role of human resource management in cybersecurity. In *Public personnel management* (pp. 175–184). Routledge. DOI: 10.4324/9781003403401-13

Loevenich, J. F., Adler, E., Bécue, A., Velazquez, A., Wrona, K., Boshnakov, V., . . . Lopes, F. (2024, October). Training Autonomous Cyber Defense Agents: Challenges & Opportunities in Military Networks. In MILCOM 2024-2024 IEEE Military Communications Conference (MILCOM) (pp. 158-163). IEEE.

Lysaght, T., Ballantyne, A., Toh, H. J., Lau, A., Ong, S., Schaefer, O., Shiraishi, M., van den Boom, W., Xafis, V., & Tai, E. S. (2021). Trust and trade-offs in sharing data for precision medicine: A national survey of Singapore. *Journal of Personalized Medicine*, *11*(9), 921. DOI: 10.3390/jpm11090921 PMID: 34575698

Maciel, C., Mendes, F. F., Pereira, V. C., & Yamauchi, E. A. (2021, April). Defining Digital Legacy Management Systems' Requirements. In *International Conference on Enterprise Information Systems* (pp. 256-279). Cham: Springer International Publishing.

Madhumita, G., Das, T., Das, S., Khatri, E., Ravisankar, P., & Hemachandu, P. (2024, April). IoT and AI for Real-Time Customer Behavior Analysis in Digital Banking. In 2024 5th International Conference on Recent Trends in Computer Science and Technology (ICRTCST) (pp. 198-203). IEEE.

Maharjan, P. (2023). *The Role of Artificial Intelligence-Driven Big Data Analytics in Strengthening Cybersecurity Frameworks for Critical Infrastructure*. Global Research Perspectives on Cybersecurity Governance, Policy, and Management.

Mahboubi, A., Luong, K., Aboutorab, H., Bui, H. T., Jarrad, G., Bahutair, M., & Gately, H. (2024). Aralık). Evolving techniques in cyber threat hunting: A systematic review. *Journal of Network and Computer Applications*, •••, 232.

Mahmood, H. S., Abdulqader, D. M., Abdullah, R. M., Ismael, H. R., Rashid, Z. N., & Sami, T. M. (2024). Conducting In-Depth Analysis of AI, IoT, Web Technology, Cloud Computing, and Enterprise Systems Integration for Enhancing Data Security and Governance to Promote Sustainable Business Practices. [JITI]. *Journal of Information Technology and Informatics*, *3*(2), 297–332.

Mahnamfar, A., & Ünlü, N. (2022). Siber Fiziksel Sistemler ve Güvenlik Sorunları. *Savunma Bilimleri Dergisi*, *41*, 97–118. DOI: 10.17134/khosbd.1100660

Majam, T., & Jarbandhan, D. B. (2022). Data-driven human resource management in the Fourth Industrial Revolution (4IR). *Africa's Public Service Delivery and Performance Review*, *10*(1), 588. DOI: 10.4102/apsdpr.v10i1.588

Majerník, M., Daneshjo, N., Malega, P., Drábik, P., Ševčíková, R., & Vravec, J. (2023). Integrated Management of the Environment-Safety Risks in the Thermal Power Station. *Polish Journal of Environmental Studies*, *32*(5), 4725–4738. DOI: 10.15244/pjoes/168290

Makedon, V., Hetman, O., Yemchuk, L., Paranytsia, N., & Petrovska, S. (2019). Human resource management for secure and sustainable development. *Journal of Security & Sustainability Issues*, *8*(3), 345–354. DOI: 10.9770/jssi.2019.8.3(5)

Malik, S., Malik, P. K., & Naim, A. (2024). Opportunities and challenges in new generation cyber security applications using artificial intelligence, machine learning and block chain. *Next-generation cybersecurity: AI, ML, and Blockchain*, 23-37.

Mandadi, S., Gochhayat, S. P., Torremocha, V., & Kethar, J. (2024). Cybersecurity risks in remote work and learning environments and methods of combating them. *Journal of Student Research*, *13*(2). Advance online publication. DOI: 10.47611/jsrhs.v13i2.6808

Manikyala, A., Kommineni, H. P., Allam, A. R., Nizamuddin, M., & Sridharlakshmi, N. R. B. (2023). Integrating Cybersecurity Best Practices in DevOps Pipelines for Securing Distributed Systems. *ABC Journal of Advanced Research*, *12*(1), 57–70. DOI: 10.18034/abcjar.v12i1.773

Manoharan, A., & Sarker, M. (2022, December). Evolutionizing Cybersecurity: Unleashing The Power Of Artificial İntelligence And Machine Learning For Next Generation Threat Detection. *International Research Journal of Modernization in Engineering Technology and Science*, *04*(12).

Manoharan, P. (2024). A review on cybersecurity in HR systems: Protecting employee data in the age of AI. *Regul. GDPR*, *4*, 605–612. DOI: 10.48175/IJARSCT-18492

Mao, R., Li, Y., Li, G., Hildre, H. P., & Zhang, H. (2025). A Systematic Survey of Digital Twin Applications: Transferring Knowledge From Automotive and Aviation to Maritime Industry. *IEEE Transactions on Intelligent Transportation Systems*, *26*(4), 4240–4259. DOI: 10.1109/TITS.2025.3535593

Maqueira Marín, J. M., Oliveira-Dias, D. D., Jafari Navimipour, N., Gardas, B., & Unal, M. (2022). Cloud computing and human resource management: Systematic literature review and future research agenda. *Kybernetes*, *51*(6), 2172–2191. DOI: 10.1108/K-05-2021-0420

MARCHIAFAVA., G. (2022). Cybercrime and cybersecurity in shipping. Rivista di Studi Politici Internazionali, 89(2 (354), 239-258. Johnson, C. W. (2014, October). Tools and techniques for reporting and analysing the causes of cyber-security incidents in safety-critical systems. In *9th IET International Conference on System Safety and Cyber Security* (2014) (pp. 3-2).

Marchini, K., & Pascual, A. (2019). *2019 identity fraud study: Fraudsters seek new targets and victims bear the brunt*. Javelin, 45.

Marforio, C., Masti, R. J., Soriente, C., Kostiainen, K., & Capkun, S. (2015). Personalized security indicators to detect application phishing attacks in mobile platforms. Working paper, https://arxiv.org/abs/1502.06824

Martins, B. F., Serrano Gil, L. J., Reyes Román, J. F., Panach, J. I., Pastor, O., Hadad, M., & Rochwerger, B. (2022). A framework for conceptual characterization of ontologies and its application in the cybersecurity domain. *Software & Systems Modeling*, *21*(4), 1437–1464. DOI: 10.1007/s10270-022-01013-0

Masombuka, M., Grobler, M., & Duvenage, P. (2021, June). Cybersecurity and local government: Imperative, challenges and priorities. In *ECCWS 2021 20th European Conference on Cyber Warfare and Security* (Vol. 285). Academic Conferences Inter Ltd.

Masseno, M. D., & Santos, C. (2019). Personalization and profiling of tourists in smart tourism destinations–a data protection perspective. *Revista Argumentum-Argumentum Journal of Law*, *20*(3), 1–215.

Mat, N. I. C., Jamil, N., Yusoff, Y., & Kiah, M. L. M. (2024). A systematic literature review on advanced persistent threat behaviors and its detection strategy. *Journal of Cybersecurity*, *10*(1).

Mchirgui, N., Quadar, N., Kraiem, H., & Lakhssassi, A. (2024). The applications and challenges of digital twin technology in smart grids: A comprehensive review. *Applied Sciences (Basel, Switzerland), 14*(23), 10933. DOI: 10.3390/app142310933

Medina, C., & Dela Cruz, R. (2023). Hawai'i state department of education: Strategic transformation of secure education infrastructure. In *Proceedings of the 2023 International Conference on Digital Learning Ecosystems.*

Merlo, T. R. (2024). Emerging role of artificial intelligence (AI) in aviation: using predictive maintenance for operational efficiency. In *Harnessing Digital Innovation for Air Transportation* (pp. 25–41). IGI Global. DOI: 10.4018/979-8-3693-0732-8.ch002

Michota, A., & Polemi, N. (2022, July). A Supply Chain Service Cybersecurity Certification Scheme based on the Cybersecurity Act. In *2022 IEEE International Conference on Cyber Security and Resilience (CSR)* (pp. 382-387). IEEE. DOI: 10.1109/CSR54599.2022.9850323

Microsoft. (2024). *Azure IoT Hub*. Retrieved from https://azure.microsoft.com/en-us/products/iot-hub/

Mihailović, A., Cerović Smolović, J., Radević, I., Rašović, N., & Martinović, N. (2021). COVID-19 and beyond: Employee perceptions of the efficiency of teleworking and its cybersecurity implications. *Sustainability (Basel), 13*(12), 6750. DOI: 10.3390/su13126750

Mirtsch, M. (2023). Adoption of the information security management system standard ISO/IEC 27001-A study among German organizations. *International Journal of Qualitative Research, 17*(3), 747–768. DOI: 10.24874/IJQR17.03-08

Mızrak, F. (2023). Integration of Fuzzy AHP for Cybersecurity Strategy Development in International Organizations. *Premium e-Journal of Social Sciences (PEJOSS), 7*(35), 1272-1292.

Mızrak, F. (2023b). Integration of Fuzzy AHP for Cybersecurity Strategy Development in International Organizations. *Premium e-Journal of Social Sciences (PEJOSS), 7*(35), 1272-1292.

Mızrak, F. (2024). *Strategic Innovations for Dynamic Supply Chains.* IGI Global.

Mızrak, F. (2023). Integrating cybersecurity risk management into strategic management: A comprehensive literature review. *Research Journal of Business and Management, 10*(3), 98–108. DOI: 10.17261/Pressacademia.2023.1807

Mızrak, F. (2024). Integrating AI with aviation cybersecurity: The strategic role of human resources. *Business & Management Studies: An International Journal, 12*(3), 610–628. DOI: 10.15295/bmij.v12i3.2396

Mızrak, F. (2024a). Enhancing Cybersecurity risk management through conceptual analysis of Hrm integration. *Yönetim Bilimleri Dergisi, 22*(51), 96–118. DOI: 10.35408/comuybd.1342408

Mizrak, F., & Akkartal, G. R. (2024). Prioritizing cybersecurity initiatives in aviation: A dematel-QSFS methodology. *Heliyon, 10*(16), e35487. DOI: 10.1016/j.heliyon.2024.e35487 PMID: 39687858

Mizrak, F., Demirel, H. G., Yaşar, O., & Karakaya, T. (2025). Digital detox: Exploring the impact of cybersecurity fatigue on employee productivity and mental health. *Discover Mental Health, 5*(1), 1–21. DOI: 10.1007/s44192-025-00149-x PMID: 39998759

Mizrak, F., Polat, L., & Tasar, S. A. (2024). Applying Entropy Weighting and 2-Tuple Linguistic T-Spherical Fuzzy MCDM: A Case Study of Developing a Strategic Sustainability Plan for Istanbul Airport. *Sustainability (Basel), 16*(24), 11104. DOI: 10.3390/su162411104

Mobi, S. (2019). Siber Saldırılar Nesnelerin İnternetini (IoT) Etkiler mi? Sanal Mobi. Retrieved from https://sanal.mobi/tr/Blog/165-siber-saldirilar-nesnelerin-internetini-iot-etkiler-mi?utm_source

Moghadasi, N., Collier, Z. A., Koch, A., Slutzky, D. L., Polmateer, T. L., Manasco, M. C., & Lambert, J. H. (2022). Trust and security of electric vehicle-to-grid systems and hardware supply chains. *Reliability Engineering & System Safety, 225*, 108565. DOI: 10.1016/j.ress.2022.108565

Mohammed, T. J., & Jasim, N. A. (2022). Designing a model to protect documented information according to the integration of some international standards (ISO 27001: 2013)(ISO 10013: 2021): A case study. *International Journal of Health Sciences*, (III), 431069. DOI: 10.53730/ijhs.v6nS3.8376

Möhlmann, M., & Zalmanson, L. (2017). Hands on the wheel: Navigating algorithmic management and Uber drivers' autonomy. *Journal of Business Ethics, 152*(1), 1–16. DOI: 10.1007/s10551-019-04204-w

Möller, D. P. (2023). Cybersecurity in digital transformation. In *Guide to cybersecurity in digital transformation: Trends, methods, technologies, applications and best practices* (pp. 1–70). Springer Nature Switzerland. DOI: 10.1007/978-3-031-26845-8_1

Mor, S., & Ashta, A. (2018). Fostering the culture of learning and experimentations: An introduction. *Culture of learning and experimentation for well-being*, 1-18.

Moura, J., & Serrão, C. (2016). Security and Privacy Issues of Big Data. arXiv. https://arxiv.org/pdf/1601.06206

Moyo, S. (2022). *Executive's Guide to Cyber Risk: Securing the Future Today*. John Wiley & Sons. DOI: 10.1002/9781394320578

Mugarza, I., Flores, J. L., & Montero, J. L. (2020). Security Issues and Software Updates Management in the Industrial Internet of Things (IIoT) Era. Sensors MDPI.

Muneer, S., Farooq, U., Athar, A., Raza, M. A., Ghazal, T. M., & Sakib, S. (2024). A Critical Review of Artificial Intelligence Based Approaches in Intrusion Detection: A Comprehensive Analysis. Hindawi Journal of Engineering.

Muppalaneni, R., Inaganti, A. C., Ravichandran, N., & Nersu, S. R. K. (2025). AI-powered role-based access control (RBAC): Automating policy enforcement in enterprise environments. *Journal of Advanced Computing Systems*, *5*(2), 1–12.

Murat, D., Berkan, U., & Ali, I. (2024, October). An Overview of Secure by Design: Enhancing Systems Security through Systems Security Engineering and Threat Modeling. In 2024 17th International Conference on Information Security and Cryptology (ISCTürkiye) (pp. 1-6). IEEE.

Mustak, M., Salminen, J., Mantymaki, M., Rahman, A., & Dwivedi, Y. K. (2023). Deepfakes: Deceptions, mitigations, and opportunities. *Journal of Business Research*, •••, 154.

Mutalib, N. H. A., Sabri, A. Q. M., Wahab, A. W. A., Abdullah, E. R. M. F., & AlDahoul, N. (2024). Explainable deep learning approach for advanced persistent threats (APTs) detection in cybersecurity: A review. *Artificial Intelligence Review*, *57*(11), 297. DOI: 10.1007/s10462-024-10890-4

Muvva, S. (2021). Ethical AI and Responsible Data Engineering: A Framework for Bias Mitigation and Privacy Preservation in Large-Scale Data Pipelines. *International Journal of Scientific Research in Engineering and Management*, *5*(09).

Mwesiumo, D., Halpern, N., Bråthen, S., Budd, T., & Suau-Sanchez, P. (2023). Perceived benefits as a driver and necessary condition for the willingness of air passengers to provide personal data for non-mandatory digital services at airports. *Transportation Research Part A, Policy and Practice*, *171*, 103659. DOI: 10.1016/j.tra.2023.103659

Mylrea, M., Fracchia, C., Grimes, H., Austad, W., Shannon, G., Reid, B., & Case, N. (2021). BioSecure digital twin: manufacturing innovation and cybersecurity resilience. *Engineering Artificially Intelligent Systems: A Systems Engineering Approach to Realizing Synergistic Capabilities*, 53-72.

Nambundo, J. M., Gomes, O. S. M., De Souza, A. D., & Machado, R. C. S. (2025). Cybersecurity and major cyber threats of smart meters: A systematic mapping review. *Energies*, *18*(6), 1445. DOI: 10.3390/en18061445

National Institute of Standards and Technology. (2018). *Framework for Improving Critical Infrastructure Cybersecurity*(Version 1.1). NIST. DOI: 10.6028/NIST.CSWP.04162018

Nature. (2021). *How federated learning is transforming healthcare AI*. Retrieved from https://www.nature.com/articles/d41586-021-00003-w

Neri, M., & Niccolini, F. (2025). On the path to cyber organizational resilience: Shedding light on the context of SMEs. *The International Journal of Organizational Analysis*, *33*(12), 105–131. DOI: 10.1108/IJOA-06-2024-4572

Nespoli, P., Dimitrios Papamartzivanos, F. G., & Kambourakis, G. (2018). Optimal Countermeasures Selection Against Cyber Attacks: A Comprehensive Surveyon Reaction Frameworks. *IEEE Communications Surveys and Tutorials*, *20*(2), 1361–1396. DOI: 10.1109/COMST.2017.2781126

New Prairie Press. (2020). *Cybersecurity threats in commercial drone usage: A review of vulnerabilities and risk controls*. Retrieved from https://newprairiepress.org

Nica, E., Burcea, . G., & Sabie, O. M. (2024). The critical role of human resources in mitigating and managing cybersecurity risks in modern organizations: A strategic approach. *Psychosociological Issues in Human Resource Management*, *12*(2).

Nikookar, E., Stevenson, M., & Varsei, M. (2024). Building an antifragile supply chain: A capability blueprint for resilience and post-disruption growth. *The Journal of Supply Chain Management*, *60*(1), 13–31. DOI: 10.1111/jscm.12313

NIST. (2011). NIST Special Publication 800-39: Managing Information Security Risk; NIST: Gaithersburg, MD, USA.

NIST. (2018). Framework for Improving Critical Infrastructure Cybersecurity (Version 1.1). ABD: National Institute of Standards and Technology.

NIST. (2023). *How digital twins could protect manufacturers from cyberattacks*. National Institute of Standards and Technology. Retrieved from https://www.nist.gov/news-events/news/2023/02/how-digital-twins-could-protect-manufacturers-cyberattacks

NIST. (2024). *Securing Drone Fleets with BFDI-AP: Real-World Applications and Demonstrations*. National Institute of Standards and Technology. Retrieved from https://www.nist.gov

Nkomo, L., & Kalisz, D. (2023). Establishing organisational resilience through developing a strategic framework for digital transformation. *Digital Transformation and Society*, *2*(4), 403–426. DOI: 10.1108/DTS-11-2022-0059

NPR. (2020, April 7). *'Zoombombing' is a wake-up call: Online education faces security scrutiny*. Retrieved from https://www.npr.org/2020/04/07/zoombombing-cybersecurity-education

NTT. (2023). Global Threat Intelligence Report. Information Asset Classification: Public NTT Security Holdings.

Nugraha, A. A., & Nasyuha, A. H. (2024). Integrating ISO 27001 and Indonesia's Personal Data Protection Law for Data Protection Requirement Model. *Journal of Information Systems and Informatics*, *6*(2), 1052–1069. DOI: 10.51519/journalisi.v6i2.754

Nwankpa, J. K., & Datta, P. M. (2023). Remote vigilance: The roles of cyber awareness and cybersecurity policies among remote workers. *Computers & Security*, *130*, 103266. DOI: 10.1016/j.cose.2023.103266

O'Kane, P., Sezer, S., & Carlin, D. (2018). Evolution of ransomware. *IET Networks*, *7*(5), 1–7. DOI: 10.1049/iet-net.2017.0207

Odebade, A. T., & Benkhelifa, E. (2023). A comparative study of national cyber security strategies of ten nations. *arXiv preprint arXiv:2303.13938.*

Odimarha, A. C., Ayodeji, S. A., & Abaku, E. A. (2024). Securing the digital supply chain: Cybersecurity best practices for logistics and shipping companies,'. *World Journal of Advanced Science and Technology*, *5*(1), 026-030.

Okwuibe, J., Haavisto, J., Kovacevic, I., Harjula, E., Ahmad, I., Islam, J., & Ylianttila, M. (2021). SDN-enabled resource orchestration for industrial IoT in collaborative edge-cloud networks. *IEEE Access : Practical Innovations, Open Solutions*, *9*, 115839–115854. DOI: 10.1109/ACCESS.2021.3105944

Oláh, J., Aburumman, N., Popp, J., Khan, M. A., Haddad, H., & Kitukutha, N. (2020, June 8). Impact of Industry 4.0 on Environmental Sustainability. *MDPI, 12*(11).

Olaniyi, O. O., Omogoroye, O. O., Olaniyi, F. G., Alao, A. I., & Oladoyinbo, T. O. (2024). CyberFusion protocols: Strategic integration of enterprise risk management, ISO 27001, and mobile forensics for advanced digital security in the modern business ecosystem. *Journal of Engineering Research and Reports*, *26*(6), 31–49. DOI: 10.9734/jerr/2024/v26i61160

Olsen, M. (2019). Using data analytics in the management of employees: Digital means of tracking, monitoring, and surveilling worker activities. *Psychosociological Issues in Human Resource Management*, *7*(2), 43–48. DOI: 10.22381/PIHRM7220197

Omar, M. (2022). *Machine learning for cybersecurity: Innovative deep learning solutions*. Springer Nature. DOI: 10.1007/978-3-031-15893-3

Onwuegbuzie, I. U., & Alabi, O. A. (2025). A Review of Authentication and Authorization Mechanisms in Zero Trust Architecture: Evolution and Efficiency. *Tech-Sphere Journal for Pure and Applied Sciences, 2*(1).

Oriekhoe, O. I., Oyeyemi, O. P., Bello, B. G., Omotoye, G. B., Daraojimba, A. I., & Adefemi, A. (2024). Blockchain in supply chain management: A review of efficiency, transparency, and innovation. *International Journal of Science and Research Archive*, *11*(1), 173–181. DOI: 10.30574/ijsra.2024.11.1.0028

Orlando, A. (2021). Cyber risk quantification: Investigating the role of cyber value at risk. *Risks*, *9*(10), 184. DOI: 10.3390/risks9100184

Ötleş, S. (2016). *Vasfiye Hazal Özyurt, "Büyüme ve Verimlilik İçin Dijitalleşme"*. Ege Üniversitesi Gıda Mühendisliği Bölümü Dergisi.

Otoom, S. (2025). Risk auditing for Digital Twins in cyber physical systems: A systematic review. *Journal of Cyber Security and Risk Auditing*, *2025*(1), 22–35. DOI: 10.63180/jcsra.thestap.2025.1.3

Oukes, T., Beninger, S., Derks, M., & Nijhof, A. (2024). Navigating disturbances in developing countries: Resilience strategies for cross-sector partnerships. *Business Strategy & Development*, *7*(4), e70020. DOI: 10.1002/bsd2.70020

Oyewole, A. T., Okoye, C. C., Ofodile, O. C., & Ugochukwu, C. E.Adedoyin Tolulope OyewoleChinwe Chinazo OkoyeOnyeka Chrisanctus OfodileChinonye Esther Ugochukwu. (2024). Cybersecurity risks in online banking: A detailed review and preventive strategies application. *World Journal of Advanced Research and Reviews*, *21*(03), 625–643. DOI: 10.30574/wjarr.2024.21.3.0707

Özçetin, N. (2024). Endüstri 4.0 ve Endüstri 5.0 perspektiflerinde muhasebe: Teorik bir inceleme [Accounting in Industry 4.0 and Industry 5.0 Perspectives: A Theoretical Review]. Yönetim Bilimleri Dergisi- Journal of Administrative Sciences, 22(Özel Sayı), 1324-1344. DOI: 10.35408/comuybd.1490646

Ozer, M., Kose, Y., Bastug, M., Kucukkaya, G., & Varlioglu, E. R. (2024). The Shifting Landscape of Cybersecurity: The Impact of Remote Work and COVID-19 on Data Breach Trends. *arXiv preprint arXiv:2402.06650.*

Ozobu, C. O., Adikwu, F. E., Cynthia, O. O., Onyeke, F. O., & Nwulu, E. O. (2025). Developing an AI-powered occupational health surveillance system for real-time detection and management of workplace health hazards. *World Journal of Innovation and Modern Technology*, *9*(1), 156–185.

Öztuna, B. (2017). *The Future of Working Life with Industry 4.0 (The Fourth Industrial Revolution)* (1st ed.). Gece Kitaplığı.

Padmanabhan, A., & Zhang, J. (2018). Cybersecurity risks and mitigation strategies in additive manufacturing. *Progress in Additive Manufacturing*, *3*(1-2), 87–93. DOI: 10.1007/s40964-017-0036-9

Pandey, S., Singh, R. K., Gunasekaran, A., & Kaushik, A. (2020). Cyber security risks in globalized supply chains: Conceptual framework. *Journal of Global Operations and Strategic Sourcing*, *13*(1), 103–128. DOI: 10.1108/JGOSS-05-2019-0042

Panko, R. R. (2020). *Corporate computer and network security*. Pearson Education.

Pan, S., Trentesaux, D., McFarlane, D., Montreuil, B., Ballot, E., & Huang, G. Q. (2021). Digital interoperability in logistics and supply chain management: State-of-the-art and research avenues towards Physical Internet. *Computers in Industry*, *128*, 103435. DOI: 10.1016/j.compind.2021.103435

Paracha, M. A., Jamil, S. U., Shahzad, K., Khan, M. A., & Rasheed, A. (2024). Leveraging ai for network threat detection—A conceptual overview. *Electronics (Basel)*, *13*(23), 4611. DOI: 10.3390/electronics13234611

Parsons, K., McCormac, A., Butavicius, M., Pattinson, M., & Jerram, C. (2014, May). Determining employee awareness using the Human Aspects of Information Security Questionnaire (HAIS-Q). *Computers & Security*, *42*, 165–176. DOI: 10.1016/j.cose.2013.12.003

Patel, A., & Chaudhary, M. (2024). Zero Trust Architecture: A Comprehensive Guide to Modern IT Security. *Baltic Multidisciplinary Research Letters Journal*, *1*(3), 44–53.

Patrano, L., Atzori, L., Solic, P., Mongiello, M., & Almeida, A. (2020). Challenges to be addressed to realize Internet of Things solutions for smart environments. *Future Generation Computer Systems, 111*, 873–878. DOI: 10.1016/j.future.2019.09.033

Payne, B., Cigularova, D., Costanzo, J., Das, S., Mann, M., & Perez, K. (2022). Impact of articulation agreements on student transfer between higher education institutions: A case study of a cybersecurity program. *Community College Journal of Research and Practice, 46*(8), 573–588. DOI: 10.1080/10668926.2021.1887007

Pereira, B. A., Lohmann, G., & Houghton, L. (2022). Technology trajectory in aviation: Innovations leading to value creation (2000–2019). *International Journal of Innovation Studies, 6*(3), 128–141. DOI: 10.1016/j.ijis.2022.05.001

Petrosyan, A. (2024). The annual number of malware attacks worldwide from 2015 to 2023. https://www.statista.com/statistics/873097/malware-attacks-per-year-worldwide/

Phillips, S. C., Taylor, S., Boniface, M., Modafferi, S., & Surridge, M. (2024). Automated knowledge-based cybersecurity risk assessment of cyber-physical systems. *IEEE Access : Practical Innovations, Open Solutions, 12*, 82482–82505. DOI: 10.1109/ACCESS.2024.3404264

Pigola, A., & da Costa, P. R. (2025). Cybersecurity management: An empirical analysis of dynamic capabilities framework for enhancing cybersecurity intelligence. *Information and Computer Security*. Advance online publication. DOI: 10.1108/ICS-08-2024-0185

Pina, N., Brito, C., Vitorino, R., & Cunha, I. (2023). Promoting sustainable and personalised travel behaviours while preserving data privacy. *Transportation Research Procedia, 72*, 2768–2775. DOI: 10.1016/j.trpro.2023.11.819

Pochmara, J., & Swietlicka, A. (2024). Cybersecurity of industrial systems- A 2023 report. *Electronics (Basel), 13*(7), 1191. DOI: 10.3390/electronics13071191

Podrecca, M., Culot, G., Nassimbeni, G., & Sartor, M. (2022). Information security and value creation: The performance implications of ISO/IEC 27001. *Computers in Industry, 142*, 103744. DOI: 10.1016/j.compind.2022.103744

Ponemon (2022). Cost of a Data Breach Report 2022.

Ponnusamy, S., Assaf, M., Antari, J., Singh, S., & Kalyanaraman, S. (Eds.). (2024). *Digital twin technology and AI implementations in future-focused businesses*. IGI Global. DOI: 10.4018/979-8-3693-1818-8

Prabhu, S., & Thompson, N., A primer on insider threats in cybersecurity. (2022). Information. *Security Journal*, *31*(5), 602–611.

Qasim, S. S., & Nsaif, S. M. (2024). Advancements in time series-based detection systems for distributed denial of service (DDoS) attacks: A comprehensive review. *Babylonian Journal of Networking*, *2024*, 9–17. DOI: 10.58496/BJN/2024/002

Qiangmin, W., Mengquan, L., & Jianhua, L. (2007). Method on network information system security assessment based on rough set. In *Proceedings of the 2007 Third International IEEE Conference on Signal-Image Technologies and Internet-Based System*, Shanghai, China. DOI: 10.1109/SITIS.2007.114

Rahardja, U., Miftah, M., Rakhmansyah, M., & Zanubiya, J. (2025). Revolutionizing Financial Services with Big Data and Fintech: A Scalable Approach to Innovation. *ADI Journal on Recent Innovation*, *6*(2), 118–129. DOI: 10.34306/ajri.v6i2.1180

Rahul, K., Banyal, R. K., & Arora, N. (2023). A systematic review on big data applications and scope for industrial processing and healthcare sectors. *Journal of Big Data*, *10*(1), 133. DOI: 10.1186/s40537-023-00808-2

Raimundo, R. J., Baltazar, M. E., & Cruz, S. P. (2023). Sustainability in the airports ecosystem: A literature review. *Sustainability (Basel)*, *15*(16), 12325. DOI: 10.3390/su151612325

Rajan, R., Rana, N. P., Parameswar, N., Dhir, S., & Dwivedi, Y. K. (2021). Developing a modified total interpretive structural model (M-TISM) for organizational strategic cybersecurity management. *Technological Forecasting and Social Change*, *170*, 120872. DOI: 10.1016/j.techfore.2021.120872

Rajenda, S., & Kaliappan, V. K. (2022). Sensor Data Based Anomaly Detection in Autonomous Vehicles using Modified Convolutional Neural Network. *Intelligent Automation & Soft Computing*, *32*(2), 859–875. DOI: 10.32604/iasc.2022.020936

Rakhade, V. M. (2024, December). Security challenges in edge computing. Paper presented at the International Journal of Futuristic Innovation in Arts, Humanities and Management (IJFIAHM), Shri Sai College of Engineering & Technology, Chandrapur, India.

Ramya, G., & Srinivasagan, K. G. Integrating Cybersecurity Threats into Smart Manufacturing: Best Practices and Frameworks. In *Artificial Intelligence Solutions for Cyber-Physical Systems* (pp. 120-138). Auerbach Publications.

Ranawaka, A., Alahakoon, D., Sun, Y., & Hewapathirana, K. (2024). Leveraging the Synergy of Digital Twins and Artificial Intelligence for Sustainable Power Grids: A Scoping Review. *Energies*, *17*(21), 5342. DOI: 10.3390/en17215342

Ranganathan, P., Jangula, J., Kose, U., Goveas, N., & Balaji, S. R. A. (2024). Designing Effective Cybersecurity Curriculum: Bridging Disciplines for Next Generation Workforce.

Rantos, K., Fysarakis, K., & Manifavas, H. (2012). *How effective is your security awareness program? An evaluation methodology*. Inf Sec J Global Perspect. DOI: 10.1080/19393555.2012.747234

Raywood-Burke, G., Bishop, L. M., Asquith, P. M., & Morgan, P. L. (2021, July). Human individual difference predictors in cyber-security: exploring an alternative scale method and data resolution to modelling cyber secure behavior. In *International Conference on Human-Computer Interaction* (pp. 226-240). Cham: Springer International Publishing. DOI: 10.1007/978-3-030-77392-2_15

Reddy, R. P. (2024). A survey of Distributed Denial Service (DDoS) attack mitigation techniques. *International Journal of Computer Trends and Technology*, *72*(12), 69–77. DOI: 10.14445/22312803/IJCTT-V72I12P108

Reichert, B. M., & Obelheiro, R. R. (2024). Software supply chain security: A systematic literature review. *International Journal of Computers and Applications*, *46*(10), 853–867. DOI: 10.1080/1206212X.2024.2390978

Rejeb, A., Keogh, J. G., Simske, S. J., Stafford, T., & Treiblmaier, H. (2021). Potentials of blockchain technologies for supply chain collaboration: A conceptual framework. *International Journal of Logistics Management*, *32*(3), 973–994. DOI: 10.1108/IJLM-02-2020-0098

Rivera, J. J. D., Muhammad, A., & Song, W. C. (2024). Securing digital identity in the zero trust architecture: A blockchain approach to privacy-focused multi-factor authentication. *IEEE Open Journal of the Communications Society*.

Rogers, R. (1975). A protection motivation theory of fear appeals and attitude change. *The Journal of Psychology*, *91*(1), 93–114. DOI: 10.1080/00223980.1975.9915803 PMID: 28136248

Rosenkranz, S., Staegemann, D., Volk, M., & Turowski, K. (2024). Explaining the Business-Technological Age of Legacy Information Systems. *IEEE Access : Practical Innovations, Open Solutions*, *12*, 84579–84611. DOI: 10.1109/ACCESS.2024.3414377

Roshanaei, M., Khan, M. R., & Sylvester, N. N. (2024). Enhancing cybersecurity through AI and ML: Strategies, challenges, and future directions. *Journal of Information Security*, *15*(3), 320–339. DOI: 10.4236/jis.2024.153019

Roul, J., Mohapatra, L. M., Pradhan, A. K., & Kamesh, A. V. S. (2024). Analysing the role of modern information technologies in HRM: Management perspective and future agenda. *Kybernetes*. Advance online publication. DOI: 10.1108/K-11-2023-2512

Rubio-Andrada, L., Celemín-Pedroche, M. S., Escat-Cortés, M. D., & Jiménez-Crisóstomo, A. (2023). Passengers satisfaction with the technologies used in smart airports: An empirical study from a gender perspective. *Journal of Air Transport Management*, *107*, 102347. DOI: 10.1016/j.jairtraman.2022.102347

Rughiniş, C., & Rughiniş, R. (2014). Nothing ventured, nothing gained. Profiles of online activity cyber-crime exposure, and security measures of end-users in european union. *Computers*, •••, 111–125.

Sabet, S., & Farooq, B. (2023). Energy-smart transportation systems: Role of connectivity, automation, big data, and machine learning. In *Handbook of Smart Energy Systems* (pp. 2003–2023). Springer International Publishing. DOI: 10.1007/978-3-030-97940-9_126

Sabillon, R., & Bermejo Higuera, J. R. (2023, July). The importance of cybersecurity awareness training in the aviation industry for early detection of Cyberthreats and vulnerabilities. In *International Conference on Human-Computer Interaction* (pp. 461-479). Cham: Springer Nature Switzerland. DOI: 10.1007/978-3-031-48057-7_29

Sadeghi, A., Bellavista, P., Song, W., & Yazdani-Asrami, M. (2024). Digital twins for condition and fleet monitoring of aircraft: Towards more-intelligent electrified aviation systems. *IEEE Access : Practical Innovations, Open Solutions*, *12*, 99806–99832. DOI: 10.1109/ACCESS.2024.3371902

Sadeghi, K., Azadegan, A., & Ojha, D. (2023). A path to build supply chain cyber-resilience through absorptive capacity and visibility: Two empirical studies. *Industrial Marketing Management*, *111*, 202–215. DOI: 10.1016/j.indmarman.2023.04.001

Saeed, S., Altamimi, S. A., Alkayyal, N. A., Alshehri, E., & Alabbad, D. A. (2023). Digital transformation and cybersecurity challenges for businesses resilience: Issues and recommendations. *Sensors (Basel)*, *23*(15), 6666. DOI: 10.3390/s23156666 PMID: 37571451

Saeed, S., Suayyid, S. A., Al-Ghamdi, M. S., Al-Muhaisen, H., & Almuhaideb, A. M. (2023). A systematic literature review on cyber threat intelligence for organizational cybersecurity resilience. *Sensors (Basel)*, *23*(16), 7273. DOI: 10.3390/s23167273 PMID: 37631808

Safitra, M. F., Lubis, M., & Fakhrurroja, H. (2023). Counterattacking cyber threats: A framework for the future of cybersecurity. *Sustainability (Basel), 15*(18), 13369. DOI: 10.3390/su151813369

Salah, K., Elbadawi, K., & Boutaba, R. (2012, March). Performance Modeling and Analysis of Network Firewalls. *IEEE Transactions on Network and Service Management, 9*(1), 12–21. DOI: 10.1109/TNSM.2011.122011.110151

Sallos, M. P., Garcia-Perez, A., Bedford, D., & Orlando, B. (2019). Strategy and organisational cybersecurity: A knowledge-problem perspective. *Journal of Intellectual Capital, 20*(4), 581–597. DOI: 10.1108/JIC-03-2019-0041

Salman, O. H., Alawida, M., Hazeem, R. M. A., Zeyadeh, M. S., & Alameri, M. R. (2023, December). CyberSafe: A Gamified Cyber Security Training Method. In *2023 International Conference on Electrical, Communication and Computer Engineering (ICECCE)* (pp. 1-6). IEEE. DOI: 10.1109/ICECCE61019.2023.10442243

Sampigethaya, K., Kopardekar, P., & Davis, J. (2018, April). Cyber security of unmanned aircraft system traffic management (UTM). In *2018 Integrated Communications, Navigation, Surveillance Conference (ICNS)* (pp. 1C1-1). IEEE.

Samsung, S. D. S. (2024). *Smart manufacturing and blockchain-powered logistics solutions*. Retrieved from https://en.wikipedia.org/wiki/Samsung_SDS

Sanchez-Garcia, I. D., Mejia, J., & Gilabert, T. S. F. (2023). Cybersecurity risk assessment: A systematic mapping review, proposal, and validation. *Applied Sciences (Basel, Switzerland), 13*(1), 395. DOI: 10.3390/app13010395

Sanlı, Y., Baltacı, F., Güven, E., & Eren, T. (2024, July). Siber Güvenlik Çalışmaları Üzerine Bibliyometrik Analiz. Bilişim Teknolojileri Dergisi, s. 223-229.

Sarker, I. H., Kayes, A. S. M., Badsha, S., Alqahtani, H., Watters, P., & Ng, A. (2020). Cybersecurity data science: An overview from machine learning perspective. *Journal of Big Data, 7*(41), 1–29. DOI: 10.1186/s40537-020-00318-5

Sarker, O., Jayatilaka, A., Haggag, S., Liu, C., & Babar, M. A. (2024). A multi-vocal literature review on challenges and critical success factors of phishing education, training, and awareness. *Journal of Systems and Software, 208*, 111899. DOI: 10.1016/j.jss.2023.111899

Schwartz, R., Schwartz, R., Vassilev, A., Greene, K., Perine, L., Burt, A., & Hall, P. (2022). *Towards a standard for identifying and managing bias in artificial intelligence* (Vol. 3, p. 00). Gaithersburg, MD: US Department of Commerce, National Institute of Standards and Technology.

Scott, B. I., & Andritsos, K. I. (2023). A drone strategy 2.0 for a smart and sustainable unmanned aircraft eco-system in Europe. *Air and Space Law*, *48*(3). Advance online publication. DOI: 10.54648/AILA2023041

Sellitto, G. P., Masi, M., Pavleska, T., & Aranha, H. (2021, November). A cyber security digital twin for critical infrastructure protection: The intelligent transport system use case. In *IFIP Working Conference on The Practice of Enterprise Modeling* (pp. 230-244). Cham: Springer International Publishing. DOI: 10.1007/978-3-030-91279-6_16

Sengupta, J., Ruj, S., & Bit, S. D. (2020). A Comprehensive Survey on Attacks, Security Issues and Blockchain Solutions for IoT and IIoT. *Journal of Network and Computer Applications*, *149*, 149. DOI: 10.1016/j.jnca.2019.102481

Serter, H., & Serinkan, C. (2020). Endüstri 4.0 ve yenilik yönetimi. In M. Dalkılıç (Ed.), New Developments in Education and Social Sciences (Bölüm 34, s. 677-692). Gece Kitaplığı.

Shah, I. A., Jhanjhi, N. Z., & Brohi, S. (2024). Cybersecurity issues and challenges in civil aviation security. *Cybersecurity in the Transportation Industry*, 1-23.

Shahidinejad, A., Ghobaei-Arani, M., Souri, A., Shojafar, M., & Kumari, S. (2021). Light-edge: A lightweight authentication protocol for IoT devices in an edge-cloud environment. *IEEE Consumer Electronics Magazine*, *11*(2), 57–63. DOI: 10.1109/MCE.2021.3053543

Shaikh, E., Al-Ali, A. R., Muhammad, S., Mohammad, N., & Aloul, F. (2023). Security analysis of a digital twin framework using probabilistic model checking. *IEEE Access : Practical Innovations, Open Solutions*, *11*, 26358–26374. DOI: 10.1109/ACCESS.2023.3257171

Sha, K., Yang, T. A., Wei, W., & Davari, S. (2020). A survey of edge computing-based designs for IoT security. *Digital Communications and Networks*, *6*(2), 195–202. DOI: 10.1016/j.dcan.2019.08.006

Sharma, R. (2012). Study of latest emerging trends on cyber security and its challenges to society. *International Journal of Scientific and Engineering Research*, *3*(6), 1–4.

Shea, S., Gillis, A. S., & Clark, C. (2023). What is cybersecurity? https://www.techtarget.com/searchsecurity/definition/cybersecurity

Sheikh, A. M., Islam, M. R., Habaebi, M. H., Zabidi, S. A., Najeeb, A. R. B., & Kabani, A. (2025). A survey on edge computing (EC) security challenges: Classification, threats, and mitigation strategies. Preprints, Version 1. DOI: 10.20944/preprints202502.1500.v1

Sheppard, D. (2011). *ID theft down 28 percent in U.S. in 2010: A survey*. Reuters.

Siddiqi, M. A., Pak, W., & Siddiqi, M. A. (2022). A study on the psychology of social engineering-based cyberattacks and existing countermeasures. *Applied Sciences (Basel, Switzerland)*, *12*(12), 6042. DOI: 10.3390/app12126042

Sinclair, S. (2020, November 3). *HSBC carries out Bangladesh's first blockchain letter-of-credit transaction. CoinDesk*. Retrieved from https://www.coindesk.com/markets/2020/11/03/hsbc-carries-out-bangladeshs-first-blockchain-letter-of-credit-transaction/

Sindiramutty, S. R., Tan, C. E., Goh, W. W., Balakrishnan, S., Hamzah, N., & Akbar, R. (2024). Securing the Supply Chain: Cybersecurity Strategies for Logistics Resilience. In *Navigating Cyber Threats and Cybersecurity in the Logistics Industry* (pp. 300-365). IGI Global.

Singh, P. K. (2023). Digital transformation in supply chain management: Artificial Intelligence (AI) and Machine Learning (ML) as Catalysts for Value Creation. *International Journal of Supply Chain Management*, *12*(6), 57–63. DOI: 10.59160/ijscm.v12i6.6216

Singh, S., Hosen, A. S., & Yoon, B. (2021). Blockchain security attacks, challenges, and solutions for the future distributed iot network. *IEEE Access : Practical Innovations, Open Solutions*, *9*, 13938–13959. DOI: 10.1109/ACCESS.2021.3051602

Smith, R., & Brooks, D. J. (2020). *Security Science: The Theory and Practice of Security*. Butterworth-Heinemann.

Smmarwar, S., Gupta, G., & Kumar, S. (2024). Android malware detection and identification frameworks by leveraging the machine and deep learning techniques: A comprehensive review. *Telematics and Informatics Reports*, *14*, 100130. DOI: 10.1016/j.teler.2024.100130

Sneps-Sneppe, M., & Namiot, D. (2022, December). On Digital Twin Software and Cyber Threats. In *International Conference on Next Generation Wired/Wireless Networking* (pp. 481-493). Cham: Springer Nature Switzerland.

Softeq. (2023). SkyCell: Blockchain and IoT for pharmaceutical cold chain. Retrieved from https://www.softeq.com

Sonesson, T. R., Johansson, J., & Cedergren, A. (2021). Governance and interdependencies of critical infrastructures: Exploring mechanisms for cross-sector resilience. *Safety Science*, *142*, 105383. DOI: 10.1016/j.ssci.2021.105383

Soori, M., Arezoo, B., & Dastres, R. (2023). Internet of things for smart factories in industry 4.0, a review. *Internet of Things and Cyber-Physical Systems*, *3*, 192–204. DOI: 10.1016/j.iotcps.2023.04.006

Stallings, W., & Brown, L. (2018). *Computer security: Principles and practice* (4th ed.). Pearson Education.

Stankevičiūtė, Ž. (2024). Data-driven decision making: Application of people analytics in human resource management. In *Digital transformation: Technology, tools, and studies* (pp. 239–262). Springer Nature Switzerland. DOI: 10.1007/978-3-031-55952-5_12

Stastny, P., & Stoica, A. M. (2022, February). Protecting aviation safety against cybersecurity threats. [). IOP Publishing.]. *IOP Conference Series. Materials Science and Engineering*, *1226*(1), 012025. DOI: 10.1088/1757-899X/1226/1/012025

Steen, T. (2025). Developing a behavioural cybersecurity strategy: A five-step approach for organisations. *Computer Standards & Interfaces*, *92*, 1–8. DOI: 10.1016/j.csi.2024.103939

Stefanidou, M., Maraslidis, G. S., Antoniadis, I., & Fragulis, G. F. (2024, October). Cloud-driven network security: A survey of methods, challenges, and innovations. In *AIP Conference Proceedings* (Vol. 3220, No. 1). AIP Publishing. DOI: 10.1063/5.0234978

Stevenage UK: IET. Svanadze, V. (2020). Cybersecurity in the civil aviation and existing challenges. Юридичний вісник. Повітряне і космічне право, (4), 27-33.

Suhail, S., Hussain, R., Jurdak, R., Oracevic, A., Salah, K., Hong, C. S., & Matulevičius, R. (2022). Blockchain-based digital twins: Research trends, issues, and future challenges. *ACM Computing Surveys*, *54*(11s), 1–34. DOI: 10.1145/3517189

Su, Y., Xiong, D., Qian, K., & Wang, Y. (2024). A comprehensive survey of Distributed Denial of Service detection and mitigation technologies in software-defined network. *Electronics (Basel)*, *13*(4), 807. DOI: 10.3390/electronics13040807

Sycheva, E., & Shpak, P. (2022). Practical application of the concept of digital twins in the aviation sector. In *Digital Transformation in Industry: Digital Twins and New Business Models* (pp. 29–42). Springer International Publishing. DOI: 10.1007/978-3-030-94617-3_3

Synced Review. (2020, October 7). *NVIDIA and Mass General Brigham use federated learning to predict COVID-19 patient oxygen needs*. Retrieved from https://syncedreview.com/2020/10/07/nvidia-and-mass-general-brigham-use-federated-learning-to-predict-covid-19-patient-oxygen-needs/

Szathmari, G. (2019). Owning your legal practice's cybersecurity. https://get.cofense .com/CRA- Keeping- Up- With- Phishing.html

Tabim, V. M., Ayala, N. F., & Frank, A. G. (2024). Implementing vertical integration in the industry 4.0 journey: Which factors influence the process of information systems adoption? *Information Systems Frontiers*, *26*(5), 1615–1632. DOI: 10.1007/ s10796-021-10220-x PMID: 34776762

Taeihagh, A., Ramesh, M., & Howlett, M. (2021). Assessing the regulatory challenges of emerging disruptive technologies. *Regulation & Governance*, *15*(4), 1009–1019. DOI: 10.1111/rego.12392

Taher, R., Mehrnezhad, M., & Morisset, C. (2022, September). "I feel spied on and i don't have any control over my data": user privacy perception, preferences and trade-offs in university smart buildings. In *International Workshop on Socio-Technical Aspects in Security* (pp. 73-92). Cham: Springer Nature Switzerland.

Tasar, S. A. (2023). Siber Güvenlik ve İç Denetim. In *Sosyal Bilimlerde Güncel Çalışmalar 2*. İksad Publishing House.

Tay, M., & Şentürk, A. (2021). Kenar, Sis ve Bulut Bilişimin IoT Açısından İncelenmesi. *Avrupa Bilim ve Teknoloji Dergisi*, (32), 68–75.

TechCrunch. (2022). DoorDash confirms data breach impacted millions of customers. Retrieved from https://www.techcrunch.com

Teknolojileri, B., & Kurumu, İ. (2020). Sektörel Araştırma ve Strateji Geliştirme Dairesi.

Thabit, F., Alhomdy, S. A.-H., Alahdal, A., & Jagtap, S. B. (2020). Exploration of security challenges in cloud computing: Issues, threats, and attacks with their alleviating techniques. *Journal of Information and Computational Science*, *12*(10). https://ssrn.com/abstract=3749271

The Open Group. (2019). *FAIR Factor Analysis of Information Risk*. https://www .opengroup.org/fair

The Things Network. (2023). LoRaWAN security fundamentals: How AES encryption protects agricultural IoT. https://www.thethingsnetwork.org

Thompson, E. C. (2018). Cybersecurity incident response: How to contain, eradicate, and recover from incidents, 1st ed. Apress, Lisle, Illinois, USA. BookWhole.

Thummala, V. R., & Bindewari, S. (2024). Optimizing Cybersecurity Practices through Compliance and Risk Assessment. *International Journal of Research Radicals in Multidisciplinary Fields, ISSN*, 910-930.

Tipton, H. F., & Krause, M. (Eds.). (2022). *Information security management handbook* (6th ed.). Auerbach Publications.

Tomlinson, E. C., & Schnackenberg, A. (2022). The effects of transparency perceptions on trustworthiness perceptions and trust. *Journal of Trust Research, 12*(1), 1–23. DOI: 10.1080/21515581.2022.2060245

Topping, C., Dwyer, A., Michalec, O., Craggs, B., & Rashid, A. (2021). Beware suppliers bearing gifts!: Analysing coverage of supply chain cyber security in critical national infrastructure sectorial and cross-sectorial frameworks. *Computers & Security, 108*, 102324. DOI: 10.1016/j.cose.2021.102324

Trim, P. R., & Lee, Y. I. (2021). The global cyber security model: Counteracting cyber attacks through a resilient partnership arrangement. *Big Data and Cognitive Computing, 5*(3), 32. DOI: 10.3390/bdcc5030032

Tronnier, F., Pape, S., Löbner, S., & Rannenberg, K. (2022). A discussion on ethical cybersecurity issues in digital service chains. In *Cybersecurity of digital service chains: challenges, methodologies, and tools* (pp. 222–256). Springer International Publishing. DOI: 10.1007/978-3-031-04036-8_10

Tu, Y., Gan, J., Hu, Y., Jin, R., Yang, Z., & Liu, M. (2019, November). Decentralized identity authentication and key management scheme. In *2019 IEEE 3rd Conference on Energy Internet and Energy System Integration (EI2)* (pp. 2697-2702). IEEE. DOI: 10.1109/EI247390.2019.9062013

Uchendu, B. R. C., Nurse, J., Bada, M., & Furnell, S. (2021, June 30). Developing a cyber security culture: Current practices and future needs. *Computers & Security, 109*, 1–23. DOI: 10.1016/j.cose.2021.102387

Uğuz, S. (2018). Kurumsal Bilgi Güvenliği Yönetim Sistemi Yazılımları: Örnek Bir Yazılım Geliştirilmesi. Uluslararası Yönetim Bilişim Sistemleri ve Bilgisayar Bilimleri Dergisi, 2(1).

Ukwandu, E., Ben-Farah, M. A., Hindy, H., Bures, M., Atkinson, R., Tachtatzis, C., Andonovic, I., & Bellekens, X. (2022). Cyber-security challenges in aviation industry: A review of current and future trends. *Information (Basel), 13*(3), 146. DOI: 10.3390/info13030146

Ullah, F., Naeem, H., Jabbar, S., Khalid, S., Latif, M. A., Al-Turjman, F., & Mostarda, L. (2024). Cyber security threats detection in Internet of Things using deep learning approach. *IEEE Access : Practical Innovations, Open Solutions*, •••, 7.

Ulnicane, I., Eke, D. O., Knight, W., Ogoh, G., & Stahl, B. C. (2021). Good governance as a response to discontents? Déjà vu, or lessons for AI from other emerging technologies. *Interdisciplinary Science Reviews*, *46*(1-2), 71–93. DOI: 10.1080/03080188.2020.1840220

UPS. (2024). Investor Relations: Cybersecurity risk and resilience. Retrieved from https://investors.ups.com

Uzougbo, N. S., Ikegwu, C. G., & Adewusi, A. O.Ngozi Samuel UzougboChinonso Gladys IkegwuAdefolake Olachi Adewusi. (2024). Regulatory frameworks for decentralized finance (DEFI): Challenges and opportunities. *GSC Advanced Research and Reviews*, *19*(02), 116–129. DOI: 10.30574/gscarr.2024.19.2.0170

Vagal, V., & Dillon, R. (2021). Reducing cyber risk in remote working. In *Digital Transformation in a Post-Covid World* (pp. 155–170). CRC Press. DOI: 10.1201/9781003148715-8

Vaia Rousopoulou, T. V., Nizamis, A., Iakovidis, I., Samaras, L., Kirtsoglou, A., Georgiadis, K., & Tzovaras, D. (2022). Cognitive analytics platform with AI solutions for anomaly detection. *Computers in Industry*, *134*, 134. DOI: 10.1016/j.compind.2021.103555

Vailshery, L. S. (2022). Internet of Things (IoT) and non-IoT active device connections worldwide from 2010 to 2025. Statista. https://www.statista.com/statistics/1101442/iot-number-of-connected-devices-worldwide/#:~:text=The total installed base of,that are expected in 2021.

Varshney, G., Kumawat, R., Varadharajan, V., Tupakula, U., & Gupta, C. (2024). Anti-phishing: A comprehensive perspective. *Expert Systems with Applications*, *238*, 122199. DOI: 10.1016/j.eswa.2023.122199

Vashishth, T. K., Sharma, V., Sharma, K. K., Kumar, B., Chaudhary, S., & Panwar, R. (2024). Environmental sustainability and carbon footprint reduction through artificial intelligence-enabled energy management in electric vehicles. In *Artificial Intelligence-Empowered Modern Electric Vehicles in Smart Grid Systems* (pp. 477–502). Elsevier. DOI: 10.1016/B978-0-443-23814-7.00017-1

Vasudevan, S., Piazza, A., & Carr, M. (2023, March). A decade of studies on cyber security training in organizations using social network analysis: a systematic literature review through keyword co-occurrence network. In *2023 International Conference on Business Analytics for Technology and Security (ICBATS)* (pp. 1-6). IEEE. DOI: 10.1109/ICBATS57792.2023.10111127

Veiga, G. L., Lima, E. P., & Costa, S. E. (2019). Ağustos). Efficiency Frontier Identification Based on Operations Strategy- A Retrospective Analysis of Leading Authors. *Procedia Manufacturing, 39*, 775–785. DOI: 10.1016/j.promfg.2020.01.431

Verma, A., Bhattacharya, P., Madhanı, N., Trıvedı, C., Bhushan, B., Tanwar, S., Sharma, G., Bokoro, P. N., & Sharma, A. R. (2022, July 5). Blockchain for Industry 5.0: Vision, Opportunities, Key Enablers, and Future Directions. *IEEE Access : Practical Innovations, Open Solutions, 10*, 69160–69199. DOI: 10.1109/ACCESS.2022.3186892

Victor-Mgbachi, T. O. Y. I. N. (2024). Navigating cybersecurity beyond compliance: Understanding your threat landscape and vulnerabilities. *Iconic Research and Engineering Journals*, •••, 7.

Villalón-Fonseca, R. (2022). The nature of security: A conceptual framework for integral-comprehensive modeling of IT security and cybersecurity. *Computers & Security, 120*, 102805. DOI: 10.1016/j.cose.2022.102805

Von Solms, R., & Van Niekerk, J. (2013). From information security to cyber security. *Computers & Security, 38*, 97–102. DOI: 10.1016/j.cose.2013.04.004

Vredenborg, M., van Kasteren, A., & Masthoff, J. (2025). Personalization in Public Transport Passenger Information Systems: A Systematic Review and Framework. *ACM Computing Surveys, 57*(9), 1–38. DOI: 10.1145/3721478

Waheed, N., He, X., Ikram, M., Usman, M., Hashmi, S. S., & Usman, M. (2020). Security and privacy in IoT using machine learning and blockchain: Threats and countermeasures. [csur]. *ACM Computing Surveys, 53*(6), 1–37. DOI: 10.1145/3417987

Waizenegger, L., McKenna, B., Cai, W., & Bendz, T. (2020). An affordance perspective of team collaboration and enforced working from home during COVID-19. *European Journal of Information Systems, 29*(4), 429–442. DOI: 10.1080/0960085X.2020.1800417

Wamala, F. (2012). *ITU National Cybersecurity Strategy Guide*. International Communication Union.

Wang, H., Ding, H., & Kong, X. (2023). Understanding technostress and employee well-being in digital work: The roles of work exhaustion and workplace knowledge diversity. *International Journal of Manpower, 44*(2), 334–353. DOI: 10.1108/IJM-08-2021-0480

Wang, T., Liang, Y., Shen, X., Zheng, X., Mahmood, A., & Sheng, Q. Z. (2023). Edge computing and sensor-cloud: Overview, solutions, and directions. ACM Computing Surveys, 55(13s). *ACM Computing Surveys, 281*(13s), 1–37. DOI: 10.1145/3582270

Wang, W., Li, X., Xie, L., Lv, H., & Lv, Z. (2021). Unmanned aircraft system airspace structure and safety measures based on spatial digital twins. *IEEE Transactions on Intelligent Transportation Systems*, *23*(3), 2809–2818. DOI: 10.1109/TITS.2021.3108995

Warner, M. (2012). Cybersecurity: A pre-history. *Intelligence and National Security*, *27*(5), 781–799. DOI: 10.1080/02684527.2012.708530

Waschbusch, L., & Mundt, E. (2019, 27. Mai). Was bedeutet Industrie 4.0? Definition, Merkmale und Anwendung. Industry of Things. https://www.industry-of-things.de/was-bedeutet-industrie-40-definition-merkmale-und-anwendung-a-828236/

Westerlund, M., Isabelle, D. A., & Leminen, S. (2021). The acceptance of digital surveillance in an age of big data. *Technology Innovation Management Review*, *11*(3), 32–44. DOI: 10.22215/timreview/1427

Westerlund, M.MikaWesterlund. (2019). Ekim). The Emergence of Deepfake Technology: A Review. *Technology Innovation Management Review*, *9*(11), 39–52. DOI: 10.22215/timreview/1282

West, J. P., & Bowman, J. S. (2016). Electronic surveillance at work: An ethical analysis. *Administration & Society*, *48*(5), 628–651. DOI: 10.1177/0095399714556502

Wikipedia. (2024). *China RealDID*. Retrieved from https://en.wikipedia.org/wiki/China_RealDID

Willie, M. M. (2023). The role of organizational culture in cybersecurity: Building a security-first culture. *Journal of Research. Innovation and Technologies*, *2*(2 (4)), 179–198.

WJARR. (2023). Security analysis of IoT devices used in agricultural supply chains. *World Journal of Advanced Research and Reviews*, *22*(1), 1023–1037.

World Economic Forum. (2024). Global cybersecurity outlook 2024: Insight report. https://www3.weforum.org/docs/WEF_Global_Cybersecurity_Outlook_2024.pdf

Wright, D., & Kreissl, R. (Eds.). (2014). *Surveillance in Europe*. Routledge. DOI: 10.4324/9781315851365

Wu, Y., Dai, H. N., & Wang, H. (2020). Convergence of blockchain and edge computing for secure and scalable IIoT critical infrastructures in industry 4.0. *IEEE Internet of Things Journal*, *8*(4), 2300–2317. DOI: 10.1109/JIOT.2020.3025916

Xie, Y., Gardi, A., & Sabatini, R. (2022, September). Cybersecurity trends in low-altitude air traffic management. In *2022 IEEE/AIAA 41st Digital Avionics Systems Conference (DASC)* (pp. 1-9). IEEE. DOI: 10.1109/DASC55683.2022.9925840

Xiong, M., & Wang, H. (2022). Digital twin applications in aviation industry: A review. *International Journal of Advanced Manufacturing Technology, 121*(9), 5677–5692. DOI: 10.1007/s00170-022-09717-9

Yallop, A. C., Gică, O. A., Moisescu, O. I., Coro , M. M., & Séraphin, H. (2023). The digital traveller: Implications for data ethics and data governance in tourism and hospitality. *Journal of Consumer Marketing, 40*(2), 155–170. DOI: 10.1108/JCM-12-2020-4278

Yang, C., Lan, S., Zhao, Z., Zhang, M., Wu, W., & Huang, G. Q. (2022). Edge-cloud blockchain and IoE-enabled quality management platform for perishable supply chain logistics. *IEEE Internet of Things Journal, 10*(4), 3264–3275. DOI: 10.1109/JIOT.2022.3142095

Yan, Q., & Yu, F. R. (2015). Distributed denial of service attacks in software-defined networking with cloud computing. *IEEE Communications Magazine, 53*(4), 52–59. DOI: 10.1109/MCOM.2015.7081075

Yaseen, A. (2024). Enhancing Cybersecurity through Automated Infrastructure Management: A Comprehensive Study on Optimizing Security Measures. *Quarterly Journal of Emerging Technologies and Innovations, 9*(1), 38–60.

Yeo, L. H., & Banfield, J. (2022). Human factors in electronic health records cybersecurity breach: An exploratory analysis. *Perspectives in Health Information Management, 19*(Spring), 1i. PMID: 35692854

Yıldız Tonga, M., & Tonga, M. (2022). Endüstri 4.0'a genel bir bakış: Sanayinin geleceği [Overview of Industry 4.0: The Future of the Industry]. G. Ü. İslahiye İİBF Uluslararası E-Dergi, 6(6), 40-60.

Yoşumaz, İ., & Özkara, B. (2019). Endüstri 4.0 sürecinin hazır giyim işletmeleri üzerindeki etkileri: hugo boss türkiye örneği. İşletme Araştırmaları Dergisi, 11(4), 2587-2600.

Yüksel, A., Eren, T., & Güven, E. (2024). Siber fiziksel sistemler alanında Türkiye'deki akademik eğilimler: Bir bibliyometrik analiz. *Bilgisayar Bilimleri ve Teknolojileri Dergisi, 5*(2), 24–35. DOI: 10.54047/bibted.1530609

Yu, S., & Carroll, F. (2022). Implications of AI in national security: understanding the security issues and ethical challenges. In *Artificial intelligence in cyber security: Impact and implications: Security challenges, technical and ethical issues, forensic investigative challenges* (pp. 157–175). Springer International Publishing.

Zaman, S., Alhazmi, K., Aseeri, M. A., Ahmed, M. R., Khan, R. T., Kaiser, M. S., & Mahmud, M. (2021). Security threats and artificial intelligence based countermeasures for internet of things networks: A comprehensive survey. *IEEE Access : Practical Innovations, Open Solutions*, *9*, 94668–94690. DOI: 10.1109/ACCESS.2021.3089681

Żebrowski, P., Couce-Vieira, A., & Mancuso, A. (2022). A Bayesian framework for the analysis and optimal mitigation of cyber threats to cyber-physical systems. *Risk Analysis*, *42*(10), 2275–2290. DOI: 10.1111/risa.13900 PMID: 35229333

Zetter, K. (2015). *Countdown to zero day: Stuxnet and the launch of the world's first digital weapon*. Crown.

Zhang, Y., Wen, Y., Guan, Y., Wu, Z., & Huang, D. (2014). Security and privacy for the Internet of Things: A survey. *IEEE Internet of Things Journal*, *1*(5), 381–394.

Zhan, H., Hwang, B. G., & Krishnankutty, P. (2023). Embracing digital transformation for sustainable development: Barriers to adopting digital twin in asset management within Singapore's energy and chemicals industry. *Sustainable Development*.

Zhan, Y., Ahmad, S. F., Irshad, M., Al-Razgan, M., Awwad, E. M., Ali, Y. A., & Bani Ahmad Ayassrah, A. Y. A. (2024). Investigating the role of Cybersecurity's perceived threats in the adoption of health information systems. *Heliyon*, *10*(1), 1–16. DOI: 10.1016/j.heliyon.2023.e22947

Zhao, G., Song, J., & Li, X. (2020). Network security model based on active defense and passive defense hybrid strategy. *Journal of Intelligent & Fuzzy Systems*, *39*(6), 8897–8905. DOI: 10.3233/JIFS-189287

Zheng, T., Liu, M., Puthal, D., Yi, P., Wu, Y., & He, X. (2022). Smart grid: Cyber attacks, critical defense approaches, and digital twin. *arXiv preprint arXiv:2205.11783*.

Zhou, Y. (2022). Low-carbon transition in smart city with sustainable airport energy ecosystems and hydrogen-based renewable-grid-storage-flexibility. *Energy Reviews*, *1*(1), 100001. DOI: 10.1016/j.enrev.2022.100001

Zhou, Y., Cheng, G., Zhao, Y., Chen, Z., & Jiang, S. (2022, April). Toward Proactive and Efficient DDoS Mitigation in IIoT Systems: A MovingTarget Defense Approach. *IEEE Transactions on Industrial Informatics*, *18*(4), 2734–2744. DOI: 10.1109/TII.2021.3090719

Zighan, S. (2024, February). Navigating the cyber landscape: A framework for transitioning from business continuity to digital resilience. In *2024 2nd International Conference on Cyber Resilience (ICCR)* (pp. 01-06). IEEE. DOI: 10.1109/ICCR61006.2024.10532999

Zissis, D., & Lekkas, D. (2012). Addressing cloud computing security issues. *Future Generation Computer Systems*, *28*(3), 583–592. DOI: 10.1016/j.future.2010.12.006

Zografopoulos, I., Ospina, J., Liu, X., & Konstantinou, C. (2021). Cyber-physical energy systems security: Threat modeling, risk assessment, resources, metrics, and case studies. *IEEE Access : Practical Innovations, Open Solutions*, *9*, 29775–29818. DOI: 10.1109/ACCESS.2021.3058403

Zolanvari, M., Teixeira, M. A., Gupta, L., Khan, K. M., & Jain, R. (2019). *Machine Learning Based Network Vulnerability Analysis of Industrial Internet of Things*. IEEE. DOI: 10.1109/JIOT.2019.2912022

Zwilling, M. (2022). Trends and challenges regarding cyber risk mitigation by CISOs- A systematic literature and experts' opinion review based on text analytics. *Sustainability (Basel)*, *14*(3), 1311. DOI: 10.3390/su14031311

About The Contributors

Filiz Mızrak completed her undergraduate studies in the Department of American Culture and Literature at Istanbul University in 2009. Subsequently, in 2015, she earned her Master's degree in Executive MBA from Bahçeşehir University. Between 2017 and 2021, she conducted doctoral studies in the field of Management and Strategy at Istanbul Medipol University. Starting from September 2023, Filiz Mızrak has been working as an Assistant Professor in the Logistics Management department at Beykoz University. Her academic research areas include Strategic Management, Supply Chain Management, Human Resources Management, and Aviation Management.

***

Pervin Ahu Çerçi is an academic specializing in behavioral economics and international trade. She holds a BA in Economics from Istanbul University, an MA in Economic Theory from Marmara University, and a non-thesis MA in International Trade and Investment Management from Istanbul Medeniyet University. Her interdisciplinary academic background enables her to blend theoretical and applied approaches in her research. Her work focuses on the intersection of behavioral economics and international trade policies, particularly exploring consumer behavior, irrational decision-making, trade performance, and sustainable economic strategies. She teaches various courses at different levels in higher education, sharing her interdisciplinary perspective with students. In addition to her publications in national and international platforms, she participates in research projects and conducts field-based policy analyses.

Esra Nur Gökhan completed her undergraduate studies in Business Administration and pursued both a thesis-based Executive MBA and a Ph.D. in Business Administration at Yeditepe University. She is currently a faculty member in the Department of Logistics Management (English) at the Faculty of Business and Administrative Sciences, Beykoz University. In addition to her academic role, she also serves as the Director of the Graduate School at Beykoz University. Her academic interests focus on marketing, supply chain strategies, digital transformation in logistics, and sustainable logistics practices. Dr. Gökhan combines strong theoretical knowledge with practical insights, contributing to both academic literature and applied projects. She is committed to delivering a high-impact learning experience by bridging academia and industry in her teaching and research.

Index

A

B

C

D

S

www.ingramcontent.com/pod-product-compliance
Ingram Content Group UK Ltd.
Pitfield, Milton Keynes, MK11 3LW, UK
UKHW050947290926
15470UKWH00005B/1684

9 798369 364178